THE HISTORY OF
WYANDOT COUNTY
OHIO

CONTAINING
A HISTORY OF THE COUNTY; ITS TOWNSHIPS, TOWNS, CHURCHES,
SCHOOLS, ETC.; GENERAL AND LOCAL STATISTICS; MILITARY
RECORD; PORTRAITS OF EARLY SETTLERS AND PROMINENT
MEN; HISTORY OF THE NORTHWEST TERRITORY;
HISTORY OF OHIO; MISCELLANEOUS
MATTERS; ETC., ETC.

— ILLUSTRATED —

VOLUME I
A GENERAL HISTORY
OF THE COUNTY

Leggett, Conaway & Company

HERITAGE BOOKS
2008

HERITAGE BOOKS
AN IMPRINT OF HERITAGE BOOKS, INC.

Books, CDs, and more—Worldwide

For our listing of thousands of titles see our website
at
www.HeritageBooks.com

A Facsimile Reprint
Published 2008 by
HERITAGE BOOKS, INC.
Publishing Division
100 Railroad Ave. #104
Westminster, Maryland 21157

Copyright © 1994 Heritage Books, Inc.

Originally published in Chicago
Leggett, Conaway & Co.
1884

The original *The History of Wyandot County, Ohio* has been split into two volumes by Heritage Books, Inc. for this publication. The first volume offers a general history of the county. The second volume is comprised of the township histories along with biographical sketches of prominent citizens.

— Publisher's Notice —

In reprints such as this, it is often not possible to remove blemishes from the original. We feel the contents of this book warrant its reissue despite these blemishes and hope you will agree and read it with pleasure.

International Standard Book Number: 978-0-7884-0061-2

PREFACE.

TO rescue from a fast engulfing oblivion the authentic events which have transpired in this region during a period of more than one hundred years, to preserve and to do honor to the memory of those who first dwelt within its boundaries, and to present an historical view of the institutions and industries of town and hamlet and township, is the object we have had in purpose in the preparation of this work. It has been our endeavor to glean the facts thoroughly, to present them simply and plainly.

As the table of contents indicates, the work is divided into four parts. Parts First and Second treat briefly the history of the Northwest Territory and the State of Ohio. Parts Third and Fourth are chiefly devoted to Wyandot County. The twelve chapters embraced by Part Third, as well as the history of the town of Upper Sandusky found in Part Fourth, have been prepared by Capt. John S. Schenck, a gentleman of wide experience in the compilation of local annals. The remainder of Part Fourth, mainly biographical in its contents, has been arranged by a staff of competent, painstaking writers, and possesses additional value from the fact that each biographical sketch has been submitted for correction and approval before going to press. This department of the work was largely prepared by C. G. Harraman. Part Third contains the general history of the county, and incidentally some fragments of the history of Northwestern Ohio. In Part Fourth, which is supplementary to Part Third, those minor details are preserved in connection with the township histories, which could not well be given place in the chapters upon a broader class of subjects. In these will be found carefully made records of the early settlements, accounts of churches, schools, etc., and much of incident illustrative of the men and manners of early days.

Returning to the general history, or Part Third, we will remark that within the first pages the effort is frequently made, not only to chronicle facts, but to show their relation as causes and effects in the great chain of events by which a portion of the American wilderness was reclaimed and added to the mighty realm of civilization. In the first few chapters of this part, succeeding Chapter I, a chronological order of arrangement is maintained, as nearly as may be, while in the later ones the topical form is resorted to as more practical and appropriate, and for other reasons which should be obvious to the reader.

Chapter I describes the location, extent, and natural features of the county. Then follows three large chapters which tell the story of the Wyandot Indians, and of other Ohio tribes, from time immemorial to 1843. Under the title "Early Settlements," etc., is given a brief history of the settlement of the county, with a few remarks showing the retarding effects caused by the Wyandot Reserve being located within its borders. Many of the trials of pioneer life are also dwelt upon in the same chapter, and the building of the log cabin, the dress, customs, and occupations of the first settlers are minutely described. A separate chapter is devoted to the civil history of the county, and outlines its formation and organization, the establishment of its courts, refers to notable public transactions, the erection of the county buildings, township divisions, and the results of elections, including also a valuable reference list of county officials, and the representatives of the county in the State and Federal Government. The Bench and Bar, the Medical Profession, the Newspaper Press and Educational Interests likewise have each separate places in the volume. The chapter styled "Material Progress" embraces a variety of topics, articles upon population, the more important county societies, post offices, productions, etc., and the public improvements in the county, from the days when the "mud road" was the only means of communication and travel down to and including the era of railroad development. The county in the dark days of the rebellion responded to the call for troops in a manner of which her people may ever be proud. For that reason the soldiers' record is given the large space which its importance demands and thus occupies a large chapter.

In conclusion, we add that this work contains the essence of many volumes of pertinent Federal, State, County and Township Archives, of almost complete newspaper files, and the invaluable recollections of the best-informed people of the county. Especial acknowledgments are also due to the editors and publishers of newspapers, to the pastors of churches, to county, village and township officials, the members of the bar and medical profession, the officers of public institutions, and the members of various secret orders, all of whom, without a single exception, have responded promptly and most courteously to requests for data. We are especially indebted to Hon. John D. Sears, for his able articles on the Newspapers of Upper Sandusky to 1871, and on the "Early Poets and Poetry" of the county, as well as for valuable assistance in other departments of the work. To R. D. Dumm, Esq., we are under many obligations for his well-written Reminiscences, and for his able and earnest co-operation in each and every department of the history; and lastly we acknowledge in a general manner, for their generous assistance, our obligations to Hon. L. A. Brunner, Pietro Cuneo, Hon. Robert McKelly, Hon. Chester R. Mott, Col. Moses H. Kirby, Hon. D. D. Hare, Hon. George W. Beery, J. G. Roberts, Thomas E. Beery, George Harper, and many others who aided materially in the preparation of the History.

As completed, the work is now presented to its patrons. That some errors will be found in the spelling of proper names, and in an occasional date furnished from memory, is not improbable. That such can be avoided, however, is equally as impossible, from the fact that the persons mentioned aggregate many thousands, traces of whom have been obtained, largely, from written records, prepared very frequently by those who were, seemingly, not particular whether they wrote legibly or spelled the proper names correctly or not. Yet, firmly believing that the History of Wyandot County will prove eminently satisfactory after a careful perusal and investigation, it is without further remark or explanation respectfully submitted.

LEGGETT, CONAWAY & CO.

CHICAGO, August, 1884.

CONTENTS.

CHAPTER I
Location and Extent-Natural Features 215

CHAPTER II
Indian Occupancy
(from time immemorial to 1872) 224

CHAPTER III
Indian Occupancy Contined
(events from 1782 to 1818) 240

CHAPTER IV
Indian Occupancy Continued
(from 1816-18 to 1843) 274

CHAPTER V
Early Settlements--Picture of Pioneer Life 302

CHAPTER VI
Civil History 312

CHAPTER VII
The Bench and Bar 353

CHAPTER VIII
The Medical Profession 374

CHAPTER IX
The Press 378

CHAPTER X
Educational Interests--Clerical Profession 402

CHAPTER XI
Material Progress 419

CHAPTER XII
The County's Military Record 438

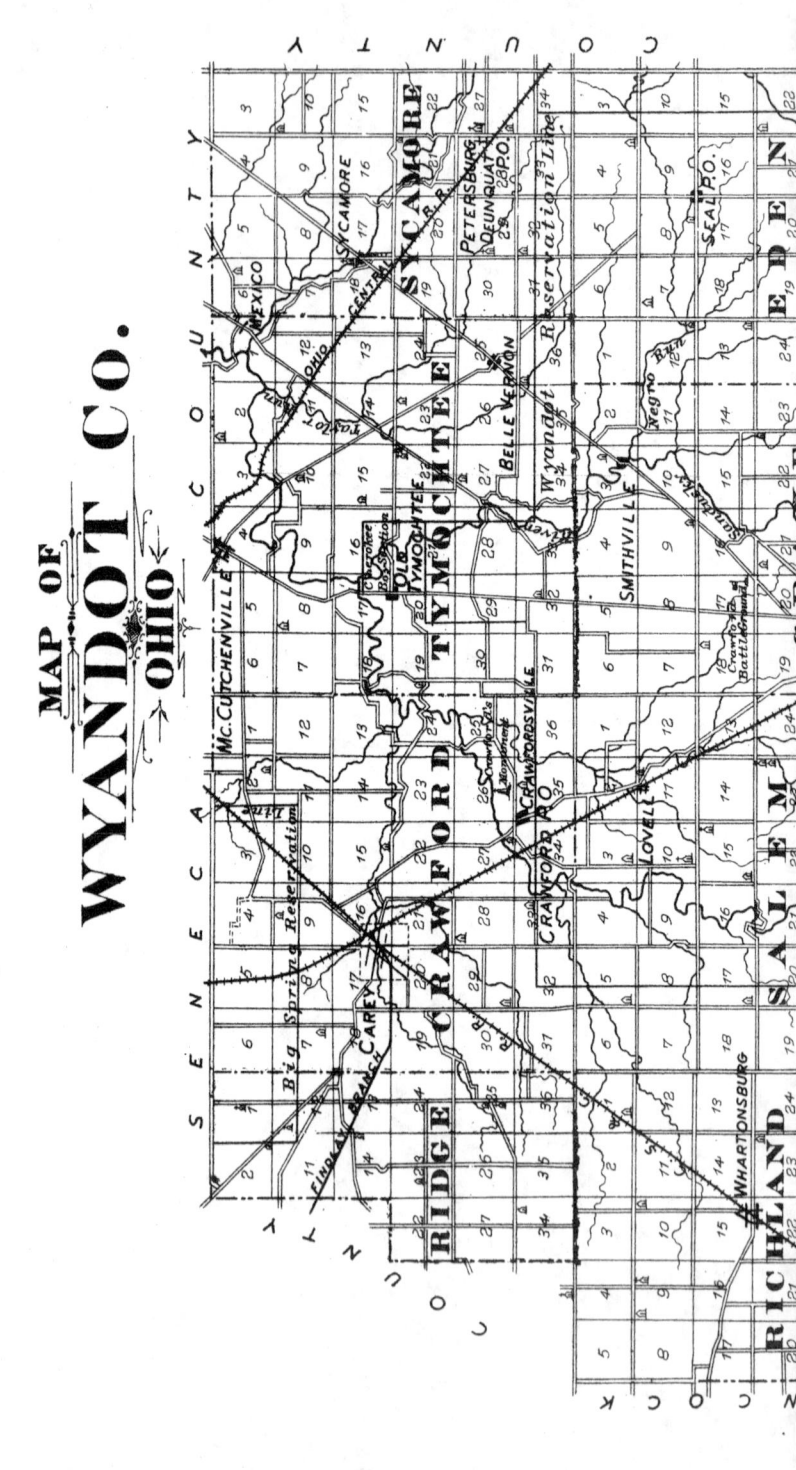

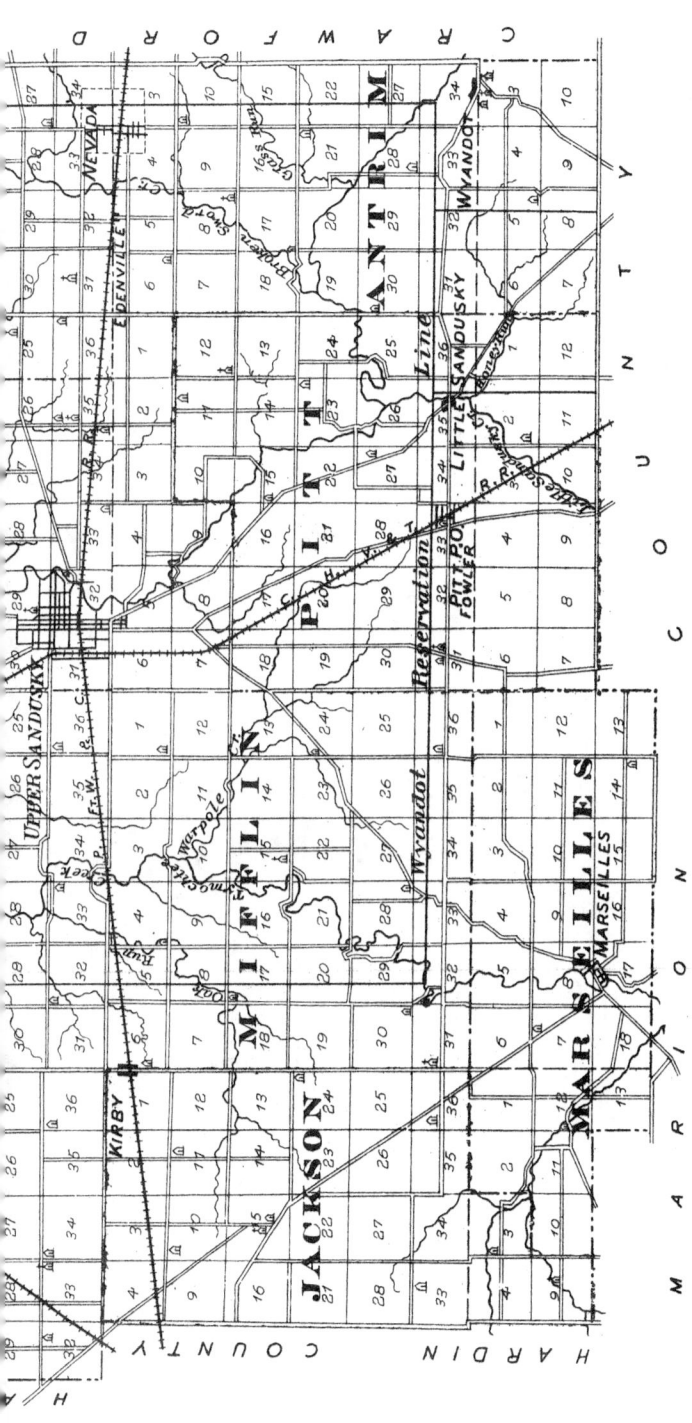

David Harpster

PART III.

HISTORY OF WYANDOT COUNTY.

BY JOHN S. SCHENCK.

HISTORY OF WYANDOT COUNTY.

CHAPTER I.

LOCATION AND EXTENT—NATURAL FEATURES.

SITUATION—BOUNDARIES—AREA — STREAMS — SURFACE — SOIL—GEOLOGICAL STRUCTURE—MATERIAL RESOURCES.

LOCATION AND EXTENT.

BY reference to the State maps, the reader will observe that Wyandot County lies in the northwest quarter of the State of Ohio, nearly equidistant from Lake Erie on the north, and the Indiana State line on the west. That the counties bordering upon it are Seneca on the north; Crawford on the east; Marion and Hardin on the south; Hardin and Hancock on the west; and that its thirteen subdivisions, known respectively as Antrim, Crane, Crawford, Eden, Jackson, Marseilles, Mifflin, Pitt, Richland, Ridge, Salem, Sycamore and Tymochtee Townships, contain eight square miles more than eleven surveyed townships, or 258,560 acres.

NATURAL FEATURES.

Its Streams.—Lying near the great water-shed of the State, just on its northern slope, it contains no large streams. Tymochtee Creek with its tributaries, and the head-waters of the Sandusky River, comprising the Little Sandusky and the Broken Sword Creeks, and the small streams known as Sycamore Creek, Tyler's Run, Sugar Run, Negro Run and Rock Run, are the drainage system of the county. Their general course is due north, except that the eastern tributaries of the Sandusky have a direction westerly or southwesterly, until they descend upon the area of the water-lime, and are well within the drainage valley of the Sandusky. The Tymochtee Creek, throughout the most of its course in Wyandot County, is a slow stream and has a clay bottom. Its valley is as wide and its banks as high as those of the Sandusky itself, although less water actually passes down its channel. The Sandusky, on the contrary, more frequently runs on a rock bottom, and its current is more rapid. It affords occasional water-power privileges. The same is true of the small creeks entering it from the east.

The Surface.—The topography of the county is quite simple. The western half is gently undulating or flat. The excavated valley of the Tymochtee Creek, which is usually about a hundred rods wide, and rarely exceeds two hundred rods, presents, in its abrupt descents, the most noticeable changes of level. There are several extensive prairie-like tracts, which have a black soil and were never clothed with forest. They are in the higher levels, and give rise to some of the tributaries of Tymochtee Creek. One is north and west of Carey, extending largely into Seneca and Hancock Counties, known as Big Spring Prairie. Another covers much of the township of Richland, known as Potatoe Swamp, and a third occupies the southeastern part of Mifflin and the southwestern part of Pitt Townships, extending also into Marion County. The Cranberry Marsh, in Jackson Township, also extends largely into Hancock County. That tract known as Cranberry Marsh, in Crane Township, and the marshy tract in the center of Tymochtee Township, are of less extent but in every way analogous to the rest. These marshes were probably, once the sites of lakes, which have become filled by the slow accumulation of vegetable matter, and the washing in from the adjoining land of the finer materials of the drift. This is particularly noticeable about the ridges and knolls which inclose Big Spring Prairie. Besides these untillable marshes, most of the territory lying between the Tymochtee Creek and the Sandusky River, has a black, loamy soil, and was once, probably, subject to inundation by those streams, although now it is generally laid out in fine farms.

East of the Sandusky River the surface is more broken, and there is a noticeable ascent from the area of the water-lime to that of the corniferous. There is a tract of elevated land, like a fragment of a glacial moraine, along the west side of Broken Sword Creek, extending from Eden Township to the Little Sandusky in Pitt Township. Besides these undulations in the original surface of the drift, that part of the county east of the Sandusky is subject to erosions by frequent small streams, which have worn channels in the drift and sometimes in the rock itself.

Where the streams of the county run through level tracts, they present the usual terrace and flood-plain. The former is the old drift surface, and rises from twenty to forty feet above the level of the water. The latter, which is constantly changing its position and its contents, is, of course, dependent on the greatest freshet rise of the stream. Along the Tymochtee Creek it is sometimes twelve feet or more above the summer stage of the stream.

The Soil.—The prevailing feature of the soil is clay. This, however, is variously modified. In the higher parts of the county, it is gravelly, and often contains stones and bowlders. It is compact, and almost entirely without stones or even gravel in the level tracts, especially where there has been a gradual filling up, with slow or imperfect drainage. The soil of the prairies, which is black, consists very largely of vegetable matter in various stages of decay. Drainage is especially needed in the western part of the county.

The Geological Structure.*—The Niagara limestone underlies a tier of townships along the western side of the county, spreading to the east so as to include the village of Marseilles. The western boundary of the Lower Corniferous enters the county from the north, about two miles east of Mexico, passes through Bellevernon and Little Sandusky, and leaves the county in Section 11, Pitt Township. Hence the most of the county, which is specially characterized by its flat surface, is underlain by the water-lime formation. It is necessary to say, however, that the western central portions of the county are entirely without rocky outcrops, and it may be that the Niagara underlies more area than has been ascribed to it; also that the boundary between the water-lime and the corniferous, as above located, is to a certain extent conjectural.

---

*Compiled from the report of N. H. Winchell, as published by authority of the State Legislature, in 1873.

The Niagara limestone has near Carey an unusual and somewhat remarkable exposure The surface of the country for many miles in every direction is flat, without exposure of rock. At this point the Niagara swells up suddenly in two separate mounds or ridges, which rise so obtrusively that the drift has been in many places entirely denuded. They rise to the height of forty to fifty feet. They are each about five miles long, and are so situated toward each other, and in relation to the direction of the natural drainage, that they inclose the marsh known as Big Spring Prairie. They are distinguished as the North Ridge and the West Ridge. The included prairie is of the shape of a horseshoe, the toe turned a little east of north, the West Ridge filling in the bow. It is usually about a mile wide, with a length of ten miles. It is drained in opposite directions. Spring Run drains it into the Sandusky River, and a stream known as the "Outlet" drains it into the Blanchard. The soil is so wet that at present it is impossible to till it. Good progress has, however, been made in draining some portions, which now produce corn of prodigious growth. The descent to the prairie from the north or from the west, so as not to be intercepted by either of the limestone ridges, is very gradual, even unobservable. The soil changes imperceptibly from a more or less gravelly clay to a fine, tough clay; then by the addition of vegetable matter the surface soil becomes black and moist, and all vegetable growth disappears except grasses and sedges. Efforts were made to ascertain the thickness of this black muck, but no result was obtained other than the fact, that while it exceeds eight feet in some places, it is usually but four or five. It is thin about the margin of the marsh, and seems to be generally underlain by a tough, blue clay, often so calcareous as to constitute a marl. This blue clay is sometimes itself overlain by a bed of quicksand. Within the muck the horns of elk are said to have been found, and logs several feet in diameter. Along the south margin of the prairie, within the bow, there is considerable sand, as if the deposit of a lake shore. Within the bow of the prairie there is also considerable flat land not marshy, the surface rising very gently toward the south for the distance of nearly one mile, when the West Ridge rises suddenly to the height of nearly fifty feet. The prairie is crossed by three public roads. These are constructed by throwing together the dirt from two parallel ditches, on which is placed first corduroy, and afterward, when repairs are needed,.stone hauled from the ridges, giving the road a rough macadamizing. Many months in the year the prairie is covered with water, and it is only in the driest months that cattle venture on it for grazing. Within it are sometimes little undulations or hillocks, on which grow bunches of shrubs and large herbs.

The rock here exposed has been found to contain characteristic Niagara fossils only in the North Ridge. There are no perpendicular sections of the bedding, except in small quarries on the slopes of the ridges near their bases. In these openings the stone appears very different from that seen in bare places higher up the ridges and on their summits, and the dip is uniformly toward the low ground, whatever the position of the quarry.

The quarry of Mr. Samuel Shoup, situated on the western slope of the West Ridge, about three miles from Carey, shows the rock dipping about fifteen or eighteen degrees toward the southwest; that is, toward the nearest low ground. It is in thin, fragile beds, of a light drab or buff color, porous, and soft under the hammer, showing no distinguishable fossils.

In the quarry of Mr. Thomas Shepherd, northeast quarter Section 11, Ridge Township, about a mile northwest of Mr. Shoup's, the beds are thin and so carious they can hardly be lifted, in even sheets of a buff color, sometimes reduced to sand by the weather. Then comes a bed three to eight inches thick; vesicular; of a buff color; easily worked. Then it is irregularly bedded; lenticular or massive; buff color; carious; with traces of fossils.

Mr. F. J. Worrello's quarry, northeast quarter Section 16, Crawford Township, is in the same kind of stone, but it is so far removed from the ridge that beds have not been tilted by it. They lie horizontal, or with a very slight inclination southwest. The rock is here very near the surface. The same is true at Carey, where it is sometimes reached in digging post-holes for fences.

The quarry of Mr. Jonas Huffman is in the west slope of the North Ridge, situated in the northwest quarter of Section 4, Crawford Township, and shows the following descending section. Dip toward the west, $10°$. The rock here is overlain by about two feet of drift and loose fragments; then comes about two feet of confused and lenticular in the bedding, with larger pores or cavities, sometimes filled with calcite; fossiliferous, showing two species of bivalves, cyathophylloids and favositoids. Then two feet of hard, close-grained; light drab; beds four to eight inches. The close-grained has a bluish tint.

Mr. Peter Kibbler's quarry at Springville affords a slight exposure of the same kind of stone, with a gentle dip west or toward the prairie. The stone here seems a little more firm, but is generally porous, with fine cavities; fossils wanting or so absorbed as to be undistinguishable. The color is a light drab, varying to buff, and also to gray, especially when thrown in piles. The stone is not handsome, the beds being uneven and containing some white chert. At Mr. David Smith's quarry, in the northeast quarter of Section 3, in Amanda Township, Hancock County, the stone is buff, porous and thin, the beds being only about two inches thick. Stone thrown out from these quarries becomes a light buff, sometimes almost white under the weather, and although not of a durable quality, it has been used considerably in ordinary walls and foundations.

In passing over the ridges which are occupied by good farms, stones are often seen gathered from the fields and deposited in piles or in the corners of the fences, or laid up in walls. They consist of fragments from the underlying rock, and of northern bowlders, the former greatly predominating. Along the road the rock is frequently seen bare, and, as already remarked, it is different, lithologically, from that seen in the foregoing quarries. It is most frequently a dark drab or brown, hard, crystalline rock, apparently in a rough, massive condition, containing cavities sometimes two or three inches in diameter. It nowhere appears in even beds. It is rarely vesicular, like the stone seen in the quarries described, but contains large cavities, irregularly scattered through it. The color is sometimes a bluish drab, and it not unfrequently shows obscure traces of fossil remains. These occur sometimes in rock otherwise compact and solid, or they may be so numerous as to make the rock porous and loose, the interior shell being entirely wanting. The fragments furnishing these fossils are, however, more vesicular and lighter colored than the stone usually seen scattered over the surface of the ridges. They have the lithological characters of that phase of the Niagara seen in the Sandusky River at Tiffin, Seneca County, and at Genoa, in Ottawa County. In the northeast quarter of Section 32, Crawford Township, a ridge may be seen of the same kind of stone as those north of Carey, running north and south, visible about one-half mile, slightly exposed on land of Joseph Pahl.

It would seem as if the conditions of the ocean's bed in which the Niagara was formed were not uniform. While regular strata were being deposited in a wide area, including portions of Seneca and Hancock Counties, without disturbance or contortions, a concretionary and crystallizing force sprang into operation in the northwest corner of Wyandot County, which in working from below, caused the even beds of deposition to swell upward or over the growing mass or masses. In some cases, it aided in the preservation of fossil remains; in others it hastened their absorption into the mass of the rock. This is a peculiarity of the rock formation not confined to the Niagara, but is displayed conspicuously in the water-lime above, and it has been seen in the Lower Corniferous. When the lapse of time brings such hardened masses into contact with the erosions of ice and water, they cause the prominent features of the landscape by the removal of the more destructible parts about them. Such may be the explanation of the remarkable ridges about Carey, the even, friable beds seen in the quarries about their flanks having once been continuous over the summits, but, unable to resist the forces of the glacial epoch, were denuded down to the more enduring rock.

Within these ridges are several caves, the entrances to which are small and have been accidentally discovered, sometimes by men plowing in the field. One particularly, on the farm of Mr. Adam Keller, northwest quarter Section 2, in Ridge Township, is described as having a perpendicular descent of sixty-five feet to a stream of water which is very deep and separates one apartment by a narrow passage from another. The entrance is about five feet across and the sides are of rock.

The Niagara, in the southwest corner of the county, rises rapidly in the same way from below the water-lime which lies to the north, the dip being northeast and to the amount of twenty-five degrees along Sections 18 and 13 near the county lines. It here appears as a thick-bedded gray and crystalline limestone. It also shows in the Tymochtee Creek, at the village of Marseilles, in a characteristic surface exposure. About five feet of thick, hard beds may be seen along the creek, lying nearly horizontal, or with a very slight dip south-southwest. It is slightly porous and fossiliferous. It is sometimes blotched with blue and drab. These are the beds that rise so rapidly about a mile further south, forming a little ridge or brow of prominent land facing north. On this brow is situated the residence of Mrs. Socrates Hartle. The rock is shown in the excavation for the cellar about the center of Section 13, in Marseilles Township, also, in a ditch by the roadside in Section 18, about sixty rods east of Mrs. Hartle's house, where the rapidity of the current of water has cleaned off the smoothed and striated rock in a handsome exposure. A little stream, locally known as Little Tymochtee Creek, makes eastward along the north side of this brow of land, and on Section 13, less than a quarter of a mile north of Mrs. Hartle's house, and perhaps thirty feet below the Niagara outcrop near it, the blue slaty beds of the water-lime may be seen in the creek.

In the southeast quarter Section 13, in Marseilles Township, Mr. Heckathorn has a quarry in the Niagara. The beds here are three to six inches in thickness. The stone is rather firm, though somewhat porous. It is used for quicklime and for general building purposes. Southeast quarter Section 11, in Marseilles Township, D. Heckathorn burns lime from the Niagara; dip north; beds about four inches. Within forty rods north of Mr. H.'s quarry the water-lime appears in the Little Tymochtee Creek. In northeast quarter Section 11, Marseilles Township, H. H. Cary burns lime and supplies building stone from the Niagara; beds three to five inches; dip east exposed eighteen inches. Near the village of Marseilles, in the same township, Mr. Charles Norris and Michael Keckler have small quarries of Niagara limestone.

The water-lime formation, which in counties further north presents three distinct, general lithological characters, in Wyandot County, is mainly reduced to one. That aspect of the water-lime designated "Phase No. 3," passes, with the addition of much bituminous matter, into a thin bedded, even, slaty condition, which, first black, weathers blue on the sides of the bedding, or lastly a chocolate color, while the fractured edge is a very drab. Throughout the country it is known in this condition as "blue slate." When the bituminous matter is more evenly distributed through the rock, instead of being confined to the thin partings, the beds are thicker and of a blue color.

The principal outcrop of the water-lime within the county is along the left bank of the Tymochtee Creek, in Section 27 and 34, in Crawford Township. The banks of the creek expose perpendicular sections of four to eight feet of these thin beds. The dip being continuously toward the southwest, a connected section of eighty-four feet ten inches may be made out in a descending order. The beds are homogenous, tough, thin, sometimes having so much bituminous matter as to appear like the great black slate. The thinnest beds are, however, streaked with alternations of dark drab, and a bituminous brown. When wet the brown is almost black, but when dry and weathered it sometimes assumes a blue color, and if long weathered it becomes chocolate. There are among these occasional patches of thicker, even drab beds, which finally become so persistent upward as to require a special designation.

Mr. McD. M. Carey has a quarry in these thin, blue beds and on Section 27, which has acquired considerable notoriety for the large, smooth slabs or flagging it affords. Some of the thicker beds furnish also a handsome and useful stone for building. The dip is toward the south-southwest exposure about twelve feet perpendicular. The stone here shows the characteristic Leperditia altu. The quarry is in the old river bank or hard-pan terrace, about forty rods from the stream. This water-lime is seen in the following places in Wyandot County:

In Section 16, southwest quarter, in Crane Township, at the old "Indian Mill," these blue flags have been taken out of the bed of the Sandusky and used for foundations for the mill. But in the construction of the bridge at the same place, the stone used is said to have come from Leesville, Crawford County.

In Section 21, Crane Township, at Carter's dam, in the Sandusky River, Mr. John Strasser has opened the water-lime. The stone is in irregular, thick and thin beds. When freshly quarried, it is blue-drab, and of a fine grain. Exposed a short time to the weather, the whole pile becomes a bright blue. The fracture of the beds, however, becomes a much more ashen or drab-blue than the sides of the bedding. The dip in W. Strasser's bed is about nine feet deep. About thirty rods east of Strasser's quarry, in the bed of the Sandusky, blue flagging is taken out like that of Mr. Carey's quarry on the Tymochtee Creek, except that here the blue color pervades the white mass. Fragments of this, whenever bituminous and jointed, come out in long tapering pieces. These flags show a fossil which appears like a species of *modiolopsis*. In Crane Township, southwest quarter, Section 22, in a bed of Rock Run, a fine-grained blue stone is quarried and used for

HISTORY OF WYANDOT COUNTY. 221

foundations. It weathers a drab color to the depth of a half-inch or an inch, all over the outside. One only of six inches is exposed. In the northwest quarter of Section 27, in the same township, along the bed of Rock Run the water-lime is abundantly exposed, with a general dip southeast, changing to west at the west end of the outcrop. Mr. Peter Weinandy here burns lime and sells stone. This bed has a depth of about fifty-seven feet. Beds which certainly cannot have been fractured more than a few months, were seen to have already acquired a coating of drab one-eighth to one-fourth of an inch thick over the fractured surface. The layers themselves, before quarrying, are sometimes one-half to two-thirds drab, with a blue streak through the center. It would seem as if the drab were entirely an acquired color, and that perhaps the whole water-lime was at first a blue rock. The access of air or aërated water seems to cause the change. The fact that the lower, regular beds (as at this quarry), shut off the percolations of water through the rock, may account for the longer preservation of the blue. Whenever the beds are lenticular or irregular, or are so situated that the atmosphere finds free access to them, they are drab. They are seen to be blue only when deep-seated or lying very true.

In Section 28, east side of Tymochtee Township, the Tymochtee slate is seen in the bed of the Sandusky, at Hayman's mill. Handsome flags, about two inches thick, are taken out. In Section 22, Pitt Township, Mr. James Anderson's quarry shows the following section in the bank of the Sandusky : Bituminous drab, ten inches ; very hard, flinty, irregular beds, five feet.

There are sometimes bituminous films visible on the fractured edge ; no fossils. In Pitt Township, on the southwest quarter of Section 10, Mrs. Rebecca Smith owns a quarry in the Sandusky, from which a fine-grained, even-bedded blue stone is taken, which weathers an ashen color. Here are some handsome beds, six to eight inches thick, affording a fine building material. Dip southeast. At various points in Pitt Township, the same features of the water-lime may be seen. No reliable estimate can be made of the thickness exposed, or of their relative places in the formation, the outcrops are so isolated, and show so nearly the same characters. The same stone is quarried in the river at Upper Sandusky by Mr. William Frederick. The same stone is found in Section 17, in Crawford Township, on lands of Mr. George Mullholand, and on Section 24, in the quarries of Messrs. Mitten and O'Brien, in the water-lime. The stone from these openings is in thick beds, much like the gray, hard beds of the quarries at Tiffin.

The lower corniferous may be seen in interrupted outcrop along the Sycamore Creek, from Benton, in Crawford County, to Section 18, in Sycamore Township, Wyandot County. Through the whole of this distance it is so hid by drift that no reliable section can be obtained. It is of the coarse-grained, thick-bedded, harsh and magnesian type until just within Section 17, Sycamore, the character of the rock changes. It assumes very much the aspect of the drab, thin-bedded water-lime. A little further down the creek the soft, thick beds of the lower corniferous return. Further still, there is another similar change to a fine-grained, compact, light-blue stone, without fossils. This character continues through the most of Section 27, and some in Section 21, evinced not often by rock *in situ*, but by the angular, bluish, fine-grained pieces in the stream. This member of the lower corniferous was also seen near Melmore, in Seneca County. No opportunity has been offered to ascertain its thickness, but, judging from the superficial expose, it may have a thickness of thirty or even forty feet. In the northwest quarter of Section 21, Sycamore, about eighteen inches of similar compact blue limestone may be seen in the creek, underlain by a blue shale, which crumbles conchoidally and shows spots of darker blue or purple. It is sometimes quite rocklike, yet when long weathered it crumbles. Its thickness cannot be stated, though there cannot be less than ten feet, judging from the distance it occupies the bed of the creek. On Section 18 of the same township, a thick-bedded, even-grained rock, harsh, like a sandstone, is slightly exposed. It is gray, without visible fossils, and weathers buff. It is impossible to give its dip, thickness, or relation to the shale just mentioned. It is probably below that. Near the same place, land of Andrew Bretz, there are also large fragments of a fragile, bituminous, crinoidal limestone, seen in the bed of the creek. In Pitt Township, southwest quarter of Section 25, on the land of Jacob Brewer, the lower corniferous is slightly exposed in the upper bank of the Sandusky River. The rock consists almost entirely of the coral *Coenostroma monticulifera* vein. On a thickness of about a foot can be *in situ*, but a mass of two feet thickness is tilted up so as to present the edges of the beds in a perpendicular position.

The Drift.—Wherever sections were observed throughout the county, the drift shows, as in counties further north, the two usual colors. The first is light brown, or ashen, and extends downward about twelve feet. It may be stratified or entirely unstratified, and forms the soil where it has not been covered with alluvial or marshy accumulations. Its color alone distinguishes it from the underlying blue or Erie clay. They both contain bowlders that show glacial action. On Section 24, Crawford Township, the lower member was seen exposed twenty-seven feet four inches in the bank of Tymochtee Creek, embracing beds of gravel and sand. The upper overlaying was twelve feet, and entirely unassorted, yet on Section 18, Tymochtee Township, both are more or less stratified. No two sections of this bank would be the same. The greatest uniformity in the order of alternation is in the upper part. The blue hard pan sometimes extends upward quite to the brown clays and sands, and in one case the whole bank consists of hard pan, the upper portion having the brown color. Hence the general character of this bank, and of the drift in Wyandot County, is as follows: Brown clay and sand, stratified; brown hard pan; statified brown clay; stratified blue clay and sand; finer blue clay and blue hard pan; brown clay; blue clay; *debris*, bowlders and slides. On the opposite side of the creek this bank is entirely wanting. There is a bank of a trifle over twelve feet, composed of agglutinated, rusty sand, without gravel or bowlders, at the base of which, near the water, is a bed of vegetable remains containing some pretty large limbs, and numerous branches of wood. Such deposits are common in the alluvial bottoms bordering the streams. There is a gradual ascent from the level of this bank to the height of the bank on the opposite side of the river, attaintain that elevation in a distance of forty rods.

Material Resources.—The chief source of material wealth in Wyandot County, as with other counties in Northwestern Ohio, lies in its rich and exhaustless soil. The streams are generally too small or too sluggish to be reliable for water-powers. The rocks themselves are not known to possess any deposits of valuable minerals. They will serve for common use in building, and will make an excellent quicklime. There is reason to believe, also, that the water-lime, when having the characters seen in the quarry of Mrs. Smith, Section 10, Pitt Township, will afford a cement of hydraulic properties.

Good brick, of a red color, are made in different places in the county from the surface of the drift. Such establishments are owned at Upper Sandusky by Jacob Gottfried & Brother, and by Ulrich & McAfee; also on the southeast quarter of Section 11, Salem, and on the Infirmary Farm, by Jacob Ulrich. Sand for mortar is easily obtained from the numerous natural sections of the drift along the drainage valleys. A sand bank at Upper Sandusky was observed to underlie a deposit of eighty feet of brown hard pan, and was excavated to the depth of ten feet. The layers of sand lay nearly horizontal.

CHAPTER II.

INDIAN OCCUPANCY.

(FROM TIME IMMEMORIAL TO 1782.)

INTRODUCTORY REMARKS—LEGENDARY ACCOUNTS CONCERNING THE DELAWARE AND IROQUOIS INDIANS—THEIR WARS—THE IROQUOIS FINALLY VICTORIOUS—THE SHAWANESE—THE ERIES—THE HURON-IROQUOIS, OR WYANDOTS—CARTIER DISCOVERS THE LATTER ON THE SHORES OF LAKE HURON IN 1535—CHAMPLAIN'S OPERATIONS—THE FRENCH AND HURONS DEFEAT THE FIVE NATIONS—THE LATTER BIDE THEIR TIME, AND FINALLY TOTALLY DEFEAT AND DISPERSE THE HURONS—UNDER FRENCH PROTECTION, THE HURONS ARE AGAIN ASSEMBLED NEAR DETROIT—THEIR CHARACTERISTICS IN A SAVAGE STATE—THEIR WARS—THEY OCCUPY THE SANDUSKY COUNTRY—AS ALLIES OF THE BRITISH, THEY COMMIT MANY ATROCITIES ON THE AMERICAN FRONTIER SETTLEMENTS—THE AMERICANS RETALIATE BY SENDING VARIOUS EXPEDITIONS INTO THE INDIAN COUNTRY.

PROBABLY no county in the State of Ohio is richer in historical data concerning its aboriginal inhabitants than this, and to none were left so many landmarks indicating the life, habits and characteristics of its former occupants—the Indians. Here, within its borders, the brave but unfortunate Colonel Crawford fought his last battle, and suffered a death which will render his name conspicuous for all time in American annals; and here the Wyandots (who owned the land, who roamed at will beneath its forest shades, who chased the wild game through its tangled thickets, and who, under the fostering care of Christian ministers, had made many advances toward civilization) remained until within the memory of many now living—until they were the last of the Ohio tribes to be removed to new homes beyond the Missouri. For these reasons, therefore, no further apology is deemed necessary in explanation of the large amount of space which is here devoted to the Indians, and to their occupancy of this and adjacent regions.

Respecting the early history of the tribes once the claimants and occupants of these regions, the most rational and lucid accounts are obtained from the journals of the Jesuit and Moravian Missionaries, men who, during the seventeenth and eighteenth centuries, penetrated into this territory far in advance of the boldest hunters and trappers. They were informed by the old men of the Delawares (the Lenni Lenape, or original people, as they called themselves) that many centuries previous, their ancestors dwelt far away in the western wilds of the American Continent, but emigrating eastwardly, arrived after many years on the west bank of the "Namoesi Sipu" (the Mississippi), or river of fish, where they fell in with the Mengwes (Iroquois), who had also emigrated from a distant country in the direction of the setting sun, and approached this river somewhat nearer its source. The spies of the Lenape reported the country on the east of the Mississippi to be inhabited by a powerful nation, dwelling in large towns erected upon the shores of their principal streams.

This people bore the name of Allegewi. They were tall and strong, some were of gigantic size, and from them were derived the names of the

INDIAN JAIL.

Allegheny River and Mountains. Their towns were defended by regular fortifications or intrenchments of earth, vestiges of which are yet seen in a greater or less degree of preservation throughout the Mississippi and Ohio valleys and in the regions of the great lakes. The Lenape requested permission to establish themselves in their vicinity, a request which was refused, but leave was given them to pass the river and seek a country farther to the eastward. But while the Lenape were crossing the river, the Allegewi, becoming alarmed at their number, assailed and destroyed many of those who had reached the eastern shore, and threatened a like fate to others should they attempt the passage of the stream. Frenzied at the loss they had sustained, the Lenape eagerly accepted the proposition from the Mengwes, who had hitherto been spectators only of their enterprise, to conquer and divide the country of the Allegewi. A war of many years' duration was waged by the combined nations, marked by great havoc and loss of life on both sides, which finally resulted in the conquest and expulsion of the Allegewi, who fled by the way of the Mississippi River, never to return. Their country was apportioned among the conquerors—the Mengwes or Iroquois choosing the neighborhood of the great lakes, and the Lennape or Delawares possessing themselves of the lands to the southward.

Many ages after, during which the victors lived together in great harmony, the enterprising hunters of the Lenape tribes crossed the Alleghany Mountains and discovered the Susquehanna and Delaware Rivers and the bays into which they flowed. Exploring the Sheyichbi country (New Jersey), they arrived on the Hudson River, to which they subsequently gave the name of the Mohicannittuck. Returning to their nation after a long absence, they reported their discoveries, describing the country they had visited as abounding in game and fruits, fish and fowl, and destitute of inhabitants. Concluding this to be the country destined for them by the Great Spirit, the Lenape proceeded to establish themselves upon the principal rivers of the east, making the Delaware, to which they gave the name of Lenape—Wihittuck (the river of the Lenape) the center of their possessions.

All of the Lenape Nation, however, who crossed to the east side of the Mississippi, did not move toward the Atlantic coast, a part remaining behind to assist that portion of their people who, frightened by the reception which the Allegewi had given to their countrymen, fled far to the west of the Namoesi Sipu. Finally the Lenape became divided into three great bodies. The larger half of all settled on the Atlantic and the great rivers which flow into it. The other half was separated into two parts; the stronger continued beyond the Mississippi, the other remained on the eastern bank.

Ultimately, that part of the Lenape Nation who located on the east side of the Mississippi, became divided into many small tribes, receiving names from their places of residence, or from some circumstance remarkable at the time of its occurrence. Thus originated the Delawares, Shawanese, Nanticokes, Susquehannas, Nishamines, Conoys, Minsis, Abenaquis, Pequots, Narragansetts, Miamis, Illinois, Sauks, Foxes, Menomonees, Chippewas, Ottawas, Pottawatomies, and the Southern Cherokees and Choctaws. According to those who have made a special study of Indian history, all of the tribes above named belonged to the great Algonquin race, and spoke dialects of the Algonquin language, so similar that the members of any tribe could communicate with those of all others without the aid of an interpreter.

For some years the Mengwes (Iroquois), who, as before stated, constituted a separate race, remained near the Great Lakes with their canoes, in readiness to fly should the Allegewi return. The latter failed to appear again, however, and becoming emboldened and their numbers rapidly increasing, they stretched themselves eastward along the St. Lawrence, and finally locating, for the most part, in the present State of New York, became, on the north, immediate neighbors of the Lenape or Algonquin tribes. In the course of time, the Mengwes and Lenape became enemies, and, dreading the power of the Lenape, the Mengwes resolved to involve them in war —one Lenape tribe with another—to reduce their strength. They committed murders upon the members of one tribe, and induced the injured party to believe they were perpetrated by another. They stole into the country of the Delawares, surprised and killed their hunters, and escaped with the plunder.

The nations or tribes of that period had each a particular mark upon its war clubs, which, left beside a murdered person, denoted the aggressor. The Mengwes committed a murder in the Cherokee country, and left with the dead body a war-club bearing the insignia of the Lenape. The Cherokees in revenge fell upon the latter, and thus commenced a long and bloody war. The treachery and cunning of the Mengwes were at length discovered, and the Delaware tribe of the Lenape turned upon them with the determination to utterly extirpate them. They were the more strongly induced to take this resolution, as the man-eating propensities of the Mengwes, according to Heckewelder, had reduced them in the estimation of the Delawares below the rank of human beings.

To this time, each tribe of the Mengwes had acted under the direction of its particular chiefs, and, although the nation could not control the conduct of its members, it was made responsible for their outrages. Pressed by the Lenape, they resolved to form a confederation, which might enable them better to concentrate their forces in war, and to regulate their affairs in peace. Thannawage, an aged Mohawk, was the projector of this alliance. Under his auspices, *five* nations*—the Mohawks, Oneidas, Onondagas, Cayugas and Senecas—formed a species of republic, governed by the united councils of their aged and experienced chiefs. The beneficial effects of this confederation early displayed themselves. The Lenape were checked, and the Mengwes, whose warlike disposition soon familiarized them with firearms procured from the Dutch on the Hudson River, were enabled at the same time to contend with their ancient enemies and to resist the French, who now attempted the settlement of Canada, and the extension of their dominion over a large portion of the country lying between the Atlantic Ocean and the Mississippi River.

However, becoming hard pressed by the Europeans, the Mengwes, or Five Nations, sought reconciliation with their old enemies, the Lenape; and for this purpose, if the traditions of the Delawares be accredited, they affected one of the most extraordinary strokes of policy which aboriginal history has recorded.

When Indian nations are at war, the mediators between them are the women. However weary of the contest, the men hold it cowardly and disgraceful to seek reconciliation. They deem it inconsistent in a warrior to speak of peace with bloody weapons in his hands. He must maintain a determined courage, and appear at all times as ready and willing to fight as at the commencement of hostilities. With such dispositions, Indian wars

---

*To these a sixth nation, the Tuscaroras, was added in 1712. This last tribe originally dwelt in the western part of the present State of North Carolina, but having become involved in a war with their neighbors, were driven from their country northward, and adopted by the Mengwes or Iroquois confederacy.

would never cease if the women did not interfere and persuade the combatants to bury the hatchet and make peace with each other. On such occasions, the women would plead their cause with much eloquence. "Not a warrior," they would say, "but laments the loss of a father, a son, a brother or a friend. And mothers, who have borne with cheerfulness the pangs of childbirth and the anxieties that wait upon the infancy and adolescence of their sons, behold their promised blessings crushed in the field of battle, or perishing at the stake in unutterable torments. In the depths of their grief, they curse their wretched existence, and shudder at the idea of bearing children." They conjured the warriors, therefore, by their suffering wives, their helpless children, their homes and their friends, to interchange forgiveness, to cast away their arms, and, smoking together the pipe of peace, to embrace as friends those whom they had learned to esteem as enemies.

Such prayers thus urged seldom failed of the desired effect. The Mengwes solicited the Lenape to assume the function of peacemakers. "They had reflected," said the Mengwes, "upon the state of the Indian race, and were convinced that no means remained to preserve it unless some magnanimous nation would assume the character of the *woman*. It could not be given to a weak and contemptible tribe; such would not be listened to; but the Lenape and their allies would at once possess influence and command respect." The facts upon which these arguments were founded were known to the Delawares, and in a moment of blind confidence in the sincerity of the Iroquois they acceded to the proposition and assumed the *petticoat*. This ceremony was performed at Fort Orange (now Albany, N. Y.) amid great rejoicings in 1617, in the presence of the Dutch, whom the Lenape afterward charged with having conspired with the Mengwes for their destruction.

The Iroquois now assumed the rights of protection and command over the Delawares, but, still dreading their strength, they cunningly involved them again in a war with the Cherokees, promised to fight their battles, led them into an ambush of their foes and deserted them. The Delawares at length comprehended the treachery of their so-called friends of the North, and resolved to resume their arms, and, being still superior in numbers, to crush them. It was too late, however. The Europeans were now making their way into the country in every direction, and gave ample employment to the astonished Lenape.

On the other hand, the Mengwes denied the story told by the Lenape. They always asserted that they had conquered the Delawares by force of arms, and made them a subject people. And though it was said they were unable to detail the circumstance of this conquest, it is more reasonable to suppose it true than that a numerous and warlike people should have voluntarily suffered themselves to be disarmed and enslaved by a shallow artifice, or that, discovering the fraud practiced upon them, they should unresistingly have submitted to its consequences. This conquest was not an empty acquisition to the Mengwes. They claimed dominion over all the lands occupied by the Delawares—from the head-waters of the Delaware and Susquehanna Rivers on the north, to the Potomac on the south, and from the Atlantic Ocean westward to the Allegheny and Ohio Rivers—and their claims were distinctly acknowledged by the early whites when treating for the cession of lands. It is also recorded in history that from about 1617, until the Indian title to the territory just described was extinguished, parties of the Iroquois or Five Nations (afterward known as the Six Nations) occupied and wandered over the country of the Delawares at pleasure. True, the cowardly Delawares and the perfidious Shawanese always boldly claimed these grounds as their own (except when confronted and rebuked by the chiefs and head men of the Six Nations), yet the proprietaries wisely recognized the claim of the Six Nations, and it was with that great confederation of red men they treated when purchases of territory were made.

The Shawanese came from the South. They were a restless, wandering tribe, and had occupied regions now embraced by the States of Tennessee, Kentucky, Georgia and the Carolinas, before locating with their allies, the Delawares, in the province of Pennsylvania. After passing a few decades in that province, they migrated, or rather were driven, westward, and by the middle of the eighteenth century the entire tribe had settled on the Ohio River and its large tributaries.

Meanwhile the Six Nations were ceding to the Penns the lands occupied by the Delawares in Pennsylvania. Hence the latter were gradually yet peaceably pushed back to the westward by the constantly advancing tide of European emigration, until the beginning of the "Old French and Indian war" of 1754-63, when they, together with the Shawanese, Wyandots and other tribes of the great Northwest, became the allies of the French, and for many years thereafter ravaged at frequent intervals the western frontiers of Pennsylvania, Maryland and Virginia. Immediately after their defeat at Kittanning by Col. Armstrong in September, 1756, the Delawares fled into Ohio; they refused to settle again on the east of Fort Du Quesne, and seemed quite willing to have that fortress and its French garrison placed between them and the English. However, while extremely careful to maintain their old men, wives and children far to the westward of Fort Du Quesne, afterward Fort Pitt, the Delaware and Shawanese warriors (assisted until 1763 by the French) dominated over all of the country (with the exception of small circles surrounding Forts Pitt and Ligonier) lying immediately west of the Alleghenies, until 1764, when Gen. Henry Boquet, with a strong force of Pennsylvania and Virginia provincials marched into the "Muskingum country." He defeated the savages in several encounters, and caused them to sue for a peace which continued until after the beginning of the war for American independence. The British then rendered their name forever odious by marshaling under their banners the Delawares, Shawanese, Wyandots, Pottawatomies and other Northwestern tribes, besides the Six Nations of New York, whose warriors, after being fully supplied with English munitions of war, were sent forward to massacre, irrespective of age, sex or condition, the unfortunate residents of American border settlements.

Having related thus much of the traditional and authentic history of the Delawares and Shawanese—tribes which many years ago were prominent in the region now embracing Wyandot County—we turn our attention to the "Erigas," or Eries, and the Huron Iroquois, otherwise known as "Yendots," or Wyandots.

Of the Eries but little is known, and that little consists mainly of a few meager traditions. Indeed, some writers doubt whether such a tribe ever existed on the southern shores of Lake Erie, as claimed. However that may be, it is fair to presume that if such a race did once occupy the lake shore described, they were at the same time occupants of the territory now within the limits of Wyandot County. The early French priests, or missionaries, are quoted as authority for the statements, that about 230 years ago a powerful tribe of savages, termed variously the Eries or "Cat Nation," the Erigas or "Neutral Nation," occupied a wide expanse of country on the

HISTORY OF WYANDOT COUNTY. 231

southern border of Lake Erie, extending from the Niagara River on the east to the Miami River on the west; that they possessed fortified towns, and could muster four thousand warriors or fighting men, famed for their exploits in archery. Finally, however, they became involved in a war with the Iroquois or Five Nations, which continued until the entire tribe of Eries was either killed, adopted into the powerful confederacy of the Five Nations, or driven to other regions far to the westward. This misfortune, we are told, befell the Eries about the year 1656, and it is supposed that from the date last mentioned until the coming of the Wyandots or Huron-Iroquois, the territory lying immediately to the southward of Lake Erie remained as abandoned or neutral ground.

THE HURONS OR WYANDOTS.

The first European to make mention of the tribe of Indians, since known to history as the Wyandots, was the celebrated French navigator and explorer Jacques Cartier, who in the summer of 1535, sailed up the St. Lawrence River to a place called by him Mont Royal (afterward changed by the English to Montreal), and formally took possession of all the country round about (in the name of King Francis the First), under the title of New France. Soon after, Cartier and his men extended their explorations along the Huron Lake, where, on its southern shores, they suddenly discovered themselves to be intruders upon the territory of a powerful tribe of savages, who called themselves, as did the New York Iroquois, Ontwaonwes, meaning "real men," but known in French and English history as the Huron-Iroquois, or more commonly the Hurons from their proximity to the lake of that name. The immediate territory occupied by them (lying about 100 miles south of the mouth of the Ottawa or French River), was only about sixty miles in extent, yet, according to French writers, they then had twenty-five towns, and were about 30,000 in number.

The Hurons, like all untutored aboriginal tribes, were chiefly employed in pursuits of the chase and warring with their no less savage neighbors. Yet it cannot be said of them, as of the Five Nations, that they were particularly a warlike and vindictive people. However, they could not for a moment tolerate a tribal insult. Though they were, without a doubt, Mengwes or Iroquois Indians, possessing many characteristics in common with their New York brethren, yet they were sworn enemies, and their tribal and personal vindictiveness was proverbial among all Indians. As the New York Iroquois was a confederation of the Mohawks, Oneidas, Onondagas, Cayugas and Senecas, so the Huron-Iroquois was a league of the Hurons proper, and various tribes of the Algonquin race, and long before Cartier navigated the waters of the St. Lawrence these leagues and confederations of red men had waged wars of extermination against each other. Cartier made some attempts at colonization along the St. Lawrence, but in 1543 the few French settlements had all been abandoned and for more than half a century thereafter, the disturbed condition of France entirely prevented its people from utilizing his discoveries.

In 1603, however, Samuel de Champlain, another distinguished French mariner and explorer, led an expedition to Quebec, made a permanent settlement there, and, in fact, founded the colony of Canada. From Quebec and from Mont Royal, which was soon after established, the adventurous French explorers, fur traders, *voyageurs* and missionaries, pushed rapidly into the Western wilderness, and as early as 1615, Champlain himself visited the Hurons on the shores of Lake Manitouline. Quite as early, too, priests of the Récollet or Franciscan order, established missions in the same locality.

As before indicated, the Hurons had been reared to hate the very name of the Iroquois—their Southern brethren—and from the remotest period of their tribal existence, the defiant warwhoop, sounded by either of the belligerents, was sufficient for the commencement of another bloody chapter in the unwritten history of their career. The Hurons, therefore, hailed the arrival of Champlain with delight. They considered the brave bearing, and improved weapons of the French soldiery (added to their numerical strength, and their perfect acquaintance with the nature of the territory of their mortal enemies), would be a force sufficiently effective for the annihilation of the vindictive Iroquois. Terms of alliance with the French were soon proposed by the Hurons to Champlain, who not willing that his power should be unknown and unfelt in the Western wilds, and particularly that his dusky neighbors should be acquainted with the fact that opposition to his policy meant that they had in their own midst an enemy of terrific vengeance, whom it was always better to placate than offend, terms of alliance were at once consummated, by which, either in times of war or peace, the Hurons and French were to act as one people.

Very naturally the Southern Iroquois, or Five Nations, looked upon the French settlements on their Northern border with deep aversion. Already the Dutch had established themselves at New Amsterdam (New York) and along the Hudson River, the Swedes were occupying the Lower Delaware Valley, the English were making settlements at Plymouth Rock, and Salem, and Dorchester in New England, also in Virginia, and now the French encroachments upon the north aroused all their slumbering suspicions as to the final result, if foreign peoples were permitted to invade their territory, curtail their hunting-grounds, and thus trifle with their hitherto unlimited authority. Therefore, the ever alert and fiery Monawks soon found an occasion for taking up the tomahawk against the French and the Hurons. Their example became infectious, and soon the whole confederation—the Mohawks, Oneidas, Onondagas, Cayugas and Senecas—took the war-path against their enemies in the North. Advised of the approach of the Iroquois, Champlain made choice of his battle-field on the lake, which still bears his name, and with his own ships, surrounded by a fleet of bark canoes bearing his Huron allies, he met the enemy in mid-lake. Of course the advantages were all with the French, for water is never the selected battle-field of the Indian and bows and arrows were no match for musketry, and after a short, though stubbornly contested fight, the Iroquois gave way, and rowed their light, birch-bark canoes almost with the bounding of the deer to the shore from which they had embarked, hotly pursued by the equally light canoes of the Hurons. By the time they had reached the shore, the panic was complete. The forest offered them no encouragement to make a stand, so on they went, followed by the musketry of the French and the victorious whoop of the Hurons, till further pursuit was useless, and the chase was abandoned.

The defeat sustained by the Five Nations on Lake Champlain, at the hands of the French and Hurons, as well as the constantly spreading out of white settlements in New England and New York, caused the terrible Iroquois confederates first mentioned to confine their attention to matters nearer home, and to remain *comparatively* (though not wholly) peaceable for many years. Meanwhile, or about 1625, there had arrived on the shores of the St. Lawrence a few Jesuits, the vanguard of a host of those fiery champions of the cross who were destined, it appears, to crowd aside the more peaceful or more inert Franciscans throughout the whole river and lake region in the North, and substantially to appropriate that missionary ground to themselves. Their course was generally across Canada by land to Lake Manitouline, and thence in canoes through Lakes Huron, Michigan and Superior; for the more convenient route by way of the Niagara River and Lake Erie was guarded by the ferocious Iroquois, whom Champlain, by his ill-advised attack, had made the implacable enemy of the French. During the period referred to, the Jesuit fathers were assiduous in their attention to the Hurons; many of the latter were willingly made converts of the Catholic faith, and also showed a rapid advancement in the ways of civilization, particularly in the cultivation of the soil, and the production of corn, beans, pumpkins, squashes, etc. A number of schools and churches were likewise established at St. Louis, St. Ignatius, and other of their chief towns, and stockades erected to protect them from surprise by the dreaded Iroquois.

The Iroquois, however, were only biding their time. For about two score years had they smarted under the stigma of the defeat received at the hands of Champlain. Another generation of warriors had grown up among them, and the sons were eager seekers of an opportunity by which the shame of the past might be obliterated in the glory of the future. This opportunity was afforded them as early as 1648, when, by a treaty with the Dutch, they became well supplied with firearms, which previous to that time had been denied them by the Dutch authorities. The tireless, irreconcilable, unforgetting and unforgiving Iroquois were now ready for the war-path. The terms of the treaty above mentioned prevented the possibility of a conflict with the Dutch along the Hudson River, and as a similar peaceful state of affairs prevailed between them and the New England colonists, the young and restless warriors of the confederation turned to more remote fields in search of an enemy upon whom to test the virtues of their newly acquired implements of war.

Such an enemy was soon found (if any credence be given to traditional narration) in the persons of the Eries, who then inhabited the country lying to the southward of Lake Erie, and as a result, the latter were vanquished and destroyed. Our "Romans of America," the confederated Iroquois, then turned upon their ancient enemy, the Hurons. This war between the Hurons and Iroquois raged for several years, or until about 1659, when the latter invaded the country of the former in great forces, defeated them at every point, massacred large numbers, including several French priests, destroyed their crops and towns, and pursued the panic-stricken fugitives to remote quarters. Some of the Hurons sought protection under the walls of Quebec; others made their way to the frozen borders of Hudson's Bay; others again reached in safety the upper part of the Lower Peninsula of Michigan; but the greater portion fled to the Ojibwáy, or as now termed, Chippewa hunting-grounds, on the southern shore of Lake Superior. The implacable Iroquois even followed the fugitives westward to their new haunts, but the latter, by the help of the Chippewas, were enabled to repulse their arrogant enemies, who thenceforth seldom sought a war-path which led so far to the Northwest.

For a number of years the Hurons, the Ottawawas, or Ottawas, and the Dinondadies —tribes which had been driven from Canada by the fierce Iroquois—led a restless, nomadic life in the Lake Superior region. At length they were visited by Fathers Jacques Marquette and Claude Dablon, who began to organize the Hurons, under their various chiefs, as a permanently established, self-reliant people, and had succeeded in a measure, when a war with the Sioux compelled their removal to Michillimacinac, now known as Mackinaw. The assembling at Mackinaw of the Hurons and other tribes friendly to the French, took place about the year 1671, and there they remained until 1701; when La Motte Cadillac, who had been for several years the commandant at Mackinaw, established a permanent post on the "detroit," or strait, between Lakes Erie and St. Clair, which was at first known as Fort Ponchartrain, but soon after received the appellation of Detroit, which, as post, village and city it has retained to this day. Cadillac immediately made strenuous efforts to induce all the various tribes of the Northwest who were friends of the French to locate around and near Fort Ponchartrain, evidently desirous to have them well in hand, so that the French commanders could more easily lead them on warlike expeditions against the English and Iroquois. The Hurons at Mackinaw (as well as various other tribes) promptly accepted his invitation. At Detroit, they were joined by quite large bands of Hurons and Dinondadies from Charity and Great Manitouline Islands. Subsequently new tribal compacts were perfected, and the reunited and combined tribes of Hurons and Dinondadies then became known as the Wyandots, meaning "Traders of the West."

The warriors of the various tribes assembled at Fort Ponchartrain usually acted together in their numerous warlike expeditions. Of the conflicts which they waged with other savages, however, there is seldom any record unless they fought in connection with the French. Even in that case the accounts are few and meager. It appears that the Indians in Michigan under French control were almost continually at war with the Iroquois, and, notwithstanding the acknowledged valor and sagacity of the Six Nations, the former (having the support and sometimes the active assistance of the French) were able after 1707 to hold their ground, and to remain in possession of that peninsular throughout the century.

Early in May, 1712, when the warriors at Cadillac's settlement at the "detroit" were nearly all absent, hunting, a large body of Outagamie (Fox) and Mascoutin Indians, supposed to be in league with the Iroquois, suddenly appeared before Fort Ponchartrain, erected a breastwork, and made other preparations for an assault. Du Buisson, the commandant, who had only about twenty men with him, sent runners to call in the hunting-parties, and then awaited the assault of his foes. It was made on the 13th of May, and, though temporarily repulsed, there was every prospect that it would be successful on account of the comparatively large numbers of the assailants.

While the fight was going on, however, the Wyandots, Ottawa, and Pottawatomie warriors returned, and immediately attacked Du Buisson's assailants. The latter were driven into their own defenses; those defenses were assaulted by the French and their allies, and these in turn were repulsed by the Foxes and Mascoutins. Thus the conflict continued with varying fortunes for no less than nineteen days, when the invaders fled. Several miles north of Detroit they halted, and built a rude fortification, but the French and their allies attacked them with two small pieces of artillery, and routed them after three days more of fighting, when the Wyandots, Pottawatomies and Ottawas massacred *eight hundred men, women and children.*

In fact, the Fox nation was reported completely destroyed, but this was not the case. Some of its warriors joined the Iroquois, while the main body fled to the west side of Lake Michigan, where they were long distinguished for their especial hatred of the French. On the other hand, the friendship then cemented between the French and the Wyandots, Pottawatomies and Ottawas, endured through more than half a century of varied fortunes, and was scarcely severed when, throughout Canada and the West, the Gallic flag went down in hopeless defeat before the conquering Britons.

From Detroit the Wyandots gradually extended their hunting-grounds to the southward (the strength of the Iroquois, after a thirty years' war with the French, having been much reduced, and their hostile incursions into the Lake Erie region successfully repelled), and as early as 1725 were in quiet possession of the country about Sandusky Bay, and also claimed ownership to all the lands lying between Lake Erie and the Ohio River. In 1740, they consented to the proposition that a considerable body of Delawares, who had been driven out of Pennsylvania by the Iroquois, should occupy the Muskingum country. Finally, the entire Delaware nation, as well as the major portion of the Shawanese, became established in the present State of Ohio, and in conjunction with the Wyandots (all allies of the French), desolated and laid waste the border settlements of Pennsylvania, Maryland and Virginia for many years.

Our researches have not led us to believe that the Wyandots were any worse or any better than the average North American savage. They had the usual characteristics of the Indians, both of the Algonquin and Iroquois races, of which races, indeed, during the later years, they were a mixture. Less terrible in battle, less sagacious in council, than the men of the Six Nations, they were, nevertheless, like the rest of their red brethren, brave, hardy and skillful warriors, astute managers so far as their knowledge extended, generally faithful friends, and invariably most implacable enemies. Their own time they devoted to war, the chase or idleness, abandoning to the women all the labors which could be imposed upon their weary shoulders.

They lived in the utmost freedom which it is possible to imagine, consistent with any civil or military organization whatever. Their sachems exercised little authority, save to declare war or make peace, to determine on the migrations of the tribes, and to give wise counsels allaying any ill feelings which might exist among the people. There was no positive law compelling obedience.

Even in war there was no way by which the braves could be forced to take the war-path. Any chieftain could drive a stake into the ground, dance the war dance around it, strike the tomahawk into it with a yell of defiance, and call for warriors to go forth against the foe. If his courage or capacity was doubted, he obtained but few followers. If he was of approved valor and skill, a larger number would grasp their weapons in response to his appeal; while if he was a chieftain distinguished far and wide for deeds of blood and craft, the whole nation would spring to arms, and all its villages would resound with the terrific notes of the war song, chanted by hundreds of frenzied braves. Even after they had taken the field (or more properly speaking, the woods) against their enemies, they could not be compelled to fight, except by the fear of being called a "squaw," which, however, to the Indian mind was a very terrible punishment.

With the Indian method of warfare, the American mind is pretty well acquainted, so that we need not give a detailed description of it here. Few have not read how the warriors went forth against their foes, clad chiefly in hideous paint, but armed with tomahawk and scalping-knives, and those who have been sufficiently successful in fur-catching, carrying also the coveted muskets of the white man; how they made their way with the utmost secrecy through the forest until they reached the vicinity of their enemies, whether red or white; how, when their unsuspecting victims were wrapped in slumber, the whole crowd of painted demons would burst in among them, using musket, knife and tomahawk with the most furious zeal; and how, when the torch had been applied, men, women and children were stricken down in indiscriminate slaughter by the luried light of their blazing homes.

It is well known, too, that those who escaped immediate death were often reserved for a still more horrible doom; that the fearful sport of running the gauntlet when a hundred weapons were flung by malignant foes at the naked fugitive, was but the preliminary amusement before the awful burning at the stake, accompanied by all the refinements of torment which a baleful ingenuity could invent, yet supported with unsurpassable fortitude by the victim, who often shrieked his defiant death song amid the last convulsions of his tortured frame. Their religion was what might have been expected from their practices—a mass of senseless and brutal superstition—and Pere Marquette, the most zealous of missionaries, after several years of labor among the Northwestern Indians, could only say that the Hurons "retained a little Christianity."

It would be foreign to the design of this work to attempt to give an extended account of all the wars, movements, etc., of the Wyandot Indians, subsequent to their occupation of the Sandusky River country, even if such were possible. They were simply in common with all other tribes in the neighborhood of the great lakes, the friends and allies of the French, the foes of the English and Iroquois, and until the termination of the French power in America, had assisted the troops of that nation to fight many battles. Thus in 1744, when war broke out between France and England, numerous bands of savages from all the Northwestern tribes sought the service of the French. Some of them assailed the frontiers of Pennsylvania and Virginia, while others made their way to Montreal, where they were furnished with arms and ammunition, and were sent forth against the settlers of New York and New England. In 1745, one of the numerous records made by the Canadian officials states that fifty "Poutewatamies," fifteen "Puans" and ten "Illinois" came to go to war. Another mentions the arrival of thirty-eight "Outawois," seventeen "Santernes," twenty-four *Hurons*, and fourteen "Poutewatamies." Similar official memoranda show the sending out of not less than twenty marauding expeditions against the English colonists in one year, frequent mention being made of the part taken by the Hurons or Wyandots in these bloody raids.

After the close of that war by the treaty of Aix-la-Chapelle in 1748, there was comparative quiet among the red men of the Northwest until the opening of the great conflict known in Europe as the seven-years' war, but in America called the "Old French and Indian War." This contest was commenced in the spring of 1754, by a fight between a body of Virginia rangers, under Lieut. Col. George Washington, and a company of French sent out from Fort DuQuesne, and continued until toward the close of 1762, when, by a treaty of peace between France and England, the former power gave up all claims to the Northwest Territory, and from that date their authority here ceased forevermore.

Meanwhile, true to their promises and their friendships, the Hurons or Wyandots had participated side by side with the French in numerous conflicts. They assisted to defeat Braddock in front of Fort Du Quesne. Subsequently, nearly every Wyandot who could lift a tomahawk, went forth upon the war-path against the hapless inhabitants of the Pennsylvania and Virginia frontiers. They served under Montcalm in Canada. Again were they summoned to the defense of Fort Du Quesne when it was threatened by Gen. Forbes' army, and the following year, under D'Aubry, they proceeded to the relief of Fort Niagara. That fortress soon surrendered to the English, however, and a little later the fall of Quebec (at which a large body of the Northwestern Indians was present) virtually decided the fate of Canada and the Northwest. The Indians then began to lose faith in the omnipotence of their French friends, and our Wyandots, together with other tribes, returned to their homes on the shores of the Great Lakes and rivers of the West, and gloomily awaited the results referred to at the close of the preceding paragraph.

When, in 1763, Pontiac, the renowned Ottawa chieftain, marshaled under his leadership the Northwestern tribes for the purpose of overthrowing British supremacy in that region, the Wyandots joined him. After the siege of Detroit had continued for several weeks, the Wyandots and Pottawatomies made a treaty of peace with Maj. Gladwyn, the besieged English commander, but when Maj. Rogers and Capt. Dalzell led a party from the fort to attack Pontiac in his camp, the treacherous Wyandots and Pottawatomies fiercely assaulted the flank of the British column. Dalzell was killed, and it was only by the most desperate exertions that his successor, Capt. Grant, with the aid of Maj. Rogers and his American rangers, was able to make good his retreat to the fort, after a fourth of his men were killed or wounded.

The next summer, 1864, Gen. Bradstreet* occupied Detroit with a considerable force of English, Americans and Iroquois, the appearance of whom, together with Gen. Boquet's successful campaign into the Muskingum Country, doubtless tended to strongly impress the power of England on the hitherto hostile tribes. In 1765, George Croghan, Deputy Superintendent of Indian Affairs, under the celebrated Sir William Johnson, baronet, his Majesty's sole agent and Superintendent of Indian Affairs in the Northern Department of North America, etc.,etc., etc., held a grand council meeting at Fort Pitt, and also at Detroit, with the Northwestern tribes. They had by that time become thoroughly humbled, and were sincerely desirous of peace and the re-opening of the fur trade. After the treaties then made, all these tribes remained steady friends of the British, so long as that nation had any need of their services.

Pontiac himself gave in his submission at another council held in August of the same year. This celebrated chieftain was murdered by an Illinois Indian near St. Louis, in 1769. The Wyandotts, the Ottawas, and other tribes which had followed his lead, sprang to arms to avenge the murder, and almost exterminated the Illinois. Except this and similar conflicts with neighboring savages, also a slight participation in Dunmore's war, the Wyandotts remained at peace until the out-break of the Revolutionary war.

The British then made strong and, as we shall see, successful efforts to obtain their assistance, and in the summer of 1777, several hundred Wyandots, Ottawas, Pottawatomies, Chippewas, Winnebagoes and others from the region of the Great Lakes, all under Charles de Langdale, a French and

---

*During the same season, Gen. Bradstreet, with his forces, ascended the Sandusky River as far as it was navigable for boats, where a treaty of peace was signed by the chiefs and head men of the Wyandot nation. It is probable that he penetrated as far inland as the old Indian town of Upper Sandusky, which stood on the right bank of the river, about three miles above the present town of Upper Sandusky. Gen. Israel Putnam, then a Major in command of a battalion of American provincials, was with Bradstreet.

Indian half-breed, and another French officer, joined the English Army of Gen. Burgoyne. They accompanied him in his invasion of New York, but accomplished little, except to burn some houses and slaughter a few families. Burgoyne made some efforts to restrain their ferocity, which so disgusted them that they nearly or quite all returned home before his surrender to Gen. Gates. They also complained that Burgoyne did not take good care of them, and that over a hundred of their number were needlessly sacrificed at Bennington, Vt.

Although the Wyandots and their neighbors—the Ottawas, Chippewas, and Pottawattomies on the north, and the Delawares and Shawanese on the south—were opposed to taking any further part in the war under the direct command of British officers, and as part of a British Army, yet as it appears, they were not at all averse to making war upon the Americans in their own way, and under the lead of their own chiefs. Hence, late in the fall of 1777, the Wyandot, Delaware and Shawanese warriors appeared in Westmoreland County, Penn., where (many of the arms-bearing population being absent as members of Washington's army) they gathered many scalps. Elated with their success, they crossed the Alleghanies and slaughtered many of the inhabitants of the region now embraced by the counties of Bedford, Blair, Huntingdon and Somerset. Neither age, sex nor condition were spared by the savages. Immediately after the French Government had relinquished control of Canada and the Northwest Territory, the Jesuit missionaries retired to the Canadian side of the Great Lakes and the river St. Lawrence, hence the Wyandots, thus left without the Christianizing influences of their former teachers, soon relapsed to a degree of barbarity and ferociousness which placed them upon an even footing with their no less savage allies, the Delawares, Shawanese, Mingoes and Miamis. The Six Nations also took the war-path in the interests of the British, and under the lead of the villains Brant, Butler and various tories, committed many murders in the frontier settlements of New York and Pennsylvania, the massacre of the Wyoming settlers and the destruction of Hannastown being among their chief exploits.

These forays and murdering expeditions on the part of the savages under British pay continued until the close of the struggle for American independence. Meanwhile, the Americans were using all the means at hand in the endeavor to defend their border settlements in the interior, while at the same time engaged in fighting the British armies, then desolating their seaport towns. To this end, in 1778, Gen. Lachlin McIntosh, commander of the Western Military Department, with headquarters at Fort Pitt (Pittsburgh), marched forth with about 1,000 men. He was vested with discretionary powers, but it was purposed that he should march his army to Detroit, or at least as far as the Indian towns on the Sandusky River, which seemed to be the general places of rendezvous for the hostile tribes of the Northwest. Gen. McIntosh, however, lacked the qualifications necessary to conduct an Indian warfare successfully, and only proceeded as far as the immediate vicinity of the present town of Bolivar, in Tuscarawas County, Ohio. He there halted, erected Fort Laurens, garrisoned it with 150 men, under the command of Col. John Gibson, returned to Fort Pitt, and soon after resigned his command of the department.

Fort Laurens—named in honor of the then President of the Continental Congress, Henry Laurens—was the first substantially built work erected within the present limits of Ohio. Yet disasters attended it from the beginning. The Indians stole the horses, and drew the garrison into several ambuscades, killing fourteen men at one time and eleven at another, besides capturing a number of others. Eight hundred warriors, among them many Wyandots, invested it and kept up the siege for six weeks! The provisions grew short, and when supplies from Fort Pitt had arrived within a hundred yards of the fort, the garrison, in their joyousness, fired a general salute with musketry, which so frightened the loaded packhorses as to produce a general stampede through the woods, scattering the provisions in every direction, so that most of the much-needed supplies were lost. Although it was regarded very desirable, for various military reasons, to have a garrisoned fort and depot of supplies at a point about equidistant from the forts on the Ohio River and the hostile Indians on the Sandusky Plains, yet so disastrous had been the experiences at Fort Laurens that it was abandoned in August, 1779.

During subsequent years, other expeditions were organized in Pennsylvania and Kentucky for the purpose of chastizing with powder and ball the hostile Indians of Ohio. Thus Col. John Bowman took the field with 160 Kentuckians in July, 1779; Col. George Rogers Clark, with about 1,000 Kentuckians, in July, 1780; Gen. Daniel Brodhead, with 300 men from Fort Pitt, in April, 1781; and Col. Archibald Lochry, with about 100 men from Westmoreland County, Penn., in July, 1781. These expeditions were attended with varying success, but as they had in view the punishment of the savages occupying the southern half of the present State, no special significance, as regards the history of Wyandot County, can be attached to their movements.

However, notwithstanding the efforts put forth by the Americans, the savages remained masters of the field in Ohio, the neighborhood of the Great Lakes, and along the River St. Lawrence. The Wyandots of the Sandusky Plains (together with large numbers of the Delawares and Shawanese, who, driven from haunts farther South by the expeditions already mentioned, had established themselves near the Wyandots), fully supplied with war material from the British post at Detroit, still continued their massacres of the inhabitants of the frontier settlements of Pennsylvania. The fiendishness displayed by these savages in their attacks upon isolated white settlements was unbounded, and frequently every member of a family was found slain, scalped, their bodies otherwise horribly mutilated, and their dwelling burned to ashes. The prattling babe, as well as the tottering decrepit grandparents, all, all fell victims to a ferocity of disposition and studied cruelty of purpose that is harrowing to contemplate, even after the lapse of more than one hundred years. At last, stung to desperation by the loss of parents, brothers, sisters, wives and children, at the hands of the savages, the sturdy Scotch-Irish residents of Westmoreland and Washington Counties, Penn., determined upon the organization of a force, under the authority of the military commander of that department, which should proceed to the Sandusky Plains (the rendezvous of all the hostile savages of the Northwest), and give battle to the Indians upon their own ground. This determination resulted in the formation and sending forward of a body of men under Col. William Crawford, whose movements, battles, etc., will be noted in the succeeding chapter.

CHAPTER III.

INDIAN OCCUPANCY.—CONTINUED.

(EVENTS FROM 1782 TO 1818.)

THE INCEPTION OF CRAWFORD'S SANDUSKY EXPEDITION—THE MARCH—BATTLE—RESULTS—DR. KNIGHT'S NARRATION—BIOGRAPHICAL SKETCH OF COL. CRAWFORD—THE TREATY OF FORT MCINTOSH—TREATY OF FORT HARMAR—SAD RESULTS ATTENDING THE EXPEDITIONS UNDER GENS. HARMAR AND ST. CLAIR—"MAD ANTHONY" IN THE FIELD—HE DEFEATS THE COMBINED SAVAGE TRIBES AT THE "FALLEN TIMBERS"—INDIAN ACCOUNTS OF THE FIGHT—TREATY OF GREENVILLE—OF FORT INDUSTRY—OF BROWNSTOWN—THE WYANDOTS THE FRIENDS OF THE AMERICANS—WAR OF 1812-15—TREATY OF THE FOOT OF THE RAPIDS OF THE MIAMI OF THE LAKE—TERMS—SUPPLEMENTARY TREATY HELD AT ST. MARY'S—THE WYANDOTS FINALLY ESTABLISHED ON RESERVATIONS, I. E., LANDS NOW EMBRACED BY WYANDOT COUNTY—DEATH OF THEIR GREAT CHIEF TARHE—ATTENDANT FUNERAL CEREMONIES—TRIBAL NAMES OF THE WYANDOTS—SKETCH OF CHIEF TARHE, AS PREPARED BY WILLIAM WALKER, A QUADROON OF THE WYANDOT NATION.

AS already indicated, the year 1782, especially along the American border settlements, was one of war, bloodshed and carnage. Urged on by the British officers at Detroit, the Indians sought every opportunity of wreaking their vengeance upon the unprotected settlers. The woods of Western Pennsylvania and Virginia teemed with savages the most vindictive, and no one was safe from attack unless protected by the walls of a fortified station. On the 28th of March, Gen. William Irvine, commander of the Western Military Department, with headquarters at Fort Pitt, issued a call to the officers of the militia of the counties of Westmoreland and Washington (which counties then comprised all that part of Southwestern Pennsylvania lying west of Laurel Hill, Washington County, having been erected from Westmoreland in 1781) to meet in council at Pittsburgh on April 5, to take into consideration the adoption of some systematic defense of the exposed settlements. The council was largely attended, and the plan then agreed upon was to divide the regular troops equally between Forts Pitt and McIntosh, and to keep flying bodies of volunteers marching from place to place along the line of the frontier.

The county of Westmoreland agreed to furnish sixty-five men to range along the border from the Allegheny River to Laurel Hill, while Washington County stipulated to keep in the field one hundred and sixty men to patrol the Ohio River from Montour's Bottom to Wheeling. It was soon apparent, however, that this experiment or system of defense was inadequate, for in spite of every precaution, and in defiance of every expedient to thwart them, the wily savages would frequently cross to the left banks of the Ohio and Allegheny rivers, fall suddenly upon some unsuspecting and helpless settlements, and after completing their work of murder and pillage, would hurriedly recross the rivers, and be far away in the western wilds before the patroling volunteers were aware of their presence. Therefore it was soon demonstrated to the entire satisfaction of the majority of the endangered inhabitants that the only security for the frontier lay in carrying the war into the Indian country, and in accordance with this feeling Col. Marshall, the commandant at Fort McIntosh, wrote to Gen. Irvine, on the 2d of April, as follows: "This is most certain, that unless an expedition be carried against some of the principal Indian towns early this summer, this country must unavoidably suffer." Again, on the 4th of the same month, he wrote: "The people in general on the frontiers are waiting with anxious expectation, to know whether an expedition can be carried against Upper Sandusky * early this spring or not."

It is claimed that Gen. Irvine was not in favor of carrying the war into the Sandusky country, but be that as it may, he soon after called a council of the officers of his department to meet at his headquarters, at Fort Pitt, on the 7th of May, to take the matter under advisement. A large number of officers were present, and many others who could not come were represented in writing. There was a wonderful unanimity of opinion, at this meeting, as to the necessity of sending an expedition into the Indian country. It was known that most of the scalping parties prowling about the borders came from Upper Sandusky, not, however, that *all* the savages invading the settlements were Wyandots, but that their town was the grand rallying point for all the Northwest tribes before starting for the frontiers. Of the men called together at Gen. Irvine's headquarters, none failed to appreciate the pressing necessity for the destruction of the Sandusky rendezvous. An expedition was determined upon, and Upper Sandusky, the favorite point of assembling for the hostile Wyandots, Delawares, Shawanese and Mingoes, was named as the point of attack.

Mingo Bottom, a point on the right bank of the Ohio River, about two and one-half miles below the present town of Steubenville, was designated as the place of rendezvous, and Monday, May 20, as the time for the assemblage of those who were to take part in the movement. However, the volunteers did not all report until Friday morning, May 24, when the last one crossed to the west side of the river. The remainder of that day was occupied in the election of regimental and company officers, and in making preparations for the march to begin the following morning. Of the troops assembled, Washington County, Penn., had furnished three hundred and twenty; Westmoreland County, Penn., one hundred and thirty; Ohio County, Va., twenty; and other localities not known, ten; making a total of four hundred and eighty officers and men. In the election which took place for chief commander of the expedition, Col. William Crawford, of Westmoreland County, and Col. David Williamson, of Washington County—he who had commanded the expedition to the Tuscarawas country† two months before—were the candidates. The vote stood two hundred and thirty-five for Col. Crawford and two hundred and thirty for Col. Williamson. Col. Crawford having been, by a small majority, placed at the head of the expedition, his competitor, Col. Williamson, was immediately chosen, by a unanimous vote,

---

* Upper Sandusky was then the place where the British paid their Western Indian allies their annuities.

†We are well aware of the fact that numbers of those who have heretofore written concerning Crawford's Sandusky expedition have managed to interweave in their narrations something about the wretched Moravian affair. The Delawares under the partial control of the easy-going Moravian missionaries may or may not have been guilty of offenses against the whites east of the Ohio River. It has been claimed that Delaware Indians who spoke the German language, and who claimed to belong to one of the Moravian villages, committed murders in a white settlement on the Pennsylvania border, also, that Williamson's men found children's clothing in one of the Moravian towns, which was identified as having been worn by little white children when killed or carried off by Indians. Be this as it may, we consider an account of the Moravian affair as not pertinent to the history of the Wyandot Indians, or of Wyandot County, and, therefore, forbear making further mention of it. If, however, it be asserted that by reason of the killing of the Delaware Indians, at the Moravian towns, the Delaware tribes were made more bloodthirsty, and burned Col. Crawford by way of retaliation, we answer, that the Delawares were always bloodthirsty, vindictive, treacherous, cowardly, and that they burned many white prisoners at the stake, both before and after the death of Crawford.

the Senior Major, or second officer in rank. The other Majors were Thomas Gaddis, John McClelland and Maj. Brinton. Daniel Leet was elected Brigade-major; Dr. John Knight was appointed Surgeon; and John Slover and Jonathan Zane accompanied the expedition as guides. The force was divided into eighteen companies, some of which were commanded by the following named captains: McGeehan, Hoagland, Beeson, Munn, Ross, Ogle, John Biggs, Craig, Ritchie, John Miller, Joseph Bean and Andrew Hood.

Gen. Irvine issued sealed orders directed to the "Commander-in-Chief of the expedition against the Indian town at or near Sandusky," in which he specifically set forth the object of his command to be "to destroy with fire and sword (if practicable) the Indian town and settlement at Sandusky, by which it was hoped to give ease and safety to the inhabitants of this country; but if that should be found impracticable, to perform such other services in his power as would, in their consequences, have a tendency to answer that great end." It was also directed to "settle all questions of rank before leaving their rendezvous; and to regulate their last day's march so as to reach said town about dawn or a little before, in order to effect a surprise." Gen. Irvine spoke of the expedition as being composed of "disinterested and virtuous men, who had the protection of this country in view, and upon whom he enjoined it specially to act in such a manner as to reflect honor on and add reputation to the American arms." The orders concluded "with the sincere wishes of the department commander for their success."

It will thus be seen that the Crawford expedition *was not*, as many have thought and asserted, an unauthorized, illegal, ill-considered or murderous raid—"a sudden and wild maraud" of "untamed borderers"—an organization put on foot by lawless men, for the destruction of the remnant of the Moravian Indians that had been, during the previous year, forcibly removed from their villages on the Tuscarawas, by the British and Delaware hostiles to the Sandusky Plains. The massacre of innocent, inoffensive Indians *was not* the purpose of the expedition, commanded by Col. Crawford, to the Sandusky country, in 1782. It *was* to chastise hostile Indian tribes who had been and still were the deadly enemies of the settlers on the Western borders—enemies of our civilization—enemies of our common country—enemies of the white race. And all those writers who have maintained that Col. Crawford's command was composed of "bandits and murderers," and that their purpose was "to destroy the remainder of the Moravian Indians," were undoubtedly mistaken. Butterfield, in his admirable history of "Crawford's Sandusky Campaign," says, that "in all examinations of the correspondence of those projecting the expedition against Sandusky, and of those who took part in it, as well as of papers and documents of that period relating thereto, and of contemporaneous publications, he had not met with a single statement or word calculated to awaken a suspicion, even of intended harm, to the Christian Indians upon the Sandusky. Whenever the objective point of the expedition is mentioned, it is invariably given as Sandusky, or the Wyandot town or towns."

Early on the morning of Saturday, May 25, Crawford's command began its march on horseback for the Sandusky Plains, distant about 150 miles. They purposed making a rapid march, avoiding, as far as practicable, the Indian trails, so as to reach the Sandusky region without the knowledge of the Indians, and thus take them by surprise. The wily nature of the sav-

WYANDOT MISSION CHURCH.
COMPLETED IN 1825.

ages, says Butterfield, was too well known to give assurance of security because no enemy was visible; hence Col. Crawford "took every precaution to guard against ambuscades and surprises." "Unceasing vigilance was the watchword." However, nothing worthy of note transpired until Monday night, the 27th, while at the third encampment. Here a number of the men lost their horses, which were hunted for the next morning without success. It was then decided by Col. Crawford that these dismounted men should return home, as their crippled condition would contribute more to the burden and inconvenience of the movement than would their services toward securing its successful issue. On Tuesday, the 28th, the fourth day of the march, the command reached the Tuscarawas River, at a point about one mile below the present town of New Philadelphia, the county seat of Tuscarawas County. During the same evening, Maj. Brinton and Capt. Bean, while a short distance from the camp, discovered two Indians lurking near by, upon whom they immediately fired, but without effect. These escaping Indians, says Dr. Knight, gave notice to the hostiles on the Sandusky of the movements of the Americans. The fact of the discovery while yet so remote from the objective point rendered the necessity greater for a rapid march. Therefore, on Wednesday morning, the 29th, the march was resumed with a rapidity not before attempted. The guides, Slover and Zane, in the advance, led off in a northwest course across the Killbuck, above the present town of Millersburg, county seat of Holmes County, leaving Wooster, the present county seat of Wayne County, about ten miles to the north, and Mansfield, now the county seat of Richland County, a few miles south, and on the evening of Saturday, June 1, the entire command encamped at a point now known as Spring Mills, about eight miles east of the present town of Crestline, in Crawford County. On the following day, Sunday, June 2, the expedition arrived at the Sandusky River near the present village of Leesville, having marched about eighty-five miles during the last five days. The Sandusky Plains were reached on Monday, the 3d day of June, and the mouth of the Little Sandusky on Tuesday, the 4th. Later on the same day, the troops reached the Wyandot town, then known as Upper Sandusky, which was situated about three miles southeast of the present town of that name, but to the utter astonishment of Crawford and his men, not an Indian was to be seen, and the village appeared as if it had been deserted for some time. It was now afternoon. The men and officers dismounted, and while the horses leisurely grazed upon the luxuriant and abundant pasturage, and the men drank from a neighboring spring, Col. Crawford and his officers consulted as to what was best to be done.

One of the guides of the expedition, Slover, had been a prisoner among the Indians, and was familiar with the localities in the Sandusky region. He communicated his opinion to Col. Crawford, that the Indians of the deserted Wyandot village, on hearing of his approach, had probably gone to one of their towns, situated about eight miles down the river. It was thereupon determined to move forward at once in search of them. A march of three miles brought them to the site of the present town of Upper Sandusky. After a further advance movement of about a mile, some of the men stated that they were short of supplies, and expressed a desire to return instead of proceeding onward. A council of war was then held, to consider the question of the probability of the concentration of the hostile Indians in their front. Crawford and the guide, Zane, were of the opinion that there were indications that the Indians were bent on a determined resistance, and were then, probably, collecting their warriors. Zane advised an immediate return home. The council, however, decided to continue the march during the remainder of that afternoon, but no longer.

Col. Crawford had previously sent forward a small body of men for the purpose of reconnoitering. This party had gone but about two miles when they discovered the enemy in full force rapidly moving toward them. Immediately one of the scouts was sent back to Col. Crawford to inform him of the presence of the enemy. The council had just adjourned, and the troops were at once formed for action. After advancing about a mile, the enemy were found moving toward a grove, evidently meaning battle. Col. Crawford ordered his men to dismount and advance upon the Indians. They did so, and ere the expiration of many minutes the savages were dislodged, and the Americans in possession of the grove. Soon, the Delawares, with whom the battle was opened, were reinforced by the Wyandots, all being under the command of Capt. Mathew Elliott, an Irishman in the service of the British Government. Very soon, the action, which commenced about 4 o'clock P. M., became general. The infamous renegade, Simon Girty, was with the savages and acted a conspicuous part. The Indians were protected, in a measure, by the tall prairie grass, and the Pennsylvanians were also afforded some protection, too, by the grove, of which they had, by gallant fighting, obtained possession. The fight at "Battle Island," in what is now termed Crane Township, Wyandot County, continued with varying success until dark, when the Indians retired farther out into the prairie, and ceased firing. The loss sustained by the Americans was four killed and nineteen wounded. Doubtless the Indians lost a greater number, but of course it was never known.

Crawford retained his position in the grove during the night, his men meanwhile suffering terribly for lack of water. At daylight on the morning of June 5 (Wednesday), the firing was renewed, but in a desultory manner, and at long range only, and so continued throughout the day. Hence little damage was done (the Americans having four more men wounded) and the relative position of the opposing forces remained unchanged. During the day, however, the enemy was re-inforced by a body of white troops, known as "Butler's Rangers," also by about 200 Shawanese Indians. Savages from other quarters also kept gathering in, so that the Americans were surrounded and greatly out-numbered. A council of war was thereupon called, which unanimously decided upon a retreat that night. The movement was to commence at 9 o'clock. Just as the hour had arrived for the retreat to begin, the enemy discovered the intentions of the Americans and opened fire from various points. Confusion followed, and some in the front line hurried off, followed by many pushing forward from the rear. The advance, under command of Maj. McClelland, was furiously attacked by the Delawares and Shawanese and suffered severely, he being fatally wounded. The rear division was also attacked and suffered considerable loss. All through the night the retreat was continued, the enemy pursuing in considerable force, with more or less vigor and efficiency. The advance of Crawford's command arrived at the old town of Upper Sandusky about daybreak of Thursday, June 6, where, after a short time, about 300 of the original force were collected.

It was then ascertained that Col. Crawford was missing. But none knew whether he was killed, captured, or was making his escape on some route other than that taken by the main body of his forces. Dr. Knight and John Slover, one of the pilots, or guides, were also among those unaccounted for. The retreating volunteers were now under the command of Col. Williamson, who is said to have conducted the movement as skillfully and successfully as could have been reasonably expected. When well along on the open country or "plains," a large body of mounted Indians and British cavalry came in sight of the retreating troops. The enemy pressed forward so closely upon their flanks and rear that the Pennsylvanians finally halted, formed their lines, and gave battle. This was at 2 o'clock P. M., on Thursday, June 6, near the eastern edge of the plains, not far from a small branch of the Olentangy Creek, a tributary of the Scioto, in what is now known as Whetstone Township, Crawford County. The enemy attacked on front, left flank and rear, but seemed glad to retire at the expiration of an hour's fighting. In this action, termed the "Battle of Olentangy," the Americans lost three men killed and eight wounded. The loss of the enemy was much greater.

The retreat then continued in a chilly, drenching rain, the enemy still pursuing and occasionally firing a shot at a respectable distance in the rear. At night the opposing forces were encamped within a mile of each other. Scarcely had the Americans formed their lines at daybreak of the 7th, when the enemy opened fire from the rear. Here they captured two of the Americans, and it is supposed tomahawked them. But the main body was not pursued further, the last hostile shot having been fired near the present town of Crestline, in Crawford County. On their further retreat they had frequent accessions of stragglers, who had been detached by various means from the main body early in the retrograde movement. The homeward march was along the trail of the troops when outward bound, as far as the Tuscarawas, which they crossed June 10. From that point to the Ohio River, Williamson's trail was followed. Mingo Bottom was reached on the 13th, where, to their great joy, they found several of their missing comrades, who had arrived before them. But the gallant Crawford was not among them, and about 100 of the 480 men that started with the expedition never returned. Among the unreturned heroes were William Harrison, son-in-law, and William Crawford, the nephew of Col. Crawford. Harrison suffered death at the stake.

John Slover, the guide, was captured by a band of Shawanese within twenty miles of the Tuscarawas River, at a point now within the limits of Wayne County. He was taken back to the Sandusky Plains, and from thence to the Shawanese towns near Mad River, now in Logan County, where he was beaten and made to run the gauntlet. Finally, he was taken to Wapatomica, an Indian village situated near the site of Zanesfield, in Logan County, where a council condemned him to die at the stake. Taken to Mack-a-chack, another Indian village, which stood near the site of the present town of West Liberty, in Logan County, he was bound to a post and a fire kindled around him. Soon after the fire began to blaze a heavy rainstorm came on and extinguished it. The savages then postponed the burning until the next day. During the night, though bound with cords and guarded, he escaped, and finally reached the settlements, having crossed the Ohio River at Wheeling, July 11, 1782.

We now give place to Dr. John Knight's narrative, which, written by him soon after his escape, tells of the march, battle, capture and death of Col. Crawford. It is as follows:

"About the latter end of the month of March or the beginning of April, of the year 1782, the Western Indians began to make incursions upon the frontiers of Ohio County, Va., and Washington and Westmoreland Counties, Penn., which had been their constant practice ever since the commencement of the present war between the United States and Great Britain.

"In consequence of these predatory invasions, the principal officers of the above-mentioned counties, named Cols. Williamson and Marshall, tried every method in their power to set on foot an expedition against the Wyandot towns, which they could effect in no other way than by giving all possible encouragement to volunteers. The plan proposed was as follows: Every man furnishing himself with a horse, a gun, and one month's provision should be exempt from two tours of militia duty. Likewise that every one who had been plundered by the Indians should, if the plunder could be found at their towns, have it again, proving it to be his property; and all horses lost on the expedition by unavoidable accidents were to be replaced by horses taken in the enemy's country.

"The place appointed for the rendezvous or general meeting of the volunteers was fixed on the west side of the Ohio River, about forty miles below Fort Pitt by land, and, I think, about seventy-five by water.

"Col. Crawford was solicited by the general voice of these western counties and districts to command the expedition. He accordingly set out as a volunteer and came to Fort Pitt two days before the time appointed for the assembling of the men. As there was no surgeon yet appointed to go with the expedition, Col. Crawford begged the favor of Gen. Irvine to permit me to accompany him (my consent having been previously asked), to which the General agreed, provided Col. Gibson did not object. Having obtained permission of the Colonel, I left Fort Pitt on Tuesday, May 21, and the next day about 1 in the afternoon arrived at the Mingo Bottom. The volunteers did not all cross the river until Friday morning, the 24th; they then distributed themselves into eighteen companies, choosing their Captains by vote. There were chosen also one Colonel commandant, four field Majors and one brigade Major. There were 465 who voted.

"We began our march on Saturday, May 25, making almost a due west course, and on the fourth day reached the old Moravian town upon the river Muskingum, about sixty miles from the river Ohio. Some of the men, having lost their horses on the night preceding, returned home. Tuesday, the 28th, in the evening, Maj. Brinton and Capt. Bean went some distance from camp to reconnoiter; having gone about one-quarter of a mile, they saw two Indians, upon whom they fired and then returned to camp. This was the first place we were discovered, as we understood afterward. On Tuesday, the 4th of June, which was the eleventh day of our march, about 1 o'clock, we came to the spot where the town of Sandusky formerly stood; the inhabitants had moved eighteen miles lower down the creek nearer Lower Sandusky; but as neither our guides or any who were with us had known anything of their removal, we began to conjecture there were no Indian towns nearer than Lower Sandusky, which was at least forty miles distant.

"However, after refreshing our horses, we advanced on in search of some of their settlements, but had scarcely got the distance of three or four miles from the old town, when a number of our men expressed their desire to return, some of them alleging that they had only five days' provisions; upon which the field officers and Captains determined in council to proceed that afternoon and no longer. Previous to the calling of this council, a small party of light horse had been sent forward to reconnoiter. Just as the council had ended, an express returned from the above-mentioned party of light horse with the intelligence that they had been about three miles in front, and had seen a large body of Indians running toward them. In a short time we saw the rest of the light horse, who joined us, and having gone one mile further met a number of Indians who had partly got possession of a piece of woods before us, whilst we were in the plains, but our men, alighting from their horses and rushing into the woods, soon obliged them to abandon that place.

"The enemy, being by this time re-inforced, flanked to the right and a part of them coming in our rear quickly made the action more serious. The firing continued very warm on both sides from 4 o'clock until the dark of the evening, each party maintaining their ground. And next morning about 4 o'clock, some guns were discharged at the distance of 200 or 300 yards; which continued till day, doing little or no execution on either side. The field officers then assembled and agreed as the enemy were every moment increasing, and we had already a number wounded, to retreat that night. The whole body was to form into three lines, keeping the wounded in the center. We had four killed and twenty-three wounded, of the latter seven very dangerously, on which account as many biers were got ready to carry them; most of the rest were slightly wounded and none so bad but they could ride on horseback. After dark the officers went on the outposts and brought in all the men as expeditiously as they could. Just as the troops were about to form, several guns were fired by the enemy, upon which some of our men spoke out and said our intention was discovered by the Indians, who were firing alarm guns, upon which some in front hurried off, and the rest immediately followed, leaving the seven men that were dangerously wounded, some of whom, however, got off on horseback by means of some good friends, who waited for and assisted them.

"We had not got a quarter of a mile from the field of action, when I heard Col. Crawford calling for his son, John Crawford, his son-in-law, Maj. Harrison, Maj. Rose, and William Crawford, his nephew, upon which I came up and told him I believed they were before us. He asked, 'Is that the doctor?' I answered, 'yes.' He then replied that they were not in front, and begged of me not to leave him. I promised him I would not. We then waited and continued calling for these men until all of the troops had passed us. The Colonel told me that his horse had almost given out, that he could not keep up with the troops, and wished some of his best friends to remain with him; presently there came two men riding after us, one of them an old man, the other a lad. We inquired if they had seen any of the above persons, and they answered they had not.

"By this time there was a very hot firing before us, and, as we judged, near where our main body must have been. Our course was then nearly southwest, but, changing it, we went north about two miles, the two men remaining in company with us. Judging ourselves now out of the enemy's lines, we took a due east course, taking care to keep at the distance of fifteen or twenty yards apart, and directing ourselves by the north star. The old man often lagged behind, and when this was the case he never failed to call for us to halt for him. When we were near the Sandusky River, he fell one hundred yards behind, and bawled out for us to stop, as usual. While we were preparing to reprimand him for making a noise, I heard an Indian halloo, as I thought, 150 yards from the man, and partly behind him. After this we did not hear the man call again, neither did he ever come up to us any more. It was now past midnight, and about daybreak Col. Crawford's and the young man's horses gave out, and they left them. We pursued our journey eastward, and about 1 o'clock fell in with Capt. Biggs, who had carried Lieut. Ashley from the field of action, who had been dangerously wounded.

"We then went on about the space of an hour, when, a heavy rain coming on, we concluded it was best to encamp, as we were encumbered with the wounded officer. We then barked four or five trees, made an encampment and a fire, and remained there all that night. Next morning we again prosecuted our journey, and having gone about three miles, found a deer which had been recently killed. The meat was sliced from the hams and bundled in the skin, with a tomahawk lying by it. We carried all with us, and, in advancing about one mile further, espied the smoke of a fire. We then gave the wounded officer into the charge of the young man, desiring him to stay behind whilst the Colonel, the Captain and myself walked up as cautiously as we could toward the fire. When we came to it we concluded, from several circumstances, some of our people had encamped there the preceding night. We then went about roasting the venison, and, when about to march, we observed one of our men coming upon our tracks. He seemed at first very shy, but having called to him, he came up and told that he was the person that killed the deer, but, upon hearing us come up, was afraid of Indians, hid in a thicket, and made off. Upon this we gave him some bread and roasted venison, proceeded altogether upon our journey, and about 2 o'clock came upon the paths by which we had gone out. Capt. Biggs and myself did not think it safe to keep the road, but the Colonel said the Indians would not follow the troops further than the plains, which we were then considerably past. As the wounded officer rode Capt. Biggs' horse, I loaned the Captain mine. The Colonel and myself went about one hundred yards in front, the Captain and wounded officer in the center, and the two young men behind. After we had traveled about one mile and a half, several Indians started up within fifteen or twenty steps of the Colonel and me. As we at first discovered only three, I immediately got behind a large black oak, made ready my piece, and raised it up to take sight, when the Colonel called to me twice not to fire; upon that, one of the Indians ran up to the Colonel and took him by the hand. The Colonel then told me to put down my gun, which I did. At that instant one of them came up to me whom I had formerly seen very often, calling me Doctor, and took me by the hand. They were Delaware Indians of the Wingenin tribe. Capt. Biggs fired amongst them, but did no execution. They then told us to call these and make them come back, else they would go and kill them, which the Colonel did, but they four got off and escaped for that time.

"The Colonel and I were then taken to the Indian camp, which was about one-half a mile from the place where we were captured. On Sunday evening five Delawares, who had posted themselves at some distance further on the road, brought back to the camp where we lay Capt. Biggs and Lieut. Ashley's scalps, with an Indian scalp, which Capt. Biggs had taken in the field of action. They also brought in Biggs' horse and mine. They told us the other two had got away from them.

"Monday morning, the 10th of June, we were paraded to march to Sandusky about thirty-three miles distant. They had eleven prisoners of us, and four scalps, the Indians being seventeen in number. Col. Crawford was very desirous to see a 'certain Simon Girty,' who lived among the Indians, and was on this account permitted to go to Tarhe the same night, with two warriors to guard him, having orders at the same time to pass by the place where the Colonel had turned out his horse, that they might if possible find him. The rest of us were taken to the old town, which was within eight miles of the new.

"Tuesday morning, the 11th, Col. Crawford was brought out to us on purpose to be marched in with the prisoners. I asked the Colonel if he had seen Mr. Girty; he told me had, and that Girty had promised to do everything in his power for him, but that the Indians were very much enraged against the prisoners, particularly Capt. Pipe, one of the chiefs. He likewise told me that Girty had informed him that his son-in-law, Maj. Harrison, and his nephew, William Crawford, were made prisoners by the Shawanese, but had been pardoned. This Capt. Pipe had come from the towns about an hour before Col. Crawford, and had painted all the prisoners' faces black.

"As he was painting me, he told me that I should go to the Shawanese towns and see my friends. When the Colonel arrived he painted him black, also told him he was glad to see him, and that he would have him shaved when he came to see his friends at the Wyandot town. When we marched the Colonel and I were kept back between Pipe and Wingenim, the two Delaware chiefs, the other nine prisoners were sent forward with another party of Indians. As we went along we saw four of the prisoners lying by the path tomahawked and scalped. Some of them were at the distance of half a mile from each other. When we arrived within half a mile of the place where the Colonel was to be executed, we overtook the five prisoners that remained alive. The Indians had caused them to sit down on the ground, as they did, also, the Colonel and me at some distance from them. I was then given in charge of an Indian fellow to be taken to the Shawanese towns.

"In the place where we were made to sit down, there were a number of squaws and boys who fell on the five prisoners and tomahawked them. There was a certain John McKinley among the prisoners, formerly an officer in the Thirteenth Virginia Regiment, whose head an old squaw cut off, and the Indians kicked it about on the ground. The young Indian fellows came often where the Colonel and I were, and dashed the scalps in our faces. We were then conducted along toward the place where the Colonel was afterward executed. When we came within about a half mile of it, Simon Girty met us, with several Indians on horseback; he spoke to the Colonel, but I was about 150 yards behind, and could not hear what passed between them. Almost every Indian we met struck us either with sticks or their fists. Girty waited until I was brought up, and asked was that the doctor. I told him yes, and went toward him reaching out my hand, but he bid me be gone, and called me a d——d rascal; upon which the fellow who had me in charge pulled me along. Girty rode up after me and told me I was to go to the Shawanese towns.

"When we were come to the fire, the Colonel was stripped naked, ordered to sit down by the fire, and then they beat him with sticks and their fists. Presently after, I was treated in the same manner. They then tied a rope to the foot of a post about fifteen feet high, bound the Colonel's hands behind his back, and fastened the rope to the ligatures between his wrists. The rope was long enough either for him to sit down or walk around the post once or twice and return the same way. The Colonel then called to Girty and asked him if they intended to burn him. Girty answered yes. The Colonel said he would take it all patiently. Upon this Capt. Pipe, the Delaware chief, made a speech to the Indians, to about thirty or forty men, sixty or seventy squaws and boys. When the speech was finished, they all yelled a hideous and hearty assent to what had been said. The Indian men then took their guns and shot powder into the Colonel's body, from his feet as far up as his neck. I think not less than seventeen loads were discharged upon his naked body. They then crowded about him and to the best of my observation cut off his ears; when the throng had dispersed a little, I saw the blood running from both sides of his head in consequence thereof.

"The fire was about six or seven yards from the post to which the Colonel was tied. It was made of small hickory poles, each about six feet long. Three or four Indians, by turns, would take up, individually, one of these burning pieces of wood, and apply it to his naked body, already burned black with the powder. These tormentors presented themselves on every side of him so that whichever way he ran around the post they met him with burning faggots and poles. Some of the squaws took wide boards upon which they would put a quantity of burning coals and hot embers, and throw on him, so that in a short time he had nothing but coals of fire and hot ashes to walk upon. In the midst of these extreme torments and tortures he called to Simon Girty, and begged of him to shoot him, but Girty making no answer, he called to him again. Girty by way of derision told the Colonel he had no gun, at the same time turning about to an Indian who was behind him, laughed heartily, and by all his gestures seemed delighted at the horrid scene.

"Girty then came up to me and bade me prepare for death. He said, however, I was not to die at this place, but to be burned at the Shawanese town. He swore by G—d, I need not expect to escape death, but should suffer it in all its extremities. He then observed that some prisoners had given him to understand that if our people had him they would not hurt him; for his part, he said, he did not believe it, but desired to know my opinion of the matter. Being at that time in great anguish and distress for the torments the Colonel was suffering before my eyes, as well as the expectation of undergoing the same fate in two days, I made little or no reply. He expressed a great deal of ill will for Col. Gibson, and said he was one of his greatest enemies, and more to the same purpose, to all of which I paid very little attention. Col. Crawford, at this period of his sufferings, besought the Almighty to have mercy on his soul, spoke very low, and bore his torments with the most manly fortitude. He continued in all the extremities of pain for an hour and three-quarters or two hours, as near as I can judge, when at last, being almost spent, he lay down on his belly. They then scalped him, and repeatedly threw the scalp in my face, telling me 'that was my Captain.' An old squaw (whose appearance every way answered the idea the people entertain of the devil) got a board, took a parcel of coals and ashes, and laid them on his back and head after he had been scalped; he then raised himself upon his feet and began to walk around the post; they next put a burning stick to him as usual, but he seemed more insensible of pain than before.

"The Indian fellow who had me in charge now took me away to Capt. Pipe's house, about three-quarters of a mile from the place of the Colonel's execution. I was bound all night, and thus prevented from seeing the last of the horrid spectacle. Next morning, being June 12, the Indian untied me, painted me black, and we set off for the Shawanese town, which he told me was somewhat less than forty miles from that place. We soon came to the spot where the Colonel had been burnt, as it was partly in our way. I saw his bones lying among the remains of the fire, almost burnt to ashes. I suppose after he was dead they had laid his body on the fire.

The Indian told me that was my 'Big Captain,' and gave the scalp-halloo. He was on horseback and drove me before him. I pretended to this Indian I was ignorant of the death I was to die at the Shawanese town; affected as cheerful a countenance as possible, and asked him if we were not to live together as brothers in one house when we should get to the town. He seemed well pleased, and said yes. He then asked me if I could make wigwams. I told him I could; he then seemed more friendly. We went that day, as near as I can judge, about twenty-five miles, the course partly southwest. The Indian told me we should the next day come to the town, the sun being in such a direction, pointing nearly south. At night, when we went to rest, I attempted very often to untie myself, but the Indian was extremely vigilant and scarce ever shut his eyes that night. About daybreak, he got up and untied me. He next began to mend the fire, and as the gnats were troublesome, I asked him if I could make a smoke behind him. He said yes. I then took the end of a dogwood fork, which had been burnt down to about eighteen inches long; it was the longest stick I could find, yet too small for the purpose I had in view; then I picked up another smaller stick, and taking a coal of fire between them, went behind him, then turning suddenly about, I* struck him on the head with all the force I was master of, which so stunned him that he fell forward with both his hands in the fire.

"Seeing him recover and get up, I seized his gun, while he ran off howling in a most fearful manner. I followed him with the determination to shoot him down, but pulling back the cock of the gun with too great violence, I believe I broke the mainspring. I pursued him about thirty yards, still endeavoring to fire the gun, but could not; then going back to the fire, I took his blanket, a pair of new moccasins, his hatchet, powder-horn, bullet-bag, together with his gun, and marched off, directing my course toward the 5 o'clock mark. About half an hour before sunset, I came to the plains, which I think are about sixteen miles wide. I laid me down in a thicket till dark, and then by the assistance of the north star made my way through them and got into the woods before morning. I pressed on the next day, and about noon crossed the paths by which our troops had gone out. These paths were nearly east and west, but I went due north nearly all that afternoon, with a view to avoid the enemy.

"In the evening I began to be very faint, and no wonder. I had been six days a prisoner, the two latter days of which I had eaten nothing, and but very little the first three or four. There were wild gooseberries in abundance in the woods, but being unripe required mastication, which at that time I was not able to perform on account of a blow received from an Indian on the jaw with the back of a tomahawk. There was a weed that grew in that place, the juice of which I knew to be grateful and nourishing. I gathered up a bundle of the same, took up my lodging under a large spreading beech tree, having sucked plentifully of the juice, and went to sleep. Next day I made a due east course, which I generally kept the rest of my journey. I often imagined my gun was only wood-bound, and tried every method I could devise to unscrew the lock, but never could effect it, having no knife nor anything fitting for the purpose. I had now the satisfaction to find my jaw began to mend, and in four or five days could chew any vegetable proper for nourishment, but finding my gun a useless burden, left her in the wilderness. I had no apparatus for making fire to sleep by, so that I could get but little rest for the gnats and mosquitoes. There are likewise a great many swamps in the beech ridge, which

---

*The Doctor was a small sized man.

occasioned me very often to lie wet. This ridge through which I traveled is about twenty miles broad; the ground in general is very level and rich, free from shrubs and brush; there are, however, very few springs, yet wells might easily be dug in all parts of the ridge. The timber on it is very lofty, but it is no easy matter to make a straight course through the same, the moss growing as high upon the south side of the trees as on the north.

"There are a great many white oak, ash and hickory trees that grow among the beech timber. There are likewise some places on the ridge, perhaps for three or four continued miles, where there is little or no beech, and in such spots, black, white oak, ash and hickory abound; sugar trees grow there also to a very great bulk. The soil is remarkably good, the ground a little ascending and descending with some rivulets and a few springs. When I got out of the beech ridge and near the River Muskingum, the land was more broken, but equally rich with those before mentioned and abounding with brooks and springs of water. There are also several small creeks that empty into that river, the bed of which is more than a mile wide in places. The wood consists of white and black oaks, walnut, hickory and sugar tree in the greatest abundance. In all parts of the country through which I came, the game was plenty, that is to say, deer, turkeys and pheasants. I likewise saw a great many vestiges of bears and elks.

"I crossed the River Muskingum about three or four miles below Fort Laurens, and crossing all paths, aimed for the Ohio River. All this time my food was gooseberries, young nettles, the juice of herbs, a few service berries and some May apples, likewise two young blackbirds and a terrapin, which I devoured raw. When my food sat heavy on my stomach, I used to eat a little wild ginger, which put all to rights. I came upon the Ohio River about five miles below Fort McIntosh, in the evening of the twenty-first day after I had made my escape, and on the twenty-second, about 7 o'clock in the morning, being the 4th of July, arrived safe, though much fatigued." In 1784, Dr. Knight married Col. Crawford's half-sister. He finally settled at Shelbyville, Ky., where he died March 12, 1838.

As shown in the foregoing narration, the Delawares, true to their savage and cowardly nature from time immemorial, and led on by the chiefs, Capt. Pipe and Wingenund, were the guilty authors of this terrible act of barbarity. This most atrocious deed, connived at by British officers, was perpetrated, it is claimed, in the present township of Crawford, on the southeast bank of Tymochtee Creek, a short distance northeast from the present town of Crawfordsville, and distant about seven miles northwest from Upper Sandusky, county seat of Wyandot County.

Col. William Crawford, a son of Scotch-Irish parents, was born in the region now known as Berkeley County, W. Va., in the year 1732. When about eighteen years of age, he became acquainted with George Washington, who was of the same age with himself, and was at that time in the service of Lord Fairfax as surveyor. Crawford's early home was in the Fairfax grant, in which Washington was surveying, being in what was called the "Northern Neck of Virginia," or the northern portion of the since famous Shenandoah Valley. Their acquaintance soon ripened into warm friendship, which was never impaired or broken, or suffered the slightest interruption while life lasted. Crawford's whole life was passed upon the frontiers. Therefore, his education was limited, but his natural abilities, good judgment and knowledge of men were very remarkable. He was generous in disposition, and in common with those of his lineage on the Pennsylvania and Virginia borders, possessed the most undaunted courage. He acquired a knowledge of surveying from Washington, and made it his business pursuit in part until the opening of the "old French and Indian war," when he joined a company of Virginia Rangers, and participated in Braddock's disastrous expedition as an Ensign. For gallantry on the battle-field, he was promoted to a lieutenancy. During the subsequent two or three years, he was employed in garrison duty, or as a scout on the frontiers. In 1758, he was commissioned Captain of a company of Virginia Riflemen, which was attached to Col. George Washington's regiment of Virginians, and performed efficient service during Gen. Forbes' successful campaign against Fort Du Quesne. Capt. Crawford remained in the service of the colony of Virginia until the close of the war mentioned.

In 1767, he moved to a point then and for years afterward known as "Stewart's Crossing" of the Youghiogheny, but afterward called New Haven, a village opposite the present town of Connellsville, in Fayette County, Penn. Crawford was among the first to settle in that part of the present State of Pennsylvania, a region which was then claimed by the province of Virginia, and of which the Indian title was not extinguished until the following year (1768). However, from Stewart's Crossing, Capt. Crawford kept up his correspondence with his old friend Washington, and to the close of his life (Washington having purchased from the Virginia authorities a large tract of land, lying in the present southwest quarter of Pennsylvania, west of Laurel Hill) served him as his land agent. In 1770, Washington and Crawford, with other gentlemen, voyaged together down the Ohio River, from Fort Pitt to the mouth of the Kanawha, and up that river, exploring with a view to the ultimate location and purchase of lands.

By an act of the General Assembly of the Province of Pennsylvania, passed on Saturday, March 9, 1771, Bedford was erected as the ninth county of the province. It embraced all of the settled regions lying west of the Tuscarora Mountain, or, in other words, the entire southwest quarter of the present State. On Monday, March 11, of the same year, John Fraser, Barnard Dougherty, Arthur St. Clair, William Proctor, Jr., Robert Cluggage, Robert Hanna, George Wilson, George Woods, William Lochry, *William Crawford*, Dorsey Pentecost, William McConnell, Thomas Gist, James Mulligan and Alexander McKee were appointed by the same General Assembly Justices of the Court of General Quarter Sessions of the Peace, and of the County Court of Common Pleas for the new county. Nearly all of these men were of Scotch or Scotch-Irish parentage, and all were stanch patriots during the Revolutionary war (which began four years later), a majority of them holding commissions high in rank.

The great extent of Bedford County, originally, the sparse and widely scattered settlements contained within it, together with the lack of highways other than those constructed years before by the armies of Braddock and Forbes, made it an extremely difficult matter to transact the public business, to assess and collect taxes, etc. Besides, as Virginia claimed all that part of the province lying west of Laurel Hill, and northward to and including Fort Pitt, and as the authorities of that province were issuing certificates for land in the disputed region at the rate of only ten shillings per 100 acres, it was but natural that a majority of those who had obtained their homesteads so cheaply should espouse the cause of Virginia (from which province they had recently removed) as against Pennsylvania, and in consequence refuse to recognize the authority of the Bedford County officials, or to pay the taxes levied upon them.

Regarding these difficulties, the following letters, written by two of the first Justices of Bedford County, will afford a partial explanation:

STEWART'S CROSSINGS, Augt. 9th, 1771.

SIR: I understand by Capt. John Harding, the Bearer of this, that there is an Agreement inter'd into be a Number of the inhabitants of Monongahalia and Readstone, ho has Entered into a bond or Articles of an Agreement that Each man will Joyn and Keep off all Officers belonging to the Law, and under the Penalty of fifty pounds for to be forfeited by the party refusing to Joyn against all Officers whatsoever.

I understand this was set on foot by a set of People who has maid a breach of the Law by Driving out a man from his home, for which there was a King's warrant Ishued against them, together with a notion Propegated by Coll. Croghan, that them posts would not fall into Pensilvania, he told me it was the Opinion of some of the best Judges that the Province Line would not Extend, by Considerable, so far, as it would be settled at 48 Miles to a Degree of Longetude which was the distance of a degree of Longitude allowd at the time the Charter was granted to Mr. Pen, and has since told those People that they had no right to Obay any presept Ishued from Pensylvania.

He has run a Line from the mouth of Rackoon up the Ohio to Fort Pitt, and from thence up Monongahalia Above Pigeon Creek, and from thence Across till it strikes Rackoon Creek, ten Miles up it, and he Says he has one more grant of 100,000 acres more to lay of in a parelele with that. Many sirways he had cut to peaces and sold to sundry People that has bin returnd into your Office, some of mine which is not above 3 or 4 Mile from Fort Pitt; one of mine he has and many others; it is a great Pity there is not a Stop.put to such Proceedings, as it will be attended with very bad Consequence.

I am informd there is a Large Number of Signers all redy to the paper, when I see it I will give you more Distinkt Account.

Sir, I am with great respect, your most Huml. Servant,

W. CRAWFORD.

To JAMES TILGHAM, ESQR, at Philadelphia.
Per CAPT. JOHN HARDING.

We supplement Col. (then known as Capt.) Crawford's communication with one written on the same topic by his colleague, Col. Wilson, not because of any pertinency to our subject, but by reason of the courage shown by the writer, and his quaint way of expressing his ideas.

MY DEAR CAPT: I am Sorey that the first Letter I ever undertook to Write you Should Contain a Detail of a Greivance so Disagreeable to me; Wars of any Cind are not agreable to aney Person Posesed of ye proper feelings of Humanity, But more Especially intestin Broyls. I no Sooner Returned Home from Court than I Found papers containing the Resolves, as they Called them, of ye inhabitants to ye Westward of ye Laurall hills, ware handing fast abowt amongst ye people, in which amongst ye rest Was one that they Were Resolved to oppose everey of Pens Laws as they Called them, Except Felonious actions at ye Risque of Life, & under ye penelty of fiftey pounds, to be Recovoured, or Leveyed By themselves, off ye Estates of ye failure. The first of them I found Hardey anugh to offer it in publick, I Emeditly ordered into Custodey, on which a large number Ware assembled as Was Seposed to Resque the Prisonar. I indavoured, By all ye Reason I was Capable of to Convince them of the ill Consequences that would of Consequence attend such a Rebellion, & Hapely Gained on the People to Consent to Relinquish their Resolves, & to Burn the peper they had Signed. When their forman saw that the Arms of His Contrie, that as hee said Hee had thrown himself into would not Resque him By force, hee Catched up his Rifle, Which was Well Loded, Jumped out of Dors, & swore if aney man Cam nigh him hee would put What Was in his throo them; the Person that Had him in Custody Called for assistance in ye King's name, & in pirtickelaur Commanded myself. I told him I Was a Subject & Was not fit to Command if not Willing to obay, on which I watched his Eye untill I Saw a Chance, Sprang in on him & sezed ye Rifle by ye Muzle and held him, So as he Could not Shoot mee, until more help got in to my assistance, on which I Disarmed him & Broke his Rifle to peeses. I Res'd a Sore Bruze on one of my arms By a punch of ye Gun in ye Strugle. Then put him under a Strong Guard, Told them ye Laws of their Contrie was Stronger then the Hardiest Ruffin amongst them.

I found it necesery on their Complyance & altering their Resolves, & his promising to Give himself no more trouble in the affair, as hee found that the people Ware not as hardey as hee Expected them to be, to Relece him on his promise of Good Behavour.

I am affraid Sum Who Have Been too much Countenanced By their King & ye province of Pensallvania are Grate accesoreys to those factions, & God knows where they May Eind. I have, in my Little time in Life, taken the oath of Alegence to His Majestie seven times, & always Did it with ye Consent of my whole Heart, & am Determined in my proper place to Seport the Contents thereof to ye outmost of my power, as I look on it as my Duty to Let those things be Known to Government & my acquaintance at Philladelphia is none. I expect you will Communicat those things to them, that the Wisdom of Government may provide Remedies in time, as there are numbers in the Lowr parts of ower Settlements still incressing ye faction.

It Givs mee Grate Pleasure that my nighbors are Determined not to joyn in the faction, & I hope the Difirant Majestrits in this side ye Mountains will use their influence to Discorage it. I understand Grate thrates are made against mee in partikolaur if possible to intimidate mee With fear & allso against the Sherifs & Constables, & all Ministers of Justice, But I hope the Laws, ye Bullworks of ower nation, will be seported in Spight of those Low Lifed trifling Raskells.

Give my Complements to Mr. George Wood, Mr. Doherty & Mr. Frazor, and Except of myn to your Self,

Who am, with Respect,
Your most obt Hble Sert
G. WILSON.*

Springhill Township, Augt 14th, 1771.
To ARTHOR ST. CLAIR, †Esq.

In 1773, when the county of Westmoreland was organized from Bedford, Capt. William Crawford was the senior Justice of the Peace, and for that reason became the presiding officer of the courts of the new county. At the same time, Capt. Arthur St. Clair was commissioned as the first Prothonotary Clerk of courts, etc., of the new jurisdiction. The latter resided at Fort Ligonier, the former at Stewart's Crossing, and both within Westmoreland County as then formed. In 1774, Capt. Crawford received another Captain's commission from the Governor of Virginia for service against the hostile Indians. He at once raised a company and served through the campaign known as "Dunmore's war." While the main body of the army was lying at Camp Charlotte, he was sent out with a force for the purpose of destroying some Mingo towns up the Scioto. The object of the expedition was successfully accomplished, and a considerable number of Indians were captured and taken to Ft. Pitt.

When the Revolutionary war began, Virginia had not yet relinquished her claim to the southwest part of the present State of Pennsylvania—a region which, as before mentioned, and had been largely settled to that time by natives of or immigrants from the Old Dominion. Hence, when volunteers were called out to defend their country against British arms, hired mercenaries and Indians; a majority of the men enlisting from the territory lying west of Laurel Hill, very naturally attached themselves to Virginia companies and regiments. Thus did it happen that in the year 1775, Col. William Crawford entered the American army as Lieutenant Colonel of the Fifth Regiment of the Virginia Line. Soon after he was commissioned Colonel, and commanded his regiment in the battle of Long Island, in the retreat through New Jersey, the crossing of the Delaware River with Gen. Washington on Christmas Day, 1776, and in the battle of Princeton, fought January 3, 1777. The next year he was in command of the Continental troops and militia at Fort Pitt. He also, during a part of the year 1778, commanded a Virginia regiment in service in the Western Military Department under Gen. McIntosh. At the time he assumed command of the ill-fated Sandusky expedition, it appears that he was not in active service, but was living in comparative retirement at his home at "Stewart's Crossing."

---
*Died at Quibbletown, N. J., in February, 1777, while serving as Lieutenant Colonel of the Eighth Regiment of the Pennsylvania Line.

†Then known as Capt. St. Clair, and serving as the first Prothonotary, Clerk of courts, etc., of the county of Bedford. He was afterward famed as Maj. Gen. St. Clair, Governor of the Northwest Territory, etc.

Says a recent writer, Smucker: "Col. Crawford was cool, brave, patriotic, and fitted by nature to be a commander. He was a man of mark, a leader, a man of courage and judgment, who rendered essential services to his country, especially to the West. He was greatly esteemed as a soldier, as a civil officer, and as a citizen, and as already remarked, his cruel death excited the sympathies of the entire country, and Gen. Washington was deeply moved by the awful death of the friend of his early years. His language shows the intensity of his feelings. He wrote: 'It is with the greatest sorrow and concern that I have learned the melancholy tidings of Col. Crawford's death. He was known to me as an officer of much care and prudence; brave, experienced and active. The manner of his death was shocking to me.' And no marvel! We can not fully estimate, and have not language adequate to express, the sum total of the agony and suffering endured by the noble Crawford; and when the terrible story of his torture was told in the border settlements among his kindred and friends who knew him well and esteemed him so highly, and when the frontiersmen came to realize that the brave soldier's life was tortured out of him by the slow burning fires kindled by the fiendish savages, and that the agony-rent soul of that pure patriot-hero, left his fire-crisped, charred, blistered body amidst the blazing flames of the stake, there was experienced such heart-rending anguish of soul as cannot be expressed in words. A gloom was spread in every countenance. Sympathy and commiseration went out from every heart. All keenly felt the tortures inflicted upon the heroic patriot soldier. Every one sorely lamented, with the Father of his Country, the melancholy, sad, sorrowful ending of the noble life of the brave companion in arms and friend of Washington. All hearts were moved by the tenderest sympathy when the announcement was made that there was such a sorrowful termination to the valuable life of the *brave pioneer of the Youghiogheny.*"

At the close of the Revolutionary war, the treaty of peace gave to the United States the Northwest Territory, which included the State of Ohio, but English troops continued to hold Detroit and various other posts for years thereafter, and, as a natural result, the Wyandots, with other tribes of this section, were still under their baneful influence.

However, on the 21st of January, 1785, a treaty was concluded at Fort McIntosh with the Wyandot, Delaware, Chippewa and Ottawa Indians, by which the boundary line between the United States and the Wyandot and Delaware nations was declared to begin "at the mouth of the river Cuyahoga, and to extend up said river to the portage, between that and the Tuscarawas branch of the Muskingum, thence down that branch to the crossing place above Fort Laurens, thence westerly to the portage of the Big Miami, which runs into the Ohio, at the mouth of which branch the fort stood which was taken by the French in 1752; then along said Portage to the Great Miami, or Omee River (now known as the Maumee), and down the south side of the same to its mouth; then along the south shore of Lake Erie to the mouth of the Cuyahoga River, where it began." The United States Government allotted all the lands contained within said lines (which the reader will observe embraced the territory now forming Wyandot County) to the Wyandot and Delaware nations, to live and hunt on, and to such of the Ottawa nation as lived thereon; saving and reserving for the establishment of trading posts, six miles square at the mouth of the Miami, or Omee River; and the same at the portage, on that branch of the Big Miami which now runs into the Ohio; and the same on the lake of Sandusky where the fort formerly stood, and also two miles square on each side of the lower rapids of Sandusky River.

On the 9th January, 1789, another treaty was made at Fort Harmer, between Gov. Arthur St. Clair and the sachems and warriors of the Wyandot, Chippewa, Pottawatomie, Sac and other nations, in which the treaty at Fort McIntosh was renewed and confirmed. But it did not produce the favorable results anticipated. . The Ohio and Michigan Indians still hated the Americans who were moving westward in a resistless column of emigration, and were continually encouraged in this feeling by the British officials. They were also equipped with guns and ammunition obtained at the British post at Detroit. Therefore, as might have been expected, the Indians the same year assumed a hostile attitude, and again all the horrors of a relentless, savage warfare were re-enacted along the line of the American border settlements. Block-houses were erected by the settlers in each of the new settlements, and in June, 1789, Maj. Doughty, with 140 men from Fort Harmer, commenced the building of Fort Washington, on a site now within the limits of Cincinnati. A few months afterward Gen. Harmer arrived with 300 men, and assumed command of the fort.

Again efforts were made to effect a peace with the hostile tribes, but by reason of British influence they proved unavailing, and as a last resort Gen. Harmer was directed to attack and destroy their towns. He marched from Fort Washington in September, 1790, with 1,300 men, of whom about one-fourth were regular troops. When near the Indian towns, on the Miami of the Lake, in the vicinity of what is now Ft. Wayne, Ind., an advanced detachment of 210 militia fell into an ambush and was defeated with severe loss. Gen. Harmer, however, succeeded in burning the Indian villages, and in destroying their standing corn. The army then commenced its march homeward. They had not proceeded far when Harmer received intelligence that the Indians had returned to their ruined towns. He immediately detached about one-third of his remaining force, under the command of Col. Hardin, with orders to bring them to an engagement. Hardin succeeded in this early the next morning; the Indians fought with desperation, and the militia and regular troops alike behaved with gallantry. However, more than one hundred of the militia, and all the regulars except nine were killed, and the rest were driven back to the main body. Dispirited by this misfortune, Harmer immediately marched to Fort Washington or Cincinnati. Thus the object of the expedition in intimidating the Indians was wholly unsuccessful.

Gaining increased confidence in their prowess and ability to successfully contend with the white troops of the Americans, by reason of their victory over a portion of Harmer's army, the Wyandots, together with other tribes composing the Miami league, continued hostile. Therefore, in 1791, a new army, superior to Harmer's, was assembled at Cincinnati under Major General, or as then termed Gov. St. Clair. The regular force amounted to 2,300 men; the militia numbered about 600. With this army St. Clair commenced his march toward the Indian towns on the Maumee. Two forts, Hamilton and Jefferson, were established and garrisoned on the route, about forty miles distant from each other, yet misfortune attended the expedition almost from its commencement. Soon after leaving Fort Jefferson, a considerable number of the militia deserted in a body. The first regiment, under Maj. Hamtranck, was ordered to pursue them and secure the advancing convoys of provisions, which it was feared they designed to plunder. Thus weakened by desertion and division, Gen. St. Clair approached the Indian villages. On the 3d of November, when at what is now the line of Drake and Mercer Counties, and within two or three miles of the Indiana State line, he halted, intending to throw up some slight fortification for the protection of baggage, and to await the return of the absent regiment. On the following morning, however, about half an hour before sunrise, the American Army was attacked with great fury by the whole disposable force of the Northwest tribes—the Wyandots, Delawares, Shawanese, Miamis, Ottawas, Chippewas and Pottawatomies. The Americans were totally defeated. Gen. Butler and more than 600 subaltern officers and enlisted men were killed.

The vigorous prosecution of the war for the protection of the Northwest Territory was now urged by President Washington, but various obstacles retarded the organization of a new army. In the spring and summer of 1794, however, an American Army was assembled at Greenville, in Darke County, under the command of Gen. Anthony Wayne, a bold, energetic and experienced officer of the Revolutionary war. His force consisted of about 2,000 regular troops and 1,500 mounted volunteers from Kentucky. To oppose him the Indian tribes above mentioned had collected their whole force, amounting to more than 2,000 warriors, near a British fort, erected since the treaty of 1783, and in violation of its obligations, at the foot of the Maumee Rapids. They were well supplied with arms and ammunition, obtained at the British posts at Detroit and on the Maumee, and felt confident of defeating Wayne. But "Mad Anthony" was a different kind of General from those who had previously commanded in the West, and when, on the 20th of August, the hostile forces of red men and white men met at the Maumee Rapids, or "the battle of Fallen Timbers," the former were completely routed and fled in the utmost precipitation from the field.

Not long afterward a trader met a Miami warrior who had fled before the terrible onslaught of Wayne's soldiers, and asked him:

"Why did you run away?"

With gestures corresponding to his words, and endeavoring to represent the effect of the cannon, he replied:

"Pop! pop! pop!—boo, woo, woo—whish, whish, boo, woo—kill twenty Indians one time—no good, by dam!"

Robinson, a young half-breed Pottawatomie, afterward one of the principal war chiefs of that tribe, was present at the battle with Wayne, and in later years was in the habit of describing it very clearly. It appears that the chiefs of the allied tribes had selected a swamp for the battleground. They formed their line, however, half a mile in front of it, on the summit of a gentle elevation, covered with an open growth of timber, with no underbrush, intending, when Wayne attacked them, to fall back slowly, thus inducing the Americans to follow them into the swamp, where the Indians would have every advantage, and where they expected a certain victory. But "Mad Anthony" soon broke up their plan. As we have shown, nearly one-half of his little army was composed of mounted Kentuckians, whom he formed in front of his infantry. After a few volleys from his artillery, always very trying to the nerves of the red men, he ordered the mounted men to advance. The Indians had never seen men fight on horseback, and supposed they would dismount before reaching the top of the ridge. But instead of that they began to trot, then drew their swords—those terrible "long knives," which always inspired the Indians with dread—then broke into a gallop, and the next moment were charging at the top of

BETWEEN-THE-LOGS

AN INDIAN CHIEF OF THE WYANDOT TRIBE AND A LICENSED PREACHER OF THE METHODIST CHURCH.

their horses' speed, " yelling like hell," as Robinson expressed it, swinging their swords, and looking like demons of wrath to the astonished red men.

"Oh," said Robinson, "you ought to have seen the poor Indians run then."

They gave but one random fire, and fled as fast as possible toward the swamp. But it was too late. The mounted Kentuckians burst through them like a whirlwind, and then wheeled about to cut off their retreat, while the infantry came up on the double-quick and barred their escape in that direction.

"Oh," the chieftain would continue, "it was awful."

Robinson admired his conqueror so much that he named one of his sons "Anthony Wayne," and always expressed the most profound respect for that dashing soldier.

Wayne's victory at the "Fallen Timbers" did not at once reduce the savages to submission. Hence their country was laid waste, and forts were erected in the heart of their territory. At length, however, they became thoroughly convinced of their inability to resist in a successful manner the American troops, and sued for peace. A grand council was therefore held at Greenville, in the summer of 1795, and on the 3d of August of that year, Gen. Wayne concluded a treaty of peace with the Wyandots, Delawares, Shawanese, Ottawas, Chippewas, Pottawatomies and Miamis, besides some less important tribes. More than one thousand Indians were present. The principal chiefs were Tarhe, or the Crane, of the Wyandots, Buckongehelas, Black Hoof, Blue Jacket and Little Turtle. A majority of the chiefs had been tampered with by the British agents and advised not to make peace with the Americans, but their people having been reduced to great extremities by the generalship of Wayne, were determined to make a permanent peace with the "Thirteen Fires" as they termed the original States of the federal Union.

The basis of the treaty of Greenville was, that hostilities were to cease, and all prisoners be restored. Article 3 defined the Indian boundary as follows:

"The general boundary line between the lands of the United States and the lands of the said Indian tribes shall begin at the mouth of Cuyahoga River, and run thence up the same to the portage, between that and the Tuscarawas branch of the Muskingum; thence down that branch to the crossing place above Fort Laurens; thence westerly to a fork of that branch of the Great Miami River, running into the Ohio, at or near which fork stood Loromie's store, and where commences the portage between the Miami of the Ohio and St. Mary's River, which is a branch of the Miami which runs into Lake Erie; thence a westerly course to Fort Recovery [erected upon the grounds where St. Clair was defeated in November, 1791], which stands on a branch of the Wabash; thence southwesterly in a direct line to the Ohio, so as to intersect that river opposite the mouth of Kentucky or Cuttawa River."

By the terms of the treaty, the Indians also ceded to the United States Government various small tracts of land surrounding military posts erected and to be erected. Also, the right to the people of the United States of a free passage by land and water through the territory still owned by the Indians. The reader will understand that the Indians relinquished all claims to the lands lying eastwardly and southwardly of the line above described, in consideration "of the peace now established; of the goods formerly received from the United States; of those now to be delivered; and of the yearly delivery of goods now stipulated to be made hereafter; and to indemnify the United States for the injuries and expenses they have sustained during the war."

On the 4th day of July, 1805, at a treaty made at Fort Industry, on the Miami of the Lake, between the United States of America and the sachems, chiefs and warriors of the Wyandot, Ottawa, Chippewa, Muncie, Delaware, Shawanese and Pottawatomie nations, it was determined that "the boundary line between the United States and the nations aforesaid shall in future be a meridian line drawn north and south through a boundary to be erected on the south shore of Lake Erie, 120 miles due west of the west boundary line of the State of Pennsylvania, extending north until it intersects the boundary line of the United States, and extending south until it intersects a line heretofore established by the treaty of Greenville." Thus, all the lands lying east of the above-described line, bounded southerly and easterly by the line established by the treaty of Greenville, and northerly by the northernmost part of the forty-first degree of north latitude, were ceded by the Indians to the United States. By Article 4 of this treaty, the United States delivered to the Wyandot, Shawanese, Muncie and Delaware nations goods to the value of $20,000, and stipulated for a perpetual annuity of $9,500, payable in goods reckoned at first cost in the city or place in the United States where they should be procured.

The Wyandots were also interested parties in the treaty of Detroit, which was concluded on the 17th day of November, 1807; but as the lands ceded were for the most part within the limits of the present State of Michigan, we refrain from further mention of its provisions, etc.

The treaty of Brownstown was made November 25, 1808, between William Hull, Governor of Michigan Territory, and the Chippewa, Ottawa, Pottawatomie, Wyandot and Shawanese nations. This treaty related mainly to the cession of lands for roads through the territory still owned by the Indians. Among the routes then ceded was "a tract of land, for a road only, of 120 feet in width, to run southwardly from what is called Lower Sandusky, to the boundary line established by the treaty of Greenville, with the privilege of taking at all times such timber and other materials from the adjacent lands as may be necessary for making and keeping in repair the said road, with the bridges that may be required along the same." This, probably, was the first highway projected by the English-speaking whites, or Americans, in a direction which would lead through the present county of Wyandot.

Meanwhile, from the date of the conclusion of the treaty of Greenville until the beginning of the last war with Great Britian—1812-15—the Wyandots, true to their treaty obligations, remained at peace with the Americans. In 1812, however, at a time when the great Shawanese Chieftain, Tecumseh, and his brother the Prophet, were endeavoring to array under arms all of the Northwestern tribes against the Americans, a great Indian council of the Northern nations was held at Brownstown in the Michigan Territory. At that meeting Tarhe, or "The Crane" and Between-the-logs* were among the chief representatives of the Wyandots. The eloquence of Tecumseh's adherents, and the glittering promises of the British

*The distinguished chief, Between-the-logs, whose portrait the reader will find in this work, was born near Lower Sandusky about the year 1780. His father was a Seneca, and his mother a member of the Bear tribe of the Wyandot nation. When still in his teens, he, with other Wyandots, fought Gen. Wayne's troops at the battle of the Maumee Rapids, or "Fallen Timbers." He then lived at Lower Sandusky. He early became prominent in his nation, and when still a young man, because of his retentive memory and ability in discussion, was made a chief and appointed chief speaker of his nation. When about twenty-five years old he was sent to fathom the doctrines and pretensions of a celebrated Seneca prophet, whose fallacy

agents, proved to be as nothing to them, and they firmly rejected all overtures to join in the war against the Americans. True, a few fiery young warriors of the Wyandot nation did enter the British service. But Tarhe, Between-the-logs, Summundewat, Big Tree, and the major portion of the Wyandots remained faithful to their pledges. These chiefs left the Brownstown council, returned to Upper Sandusky, and immediately joined the American cause. Fort Ferree, at Upper Sandusky, and Fort Meigs, at Lower Sandusky, were erected upon their lands. Here were concentrated large numbers of troops from Pennsylvania, Kentucky and Ohio, under Gen. Harrison, and here were they treated in the most friendly manner by the Wyandots. When Gen. Harrison invaded Canada, he was accompanied by a large party of Wyandot chiefs and warriors. But the principal object of his Indian friends was to detach that part of the Wyandot nation from the British interest, who, by the surrounding Indians, had in a measure been forced to join the English. This was effected.

We now come to the consideration of an event which, by its realization, placed the Wyandots upon a comparatively small tract of territory or "reservation," where they remained until within the memory of many of the present inhabitants of Wyandot County. We allude to the "treaty of the Foot of the Rapids, of the Miami of the Lake," which was concluded on the 29th day of September, 1817, between Lewis Cass and Duncan McArthur, Commissioners of the United States, and the sachems, chiefs and warriors of the Wyandot, Seneca, Delaware, Shawanese, Pottawatomie, Ottawa and Chippewa tribes of Indians. The articles of this treaty which have an especial reference to our topic are as follows:

"ARTICLE 2. The Wyandot tribe of Indians, in consideration of the stipulations herein made on the part of the United States, do hereby forever cede to the United States the lands comprehended within the following lines and boundaries: Beginning at a point on the southern shore of Lake Erie, where the present Indian boundary line intersects the same, between the mouth of Sandusky Bay and the mouth of Portage River; thence running south with said line to the line established in the year one thousand seven hundred and ninety-five, by the treaty of Greenville, which runs from the crossing place above Fort Laurens to Loromie's store; thence westerly with the last mentioned line to the eastern line of the reserve at Loromie's store; thence with the lines of said reserve north and west to the northwest corner thereof; thence to the northwestern corner of the reserve on the River St. Mary's, at the head of the navigable waters thereof; thence east to the western bank of the St. Mary's River aforesaid; thence down on the western bank of the said river to the reserve at Fort

---

he soon detected. About two years afterward he was sent on a like errand to a noted Shawanese prophet—Tecumseh's brother—with whom he staid nearly a year, and then returned, convinced and convincing others that the Prophet's pretensions were all delusion and destitute of truth.

During the war of 1812-15, he was the firm friend of the Americans, and he was instrumental in detaching from the British interests a number of the young men of the Wyandot nation who had been misled. After that war he settled permanently in the neighborhood of Upper Sandusky. He now, in common with many of the Wyandots, became addicted to habits of intemperance, and in a time of debauch and drunkenness killed his wife. When he became sober, the horror of this deed made so deep an impression un his mind that from that day he measurably abandoned the use of ardent spirits. In 1817, he made himself conspicuous by visiting Washington, and securing advantages to the Wyandots, as shown in the text of this chapter relating to the treaty at St. Mary's. When John Stewart, the colored exhorter, appeared among the Wyandots, Between-the-logs became his friend, and soon after embraced Christianity. Soon after this, he was regularly appointed an exhorter in the church, in which relation he remained until his death, a devoted friend and advocate of God. He also watched with unremitting diligence over the temporal interests of the nation; enduring the fatigues of business, and in the longest journeys, for the welfare of his people without complaint. He was uniformly an attendant upon the Ohio Annual Conference, at which he made some of the most rational and eloquent speeches ever delivered by an Indian before that body. He always manifested a deep interest in the welfare of the mission and school. He was rather above the medium height, of slight build, but well proportioned, with an open and manly countenance. He died of consumption January 1, 1827, and was buried in the grounds surrounding the Mission Church.

Wayne; thence with the lines of the last-mentioned reserve, easterly and northerly, to the north bank of the River Miami of Lake Erie; thence down on the north bank of the said river to the western line of the land ceded to the United States by the treaty of Detroit, in the year one thousand, eight hundred and seven; thence with the said line south to the middle of said Miami River, opposite the mouth of the Great Auglaize River; thence down the middle of said Miami River, and easterly with the lines of the tract ceded to the United States by the treaty of Detroit aforesaid, so far that a south line will strike the place of beginning.

* * * * *

"ART. 3. The Wyandot, Seneca, Delaware, Shawanese, Pottawatomie, Ottawa and Chippewa tribes of Indians, accede to the cessions mentioned in the two preceding articles.

* * * * * * * * *

"ART. 6. The United States agree to grant, by patent, in fee simple, to Doanquod, Howoner, Rontondee, Tauyau, Rontayau, Dawatont, Manocue, Tauyaudautauson and Haudauwaugh, chiefs of the Wyandot tribe and their successors in office, chiefs of the said tribe, for the use of the persons and for the purposes mentioned in the annexed schedule, a tract of land twelve miles square at Upper Sandusky, the center of which shall be the place where Fort Ferree stands; and also a tract of one mile square, to be located where the chiefs direct, on a cranberry swamp, on Broken Sword Creek, and to be held for the use of the tribe. * * * * * " *

"ART. 7. And the said chiefs or their successors may, at any time they may think proper, convey to either of the persons mentioned in the said schedule, or his heirs, the quantity secured thereby to him, or may refuse to do so. But the use of the said land shall be in the said person; and after the share of any person is conveyed by the chiefs to him, he may convey the same to any person whatever. And any one entitled by the said schedule to a portion of the said land, may, at any time, convey the same to any person, by obtaining the approbation of the President of the United States, or of the person appointed by him to give such approbation. And the agent of the United States shall make an equitable partition of the said share when conveyed.

"ART. 8. At the special request of the said Indians, the United States agree to grant, by patent, in fee simple, to the persons hereinafter mentioned, all of whom are connected with the said Indians, by blood or adoption, the tracts of land herein described:

"To Elizabeth Whitaker, who was taken prisoner by the Wyandots, and has ever since lived among them, 1,280 acres of land, on the west side of the Sandusky River, below Croghansville, to be laid off in a square form, as nearly as the meanders of the said river will admit, and to run an equal distance above and below the house in which the said Elizabeth Whitaker now lives.

"To Robert Armstrong, who was taken prisoner by the Indians, and has ever since lived among them, and has married a Wyandot woman, one section to contain 640 acres of land, on the west side of the Sandusky River, to begin at the place called Camp Ball, and to run up the river, with the meanders thereof, 160 poles, and from the beginning down the river, with the meanders thereof, 160 poles, and from the extremity of these lines west for quantity.

"To the children of the late William McCollock, who was killed in August, 1812, near Maugaugon, and who are quarter-blood Wyandot Indians, one section, to contain 640 acres of land, on the west side of the Sandusky River, adjoining the lower line of the tract hereby granted to Robert Armstrong, and extending in the same manner, with and from the said river.

"To John Vanmeter, who was taken prisoner by the Wyandots, and who has ever since lived among them, and has married a Seneca woman, and to his wife's three brothers, Senecas, who now reside on Honey Creek, 1,000 acres of land, to begin north, forty-five degrees west, one hundred and forty poles from the house in which the said John Vanmeter now lives, and to run thence south 320 poles, thence and from the beginning, east for quantity.

"To Sarah Williams, Joseph Williams and Rachel Nugent, late Rachel Williams, the said Sarah having been taken prisoner by the Indians, and has ever since lived among them, and being the widow, and the said Joseph and Rachel being the children of the late Isaac Williams, a half-blood Wyandot, one-quarter section of land, to contain 160 acres, on the east side of the Sandusky River, below Croghansville, and to include their improvements at a place called Negro Point.

"To Catharine Walker, a Wyandot woman, and to John R. Walker, her son, who was wounded in the service of the United States at the battle of Maugaugon, in 1812, a section of 640 acres of land each, to begin at the northwestern corner of the tract hereby granted to John Vanmeter and his wife's brothers, and to run with the line thereof south 320 poles; thence and from the beginning west for quantity.

"To William Spicer, who was taken prisoner by the Indians, and has ever since lived among them and has married a Seneca woman, a section of land to contain 640 acres, beginning on the east bank of the Sandusky River, forty poles below the lower corner of said Spicer's corn-field; thence up the river on the east side, with the meanders thereof, one mile; thence and from the beginning east for quantity.

* * * * * * * * *

"To Horonu, or the 'Cherokee Boy,' a Wyandot chief, a section of land to contain 640 acres, on the Sandusky River, to be laid off in a square form, and to include his improvements.

* * * * * * * * *

"Art. 15. The tracts of land herein granted to the chiefs, for the use of the Wyandot, Shawanese, Seneca and Delaware Indians, and the reserve for the Ottawa Indians, shall not be liable to taxes of any kind so long as such lands continue the property of said Indians.

* * * * * * * * *

"Art. 18. The Delaware tribe of Indians in consideration of the stipulations herein made on the part of the United States, do hereby forever cede to the United States all the claim which they have to the thirteen sections of land reserved for the use of certain persons of their tribe, by the second section of the act of Congress, passed March the third, one thousand eight hundred and seven, providing for the disposal of the land of the United States between the United States Military Tract and the Connecticut Reserve, and the lands of the United States between the Cincinnati and Vincennes districts.

"Art. 19. The United States agree to grant, by patent, in fee simple, to Zeeshawan, or James Armstrong, and to Sanondoyourayquaw, or Silas Armstrong, chiefs of the Delaware Indians, living on the Sandusky waters, and their successors in office, chiefs of the said tribe, for the use of the persons mentioned in the annexed schedule, in the same manner and subject to the same conditions, provisions and limitations as is hereinbefore provided for the lands granted to the Wyandot, Seneca and Shawanese Indians, a tract of land to contain nine square miles, to join the tract granted to the Wyandots of twelve miles square, to be laid off as nearly in a square form as practicable, and to include Captain Pipe's village."

* * * * * * *

By this treaty the United States stipulated to pay the Wyandots a perpetual annuity of $4,000; to the Senecas, $500; to the Shawanese, $2,000; to the Pottawatomies, annually, for fifteen years, $1,300; to the Ottawas, annually, for fifteen years, $1,000; to the Chippewas, annually, for fifteen years, $1,000, and to the Delawares, $500, but no annuity. The United States also engaged to erect a saw and grist mill, for the use of the Wyandots; and to provide and maintain two blacksmiths: one for the use of the Wyandots and Senecas, the other for the Indians at Hog Creek.

The United States further agreed to pay the sums following for property, etc., injured during the war of 1812-15: To the Wyandots, $4,319.39; to the Senecas, $3,989.24; to Indians at Lewis' and Scoutash's towns, $1,227.50; to the Delawares, $3,956.50; to the representatives of Hembis, $348.50; to the Shawanese, $420, and to the Senecas, an additional sum of $219. It was also agreed to pay the Shawanese, under the treaty of Fort Industry, $2,500. By Article 17, the value of improvements abandoned, was to be paid for.

A treaty supplementary to the "Treaty of the Foot of the Rapids of the Miami of the Lake," was concluded at St. Mary's, Ohio, on the 17th day of September, 1818, between Lewis Cass and Duncan McArthur, Commissioners of the United States, and the sachems, chiefs, and warriors of the Wyandot, Seneca, Shawanese and Ottawa tribes of Indians. The following are the articles of the supplemental treaty which were of special significance to the Wyandot nation:

"ARTICLE 1. It is agreed between the United States and the parties hereunto, that the several tracts of land described in the treaty to which this is supplementary, and agreed thereby to be granted by the United States to the chiefs of the respective tribes named therein, for the use of the individuals of the said tribes, and also the tract described in the twentieth* article of the said treaty, shall not be thus granted, but shall be excepted from the cession made by the said tribes to the United States, reserved for the use of the said Indians, and held by them in the same manner as Indian reservations have been heretofore held. But it is further agreed that the tracts thus reserved shall be reserved for the use of the Indians named in the schedule to the said treaty, and held by them and their heirs forever, unless ceded to the United States.

"ART. 2. It is also agreed that there shall be reserved for the use of the Wyandots, in addition to the reservations before made, fifty-five thousand six hundred and eighty acres of land, to be laid off in two tracts, the first to adjoin the south line of the section of six hundred and forty acres of land heretofore reserved for the Wyandot chief, the Cherokee Boy, and to extend south to the north line of the reserve of twelve miles square, at Upper Sandusky, and the other to join the east line of the reserve of twelve miles square, at Upper Sandusky, and to extend east for quantity.

"There shall also be reserved, for the use of the Wyandots residing at Solomon's town, and on Blanchard's Fork, in addition to the reservations before made, sixteen thousand acres of land, to be laid off in a square

---

* The twentieth article wholly related to a reservation granted the Ottawas, on the south side of the Miami of the lake.

form, on the head of Blanchard's Fork, the center of which shall be at the Big Spring, on the trace leading from Upper Sandusky to Fort Findlay ; and one hundred and sixty acres of land, for the use of the Wyandots, on the west side of the Sandusky River, adjoining the said river, and the lower line of two sections of land, agreed, by the treaty to which this is supplementary, to be granted Elizabeth Whitaker.

* * * . * * * *

"ART. 3. It is hereby agreed that the tracts of land, which, by the eighth article of the treaty to which this is supplementary, are to be granted by the United States to the persons therein mentioned, shall never be conveyed, by them or their heirs, without the permission of the President of the United States."

By this supplement, an additional annuity was to be given to the Wyandots of $500, forever ; to the Shawanese, $1,000 ; to the Senecas, $500, and to the Ottawas, $1,500.

The circumstances which led to the supplementary treaty at St. Mary's originated in the following manner: When the United States Government had made arrangements to extinguish the Indian title to lands in the State of Ohio, and after the Commissioners, and the sachems, chiefs and warriors of the various Indian nations had assembled at the foot of the Maumee Rapids, September 29, 1817, the Wyandots refused to sell their land. At this juncture, the Chippewas,* Pottawatomies* and Ottawas,* without any right or justice whatever, laid claim to a great part of the lands owned and occupied by the Wyandots; and Gabriel Godfroy and Whitmore Knaggs, agents for these nations, proposed in open council, in behalf of the Chippewas, etc., etc., to sell said lands. Cass and McArthur, the Commissioners, then declared that if the Wyandots would not sell their lands, they would buy them of the others—the Chippewas, Pottawatomies and Ottawas. The Wyandot chieftain, Between-the-logs, firmly opposed all of these measures; but however just his cause, or manly and eloquent in his arguments, they were lost upon men determined on their course. The Wyandots, finding themselves so circumstanced, and not being able to help themselves, were thus forced to sell on the terms proposed by the Commissioners. They did the best they could and signed the treaty; but only from a strong hope that by representing to the President and the Government the true state of things, before the treaty was ratified, they should obtain some redress from the Government. In resorting to this course, Between-the-logs acted a principal part. Accordingly, he, with other Wyandot chiefs, and a delegation from the Delawares and Senecas, immediately proceeded to Washington, without consulting the Indian agents, or any other officer of Government. When they were introduced to the Secretary of War, he remarked to them that he was surprised that he had received no information of their coming by any of the agents. Between-the-logs answered, with the spirit of a free man, "We got up, and came of ourselves. We believed the great road was free for us." He so pleaded their cause before the President, the Secretary of War and Congress, that the Wyandots obtained an enlargement of their reservations and an increase of annuities, as shown in the articles of the supplementary treaty held at St. Mary's, September 17, 1818.

During the same year, 1818, a grand Indian council was held at Upper

---

*The members then composing these tribes seem to have been exceedingly crafty and avaricious in their nature. They jointly laid claim to the greater portion of the Northwest Territory as originally formed. They were always found present when treaties and cessions of land were to be made, and thus never failed to claim the "lion's share" when reservations were granted, or annuities and goods were to be distributed.

Sandusky on the occasion of the death of Tarhe, or "the Crane," the most celebrated chieftain the Wyandot nation ever produced. Col. John Johnston, of Upper Piqua, Ohio, who for about half a century served as an agent of the United States over the Indians of the West, was present, and in his "Recollections," gives the following interesting account of the proceedings:

"On the death of the great chief of the Wyandots, I was invited to attend a general council of all the tribes of Ohio, the Delawares of Indiana, and the Senecas of New York, at Upper Sandusky. I found on arriving at the place a very large attendance. Among the chiefs was the noted leader and orator, Red Jacket, from Buffalo. The first business done was the speaker of the nation delivering an oration on the character of the deceased chief. Then followed what might be called a monody, or ceremony, of mourning or lamentation. Thus seats were arranged from end to end of a large council house, about six feet apart. The head men and the aged took their seats facing each other, stooping down, their heads almost touching. In that position they remained for several hours. Deep, heavy and long continued groans would commence at one end of the row of mourners, and so pass around until all had responded, and these repeated at intervals of a few minutes. The Indians were all washed, and had no paint or decorations of any kind upon their persons, their countenances and general deportment denoting the deepest mourning. I had never witnessed anything of the kind before, and was told this ceremony was not performed but on the decease of some great man.

"After the period of mourning and lamentation was over, the Indians proceeded to business. There were present the Wyandots, Shawanese, Delawares, Senecas, Ottawas and Mohawks. The business was entirely confined to their own affairs, and the main topics related to their lands and the claims of the respective tribes. It was evident, in the course of the discussion, that the presence of myself and people (there were some white men with me) was not acceptable to some of the parties, and allusions were made so direct to myself that I was constrained to notice them, by saying that I came there as a guest of the Wyandots by their special invitation; that as the agent of the United States, I had a right to be there as anywhere else in the Indian country; and that if any insult was offered to myself or my people, it would be resented and punished. Red Jacket was the principal speaker, and was intemperate and personal in his remarks. Accusations, pro and con, were made by the different parties, accusing each other of being foremost in selling lands to the United States. The Shawanese were particularly marked out as more guilty than any other; that they were the last coming into the Ohio country, and although they had no right but by permission of the other tribes, they were always the foremost in selling lands. This brought the Shawanese out, who retorted through their head chief, the Black Hoof, on the Senecas and Wyandots with pointed severity.

"The discussion was long continued, calling out some of the ablest speakers, and was distinguished for ability, cutting sarcasm and research, going far back into the history of the natives, their wars, alliances, negotiations, migrations, etc. I had attended many councils, treaties and gatherings of the Indians, but never in my life did I witness such an outpouring of native oratory and eloquence, of severe rebuke, taunting national and personal reproaches. The council broke up later in great confusion, and in the worst possible feeling. A circumstance occurred toward the close which more than anything else exhibited the bad feeling prevailing. In handing round the wampum belt, the emblem of amity, peace and good will, when presented to one of the chiefs, he would not touch it with his fingers, but passed it on a stick to the person next to him. A greater indignity, agreeable to Indian etiquette, could not be offered.

"The next day appeared to be one of unusual anxiety and despondency among the Indians. They could be seen in groups everywhere near the council house in deep consultation. They had acted foolishly—were sorry—but the difficulty was who would first present the olive branch. The council convened late and was very full; silence prevailed for a long time; at last the aged chief of the Shawanese, the Black Hoof, rose—a man of great influence, and a celebrated warrior. He told the assembly they had acted like children, and not men on yesterday; that he and his people were sorry for the words that had been spoken, and which had done so much harm; that he came into the council by the unanimous desire of his people present, to recall those foolish words, and did there take them back--handing strings of wampum, which passed around and were received by all with the greatest satisfaction. Several of the principal chiefs delivered speeches to the same effect, handing round wampum in turn, and in this manner the whole difficulty of the preceding day was settled, and to all appearances forgotten. The Indians are very courteous and civil to each other, and it is a rare thing to see their assemblies disturbed by unwise or ill-timed remarks. I never witnessed it except on the occasion here alluded to, and it is more than probable that the presence of myself and other white men contributed toward the unpleasant occurrence. I could not help but admire the genuine philosophy and good sense displayed by men whom we call savages, in the translation of their public business; and how much we might profit in the halls of our Legislatures, by occasionally taking for our example the proceedings of the great Indian council at Upper Sandusky."

At the time the events occurred, which have just been related, the Indian town known as Upper Sandusky, was located about four miles northeast of the present county seat (a point, it appears to which the Indians removed prior to 1782). After the death of Tarhe, however, they erected a council house on the site of the present town of Upper Sandusky (a place which was nearer the center of their reservation), gave it this name—Upper Sandusky, and called the old village Crane Town. The old council house mentioned by Col. Johnston, stood about a mile and a half north of Crane Town. It was built chiefly of bark, and in dimensions was about one hundred feet long by fifteen feet in width. Subsequently the temporary structure at the new town of Upper Sandusky gave place to a more substantial building. The frame council house known to early residents for several years, as the Wyandot County Court House, etc.— which was built probably about the year 1830, or a few years after the completion of the grist and saw* mill, provided for in the treaty of September 29, 1817, at the foot of the Maumee Rapids.

The Wyandot nation was subdivided into ten tribes. These tribes were kept up by the mother's side, and all her children belonged to her tribe. The *totem* of each of the ten tribes was as follows: The Deer, Bear, Snake,

---

*Rev. James B. Finley, in his "History of the Wyandot Mission," when speaking of building the mission house, says, under date of October, 1821; "We hauled lumber to the saw mill, and sawed it ourselves into joists and plank for the floor and other purposes." The mills referred to, which were built in 1820 for the Indians by the Government, were located about three miles northeast of Upper Sandusky, upon the Sandusky River, and supplied the wants of the Wyandots, in these particulars—flour, corn meal and lumber—until they moved to Kansas. The old buhrs and bolting chest are still in use in the present mill, which was built about twenty-two years ago, some twenty rods north of the site of the old mill.

Hawk, Porcupine, Wolf, Beaver, Big Turtle, Little Turtle and Terrapin. Each of these tribes had its chief, and these chiefs composed the grand council of the nation. The oldest man in the tribe was generally the tribal chief, and all the persons belonging to a tribe were considered as one family—all near akin. Indeed, no law or custom among them was so scrupulously regarded and adhered to with so much tenacity as the tribe law in this particular. No person was allowed to marry in his or her own tribe, or to have any sexual intercourse with one of his own tribe. It was considered that no crime could so effectually destroy their character or disgrace them so much as this. Nothing could ever restore to them their lost reputation. Murder, adultery, or fornication were not deemed half as bad as a violation of the tribe law; and in some instances such violators were put to death. When a man wished to marry a woman, he first had to obtain the consent of her tribe, and most generally he went to live with his wife in her tribe, yet the woman was not bound to live with him any longer than she pleased, and when she left him would take with her, her children and property.

From time immemorial until "Mad Anthony's" decisive battle at the foot of the Maumee Rapids, to the Deer tribe belonged the scepter and calumet of the grand sachems; but as a result of that battle, this tribe became so weak by the loss of their warriors that the nation deemed it best to take the burden off their shoulders, and placed it on the Porcupine tribe. According to Finley, the celebrated Tarhe, and his immediate successor, De un quot, as head chiefs and grand sachems of the Wyandot nation, were members of the last-mentioned tribe.

In a brief biographical sketch of the great chief, Tarhe, or "The Crane," which was published in the Wyandot *Democratic Union*, August 13, 1866, William Walker, a member of the Wyandot nation, says: "Tarhe was born in the year 1742, near Detroit, Mich., and died near Upper Sandusky in November, 1818. He belonged to the Porcupine tribe, a clan or subdivision of the Wyandot nation. * * * I can think of no man in Ohio who in anywise resembled him in general appearance but one—the Hon. Benjamin Ruggles, who for eighteen consecutive years represented the State of Ohio in the United States Senate. Between these two there was a striking resemblance, except that Tarhe's nasal organ was aquiline.

"When in his prime he must have been a lithe, withy, wiry man, capable of great endurance, as he marched on foot at the head of his warriors through the whole of Gen. Harrison's campaign into Canada, and was an tactive participant in the battle of the Thames, though then seventy-two years of age. He steadily and unflinchingly opposed Tecumseh's war policy from 1808, up to the breaking-out of the war of 1812. He maintained inviolate the treaty of peace concluded with Gen. Wayne in 1795. This brought him into conflict with that ambitious Shawanese, the latter having no regard for the plighted faith of his predecessors; but Tarhe determined to maintain that of his, and remained true to the American cause till the day of his death. Gen. Harrison, in comparing him with cotemporary chiefs of other tribes, pronounced him 'The noblest Roman of them all.' He was a man of mild aspect, and gentle in his manners when at repose, but when acting publicly exhibited great energy, and when addressing his people, there was always something that, to my youthful ear, sounded like stern command. He never drank spirits; never used tobacco in any form.

"Near the close of the war, Jonathan Pointer, a negro, who had been captured somewhere in Western Virginia by a Wyandot war party in early times, resided in Tarhe's family. Jonathan, who was not proverbial for honesty, was in the habit of abducting horses in the night belonging to teamsters who might chance to encamp in the neighborhood, and concealing them. The teamsters, of course, were in trouble and great perplexity, perhaps unable to proceed without the missing animals. Jonathan was sure to be on hand, and offer to find them for a certain pecuniary reward. The old man found out the sharp practice of his protege, and took him to task; told him that if he ever heard of his playing any more such tricks upon travelers he would remand him back to his master in Virginia. This had the desired effect, and Jonathan ceased to speculate in that direction.

"Many of the old settlers of Wyandot County will remember 'Aunt Sally Frost,' a white woman, raised among the Wyandots. Aunt Sally was Tarhe's wife when he died. He had one son, but oh, how unlike the sire! nearly an idiot, and died at the age of twenty-five.

"His Indian name is supposed to mean crane (the tall fowl); but this is a mistake. Crane is merely a soubriquet bestowed upon him by the French, thus: 'Le chef Grue,' or 'Monsieur Grue,' the chief Crane, or Mr. Crane. This nickname was bestowed upon him on account of his height and slender form. He had no English name, but the Americans took up and adopted the French nickname. Tarhe or Tarhee, when critically analyzed, means, *At him, the Tree*, or *At the Tree;* the tree personified. Thus you have in this one word a preposition, a personal pronoun, a definite article, and a noun. The name of your populous township should be Tarhe, instead of Crane. It is due to the memory of that great and good man.*"

We have now arrived at the beginning of another interesting epoch in the history of the Wyandot nation—the establishment among them of a mission of the Methodist Episcopal Church—the consideration of which will be reserved for another chapter.

---

*Rev. J. B. Finley also testifies to the noble and generous character of this chief. He says: "I was once traveling from Detroit in the year 1800, in company with two others. We came to the camp of old Tarhe, or Crane, head chief of the Wyandot nation. We had sold a drove of cattle, and had money, which we gave up to the chief in the evening. The next morning all was forthcoming, and never were men treated with more fervent kindness."

CHAPTER IV.

INDIAN OCCUPANCY—Continued.

(From 1816-18, to 1843.)

DEMORALIZED CONDITION OF THE WYANDOTS IN 1816—JOHN STEWART, THE COLORED PREACHER, APPEARS AMONG THEM—SKETCH OF HIS EARLY LIFE—COLDLY RECEIVED, BUT FINALLY GAINS THEIR CONFIDENCE—AN ACCOUNT OF HIS PROCEEDINGS—REV. JAMES B. FINLEY APPOINTED RESIDENT MISSIONARY—HIS TRIALS AND TRIUMPHS—DEUNQUOT, THE HEAD CHIEF, CREATES A SENSATION—MISSION SCHOOL OPENED—THE MISSION FARM—DEATH OF STEWART—BUILDING THE MISSION STONE CHURCH—PROSPERITY—CHIEFS VISIT EASTERN CITIES—FINLEY DEPARTS IN 1827—THE SAVAGE DELAWARES CEDE THEIR RESERVATION TO THE UNITED STATES—AN ACCOUNT OF SOME OF THEM—AN INDIAN EXECUTION—THE WYANDOTS SELL THEIR LANDS—TERMS—THEIR FINAL DEPARTURE FOR REGIONS WEST OF MISSOURI—FAREWELL SONG.

AT the time of Gen. Wayne's treaty with the Northwestern tribes, the Wyandots, under the lead of Tarhe, including men, women and children, numbered about 2,200. From that time, until the date of their settlement upon the reservation in the present county of Wyandot, they had lost but very few men in battle, yet, by reason of being on the extreme borders of civilization, and mixing with the most abandoned and vicious of the whites, they had sunk in the most degrading vices, many of them became the most debased and worthless of their race, and drunkenness, lewdness and attendant diseases, had reduced them in twenty years nearly one-half in numbers. For many years, they had been under the religious instruction of priests of the Roman Catholic Church, but, from the state of their morals, and from the declarations of those who professed to be Catholics, it seems that they had derived but little benefit. "To carry a silver cross, and to count a string of beads; to worship the Virgin Mary; to go to church and hear mass said in Latin; and be taught to believe that for a beaver's skin, or its value, they could have all their sins pardoned, was the amount of their Christianity, and served but to encourage them in their superstition and vice."[*]

Such was their condition when, in November, 1816, John Stewart first visited them. From Mr. Finley's "History of the Wyandot Mission," it is learned that John Stewart, a free-born mulatto, whose parents claimed to be mixed with Indian blood, was born in Powhatan County, Va. He became disabled in early life. When quite a youth, his parents moved to the State of Tennessee and left him behind. Subsequently he set out to join them, but on his way to Marietta, Ohio, was robbed of all his money. Discouraged over his losses, he remained at that place for a considerable period, and gave full scope to habits of intemperance, in the drinking of strong liquors, to such a degree that at one time he determined to put an end to his miserable existence by drowning himself in the Ohio River. Finally he united with the Methodist Episcopal Church at Marietta, where, subsequently, he engaged in his trade of blue-dyeing.

---

[*] J. B. Finley.

In the fall of 1814, he became very ill, and no one expected he would recover. But he invoked the blessings of God, and promised if he was spared that he would obey the call. Soon after this, he went into the fields to pray. "It seemed to me," said he, "that I heard a voice, like the voice of a woman praising God; and then another, as the voice of a man, saying to me, 'You must declare my counsel faithfully.' These voices ran through me powerfully. They seemed to come from a northwest direction. I soon found myself standing on my feet, and speaking as if I were addressing a congregation. This circumstance made a strong impression upon my mind, and seemed an indication to me that the Lord had called on me to warn sinners to flee the wrath to come. But I felt myself so poor and ignorant that I feared much to make any attempt, though I was continually drawn to travel toward the course from whence the voices seemed to come. I at length concluded that if God would enable me to pay my debts, which I had contracted in the days of my wickedness and folly, I would go. This I was soon enabled to do; and I accordingly took my knapsack and set off to the northwest, not knowing whither I was to go. When I set off, my soul was very happy, and I steered my course, sometimes in the road, and sometimes through the woods, until I came to Goshen, on the Tuscarawas River. This was the old Moravian establishment among the Delawares. The Rev. Mr. Mortimore was then its pastor." Here Stewart found a few of the Delawares, among them the old chief Killbuck and his family. He remained a few days and was kindly treated by all. And it was here doubtless that Stewart learned something of the Delawares and Wyandots further to the north; for these Delawares had many friends and relations that lived at a point on the Sandusky River called Pipetown, after the chief who lived there; and to this place he next proceeded.

At Pipetown was a considerable body of Delawares under the control of Capt. Pipe, son of the chief of the same name, who was prominent at the burning of Col. Crawford. At this place Stewart stopped, but as the Indians were preparing for a great dance they paid but little attention to him. The proceedings on the part of the Indians were all new to Stewart, and for a time their vociferations and actions alarmed him exceedingly, but at last they became somewhat quiet, when Stewart took out his hymn book and began to sing. He, as is usual with many of his race, had a most melodious voice, and as a result of his effort the Indians present were charmed and awed into perfect silence. When he ceased, Johnny-cake said in broken English, "Sing more." He then asked if there was any person present who could interpret for him; when old Lyons, who called himself one hundred and sixty years old (for he counted the summer a year and the winter a year) came forward. Stewart talked to them for some minutes and then retired for the night. In the morning, he almost determined to return to Marietta, and from thence proceed to the home of his parents in Tennessee. But so strong were his impressions that he had not yet reached the right place, though he was invited by the Delawares to remain with them, that he continued his course northwesterly and finally arrived at the house of William Walker, Sr., at Upper Sandusky.

Mr. Walker was an interpreter, and the United States Indian sub-agent at this point. At first he suspected Stewart to be a runaway slave; but the latter accounted for his presence here in such an honest, straightfoward manner, that all doubts or suspicions were at once removed. Mrs. Walker, who was a most amiable woman, of good education, and half Wyandot, also became much interested in Stewart after hearing his account of himself.

She possessed great influence in the Wyandot nation; and this whole family became his hospitable friends, and the untiring patrons to the mission which was afterward established. Mr. Walker, Sr., his wife and his sons, were all good interpreters, spoke the Indian tongue fluently, and all, except old Mr. Walker, became members of the church.

This family directed Stewart to a colored man named Jonathan Pointer. The latter, when a little boy, had been captured by the Wyandots at Point Pleasant, Va. His master and himself were cultivating corn when the Indians came upon them. They shot his master, caught Jonathan, and took him home with them. This man could speak the Indian language as well as any of the natives. When Stewart called upon him, and made known his wishes, Jonathan was very reluctant, indeed, to interpret for him, or to introduce him as a preacher. He told Stewart that "it was great folly for him, a poor colored man, to attempt to turn these Indians from their old religion to a new one." But Stewart persevered; he believed that God had sent him here, and he was unwilling to give up until he had made a trial.

Jonathan was going to a feast and dance the next day, and Stewart desired to go along, to which he rather reluctantly consented. Stewart induced him to introduce him to the chiefs, when he gave them an exhortation and sung a hymn or two. Finally he requested that all who were willing to hear him next day at Pointer's house should come forward and give him their hand. This the most of them did. But he was much disappointed the next day, for none of them came other than one old woman, to whom he preached. A meeting was appointed at the same place for the following day. The same old woman, and an old chief, named Big-Tree, were present. To these Stewart again preached. The next day being the Sabbath, he appointed to meet in the council house. At that place eight or ten came. From this time his congregations began to increase in numbers, and it is presumed that nothing contributed more to increase them and keep them up for awhile than his singing. This delighted the Indians. No people are more fond of music than they are, and for that reason Stewart mixed his prayers and exhortations with numerous songs.

Mr. Finley relates that many of the Wyandots had been Catholics, and they began to call up their old Catholic songs, and sing them, and to pray. By this means, some of them got stirred up, and awakened to see their lost condition. However, Stewart considered it to be his duty when they prayed to the Virgin Mary, and used their beads and crosses in prayer, to tell them that it was wrong. He also spoke against the foolishness of their feasts and dances, and against their witchcraft. These reproofs soon excited prejudices against him. Many that had joined in the meetings went away, and by voice and actions did all the harm they could. Some even visited the Catholic priest at Detroit, related what was going on, and asked for instructions. The priest told them, "that none had the true word of God, or Bible, but the Catholics; that none but the Catholic priests could teach them the true and right way to heaven; that if they died out of the Catholic Church they must perish forever; and that they could not be saved in any other way, but must be lost forever." They came home from Detroit in high spirits, and soon it was reported through every family that Stewart did not have the right Bible, and was leading them wrong. Some charged him with having a false Bible, but how to test the matter was the difficulty. Finally, all agreed to leave it to Mr. Walker, Sr. The time was set when the parties were to meet, and he was publicly to examine Stewart's Bible and hymn book. The parties came together at the time appointed. Deep interest was felt on both sides, and all waited in solemn suspense. After some time had been spent in the examination, Mr. Walker said that the Bible used by Stewart was a true one, and differed from the Catholic Bible only in this: one was printed in English, the other in Latin. He also affirmed that his (Stewart's) hymn book was a good one, and that the hymns it contained were well calculated to be sung in the worship of God.

This decision was received with joy by the religious party, and in a corresponding degree sunk the spirits of the other. It is believed, however, that none were so influential in putting down the superstitions of the Catholics as Mrs. Walker. She was no ordinary woman. Her mind was well enlightened, and she could expose the folly of their superstitions better than any one in the nation. As she stood so high in the estimation of all, her words had more weight than anyone else.

Stewart continued his labors among the Wyandots from November, 1816, until early in the following spring. His interpreter, Pointer, had professed to obtain religion, and also a considerable number of rather unimportant Indians; but the leading chiefs and head men of the nation stood aloof. After passing several months at Mariette, Stewart returned to Upper Sandusky in August, 1817. He found upon his return that but few of his flock had remained steadfast. Most of them had fallen back into their former habits, and one of the most hopeful of the young men had been killed in a drunken frolic. At this time Mononcue* and Two-logs, or Bloody Eyes (the last mentioned chief being a brother of Between-the-logs), raised a powerful opposition to Stewart, and represented in most glowing colors the destruction that the Great Spirit would visit upon them if they forsook their old traditions; that the Great Spirit had denounced them as a nation, and

---

*This renowned chief of the Wyandot nation was of medium stature, and remarkably symmetrical in form. Mr. Finley says he was one of the most active men he ever knew, quick in his motions as thought, and fleet as the doe in the chase.

As a speaker, he possessed a native eloquence which was truly wonderful. Few could stand before the overwhelming torrent of his eloquence. He was a son of Thunder. When inspired with his theme, he could move a large assembly with as much ease, and rouse them to as high a state of excitement, as any speaker I ever heard. There is a peculiarity in Indian eloquence which it is difficult to describe. To form a correct idea of its character, you must be in the hearing and sight of the son of the forest; the tones of his voice and the flash of his eye must fall upon you, and you must see the significant movement of his body. As an orator, Mononcue was not surpassed by any chieftain.

I will give a specimen or two of the eloquence of this gifted son of nature. Imagine yourself, gentle reader, in the depths of the forest, surrounded by hundreds of chiefs and warriors, all sunk in the degredation and darkness of paganism. They have been visited by the missionary, and several converted chiefs. One after another the chiefs rise and address the assembly, but with no effect. The dark scowl of infidelity settles on their brows, and the frequent mutterings of the excited auditors indicate that their speeches are not acceptable, and their doctrines not believed. At length Mononcue rises amidst confusion and disturbance, and ordering silence with a commanding voice, he addresses them as follows:

"When you meet to worship God, and to hear from His word, shut up your mouths, and open your ears to hear what is said. You have been here several days and nights worshipping your Indian god, who has no existence, only in your dark and beclouded minds. You have been burning your dogs and venison for him to smell What kind of a god or spirit is he, that he can be delighted with the smell of a burnt dog? Do you suppose the great God that spread out the heavens, that hung up the sun and moon, and all the stars, to make light, and spread out this vast world of land and water, and filled it with men and beasts, and everything that swims or flies, is pleased with the smell of your burnt dog? I tell you to-day, that His great eye is on your hearts, and not on your dogs, to see and smell what you are burning. Has your worshipping here these few days made you any better? Do you feel that you have gotten the victory over one evil? No! You have not taken the first step to do better, which is to keep this day holy. This day was appointed by God Himself, a day of rest for all men, and a day on which men are to worship Him with pure hearts, and to come before Him that He may examine their hearts, and cast out all their evil. This day is appointed for His minister to preach to us Jesus, and to teach our dark and cloudy minds, and to bring them to light." He here spoke of the Savior, and His dying to redeem the world; that how life and salvation are freely offered to all that will forsake sin and turn to God He adverted to the judgment day, and the awful consequences of being found in sin, and strangers to God. On this subject he was tremendously awful. He burst into tears; he caught the handkerchief from his head, and wiped them from his eyes. Many in the house sat as if they were petrified, while others wept in silence. Many of the females drew their blankets over their faces and wept. " Awful, awful day to the wicked!" said this thundering minister. " Your faces will look much blacker with your shame and guilt than they do now with your paint. I have no doubt but God was with Mononcue on this occasion, and that many were convicted of sin and a judgment to come.

Mononcue was of great service to the mission at Upper Sandusky as a local preacher, and was always prompt in the discharge of every duty. He remained a true Christian and friend of the whites until his death, which occurred some time before the removal of the Wyandots west of Missouri.

would abandon them forever, if they left His commandments, and exhorted the people never to think of turning aside from their fathers' religion.

Late in the year 1818, Stewart encountered other difficulties. It seems that certain missionaries, traveling to the northward, passed through Upper Sandusky, and finding that Stewart had been somewhat successful in his labors among the Wyandots, wanted him to join their church, saying that they would assure him a good salary. He refused on the ground of his objections to the doctrines they held. They then demanded his authority as a Methodist missionary. As he held no other authority from the church than an exhorter's license, he frankly told them he had none. Through this means, it became known that he had no authority from the church to exercise the ministerial office; although he had both solemnized matrimony and baptized several persons, both adults and children, believing that the necessity of the case justified it. This operated greatly to his disadvantage, for the missionaries aforesaid and the traders asserted that he was an impostor.

Stewart now determined to attach himself to the Methodist Episcopal Church, at some point nearer than Marietta. The same winter (1818–19), he visited a tribe of the Wyandots that lived at Solomonstown, on the Great Miami River. He there formed the acquaintance of Robert Armstrong, and some Methodist families living near Bellefontaine. From them he learned that the quarterly meeting, for that circuit, would be held near Urbana. To that place he proceeded (in company with some of the Indians), recommended by the converted chiefs and others, as a proper person to be licensed as a local preacher in the Methodist Episcopal Church. In March, 1819, his case was brought before the conference, and by a unanimous vote of that body, he was duly licensed. At this meeting, several of the local preachers present volunteered to go in turn and assist Stewart, but it appears that Rev. Anthony Banning, of Mount Vernon, anticipated their action, and was the first to aid him.

At the annual conference, held at Cincinnati in August, 1819, the Indian mission at Upper Sandusky was named as a regular field of labor in the Lebanon District, which then extended from the Ohio River northward to and including Michigan Territory. At the same time Rev. James B. Finley was appointed Presiding Elder of the district, and Rev. James Montgomery, missionary to assist Stewart. Subsequently, Montgomery was appointed by Col. John Johnston, sub-agent over the Senecas, and Moses Henkle was employed to fill the position vacated by Montgomery. As a result of these proceedings, Stewart's prominence as a missionary among the Indians began to wane, and others proceeded to occupy the field which he had opened.

Although Mononcue and other prominent men of the Wyandots opposed Stewart's efforts for a time, they were, comparatively speaking, early converts to Methodism. Thus, Finley relates that the first quarterly meeting appointed for the benefit of the Indians was held at Zanesfield, at the house of Ebenezer Zane, a half-breed, in November, 1819. About sixty Indians were present, among them the chiefs known as Between-the-logs, Mononcue, John Hicks, Peacock, Squindighty and Scuteash. Robert Armstrong and Jonathan Pointer were the interpreters. All of the chiefs mentioned, besides several others, spoke to the white men and red men there assembled. The address of Between-the-logs, interpreted, was as follows:

"Will you have patience to hear me, and I will give you a history of religion among the Indians for some time back, and how we have been

MO-NONCUE

AN INDIAN CHIEF OF THE WYANDOT TRIBE AND A LICENSED PREACHER
OF THE METHODIST CHURCH.

deceived. Our fathers had a religion of their own, by which they served God and were happy, before any white men came among them. They used to worship with feasts, sacrifices, dances and rattles; in doing which they thought they were right. Our parents wished us to be good, and they used to make us do good, and would sometimes correct us for doing evil. But a great while ago, the French sent us the good book by a Roman priest, and we listened to him. He taught us that we must confess our sins, and he would forgive them; that we must worship Lady Mary, and do penance. He baptized us with spittle and salt, and many of us did as he told us. Now, we thought, to be sure we are right. He told us to pray, and to carry the cross on our breasts. He told us, also, that it was wrong to drink whisky. But we found that he would drink it himself, and we followed his steps and got drunk too. At last our priest left us, and this religion all died away. So, many of us left off getting drunk, and we began again to do pretty well. Then the Seneca prophet arose and pretended that he had talked to the Great Spirit, and that he had told him what the Indians ought to do. So we heard and followed him. It is true, he told us many good things, and that we ought not to drink whisky; but soon we found that he was like the Roman priest—he would tell us we must not do things, and yet do them himself. So here we were deceived again. Then, after these cheats, we thought our fathers' religion was still the best, and we would take it up again and follow it. After some time the great Shawanese prophet [Tecumseh's brother] arose. Well, we heard him, and some of us followed him for awhile. But we had now become very jealous, having been deceived so often, and we watched him very closely, and soon found him like all the rest. Then we left him also. and now we were made strong in the religion of our fathers, and concluded to turn away from it no more. We made another trial to establish it more firmly, and had made some progress when the war broke out between our father, the President, and King George. Our nation was for war with the king, and every man wanted to be a big man. Then we drank whisky and fought; and by the time the war was over we were all scattered, and many killed and dead.

"But the chiefs thought they would gather the nation together once more. We had a good many collected, and were again establishing our Indian religion. Just at this time, a black man, Stewart, our brother here (pointing to him), came to us, and told us he was sent by the Great Spirit to tell us the true and good way. But we thought that he was like all the rest, that he wanted to cheat us, and get our money and land from us. He told us of all our sins; showed us that drinking whisky was ruining us; that the Great Spirit was angry with us; and that we must leave off these things. But we treated him ill, and gave him but little to eat, and trampled on him, and were jealous of him for a whole year. We are sure if the Great Spirit had not sent him, he could not have borne with our treatment. About this time our father, the President, applied to us to buy our lands, and we had to go to the great city to see him. When we came home, our old preacher was still with us, telling us the same things; and we could find no fault or alteration in him. About this time he talked about leaving us to see his friends; and our squaws told us that we were fools to let him go, for the Great God had sent him, and we ought to adopt him. But still we wanted to hear longer. They then told us what God had done for them by this man. So we attended his meeting in the council house, and the Great Spirit came upon us so that some cried aloud, some clapped their hands, some ran away, and some were angry. We held our meeting all night, sometimes singing and sometimes praying. By this time we were convinced that God had sent him to us; and then we adopted him, and gave him mother and children. About this time a few of us went to a great camp-meeting near Lebanon, Warren County, Ohio, and were much blessed and very happy. As soon as this work was among us at Sandusky, almost every week some preacher would come and tell us they loved us, and would take us and our preacher under their care, and give us schools, and do all for us that we wished. But we thought if they loved Indians so, why not go to the Senecas and Mohawks? They have no preacher; we have ours. Some told us that we must be baptized all over in the water, to wash away our sins. And now they said they cared much for us; but before Stewart came they cared nothing for us. Now some of us are trying to do good, and are happy. We find no alteration in Stewart. But when others come, and our young men will not sit still, they scold; and we believe Stewart is the best man. Some of the white people that live among us and can talk our language say, 'The Methodists have bewitched you;' and that, 'It is all nothing but the works of the devil; and the whites want to get you tamed, and then kill you, as they did the Moravian Indians on the Tuscarawas River.' I told them that if we were to be killed, it was time for us all to be praying. Some white people put bad things in the minds of our young Indians, and make our way rough." Between-the-logs concluded his address by telling of the goodness of the Lord, and requesting an interest in the prayers of his people.

In August, 1821, in accordance with the suggestions of the Methodist preachers, the chiefs, Deunquot, Between-the-logs, John Hicks, Mononcue, Andauyouah, Deandoughso and Tahuwaughtarode, signed a petition, which was drawn up and witnessed by William Walker, United States Interpreter; and Moses Henkle, Sr., Missionary, requesting that a missionary school be established among them, at Upper Sandusky, and for that purpose they donated a section of land at the place called Camp Meigs, where existed a fine spring of water and other conveniences. The Indians also requested of conference that the teacher sent them should be a preacher, thus obviating the necessity of a traveling misssonary being continued among them. Thereupon Rev. James B. Finley, was appointed resident missionary and teacher at the Wyandot Mission. He says in his history of the mission: "There was no plan of operation furnished me, no provision made for the mission family, no house to shelter them, nor supplies for the winter; and there was only a small sum of money, amounting to $200, appropriated for the benefit of the mission. However, I set about the work of preparation to move. I had a suitable wagon made, bought a yoke of oxen, and other things necessary, took my own furniture and household goods, and by the 8th of October was on my way. I had hired two young men, and one young woman, and Sister Harriet Stubbs volunteered to accompany us as a teacher. These, with my wife and self, made the whole mission family. We were eight days making our way out. Sixty miles of the road was almost as bad as it could be. From Markley's, on the Scioto, to Upper Sandusky, there were but two or three cabins. But by the blessing of kind Providence, we arrived safe, and were received by all with the warmest affection. There was no house for us to shelter in on the section of land we were to occupy, but by the kindness of Mr. Lewis, the blacksmith, we were permitted to occupy a new cabin he had built for his family. It was without door, window or chinking. Here we unloaded, and set up our Ebenezer. The Sabbath following, we held meeting in the council house, and had a large congregation. Brother Stewart was present, and aided in the exercises. We had a good meeting, and the prospect of better times. "We now selected the place for building our mission house. It was on the spot called 'Camp Meigs,' where Gov. Meigs had encamped with the Ohio Militia in time of the last war, on the west bank of the Sandusky River, about a mile below the post of 'Upper Sandusky.' We commenced getting logs to put us up a shelter for the winter. The first week one of my hands left me. A day or two after, while we were in the woods cutting down timber, a dead limb fell from the tree we were chopping on the head of the other young man, so that he lay breathless. I placed him on the wagon, drove home half a mile or more, and then bled him, before he recovered his senses. I now began to think it would be hard times. Winter was coming on, and my family exposed in an Indian country, without a house to shelter in. For years I had done but little manual labor. But the Lord blessed me with great peace in my soul. My worthy friend, George Riley, recovered from his hurt, and we worked almost day and night, until the skin came off the inside of my hands. I took oak bark, boiled it, and washed my hands in the decoction, and they soon got well and became hard. We built a cabin house, 20x23 feet, and without door, window, or loft. On the very day that snow began to fall, we moved into it. The winter soon became extremely cold. We repaired one of the old blockhouses, made a stable thereof for our cattle, and cut, hauled and hewed logs to put up a double house, forty-eight feet long by twenty wide, a story and a half high. We hauled timber to the saw mill, and sawed it ourselves into joists and plank, for the floors and other purposes. I think I can say that neither brother Riley nor myself sat down to eat one meal of victuals that winter but by candle-light, except on Sabbath days. We always went to bed at 9, and rose at 4 o'clock in the morning, and by daylight we were ready to go to work. In addition to this, I preached every Sabbath and met class, attended prayer meeting once every week, and labored to rear up the church. Brother Stewart assisted when he was able to labor, but his pulmonary affliction confined him the most of his time to the house, and I employed him to teach a small school of ten or twelve Indian children at the Big Spring; for these people were so anxious to have their children taught that they could not wait until preparations were made at the mission house, and they wanted to have a separate school by themselves. To this I would not agree; but to accommodate their wishes until we were ready at the mission house to receive their children, I consented that they might be taught at home."

Mr. Finley remained with the Wyandots at Upper Sandusky (assisted meanwhile, at different periods, by Revs. John Stewart, Charles Elliott, Jacob Hooper, John C. Brooke and James Gilruth), about seven years, and his published statements of the proceedings while here, are quite interesting and complete. Yet, except in a few instances, the scope of this work—the great variety of topics to be treated—precludes the practicability of our giving full accounts obtained therefrom, or indeed of doing but little more, while speaking further of the Wyandot Mission, than to merely make mention of some of the most prominent events.

While the chiefs and head men known as Between-the-logs, Mononcue, John Hicks, Squire Grayeyes, George Punch, Summundewat, Big-tree, Driver, Washington, Joseph Williams, Two Logs, Mathew Peacock, Harrihoot, Robert Armstrong, Scuteash, Rohnyenness, Little Chief, Big River, Squindatee and others (with a following of about one-half of those on the reservation), professed to have obtained religion, and were enrolled as members of the Mission Methodist Episcopal Church, *Deunquot*, who became the head chief of the nation upon the death of Tarhe, together with the other half of the Indians under his control, remained true to the religion (if so it may be called) of their fathers. Finley speaks of an occurrence in which Deunquot prominently figured as follows:

"Some time after this the head chief, Deunquot, and his party came one Sabbath to the council house, where we held our meetings, dressed up and painted in real Indian style, with their head-bands filled with silver bobs, their head-dress consisting of feathers and painted horse hair. The chief had a half moon of silver on his neck before and several hanging on his back. He had nose-jewels and ear-rings, and many bands of silver on his arms and legs. Around his ankles hung many buck-hoofs, to rattle when he walked. His party were dressed in similar style. The likenesses of animals were painted on their breasts and backs, and snakes on their arms. When he came in he addressed the congregation in Indian style, with a polite compliment, and then taking his seat, struck fire, took out his pipe, lighted it and commenced smoking. Others of his party followed his example. I knew this was done by way of opposition and designed as an insult. Soon after I took my text, John v, 16, 'Wilt thou be made whole?' etc.; and commenced on the diseases of man's soul, and showing from history the injustice of one nation to another; the treatment of the white people to the natives of North and South America; the conduct of man to his brother, and his conduct to himself, his drunkenness etc., and all the good we have comes from God, to make us happy. But that we, from the badness of our hearts, use these blessings to our own hurt; and that all evil proceeds out of the heart; therefore, all our hearts must be evil, and that continually; that we are proud, and of this we have an example before us in our grandfather, the head chief. Surely these things can do him no good, but to feed a proud heart. They will not warm his body when cold, nor feed him when hungry.

"As soon as I sat down, he arose with all the dignity of an Indian, and spoke as follows: 'My friends, this is a pretty day, and your faces all look pleasantly. I thank the Great Spirit that He has permitted us to meet. I have listened to your preacher. He has said some things that are good, but they have nothing to do with us. We are Indians, and belong to the red man's God. That book was made by the white man's God, and suits them. They can read it—we cannot; and what he has said will do for white men, but with us it has nothing to do. Once, in the days of our grandfathers, many years ago, this white man's God came himself to this country and claimed us. But our God met him somewhere near the great mountains, and they disputed about the right to this country. At last they agreed to settle this question by trying their great power to remove a mountain. The white man's God got down on his knees, opened a big book, and began to pray and talk, but the mountain stood fast. Then then the red man's God took his magic wand, and began to pow-wow and beat the turtle shell, and the mountain trembled, shook, and stood by him. The white man's God got scared and ran off, and we have not heard of him since, unless he has sent these men to see what they can do.' All the time he was speaking, the heathen party were on tip-toe, and often responded, saying, '*Tough gondee*'—that is, *true* or *right*; and seemed to think they had won the victory.

"As soon as he sat down, I arose and said: 'Our grandfather is a great man—he is an able warrior, a great hunter, and a good chief in many things; and in all this I am his son. But when it comes to matters of religion, he is my son and I am his father. He has told us a long and queer story. I wonder where he obtained it. He may have dreamed it, or he has heard some drunken Indian tell it; for you know that drunkards always see great sights, and have many revelations, which sober men never have. (Here my old friend Mononcue said, '*Tough gondee.*') But my friend, the head chief, is mistaken about his gods; for if it requires a God for every color, there must be many more gods. This man is black (pointing to Pointer). I am white, and you are red. Who made the black man? Where is *his* God? This book tells you and me that there is but *one* God, and that he made all things, and all nations of the earth of *one blood*, to dwell together; and a strong evidence is, that the difference of color is no obstacle to generation. God has diversified the color of the plants. Go to the plains and see how varied they are in their appearance. Look at the beasts; they are of all colors. So it is with men. God has given them all shades of color, from the jet black to the snow white. Then your being a red man, and I a white man, is no argument at all that there are two gods. And I again say that this book is true in what it states of man having a bad heart, and being wicked; and that my friend has a proud heart is evident from his dress and painting himself. God made me white and that man black. We are contented. But my friend does not think the Great Spirit has made him pretty enough; he must put on his paint to make himself look better. This is a plain proof that he is a proud man, and has an evil heart.' Seeing that the chief was angry, I said, 'My grandfather will not get angry at his son for telling him the truth, but he might if I had told him a lie.'

"He then rose, considerably excited, saying: 'I am not angry; but you cannot show in all your book where an Indian is forbid to paint. You may find where white people are forbid, but you cannot show where an Indian is.' I then arose, and read from the third chapter of Isaiah, at the sixteenth verse; and told him that these people were not white men, as the Americans, and yet were forbidden to use those foolish ornaments. He arose and said I had not read it right. I then handed the book to one of the Mr. Walkers, and he read and interpreted it; so that the old man was at last confounded, and said no more." Nevertheless, Deunquot remained steadfast in the belief of his ancestors until his death, which occurred about a year after the affair in the council house, just narrated. He was succeeded by the chief termed Warpole.

In the summer of 1823, the mission school was formally opened. It was conducted according to the manual labor system. The boys were taught the art of farming, and the girls, house-work, sewing, knitting, spinning, cooking, etc. The boys were averse to labor at first; but instead of force, stratagem was brought into play. They were divided into separate groups, and each encouraged to excel the others. Sixty scholars were enrolled in the year last mentioned, among them being a number of children sent from Canada, by members of the Wyandot nation there residing. Bishop McKendree also visited the mission and reservation during the same year. In a letter written by him in August, 1823, he said: "Our missionary establishment is at Upper Sandusky, in the large national reserve of the Wyandot tribes of Indians, which contains one hundred and forty-seven thousand eight hundred and forty acres of land; being in extent something more than nineteen miles from east to west, and twelve miles from north to south. Throughout the whole extent of this tract, the Sandusky winds its course, receiving several beautiful streams. This fine tract, with another reservation of five miles square at the Big Spring, head of Blanchard's River, is all the soil that remains to the Wyandots, once the proprietors of an extensive tract of country. The mission at Upper Sandusky is about sixty-five or seventy miles north of Columbus, the seat of government of Ohio. To the old Indian boundary line, which is about half way, the country is pretty well improved. From thence to the Wyandot Reserve, the population is thinly scattered, the lands having been but lately surveyed and brought into market."

During the same year (1823), Col. John Johnston, United States Indian Agent, likewise visited the Wyandots on their reservations. He passed several days among them, and at the close of his visit—August 23—reported as follows: "The buildings and improvements of the establishment are substantial and extensive, and do this gentleman [meaning Mr. Finley] great credit. The farm is under excellent fence, and in fine order; comprising about one hundred and forty acres, in pasture, corn and vegetables. There are about fifty acres in corn, which, from present appearances, will yield 3,000 bushels. It's by much the finest crop I have seen this year, has been well worked, and is clear of grass and weeds. There are twelve acres in potatoes, cabbage, turnips and garden. Sixty children belong to the school, of which number fifty-one are Indians. These children are boarded and lodged at the mission house. They are orderly and attentive, comprising every class from the alphabet to readers in the Bible. I am told by the teacher that they are apt in learning. and that he is entirely satisfied with the progress they have made. They attend with the family regularly to the duties of religion. The meeting-house, on the Sabbath, is numerously and devoutly attended. A better congregation in behavior I have not beheld; and I believe there can be no doubt, that there are very many persons, of both sexes, in the Wyandot nation, who have experienced the saving effects of the Gospel upon their minds. Many of the Indians are now settling on farms, and have comfortable houses and large fields. A spirit of order, industry and improvement appears to prevail with that part of the nation which has embraced Christianity, and this constitutes a full half of the population." During the year 1823, the sum of $2,254.54 was expended at the mission, which had been gathered from various sources.

The same year was also made memorable in the history of the mission by reason of the death of the colored preacher, Rev. John Stewart, who died of consumption December 17, 1823. It appears from Finley's account, that in 1820, conference appropriated money for the purpose of purchasing a horse for Stewart, and to pay for clothing he had bought; besides which, he received many presents from friends in and about Urbana. Soon after, he married a women of his own color, and wished to have a place of his own. Thereupon the venerable Bishop McKendree collected $100, with which sixty acres of land were purchased and patented in the name of Stewart. It adjoined the Wyandot Reservation, and was occupied by him from the spring of 1821 until his death. Afterward his wife and brother sold the land and appropriated the money to their own use. Stewart was the recipient of regular supplies from the mission to the time of his decease; although a year or so before that event he had withdrawn from the Methodist Episcopal Church, and joined the *Allenites*, a sect of colored Methodists.

In the spring of 1824, the Indians turned their attention to the improvement of their farms, and to the building of comfortable houses. A number of hewed-log houses were put up, with brick or stone chimneys; and great exertions were made to enclose large fields, for raising grain and grass. Many purchased sheep, and means were taken to improve their breed of cattle and hogs. With the means at their command, they did all they could to provide for the future, without following the chase, for they clearly saw that the white settlers would soon occupy all the country around them, and that they must starve unless they could procure the means of living at home. The same year, too, was built the mission church, now standing in ruins. Says Mr. Finley: " We were much in want of a place of worship, as there was no proper meeting-house. Sometimes we worshiped in the old council house, as the largest and most roomy. This was an old building, made of split slabs, laid between two posts stuck in the ground, and covered with bark peeled from the trees. No floor but the earth—no fireplace but a hearth in the middle, and logs laid on the ground on each side for seats. In the winter we met in the mission schoolhouse, which was much too small.

On my tour to the East, I visited the city of Washington, in company with the Rev. David Young. Here I had an interview with President Monroe, and gave him such information as he wished, as to the state of the mission and Indians in general. I had also an introduction to John C. Calhoun, Secretary of War. This gentleman took a deep interest in Indian afairs, and gave me much satisfactory information respecting the different missions in progress among the Indians; the amount of money expended on each establishment, and the probable success. I made an estimate of the cost of our buildings, and he gave me the Government's proportion of the expense, which amounted to $1,333. I then asked him if it would be improper to take that money, and build a good church for the benefit of the nation. His reply was, that I might use it for building a church; and he wished it made of strong and durable materials, so that it might remain a house of worship when both of us were no more. This work was performed, and the house was built out of good limestone, 30x40 feet, and plainly finished. So these people have had a comfortable house to worship God in ever since. It will stand if not torn down, for a century* to come."

---

*Such would have been the case, doubtless, if the successors of the Wyandots here—the white men—had exhibited the least particle of public spirit, or of pride, in the preservation of this, and other priceless mementoes of a past race and age. Under date of May 12, 1881, the very able editor of the Wyandot *Democratic Union* speaks of this: "The Last Landmark of the Wyandot Reservation," in the following lucid, unmistakable style: * * * "We remember with what interest we viewed, on our first visit to the town —shortly after these so-called wild men had taken their departure—the council house, the block-house, many of their cabins, and especially the church, which had witnessed so many gracious manifestations of the presence of the Holy Ghost, and which now is almost a heap of ruins. Then they were considered souvenirs of the people that for generations had occupied the land, and whose untutored minds had formed certain well defined laws much in accordance with nature for their government; and who, to enforce them, had their officers, prisons and courts of justice. All these were left as mementoes of the age that had preceded ours. They should have been protected by the people who succeeded them, and guarded as legacies handed down from those whose hands had built them. But this was not the case. A different spirit actuated those who succeeded them, although they boasted of a higher order of civilization, that had the Christian religion for its corner stone. The tide of emigration that pressed into the reservation under the new order of things, had no appreciation for the venerable relics they found standing everywhere, as monuments of the genius of the people who had preceded them, and with the greed ever manifested by the whites to gain property, and to turn everything found in their way into a channel that would lead to such results, therefore, nothing belonging to Indian mythology was deemed too sacred to be sacrificed to this unholy thirst for riches.

"After the organization of the county, the council house, which had witnessed so many grand scenes connected with the primeval history of the Wyandots, was used for holding the courts of justice, and by sheer carelessness in storing ashes in a barrel, it took fire and was burned up. The block-house or jail gave way for a more imposing building, to be used as a dwelling-house. Other memorial stones that were set up as commemorative of Indian history were thrown down, and at last the 'Old Mission Church,' the only landmark remaining, is about to fall into decay. More than this, the vandal hand was seen a few years ago in the almost total obliteration of the marble slabs that marked the last resting-place of a number of the most noteworthy of the Indian chiefs of the Wyandots, many of them having, ere they died, gloried in the power of the new birth, and believed in Him who is the resurrection and the life. But nevertheless, men calling themselves Christians, some of them ministers of the Gospel, with uplifted hands, struck piece after piece from these grave marks of the noble dead, until there does not remain a single one to tell where rests

For the year ending September 30, 1826, the following report of the mission school, etc., was rendered to the War Department of the United States: Name of the site or station, Wyandot Mission School, Upper Sandusky; by whom established, by the Bishops of the Methodist Episcopal Church, with the consent of the Ohio Annual Conference; when established, October 16, 1821; name of Superintendent, J. B. Finley; number of scholars, sixty-nine; number of teachers, one male and one female teacher, principals—ten others—in all, twelve; amount of funds received, including annual allowance of Government, $2,454.47½; amount of disbursements, $2,600; deficiency, $145.52¼; value of property belonging to the establishment, $10,000. At that time this was the most successful and prosperous Indian school and mission in the United States. We will also mention here, that the building known as the mission school and boarding-house was situated about half a mile northeast of the church. It entirely disappeared many years ago. It was commenced by Mr. Finley in the winter of 1821–22 See his account as shown on preceding pages.

In explanation of the number of white men or partly white men found among the Wyandots, it appears that this nation, although never behind other savage tribes during their wars with the whites, were more merciful than their neighbors—the Delawares, Shawanese, Miamis, Ottawas, Chippewas, etc. They saved more prisoners, and purchased many from other Indians, and adopted them into their families. Thus did they become allied with some of the best families in the country. The Browns, an old Virginia family; the Zanes, another well-known family; the Walkers of Tennessee, and the Williams, Armstrongs, McCulloughs and Magees of Pittsburgh, were all represented among them. Robert Armstrong, one of the best interpreters during Finley's time, was taken prisoner by the Wyandots about the year 1786, when a boy about four years old. His parents resided a few miles above Pittsburgh, on the banks of the Allegheny River. One Sunday morning a young man of the family, with little Robert, took a canoe and crossed over to the west side of the river to visit a camp of friendly Indians of the Cornplanter tribe. This camp was situated about four miles distant from the river. After they had made their visit and were returning home, in passing a dense thicket through which the path led, they heard a noise and stopped to look, and to their great surprise and terror, four hideously painted Indians of the Wyandot nation rose up and ordered them to stop.

the sleeping dust of Mononcue, Summundewat, Between-the-Logs, Deunquot, or any other of the braves whose remains had been deposited in the ground around this 'Old Mission Church.' It is a record at which the Christian should blush with shame. It was a vandalism of which the Goths, in their palmiest days, would have blushed to have been charged with, and yet in this advanced age, in the light of the sun shining on us in this, the nineteenth century, there were men wearing the livery of heaven that boldly, in open daylight, were guilty of this crime.

"But the past cannot be recalled. What has been done cannot be remedied. But the people of Upper Sandusky have a sacred duty to perform in the preservation of what remains of the 'Old Mission Church' from total obliteration. Last winter, had there been sufficient enterprise, the object sought for might have been attained. Through the persevering efforts of Hon. E. B. Finley, a bill passed the Senate of the United States, appropriating $3,000 for repairing the Old Mission Church, and building a suitable monument in honor of the Wyandot nation. Mr. Finley notified our citizens of this fact, and invited their co-operation. What was done by our people? Simply nothing! We made an appeal to them through the columns of the Union. Our appeal had about as much effect as pouring water upon a goose's back. We talked privately to our business men, but they turned a deaf ear to all we said, and the result was that with the expiration of the last Congress, the bill died a borning in the house, and the town is out of the $3,000 for the fitting-up of the old mission grounds If our citizens would have met in public meeting, and taken steps to co-operate with Mr. Finley, our member of Congress, and sent a delegation to Washington to work up the matter, the bill could, we have no doubt, have been passed. But as it is, we see now no hope. The church that should stand as a monument of other days and of another people is going into decay, and it will not be long until there will be nothing left of it. We are chargeable with its destruction, and the generations that will come after us, looking for these mementoes of a pre-historic race, will condemn us for our want of liberality in not preserving them. We have now had our say on this subject, and we close by reiterating our former belief, that if our citizens had moved at the proper time, Finley's bill would have passed the National Congress, and an amount sufficient would have been placed at the disposal of the proper person to have put in repair this old landmark, and to have erected a suitable monument to the memory of the sleeping braves whose bodies have returned to dust around it."

The young man attempted to make his escape by running, but had made a few steps only, when the Indians fired and he fell dead. Little Robert ran a few yards, but one of the Indians soon caught him and picked him up. Said he: "I was so scared to see the young man tomahawked and scalped that I could hardly stand, when set on my feet, for I expected it would be my lot next. One of the men took me on his back and carried me for several miles before he stopped. The company then divided. Two men took the scalp, and the other two had charge of me. In the evening they met, and traveled until it was late in the night, and then stopped to rest and sleep. The next morning I had to take it afoot as long as I could travel; and although they treated me kindly, yet I was afraid they would kill me. Thus they traveled on for several days, crossing some large rivers, until they got to an Indian town, as I learned afterward, on the Jerome's Fork of Mohickan Creek, one of the branches of Muskingum River. Here they rested awhile, and then went on until they came to Lower Sandusky."

Young Armstrong was adopted into the Big Turtle tribe of Wyandots, and named O-no-ran-do-roh. He became an expert hunter and a perfect Indian in his feelings and habits of life. He married an Indian woman or half-breed, and had so far lost the knowledge of his mother tongue that for years he could speak or understand but little of it. After Gen. Wayne's treaty he mingled more with the whites, conversed more in English, and finally learned to talk the language of his fathers equal to any of the traders or settlers. He became an excellent interpreter, and was employed in trading and interpreting the rest of his life. His wife was a daughter of Ebenezer Zane—a half Indian woman—and they raised a family of interesting children. He lived for some years at Solomonstown. Afterward he moved to Zanesfield, on Mad River, and from thence to Upper Sandusky, where he died of consumption in April, 1825. We have thus briefly sketched the career of Armstrong for the reason that it is a fair illustration, probably, of the life and experiences of many other whites who had been captured and adopted by the Wyandots.

In the summer of 1826, Rev. J. B. Finley, accompanied by the chiefs Mononcue and Between-the-logs, and Samuel Brown as interpreter, visited the cities of Buffalo, Albany, New York, Philadelphia, Baltimore and Washington. At each point great crowds gathered to see and hear them, and all expressed the utmost surprise and delight after listening to the addresses of these eloquent, Christianized sons of the forest. They returned home at the end of three months.

In the autumn of that year, Judge Leib, an agent appointed by the government to visit all the Indian mission schools to which the government had made appropriations of money, reported to the Secretary of War as follows: "On Tuesday, the 10th of November last, I left Detroit for Upper Sandusky, where I arrived on the 12th, and found this establishment in the most flourishing state. All was harmony, order and regularity under the superintending care of the Rev. Mr. Finley. Too much praise cannot be bestowed on this gentleman. His great good sense, his unaffected zeal in the reformation of the Indians, his gracious manners and conciliating disposition fit him in a peculiar manner for the accomplishment of his purpose, and the fruits of his labors are everywhere visible; they are to be found in every Indian and Indian habitation. By Indian habitation here is meant a good comfortable dwelling, built in the modern country style, with neat and well-finished apartments, and furnished with chairs, tables, bedsteads and beds, equal at least, in all respects to the generality of whites around them. The Wyandots are a fine race, and I consider their civilization accomplished, and little short in their general improvement to an equal number of whites in our frontier settlements. They are charmingly situated in a most fruitful country. They hunt more for sport than for subsistence, for cattle seem to abound among them, and their good condition gives assurance of the fertility of their soil and the rich herbage which it produces, for the land is everywhere covered with the richest blue grass.

"They mostly dress like their white neighbors, and seem as contented and happy as any other portion of people I ever saw. A stranger would believe he was passing through a white population, if the inhabitants were not seen; for besides the neatness of their houses, with brick chimneys and glazed windows, you see horses, cows, sheep and hogs grazing everywhere, and wagons, harness, plows, and other implements of husbandry in their proper places. In short, they are the only Indians within the circle of my visits whom I consider as entirely reclaimed, and whom I should consider it *a cruelty to attempt to remove.* * * * A good and handsome stone meeting-house, forty feet in length by thirty in breadth, has been erected since last year. * * * The mission farm is well supplied with horses, oxen, cows and swine, and all the necessary farming utensils. I cannot forbear mentioning a plan adopted by this tribe, under the auspices of the Superintendent, which promises the most salutary effects. A considerable store has been fitted up on their reserve, and furnished with every species of goods suited to their wants, and purchased with their annuities. An account is opened with each individual who deals thereat, and a very small profit acquired. Mr. William Walker, a quadroon, one of the tribe, a trustworthy man, and well qualified by his habits and education to conduct the business, is their agent. The benefits resulting from this establishment are obvious. The Indians can, at home, procure every necessary article at a cheap rate, and avoid not only every temptation which assails him when he goes abroad, but also great imposition. The profits of the store are appropriated to the general benefit. This plan, it seems to me, promises many advantages. The merchandise with which this store is furnished was bought in New York on good terms."

Between-the-logs died of consumption January 1, 1827. During the last part of the same year, Rev. Mr. Finley terminated his labors with the Wyandots, leaving Rev. James Gilruth in control. Among the successors of the latter were Messrs. Thompson, Shaw, Allen and Wheeler, ministers of the Methodist Episcopal Church. It is probable, however, that the mission attained its greatest degree of activity and substantial prosperity just at the close of Mr. Finley's superintendency.

By a treaty concluded at Little Sandusky August 3, 1829, between John McElvaine, Commissioner on the part of the United States, and the chiefs and head men of the Delawares, the latter ceded their reservation to the United States for the sum of $3,000, and removed west of the Mississippi. This reservation was granted to the Delawares at the treaty of the Maumee Rapids. It contained nine square miles, and adjoined the Wyandot Reserve on the southeast, thus embracing portions of the present townships of Antrim and Pitt, in Wyandot County. By permission of the Wyandots, these Indians made a village on the west bank of the Sandusky River, below the mouth of Broken Sword Creek, where a fine spring emerges from the river bank. Capt. Pipe, Jr, a son of the Capt. Pipe who burned Col. Crawford at the stake, was with them, and their village was called Pipetown, or Capt. Pipe's village. Among those named in the original grant at the treaty of the Maumee Rapids (several of whom survived until after their removal beyond the Mississippi) were Capt. Pipe, Zeshauau or James Armstrong, Mahautoo or John Armstrong, Sanoudoyeasquaw or Silas Armstrong, Black Raccoon, Billy Montour, Buckwheat, William Doudee, Thomas Lyons, Johnnycake, Capt. Wolf, Isaac Hill, John Hill, Tishatahooms or Widow Armstrong, Ayenucere, Hoomaurou or John Ming and Youdorast.

The Delawares were ever a savage, superstitious, treacherous race, and the whites of the pioneer days never placed much dependence upon their promises. Buckwheat, one of the Indians mentioned above, was part negro. About the year 1827 he was accused of witchcraft, and after having been tried and found guilty was sentenced to die by being burned alive. Maj. Anthony Bowsher, the founder of Bowsherville, and one of the very few surviving pioneers of the county, witnessed the burning. From his account, it appears that Buckwheat was first made so drunk with whisky that he was unable to stand; then he was bound and placed upon a blazing fire of brush, wood, etc., and to insure his remaining there, a heavy and long piece of green timber was placed upon his body, and that kept in place by Indians sitting upon both ends of it. Around the victim circled and danced all the Indians there assembled. All were maddened with whisky passed around by an old squaw, and the shouts and songs rendered were most terrifying. The hideous orgies continued for two days and nights. Even Bowsher was made to move around the burning remains of Buckwheat with them, but he states that he refused to taste any of the whisky. This affair took place near the bank of the river, opposite the present town of Little Sandusky.

Thomas Lyons. or "Old Tom Lyons," as he was termed by the whites, was another conspicuous character among this small band of Delawares. He claimed that Gen. Wayne gave him his name and a coat, likewise that he was more than one hundred and sixty years old. However, as old Tom counted the summer a year. and the winter a year, his alleged great age can easily be accounted for. He it was who interpreted for the colored man Stewart at Pipetown, in 1816, when the latter was traveling toward Upper Sandusky. He had lived with the Delawares in Pennsylvania before these Indians were forced to remove to Ohio. He had been a strong, powerful man, and made many enemies among the whites, by reason of his fondness in boasting of his deeds of prowess, and in relating many incidents of the wars through which he had passed. He seemed to take great delight in asserting that he had killed and scalped ninety-nine whites, including men, women and children, and only desired to make the number an even one hundred before being called to the happy hunting-grounds. Various accounts have been published concerning the time and place of his death. One statement is that Samuel Spurgeon, who, in common with many other white men of his acquaintance, did not enjoy such boasting, met him alone one day in the woods and offered Lyons an opportunity to make him the hundredth victim, but Lyons failing in his aim, Spurgeon shot him dead and left his body lying in the forest as food for wild animals. Another person claims that old Tom was shot in his wigwam, near Fort Ball, by two white hunters from Delaware County, while others assert that he died a natural death at Pipestown, on the Delaware Reservation. Lyons' wife is reputed to have been one of the finest-looking squaws in the tribe, being, in fact, a queen of beauty among them. He was very proud of her, and kept her dressed in the height of Indian fashion, and did not compel her to perform menial labor, as was the custom among the Indians.

Solomon Johnycake, the husband of Sally Williams, was well known to the early settlers of the region now known as Wyandot County. He was a well-developed, good-natured, friendly hunter, and it was customary for Sally and the children to accompany him on his hunting excursions. He usually constructed a neat bark wigwam to protect his squaw and children from the storms and exposures of the forest, while he ranged the woods in search of game. He sometimes exchanged venison for side-pork with the white settlers, and frequently parties, who had a curiosity to see Sally (who was a quarter-blood) and the children visited his wigwam. Sally was regarded as a very neat housekeeper, and preferred, as far as possible, to imitate the whites. Her mother, a white woman, by the name of Castleman, was captured in girlhood, upon the Pennsylvania frontier. Johnycake went West with his people. Three of his sons served in a Kansas Indian company of the Union army during the war of the rebellion.

Capt. Billy Doudee, or Dowdee, was, in point of notoriety, nearly equal to Old Tom Lyons. Nickels, his son-in-law, was a very bad Indian, and Dowdee's son Tom was not much better. Capt. Beckley, in his reminiscences of pioneer life, relates the following incidents, as told by Benjamin Sharrock, a former citizen of Marion County:

"About the year 1821 or 1822, there were several Indians who frequently camped and hunted on the waters of the West and Middle Forks of the Whetstone, to wit, Capt. Dowdee, his son Tom, and Capt. Dowdee's son-in-law, Nickels (the bad Indian), the subject of this narrative. He was regarded as a dangerous man among his own companions. He had become embittered against Benjamin Sharrock, his brother, Everard Sharrock, and Jacob Stateler, who, with his three sons, Andrew, James and John (the two latter were twin brothers), lived in a cabin on or near the land now owned by George Diegle, Esq., in Tully Township. The Dowdees had frequently shared the hospitalities of our cabin and we regarded them as peaceable and well-disposed citizens.

"Mr. Sharrock, in relating his difficulty with this bad Indian, says: "This Indian, Nickels, had been skulking around and watching my house, trying to get a chance to shoot me. I have seen him dodge from tree to tree when trying to get a shot at me. He also made threats of killing my stock. About this time, he and the two Dowdees were encamped on the boundary north of where Iberia now is. Mr. Catrell, my brother and myself held a consultation, whereupon we resolved that this state of things should no longer be tolerated, and the next morning was the time agreed upon to bring this matter to the test. They were to be at my house fully armed for any emergency. They were promptly on time, and as Catrell had no gun, he took my tomahawk, sheath knife, etc.

"In this plight, we went directly to their camp, called Tom Dowdee out and ordered him to take those coon skins out of "them" frames. (They are stretched in frames to dry and keep them in shape.) We next went to the tent of Tom's father, old Capt. Dowdee, and told him how Nickels had been watching my house, and that he threatened to kill me and my stock. I told him to call Nickels out, but he would not leave his hut. We told them we would not endure such treatment any longer, and that we had come to settle it right then and there, and were ready to fight it out. The Dowdees seemed to be peaceably inclined, and as Nickels did not show himself, the matter was dropped for a short time. Some time after this, as I was returning from Wooster, where I had been to enter a piece of land, I saw quite a number of moccasin tracks in the snow near Hosford's.

I thought there would be trouble, as it appeared from the tracks that there were about thirty persons, and by the way they had tumbled about, concluded that they were on a big drunk. I followed their tracks from Hosford's down the road leading to our cabin. They had not proceeded far before they left their tracks in the snow somewhat besprinkled with blood. I afterward learned that Tom Dowdee had stabbed another Indian, inflicting two dangerous wounds. They were camped north of my house on the land now owned by James Dunlap. The excitement among the settlers now became intense, and soon a number of us repaired to their camp, but we had not been there long before Tom Dowdee rushed upon me and grasped me by the collar, perhaps intending to retaliate for the visit we had made to their camp a few days before. I was not slow in returning the compliment by taking him by the throat, and my arms being the longest I could easily hold him at bay. At this moment we saw an Indian boy loading a gun. I told Dowdee several times to let me alone, but he still persisted in fighting me. I then attempted to give him a severe thrust with my gun barrel; he sprang and grasped the gun which the boy had just loaded, when several of the squaws also grasped it to prevent him from shooting me. All this time I kept my rifle up with a steady aim upon the Indian, ready to fire before he should be able to fire at me. At this crisis Joel Loverick interfered and the Indians allowed him to take possession of the gun, so the quarrel was then settled without bloodshed. But what grieves me to this day is that Bashford and Loverick both knew that my rifle was not primed all the time I was aiming it at the Indian, and they did not tell me. The next day I was out in the woods with my gun, and came upon Dowdee before he discovered me. He had no gun with him, and he begged and implored me not to kill him, promising over and over that if I would not he would never molest me, but would be my fast friend as long as he lived. I gladly agreed to his proposal, and to his credit be it said I never saw him after that time but that he met me with the kindest greetings.'

"About the same time some of the Indians told Stateler, 'Nickels, bad Indian, by and by he go to Stony Creek, before he go he say he kill Stateler and two Sharrocks, and we 'fraid that big fight. We want white man to kill Nickels, then Indians say Nickels gone to Stony Creek.'

"We never saw Nickels after about that time, but did not know at what moment he would come down upon us. I often asked the Indians whether they knew where Nickels was, and they usually replied that he had gone to Stony Creek. We had often seen a gun in the settlement, first owned by one, then by another, that I believed was Nickels' gun. Jake Stateler often stayed with us several weeks at a time, and many times when we spoke about those Indians, Jake would say, 'Nickels will never do you any harm,' but made no further disclosures until a long while after; when the subject again came up, he said:

" 'Ben, Nickels will never hurt you nor your brother.'

" 'How do you know, Uncle Jake?'

" 'I know very well how I know, Uncle Ben.'

" 'Did you never know what became of Nickels?'

" 'No, Jake, I never knew what became of him any more than what the Indians told me, that he had gone to Stony Creek.'

" 'I thought my boys had told you long ago, as they always thought so much of you. I will then tell you how I know what became of Nickels. After he was about ready to start for Stony Creek, he had only one more job to do before he could leave Pipetown, and that was to kill Stateler and you and your brother, if possible. No sooner had Nickels left Pipetown than the Indians sent another Indian by a different route to give us notice of his coming and of his intentions, desiring us to kill him and they would say he had gone to Stony Creek. The messenger arrived in time and departed. I loaded my rifle, put it in good order and went up to Coss' cabin to watch the Pipetown trail, on which I expected him to come. I did not wait long before I saw him coming, and stepping behind a tree, closely watched his movements. After he had come within easy range of my rifle, he stopped and commenced looking all around, which enabled me to take a steady aim at him; I fired, he sprang several feet from the ground with a terrific scream and fell dead, and that was the last of "Bad Indian." We took his gun, shot-pouch, tomahawk, butcher-knife, etc., and laid them by a log, and buried him under the roots of a large tree that had been blown down near the foot of the bluff bank of the Whetstone, nearly opposite the old Coss cabin. Now, Uncle Ben, that is the reason why I know Nickels will never do you, or me, or your brother any harm.'"

Capt. Pipe, Jr., son of old Capt. Pipe, who burned Col. Crawford, was a small, rather spare man, and taciturn in his disposition. He never married. He went West with his tribe and died on their reservation about 1840. Among his own people he had the reputation of being a great "medicine man." At an early day, Reuben Drake, who lived in Grand Prairie Township, Marion County, had two children bitten by a rattlesnake, one of whom died. Having heard of Capt. Pipe's reputation, he sent for him to come and cure the other child. Pipe is said to have been somewhat under the influence of whisky at the time, and refused at first to go; but being strongly urged, finally visited the cabin of Mr. Drake. Upon his arrival he looked at the child, which was in great pain, exclaiming, " great pain, very sick." He then stated he could do nothing for half an hour, and laid down by the cradle and snored soundly for some time, then arose and called for milk, which was furnished, when he pounded some roots, which he had brought with him, poured the milk over them, gave the child a portion to drink, applied more of the same in the nature of a poultice to the place bitten, rocked the child some time in its cradle, when it fell into a slumber and soon began to perspire freely. Upon seeing this effect of his remedy, the Captain said, "It get well;" and true enough the child recovered rapidly.

The Delawares as well as the Wyandots, when journeying from their reservations in search of game, almost invariably stopped at all the houses of the white settlers, and when they came to a white man's cabin, expected to receive the hospitality of its inmates; if they did not, they were much offended. They would say, "very bad man, very bad man." They would never accept a bed to sleep upon; all that was necessary was to have a good back-log on, and a few extra pieces of wood near by, especially in cold weather, for them to put on the fire when needed. They usually carried their blankets, and would spread them upon the floor before the fire, and give no further trouble. Often they would leave those who had sheltered them a saddle of venison or some other commodity which they had to spare. Says an early pioneer: " We have seen as many as twenty or thirty in a caravan pass by here, with their hunting material and equipments packed on their ponies, all in single file, on their old Sandusky and Pipetown trail. If we would meet half a dozen or more of them together, it was seldom that we could induce more than one of them to say one word in English. One of them would do all the talking or interpret for the others. Why they did so I could not say. Tommy Vanhorn once related an amusing incident.

He had been imbibing a little, and on his way home met one of those Indians who could not utter one word of English, but used the pantomimic language instead—that of gestures or motions. But it so happened that while they were thus conveying their thoughts to each other, Tommy stepped around to windward of the red man or the red man got to leeward of Tommy, and his olfactories not being at fault, inhaled the odor of Tommy's breath. He straightened up, looked Tommy square in the face, and lo! Mr. Indian's colloquial powers were now complete, saying in as good English as Lord Mansfield ever could have uttered: 'Where you get whisky?'"

In the fall of 1830, a young brave of one of the Wyandot tribes killed another of the same nation. The murderer was arrested, tried, found guilty and shot. However, this affair is best told by the chief, Mononcue, in a letter addressed to Mr. Finley, as follows:

UPPER SANDUSKY, October 29, 1830.
DEAR SIR: * * * * * * * * *

One of our young men was killed by another about two or three weeks ago. The murdered was John Barnet's half-brother, the murderer, Soo-de-nooks, or Black Chief's, son. The sentence of the chiefs was the perpetual banishment of the murderer and the confiscation of all his property. When the sentence was made known to the nation, there was a general dissatisfaction; and the sentence of the chiefs was set aside by the nation. On Thursday morning, about daylight, he was arrested and brought before the nation assembled, and his case was tried by all the men (that vote) over the age of twenty-one, whether he should live or die. The votes were counted, and there were 112 in favor of his death, and twelve in favor of his living. Sentence of death was accordingly passed against him, and on the second Friday he was shot by six men chosen for that purpose—three from the Christian party and three from the heathen party. The executioners were Francis Cotter, Lump-on-the-head, Silas Armstrong, Joe Enos, Soo-cuh-guess, and Saw-yau-wa-hoy. The execution was conducted in Indian military style; and we hope it will be a great warning to others, and be the means of preventing such crimes hereafter. I remain, yours affectionately,
REV. J. B. FINLEY. MONONCUE.

After the departure of their old neighbors—the Delawares—for the West, the Wyandots were the only considerable body of Indians remaining in the State of Ohio. Meanwhile the white settlers had encircled their reservations at Upper Sandusky and the Big Spring with towns and cultivated lands, and each year were asking Congress to purchase these reservations, and thus open the way for their occupation by the whites. Hence, in acting upon these unceasing urgent petitions, agents of the General Government had endeavored to open negotiations with the Wyandots for the purchase of their lands as early as 1825. But they firmly resisted all blandishments and pleadings to that end for nearly twenty years thereafter. However, it seems that such a condition of affairs could not always exist; they had sadly degenerated from the prosperous state in which they were left by Mr. Finley in 1827. A majority of them had gone back to their old habits of intemperance and heathenism, and at last, when poor in purse and character, they were induced to give up their narrow possessions here in lieu of a great sum of money, and thousands of broad acres lying west of Missouri. Col. John Johnston, of Piqua, Ohio, conducted the negotiations on the part of the United States, and concluded the purchase at Upper Sandusky on the 17th day of March, 1842. In speaking of this transaction and the proceedings which led to it, Col. Johnston has said:

"About 1800, this tribe contained about 2,200 souls; and in March, 1842, when, as Commissioner of the United States, I concluded with them a treaty of cession and emigration, they had become reduced to less than 800 of all ages and both sexes. Before the Revolutionary war, a large portion of the Wyandots had embraced Christianity in the communion of the Roman Catholic Church. In the early part of my agency, Presbyterians had a mission among them at Lower Sandusky, under the care of the Rev. Joseph Badger. The war of 1812 broke up this benevolent enterprise. When peace was restored, the Methodists became the spiritual instructors of these Indians, and continued in charge of them until their final removal westward of Missouri. The mission had once been in a very prosperous condition, but of late years had greatly declined, many of the Indians having gone back to habits of intemperance and heathenism; a few continued steadfast to their Christian profession. Of this number was Grey Eyes, a regularly ordained minister, of pure Wyandot blood, a holy, devoted, and exemplary Christian. This man was resolutely opposed to the emigration of his people, and was against me at every step of a long and protracted negotiation of twelve months' continuance. I finally overcame all objections; on the last vote, more than two-thirds of the whole male population were found in favor of removal. The preacher had always asserted that under no circumstances would he ever go westward. His age was about forty-eight years; his character forbade any approaches to tampering with him; and although I felt very sensibly his influence, yet I never addressed myself to him personally on the subject of the treaty. But as soon as the whole nation, in open council, had voted to leave their country and seek a new home far in the West, I sent an invitation to the preacher to come and dine with me and spend an evening in consultation; he came accordingly." As a result of this interview, it appears that Grey Eyes changed his purpose, for he removed West with his people.

By the terms of this treaty, it was stipulated that the chiefs should remove their people without other expense to the United States than $10,000, one-half payable when the first detachment should start; the remainder, when the whole nation should arrive at its place of destination. Further, that the Wyandots should receive for the lands ceded another tract of land west of the Mississippi. It contained 148,000 acres; a permanent cash annuity of $17,500; a permanent fund of $500 per annum, for educational purposes, and an appropriation of $23,860 to pay the debts of the tribe. They were also to be paid the full value of their improvements in the country ceded, and to be provided in their new home with two blacksmiths and a blacksmith shop with necessary steel, iron and tools, and with an agent and an interpreter. However, instead of the 148,000 acres promised, the Wyandots received by purchase from the Delaware Indians 24,960 acres, and by a subsequent treaty (which will be referred to in a succeeding paragraph) received in lieu of the balance of the 148,000 acres, $380,000, in three annual payments.

In the spring and summer of 1843, in accordance with the stipulations of the treaty concluded the previous year, the Wyandots under the lead of Jacques*, their head chief, completed their arrangements for the removal to the new reserve in the then wild West. The parting scenes at Upper Sandusky were most affecting. Consultations were held in the council house, and religious worship in the church, almost constantly for days before the final departure. Meanwhile, the remains of the chief, Summundewat, who was murdered by two white men in Wood County, Ohio, in the fall of 1841, also those of the colored preacher, John Stewart, were brought hither and deposited in the burial ground attached to their church. The last resting places of other loved ones were likewise tenderly cared for, and

---

*After the death of Deunquot, some difficulty occurred in making choice of his successor, and as a result of it the Wyandots changed their form of government and mode of choosing their governors. Instead of being obliged to take their head chief out of the royal tribe, they then agreed to have the head chief and eight counselors chosen by election, on New Year's Day of each year. The first head chief elected according to the new plan was Warpole.

WYANDOT COUNTY COURT HOUSE.
COMPLETED A.D. 1849.

marked with stone or marble tablets. Just before their strange and motley procession unwound its length on the highway leading southerly, Squire Grey-Eyes bade an affectionate farewell to the large number of whites present. He exhorted them to be good Christians, and to meet him in heaven. In a most sublime and pathetic manner he discoursed upon all the familiar objects of a home—no longer theirs. He bade adieu to the Sandusky, on whose waters they had paddled the light bark canoe, and in whose pools they had fished, laved and sported. He saluted in his farewell the forests and the plains of Sandusky, where he and his ancestors had hunted, roved and dwelt for many generations. He bade farewell to their habitations, where they had dwelt for many years, and where they would still wish to dwell. With mournful strains and plaintiff voice he bade farewell to the graves of his ancestors, which now they were about to leave forever, probably to be encroached upon, ere the lapse of many years, by the avaricious tillage of some irreverent white man. Here, as a savage, untutored Indian, it is probable Grey-Eyes would have stopped, but as a Christian he closed his valedictory by alluding to an object yet dearer to him; it was the church where they had worshipped, the temple of God, constructed by the good white men for their use, and within whose walls they had so often bowed down in reverence under the ministrations of Finley and his co-laborers.

At last, all being in readiness, all the sad duties having been performed, the train, consisting of horses and wagons hired from settlers living in the vicinity, Indian chiefs upon horseback, and many men and women on foot, began wending its slow way toward Cincinnati, where boats were waiting to take its members to the mouth of the Kansas River. This movement began in the last days of July, and was participated in by nearly 700 of the Wyandot nation. Many ludicrous occurrences took place en route, but we have not space, in a topic already largely drawn out, to recount them. The end of the first day's journey found the Wyandots at Grass Point, in Hardin County; the second, at Bellefontaine; the third, at Urbana; the fourth, at Springfield; the fifth, at Clifton; the sixth, within four miles of Cincinnati, and the seventh at the wharf of the latter city. The remainder of the distance to the new reservation, as before stated, was accomplished by steamboats via the Ohio, Mississippi and Missouri Rivers. The Wyandots left Cincinnati on the eighth day after leaving Upper Sandusky. Among their leading men at that time were Jacques, Bearskin, Blue Jacket, Big Tree, Black Sheep, Big River, Bull Head, Big Town, Curly Head, Caryhoe, Chop-the-logs, Lump-on-the-head, Peacock, Porcupine, Providence, Split-the-log, Stand-in-the-water, White Wing, Mudeater, Warpole, Squire Grey-eyes, William Walker, a quarter-blood, who died in 1874, John Hicks and Washington.

While the main body of the Wyandots was moving toward Cincinnati, Jacques, the head chief, accompanied by a few other leading men of the nation, visited Gov. Shannon at the State capital, when very feeling and interesting parting addresses were delivered by the chief and the Governor. Jacques' address, as printed in the *Ohio State Journal* of that date, was as follows:

"We have several objects in view in visiting you, the Governor of the State. First, it was due him, as the chief magistrate of this great State; and, secondly, it was due to the people of Ohio, to whom, through their Governor, we speak, and bid them an affectionate farewell.

"We came here, also, to ask for the extension of executive clemency to an unfortunate brother of our nation, and we thank you for granting our prayer in their behalf.

"We part with the people of Ohio with feelings the more kind, because there has not been any hostility between your people and ours ever since the treaty of Gen. Wayne, at Greenville. Almost fifty years of profound peace between us have passed away, and have endeared your people to ours; whatever may be our future fate beyond the Mississippi—whither we are bound—we shall always entertain none but feelings the most kind and grateful toward the people of Ohio. Before Wayne's treaty there had been one long war between our fathers and your ancestors. At that treaty our people promised peace, and they have kept that promise faithfully; we will forever keep that promise as long as the sun shines and the rivers run.

"When we arrive at the place of our destination, surrounded, as we shall be, by red men less acquainted with them than we are with white men, we shall always take great pleasure in telling the Indians of that western region how kind, how peaceful, how true, faithful and honest your people have been to our people. If, at any future day, any of our people should visit this State, we hope that your people will see that they do not suffer for food or any of the necessaries of life; that, when thirsty, you will give him drink; when hungry, you will give him food; or naked, you will give him clothes; or sick, you will heal him. And we, on our part, promise the same kindnesses to any of your people should they visit us in our far western future home. Our original intention was to have passed through Columbus as a nation on our departing journey from Ohio to the West; but for the purpose of shortening our route on so long a journey, the principal part of our people have passed through Urbana. But although, for the reason stated, our people have passed through Ohio by the shortest route, yet they could not forego the pleasure of sending you their chiefs and addressing you, and through you the people of Ohio, in the language of truth, friendship and sincerity.

"Our fathers have ranged this valley with your fathers in peace and friendship, and we wished your people to know that we have the same kind feelings that existed in times past, and we wish you to know that we wish to perpetuate and keep alive the same brotherly feelings. In other States and Territories the Indians have lived, surrounded by white men, with whom they had occasional outbreaks, wars and difficulties; but between us and your people the chain of peace and friendship has always continued to be bright, smooth, and free from rusty or bloody spots. You are the representative of your people; therefore be so good as to tell your people what we say on this final parting occasion, and say to them to believe us to be always hereafter—what we always have been—the friends of the people of Ohio."

From the report of the United States Commissioner of Indian affairs for the year 1843, we learn that the number of Wyandots who removed to their new reservation in July and August of that year, was 664, and that 50 still remained in Ohio who were expected to emigrate the next spring. The following year (1844), the sub-agent reported only 585 Wyandots on the new reserve. During the year 1855, another treaty was concluded with that nation, wherein it was stipulated that in lieu of the 148,000 acres (less the 24,960 acres purchased for the Wyandots from the Delawares in 1842), granted by the treaty of Upper Sandusky, the Wyandots were to receive $380,-000, in three annual payments. By this treaty, also, all provisions of former treaties guaranteeing permanent annuities, etc., were annulled. The Wyandots who remained in tribal relations and were located in the Indian Territory on the 1st day of January, 1879, numbered 260.

We conclude this chapter, likewise our account of the Indians, by adding the following poem, which, whatever its merits or demerits as a literary production, has been widely copied, frequently in works, where its mention of localities obtained for it no special significance. It was written, we believe, by a resident of Wyandot County, and was first published in *The Democratic Pioneer*, of Upper Sandusky, under date of October 24, 1845.

THE WYANDOT'S FAREWELL SONG.

"Adieu to the graves where my fathers now rest!
For I must be going afar to the West.
I've sold my possessions; my heart's filled with woe
To think I must lose them. Alas! I must go.

"Farewell, ye tall oaks, in whose pleasant green shade
In childhood I rambled, in innocence played!
My dog and my hatchet, my arrows and bow,
Are still in remembrance. Alas! I must go.

"Adieu, ye loved scenes, which bind me like chains!
Where on my gay pony, I chased o'er the plains
The deer and the turkey I tracked in the snow.
But now I must leave them. Alas! I must go.

"Adieu to the trails, which for many a year
I have traveled to spy out the turkey and deer!
The hills, trees and flowers, that pleased me so,
I must leave now forever. Alas! I must go.

"Sandusky, Tymochtee and Broken Sword streams,
Never more shall I see you except in my dreams.
Adieu to the marshes, where the cranberries grow;
O'er the great Mississippi, alas! I must go.

"Adieu to the road, which for many a year,
I travel'd each Sabbath, the Gospel to hear;
The news was so joyful, and pleased me so,
From hence where I heard it, it grieves me to go.

"Farewell, my white friends, who first taught me to pray,
And worship my Maker and Savior each day.
Pray for the poor native, whose eyes overflow
With tears at our parting. Alas! I must go."

CHAPTER V.

EARLY SETTLEMENTS—PICTURE OF PIONEER LIFE.

THE UNUSUAL CONDITIONS ATTENDING THE SETTLEMENT OF THE COUNTY—NAMES OF EARLY PIONEERS, AND DATE OF THEIR ESTABLISHMENT IN THE SEVERAL TOWNSHIPS—CABIN-BUILDING—COOKING UTENSILS AND TABLE WARE—FOOD—HABITS OF THE PIONEERS—EMPLOYMENT OF THE MEN—WOMEN'S WORK—DRESS OF THE PIONEERS—THEIR BOOKS—SENSE OF ISOLATION—HOSPITALITY—WHISKY—SCARCITY OF MONEY—OF THE NECESSITIES OF LIFE—PRIMITIVE AGRICULTURAL IMPLEMENTS—WILD HOGS—GRADUAL IMPROVEMENTS.

EARLY SETTLEMENTS.

IN the course of events, over which those who were to become its pioneers exercised little or no control, the region now denominated Wyandot County was settled (as compared with most other districts) in a manner quite anomalous, yet in a way which is very easily comprehended when once explained. As already shown, the Indians, at the treaty held at the foot of the rapids of the Miami of the Lake in 1817, ceded to the United States Government all the lands remaining in their possession in the State of Ohio, except various small reservations then and there designated. Hence when it was agreed that the principal reservation of the Wyandots should have Fort Ferree at Upper Sandusky for its center, the central and greater portion of the present county was reserved to its aboriginal owners. The small Wyandot reserve at the Big Spring, and the Delaware reserve lying southeast of the reservation first mentioned, also encroached upon the limits of the county as now formed, therefore, all of the white settlements began upon the outskirts, so to speak—to the north, east, south and west of the chief Wyandot reservation—and in either direction, distant seven to ten miles from Fort Ferree, the locality now known as the town of Upper Sandusky.

In 1819, Deputy United States Surveyors* Sylvanus Burns and Thomas Worthington ran out the townships and subdivision lines of the county, and the following year the lands not reserved to the Indians were offered for sale at the usual Government price per acre. Prior to the sale of any of these lands, however, quite a number of "squatters" had settled near the reservation lines, chiefly for the purpose of trading with the Indians and to gather in the greater portion of annuity moneys paid the red men in exchange for poor whisky, bright calicoes, brass trinkets, etc., etc. From the date last mentioned until 1842, the whites within the present limits of the county, increased but slowly in numbers, yet, on the northern border—in the townships of Crawford, Tymochtee and Sycamore—quite populous communities were to be found, long before the removal of the Wyandots. However, by the purchase of the reservations of that nation, and the disposal of the same to individual owners, the population at once increased with astonishing rapidity. This is shown by the report of Col. Huber, Receiver of the Land Office at Upper Sandusky, who stated that

---

*Samuel Holmes, Deputy Surveyor General, performed much work in the county in 1836, and William Brown in 1843.

from the 1st of September, 1845, to January 1, 1846, he received for the sale of lands in Wyandot County the sum of $211,057.06.

Having thus briefly pointed out the rather unusual conditions under which the county was peopled by the whites, the following conclusions are reached: That a few "squatters" settled in the county, outside of the Indian reservations, about the year 1817; that the first lawful settlers became established in the same localities not earlier than 1820; that the first white settlements were not made within the reservation lines until after the year 1842, and but very few in the territory last referred to until 1845.

The original settlers of the county were chiefly of English and German origin. Forty years ago, the English element largely predominated, but at the present time it is probable that those of German birth or descent, as a class, outnumber all others. The reader will find sketches concerning many of the past and present residents of Wyandot in the township histories of this work, hence it is not purposed to enter into a repetition here; yet a small number of the pioneers are named in this connection, merely for the purpose of approximating the time when each township was first occupied by the white men.

FIRST SETTLERS IN THE SEVERAL TOWNSHIPS.

Antrim—Jacob, John and Adam Coon, John Heckathorn, Jacob Snyder and Valentine Mutchler, all Germans, who came from Pickaway County, Ohio, and squatted on the Delaware Reserve in the spring of 1819, are believed to have been the first white men to attempt a settlement. Their location afterward became known as "Germantown."

Crawford—Daniel Hodges, who settled near the site of the present town of Crawfordsville, in 1821, was one of the first to locate in this township. Hon. John Carey became a resident in 1823, and he was soon followed by Thomas Gale, Jesse Gale, Samuel Ritchie, Jonathan Kear, Asa Lake, Thomas Wallace, Curtis Berry, Sr., and a number of others.

Crane—As this township was embraced by the Wyandot Reservation, its lands were not offered for sale until the latter part of 1845. Prior to that date, its residents were all located at the town of Upper Sandusky. See history of that town for a list of its inhabitants and lot owners in 1845.

Eden—Judge George W. Leith settled in what is now termed Eden Township in 1837. It had but a sparse population for a number of years, but among those who soon followed Mr. Leith to this then wild region were James Winstead, David Kisor, Z. P. Lee, John Horrick, John Leith, Solomon Brundige, Isaac Miller and Solomon York.

Jackson—Thomas C. Beaver settled in the township in 1826; John Abbott upon Section 3 in 1833, John Vanorsdall in 1834, John Flower and Jacob Dermiger in 1835, and William Fitch in 1837.

Marseilles—It is claimed that John Heckathorn, before mentioned as a "squatter" in Antrim Township, settled in the present township of Marseilles about the year 1828. Charles Merriman located on the site of the village about 1830, and Hugh Long in the same place in 1832.

Mifflin—Samuel M. Stansberry and family located within the present limits of the township in 1832. John Tanner, Daniel Straw, Israel Straw, Abraham Clark, Wesley Davenport, Jabez Halstead and Martin Dickens were also among the early settlers. Dr. Cover was the first resident physician.

Pitt—Ebenezer Roseberry, a noted hunter and frontier sportsman, was the first to settle within the limits of the township, as now formed. Anthony Bowsher found Roseberry here in the spring of 1819, and informs us that the latter had already been established two or three years, at least long enough to have caught and placed his private mark upon scores of the wild hogs. During the years 1819 and 1820, Anthony Bowsher, Peter Bowsher, William Morral, Walter Woolsey, John Wilson, Jacob Snyder, Jacob Brewer, Alexander Frazier, Samuel Morral, D. H. Bargley, Cornelius Wilson and John Wilson all settled just south of the reservation line in the vicinity of Little Sandusky.

Richland—Hescot Picket, the first settler of this township, established his residence on Section 28, in January, 1832. He came from Athens County, Ohio. Nathan Benjamin, from the same county, also settled here in 1832. The following year, Philip Cole and Charles Smith became residents.

Ridge—It is claimed that Homan and Andrew Bates became the first residents within the present township about 1833. John Salyards, Daniel Spade, T. N. Shepherd, Isaac Wohlgamuth, the Starrs and Grindles were also early pioneers.

Salem—The first settler in this township was Ezra Stewart, a native of Connecticut, who settled upon Section 5 in October, 1831. He was followed by John Stewart in 1834, John Nichols and Arnold B. Inman in 1835, Daniel and Jacob Baughman and John B. Mann, or Mason, in 1836.

Sycamore—Samuel Harper settled in the township as now formed in 1821, and built the first dwelling—a log cabin. His sons who came with him were William, James, Samuel G. and George. Samuel Harper, Sr., had served as a Revolutionary soldier, and was wounded at Bunker Hill. He died in October, 1821. The Eyestones, Luptons, Kisors, Betzers, Pontius, Griffiths and Van Gundys were also early settlers.

Tymochtee—Henry Lish, of this township, and Ebenezer Roseberry, of Pitt, were the earliest settlers in the present county of whom any record has been preserved. Lish was a native of the State of New York, and it is claimed that he settled on the site of the village of Tymochtee (where he soon after established a ferry over Tymochtee Creek) in 1816 or 1817. At his house the first election in the county was held on the 1st day of April, 1821. Thomas Leeper and family, from Ross County, Ohio, became residents in 1821, and soon after came Peter Baum, William Combs, Levi Bunn, John Taylor and George Bogart. At an early day this was the most populous district within the limits of the present county. In 1850, its inhabitants numbered 1,817.

A PICTURE OF PIONEER LIFE.

The pioneers of Wyandot as a rule, after long and tedious journeyings over Indian trails or roads rudely improved, brought very little with them with which to begin the battle of life among new surroundings. They had brave hearts and strong arms, however, and possessed invincible determinations to hew out for themselves homes which should in time become the abodes of happiness and plenty. Sometimes the men came on without their families to make a beginning, but more often all came together. The first thing to be done, after a rude temporary shelter was provided, was to prepare a little spot of ground for the growth of some kind of crop. This was done by girdling the large trees, clearing away the underbrush, and sweeping the surface with fire. The ground was then broken as thoroughly as possible with the few rude implements which the pioneer possessed. Ten, fifteen, twenty, or even thirty acres of land might be thus prepared and planted the first season. In the autumn, the crop would be carefully gathered and garnered with the least possible waste, for it was the chief food supply of the pioneer and his family, and life and comfort depended upon its safe preservation.

While the first crop was maturing, cabin-building occupied much of the attention of the pioneer. He would need a shelter from the storms and cold of the approaching winter, and perhaps a protection from wild beasts. The pioneer who was completely isolated from his fellow-men, occupied a situation truly unenviable, for without assistance he could construct only a poor habitation. In such cases a small and rough cabin was constructed of very light logs or poles, or else a three-sided, sloping-roofed shanty was improvised. In front of the fourth or open side of the shanty or "camp," as it was sometimes called, a hugh fire of logs was kept burning, and this primitive structure was occupied until other settlers should come into the owner's neighborhood, by whose help a more substantial dwelling could be built. Usually a number of families came into the country together, and located within such distance of each other that they were enabled to perform many friendly and neighborly offices. After the first year or two from the time of the primal settlements, there was no difficulty in cabin-building. Assistance was always readily given a pioneer by all of the scattered residents of the forest within a radius of several miles.

The site of the cabin home was usually selected with reference to a good water supply. It was often near a never-failing spring, or if such could not be found in a location otherwise desirable, it was not uncommon to first dig a well. If water was reached, preparations were made for building near the well; if not, the search for a situation affording it was continued, but there was little trouble on this score in the territory now known as Wyandot County.

When the cabin was to be built, the few men in the neighborhood gathered at the site, and first cut down, within as close proximity as possible, the requisite number of trees, as nearly of a size as could be found, but varying often from ten to fifteen inches in diameter. Logs, generally from fourteen to sixteen feet in length, were chopped from these, and rolled to the common center, where they were to be used in building the home of the pioneer family. Often this preliminary work was performed by the prospective occupants alone. If such was not the case, it would occupy the greater part of the first day. The entire labor of erecting a good substantial cabin, would usually require two or three days. After the ground logs were laid, the others were raised to their places by the use of hand spikes and "skid poles," and men standing at the corners with axes, notched them as fast as they were laid in position. The place of "corner man" was one of honor and distinction, and the persons chosen for these positions were supposed to be particularly skillful in the use of the ax.

Greater difficulty attended the work after the cabin was built a few logs high. It was necessary that the logs in the gables should be beveled, and that each succeeding one should be shorter than that on which it rested. These gable logs were held in place by poles which extended across the cabin overhead, serving also as rafters upon which to lay the rived "clapboard" roof. The so-called clapboards were five or six feet in length, and were split from oak logs, and made as smooth as possible. They were laid side by side, and other pieces of split stuff were laid over the cracks to keep out the rain.

The chimney was likewise an important part of the structure. In some cases it was made of stone, and in others of logs and sticks, laid up in a manner similar to those which formed the walls of the house, and plastered with mud. It was built outside of the house, and at one end. At its base a huge hole was cut through the wall for a fire-place. The back and sides of the latter were formed of large flat stones, when such could be procured, otherwise irregularly shaped stones, held to their place by a slab wall locked around them, and covered with mud, were utilized.

An opening was chopped or sawed in one side of the cabin for a doorway. Pieces of hewn timber, three or four inches thick, were fastened on each side with wooden pins, or in rare instances with heavy iron nails, and these formed the frame on which the door (if there was one) was hung, either by wooden or leather hinges. The door itself was a clumsy piece of woodwork. It was made from a plank rived from an oak log, and held together by heavy cross-pieces. There was a wooden latch upon the inside, raised from without by a string or thong of deer-skin, which passed through a gimlet hole. From this mode of construction arose the old and well-known phrase, indicating the hospitality of its inmates, "You will find the latch-string always out." When on rare occasions, it was pulled in, the door was considered fastened. Many of the pioneer cabins had no door of this kind until they had been occupied for years. Instead of the door on hinges, a blanket or some old garment was frequently suspended before the opening to guard the occupants of the cabin from sun or rain.

The window was a small opening usually near the door, and in most cases devoid of frame or glass. In lieu of the latter, greased paper was often used, in rare instances thin deer skin well greased, and sometimes an article of the housewife's limited wardrobe constituted a curtain.

The floor of the cabin was made of puncheons. These were pieces of timber split from trees about twelve to eighteen inches in diameter, and hewed smooth as possible with a broad-ax. They were usually half the length of the floor surface. Indeed some of the cabins earliest erected had nothing but earth floors. Occasionally there was one which had a cellar— that is, a small excavation under the floor— to which access was had by removing a loose puncheon. Very commonly the cabins were provided with lofts. The loft was used for various purposes, and among others as the "guest chamber," which pioneer hospitality was offered to the wayfarer and the stranger. It was reached by a ladder, the sides of which were split pieces of sapling.

Although the labor of building a rough log cabin was usually performed in two or three days, the occupants were often employed for months in finishing and furnishing it. The walls had to be "chinked and daubed," various conveniences furnished, and a few rude articles of furniture manufactured. A forked stick set in the floor and supporting the ends of two poles, the other extremities of which rested upon the logs at the side and end of the cabin, formed the basis for a bedstead. A common form of table was a split slab supported by four rustic legs, set in auger holes. Three-legged stools were formed in similar simple manner. Pegs driven in auger holes in the logs of the wall supported shelves, and upon others were displayed the few articles of wearing apparel not in use. A few other pegs, or perhaps a pair of deer horns, formed a rack where hung the rifle and powder horn, which no cabin was without. These, and a few simple articles in addition, formed the furniture and furnishings of the pioneer's cabin. In contrast with the rude furniture fashioned by the pioneer with his poor tools, there were occasionally a few souvenirs of "the old home."

The utensils for cooking and the dishes for table use were few. The best of the latter were made of pewter, and the careful housewife of the olden time kept them shining as brightly as the pretentious plate in our latter-day fine houses. Knives and forks were few, crockery very scarce, and tinware by no means abundant. Food was simply cooked and served, but it was, as a rule, of the best and most wholesome kind. The hunter kept the larder well supplied with venison, bear meat, squirrels, wild turkeys, and the many varieties of small game. Plain corn bread, baked in a kettle in the ashes, or upon a board or board chip, in front of the great, open fire-place, was a staple article of food. Corn was either pounded into coarse meal, or carried a long distance to mill to be ground. The wild fruits in their season were made use of, and afforded a pleasant variety. In the lofts of the cabins was usually to be found a collection of articles making up the pioneer's materia medica—the herb medicines and spices—catnip, sage, tansy, fennel, boneset, wormwood and pennyroyal, each gathered in its season; and there were also stores of nuts, strings of dried pumpkin, with bags of berries and fruit.

Well water was generally drawn up with what is called a "sweep," which was a long, heavy pole, hinged in a fork at the top of a tall post, and a rope or chain attached at the end over the well, with the bucket. Water could be drawn more rapidly with this simple apparatus than with the windlass or any modern pump.

The habits of the pioneers were of a simplicity and purity which was in conformance with the character of their surroundings and belongings. The days were full of toil, both for man and woman. The men were engaged constantly in the rude avocations of pioneer life—cutting away the forest, logging, burning the brush and the debris, preparing the soil, planting, harvesting, and caring for the few animals they brought with them or soon procured. The little openings around the log cabins were constantly made larger and the sunshine year after year admitted to a larger area of the virgin soil, which had been growing rich for centuries, and only awaiting cultivation to give evidence of its fertility.

While the men were engaged in the heavy work of the field or forest, their helpmeets were busied with a multiplicity of household duties, providing for the day and for the year; cooking, making or mending clothes, spinning and weaving. They were heroic in their endurance of hardship and privation and loneliness. They were, as a rule, admirably fitted by nature and experience to be the consorts of the sturdy, industrious men who came into the wilderness of Western Ohio. Their cheerful industry was well directed and unceasing. Woman's work, like man's, in the years when this country was new, was performed under many disadvantages, which have been removed by modern skill and science, and the growth of new conditions.

The pioneer woman had not only to perform what are now known as household duties, but many which were removed in later years. She not only made clothing, but the fabric for it. Money was scarce, and the markets in which satisfactory purchases could be made were far away. It was the policy of the pioneer (urged by necessity) to buy nothing which could be produced by home industry. And so it happened that in nearly all of the cabins was to be heard the drowsy sound of the softly whirring spinning wheel, and the rythmic thud of the loom, and that women were there engaged in those old, old occupations of spinning and weaving, which have been associated with her name in all ages but our own. They are occupations of which the modern world knows little, except what it has heard from the lips of those who are grandmothers now. They are occupations which seem surrounded with the glamour of romance as we look back upon them through tradition and poetry, and they invariably conjure up thoughts of the virtues and graces of the generations of dames and damsels of the olden time. The woman of pioneer times was like the woman of whom Solomon sang: "She seeketh wool and flax, and worketh willingly with her hands; she layeth her hands to the spindle, and her hands hold the distaff." Almost every article of clothing, all the cloth in use in the old log cabins, was the product of the patient woman-weaver's toil. She spun the flax, and wove the cloth, for shirts and trowsers, frocks, sheets and blankets. The linen and the wool, the "linsey-woolsey" woven by the housewife, formed nearly all of the articles of clothing worn by men and women.

These home fabrics were died with walnut bark, indigo, copperas, etc., and striped or checkered work was produced by first dyeing portions of the yarn their respective colors before it was put into the loom.

Nearly every farmer had a patch of from a quarter to half an acre of flax, which was manufactured into cloth by the family. The flax, before it was ready for spinning, had to be put through the process of "hackling" and "scutching," and the latter of these operations frequently furnished occasions for "bees," at which the people combined industry with merriment and sociability. Clothes entirely of home manufacture were almost universally worn during the early years, and the wearing of "store" clothes was thought by many to be an evidence of excessive vanity.

Men in the pioneer days commonly wore the hunting-shirt, a kind of loose frock reaching half way down the thighs, open before, and so wide as to lap over a foot upon the chest. This generally had a cape, which was sometimes fringed with a piece of raveled cloth of a color different from that of the garment. The hunting-shirt was always worn belted. The bosom of the garment answered as a pouch in which could be carried the various articles needed by the hunter or woodsman. The shirt, or more properly, coat, was made of coarse linen, of linsey or deer-skin, according to the fancy of the wearer. Breeches were made of heavy cloth or of deer-skin, and were often worn with leggings of the same material, or of some kind of leather. The deer-skin breeches or trousers were very comfortable when dry, but when they became wet, were cold to the limbs, and the next time they were put on, were almost as stiff as if made of boards. Hats or caps were made of the various native furs, in crude form, each man being his own hatter until, a few years after the first settlements, men who followed hat-making as a trade came into the country and opened little shops, in which they made woolen hats.

The pioneer women were clothed in linsey petticoats, coarse shoes and stockings, and wore buck-skin mittens or gloves, when any protection was needed for the hands. To a wardrobe of this kind were added a few articles obtained from some distant village, or brought from their old homes in the East. Nearly all of the women's wearing apparel, however, like that of the men, was of home manufacture, and was made with a view to being comfortable and serviceable. Jewelry was very rarely seen, but occasionally ornaments were worn which likewise had been brought from former homes.

The Bible was to be found in the cabins of the pioneers almost as frequently as the rifle. In the cabins of some families, a few other books were occasionally to be met with, such as "Pilgrim's Progress," Baxter's

"Saints' Rest," Hervey's "Meditations," Æsop's "Fables" and the like. The long winter evenings were spent in poring over a few well-thumbed volumes by the light of the great log fire, or in knitting, mending, curing furs, etc.

The pioneers had many discomforts to endure, and some dangers to encounter. True, when Wyandot County was settled, the danger of Indian depredations had passed away forever, but a vaguely defined apprehension existed in the minds of not a few of the first settlers, that they were not entirely secure in their forest homes. The larger wild beasts were a source of dread, and the smaller ones a source of much annoyance to those who first dwelt in this region. Added to this was the liability to sickness, which always exists in a new country. Then, too, in the midst of all the loveliness of their surroundings, there was a sense of loneliness which could not be dispelled, and this was a far greater trial to many men and women on the frontier of civilization, than is generally imagined. The deep-seated, constantly-recurring feeling of isolation made many stout hearts turn fondly back to remembrance of the older settlements, the abodes of comfort, the companionship and sociability they had abandoned.

However, the traveler always found a welcome at the pioneer's cabin. It was never "full." Although there might be already a guest for every puncheon, still there was "room for one more." If the stranger was in search of land, he was doubly welcome, and his host would volunteer to show him all the first-rate claims in "this 'ere neck of the woods," going with him for days, showing the corners and advantages of every "Congress tract" or unclaimed section within a dozen miles. To his neighbors, the pioneer was equally liberal. If a deer was killed, the choicest bits were sent to them—a half-dozen miles away, perhaps. When a "shoat" was butchered, the neighbors were also kindly remembered. If a new-comer came in too late for "cropping," the neighbors would supply his table with the same luxuries they themselves enjoyed, and in as liberal quantity, until a new crop could be raised. Often the neighbors would also cut and hew logs, and haul them to the place of the new-comer's future residence, concluding the jubilee task with a grand house-raising. The first night after completing the cabin, they would have a "house-warming" and a dance, as a sort of dedication. The very next day, the new-comer was about as wealthy as the oldest settlers.

As the settlement increased, the sense of loneliness and isolation was dispelled, the asperities of life were softened, its amenities multiplied. Social gatherings became more numerous and more enjoyable. The log-rollings, harvesting and husking bees; the occasional rifle matches for the men, and the quilting parties for the women, furnished frequent occasions for social intercourse. Hospitality in the olden time was simple, unaffected and unbounded, save by the limited means of the people. Whisky was in common use, and was furnished on all festive occasions. Those of the settlers who could afford it, had a barrel stored away, and there were very few so poor that they could not have at least a jugful. The liquor at first in use was brought from the Monongahela country. It was the good old-fashioned whisky—"clear as amber, sweet as musk, smooth as oil"—that the octogenarians and monogenarians of to-day recall to memory with an unctious gusto, and a smack of the lips, which entirely outdoes the descriptive power of words. A few years after the first settlements were made, stills were set up in the large towns to supply the home demand, and corn whisky was manufactured, which, although not held in as high esteem as the "old Monongahela," was used in large quantities.

Commercial transactions were generally carried on without money, that is, by exchanges of commodities, called "barter" in the books. In this system, sometimes, considerable ingenuity was displayed. When commodities were not even in value, credit was given. But for taxes and postage neither the barter nor the credit dodge would answer, and often letters were suffered to remain a long time in the post office for want of the 25 cents in money demanded by the Government. With all this high price on postage, by the way, the letter had not been brought several hundred miles in a day or two, as now-a-days, and delivered within a mile or two of the person addressed; but it had been weeks on the route, and delivered, probably, at a post office five, ten or twenty miles distant. Peltries came nearer being money than anything else, as it became the custom to estimate values in peltries; thus such and such articles were worth so many peltries. Even some Tax Collectors and Postmasters were known to take peltries and exchange them for the money required by the Government. Orders on the store were abundant, and served as a kind of local money. When a day's work was done by a working-man, his employer would ask: "Well, what store do you want your order on?" The answer being given, the order was drawn, which was nearly always honored.

When the first settlers came into the wilderness, they generally supposed that their hard struggle would be principally over after the first year; but alas! they often looked for "easier times next year" for many years before realizing them; and then they came in so gradually and obscurely as to be almost imperceptible. The sturdy frontiersmen thus learned to bear hardships like soldiers on duty. The less heroic would sell out cheap, return to their old homes East and spread reports of the hardships and privations on the frontier, while the sterner class would remain and also take advantage of these partially improved lands thus abandoned, and in time become wealthy.

At one time, tea retailed at $2 to $3 a pound; coffee, 75 cents; salt, from $5 to $6 a bushel of fifty pounds; the coarsest calico, $1 a yard, and whisky, $1 to $2 a gallon, and all this at a time, too, when the poor pioneers had no money to buy with, except the little they sometimes obtained for peltries.

About 1837, a farmer would haul his wheat to Sandusky City, over swampy roads, requiring six to eight days to make the trip, and sell his grain for 60 cents a bushel. On returning, they brought out merchandise, at the rate of 50 cents a hundred weight.

Flour, for some time, could not be obtained nearer than Zanesville or Chillicothe. Store goods were very high, and none but the most common kinds were brought here, and had to be packed on horses or mules from Detroit, or wagoned from Philadelphia to Pittsburgh, thence floated down the Ohio River to the mouth of the Scioto, and then packed or hauled up. The freight was enormous, often costing $4 a ton.

Bread, the "staff of life," was the most difficult of all to procure, as there were no mills in the country to grind the grain. The use of stump mortars and graters already referred to, were tedious and tiresome processes. A grater was a semi-cylindrical piece of thickly perforated tin, fastened upon a board, and operated upon as is a nutmeg grater. The corn was taken in the ear, and grated before it got dry and hard. By and by a horse grist mill was put up here and there, and then water grist mills along the principal streams; but all these together could not keep pace with the demands of the rapidly growing settlements. When there was water enough to run the mills, the roads were too muddy and small streams too high for teaming and taking the grain to the mills. Horse mills were too slow, and thus the community had to plod their weary way along until steam flouring mills were introduced.

The implements used by the first farmers in this State would, in this age of improvement, be great curiosities. The plow was of the wooden mold-board, bar-share pattern, difficult to describe. The reapers were the sickle and the cradle. Harrows, with wooden teeth, were simply brush heaps dragged over the ground. Hoes were almost as heavy as grubbing hoes. Threshing machines were flails, or the grain was trodden out by horses or oxen. A sheet or quilt, with a stout person at each end to swing it simultaneously, sometimes constituted the fanning mill; or sometimes the grain and chaff would be dipped up with a pail, held aloft and slowly poured out, while the wind was blowing. Handbreaks were used for breaking flax and hemp.

When the earliest pioneer reached this Western wilderness, game was his principal meat, until he had conquered a farm from the forest or prairie. As the country filled up with inhabitants, game grew correspondingly scarce, and by 1840–50, he who would live by his rifle would have had but a precarious subsistence had it not been for "wild hogs." These animals —the descendants of those left by home-sick emigrants who had returned East—multiplied and thrived in a wild state, their subsistence being chiefly acorns, nuts, sedge stalks, and flesh of carcasses and small vermin. The second and third immigration to the country found these wild hogs an unfailing source of meat supply for a number of years. In some sections of the West, they became altogether too numerous for comfort, and the citizens met, organized and adopted measures for their extermination.

Meanwhile, during all the early years of the settlement, varied with occasional pleasures and excitements, the great work of increasing the area of tillable lands went steadily on, and true, the implements, as already mentioned, were few and of the most primitive kind, yet the soil which held in reserve the accumulated richness of unnumbered centuries, produced splendid results. Although the development of the country and the improvement of individual condition was slow, nevertheless it was sure. Hence year by year, the log houses became more numerous, and the forest shrank away before the woodman's ax. The settlers brought stock into the country as they became able, and each one had his horses, oxen, cows, sheep and swine. Among the earliest evidences of the reward of patient toil were the double cabins of hewed logs, which took the places of the earlier hut like structures. Then frame houses began to appear, and hewed-log barns, and later, frame barns were built for the protection of stock and the housing of the crops. Simultaneously with the earliest indications of increasing thrift, society began to form itself; the schoolhouse and the church appeared, and advancement was noticeable in a score of ways.

Still there remained a vast work to perform, for as yet only a beginning had been made. The brunt of the struggle, however, was past. The pioneers had made a way in the wilderness for the advancing hosts of the army of civilization.

CHAPTER VI.

CIVIL HISTORY.

THIS REGION PRIOR TO 1845—ORGANIZATION, ETC., OF WYANDOT COUNTY—ACT OF CONGRESS RELATING THERETO—PUBLIC SALE OF TOWN LOTS IN UPPER SANDUSKY—NAMES OF PURCHASERS—TOWNSHIPS—PUBLIC BUILDINGS—NOTABLE PROCEEDINGS OF COURTS—RESULTS OF ELECTIONS—OFFICERS ELECTED.

A GLANCE AT THIS REGION PRIOR TO THE FORMATION OF WYANDOT COUNTY.

AS already explained, the Wyandot Indians were the acknowledged owners of all this region prior to September 29, 1817. They then ceded (with the exception of some small reservations, also heretofore described) their landed possession to the United States Government, and agreed to retire to, and remain within their reservations, with the privilege granted them, however, of hunting over any and all parts of the broad domain so lately theirs, until the same was required for actual occupation, and improvement by the whites. During the two or three years immediately succeeding this cession of lands, certain officials, styled Deputy Surveyor Generals, acting under the orders of 'the Surveyor General of the United States, ran out the township and sectional lines over a large portion of this, the new purchase. A region, which it appears, remained without the limits of civil jurisdiction, until by an act of the State Legislature passed February 12, 1820, to take effect on the 1st day of April following, a number of counties were erected from the new purchase, or what was then termed 'the "Old Indian Territory." Among them Crawford, Hancock, Hardin, Marion and Seneca. As these counties (except Seneca) originally embraced the territory now known as Wyandot County, we will glance at the their original dimensions.

Hancock County, to include Townships 1 and 2 south, and 1 and 2 north, in Ranges 9, 10, 11 and 12. Hardin County to include all the last-mentioned ranges, south of said second townships, and running south with the range lines to the northern boundaries of the organized counties. Crawford County to include Townships 1, 2 and 3 south, in Ranges 13, 14, 15, 16 and 17, and all that may lie between the same and the west line of Richland County. Marion County to include all of the last-mentioned ranges south of said third townships, and to run south with said range lines to the northern boundaries of the organized counties, and east with the township lines to Richland County line.

By the provisions of the same act—the act passed February 12, 1820—Crawford County was attached to Delaware for judicial purposes. The former county in part then embraced all that portion of the present county of Wyandot designated Townships 1, 2 and 3 south, in Ranges 13, 14 and 15 east, and it was while under the jurisdiction of the Delaware County officials, and by virtue of an order issued from the Court of Common Pleas of Delaware County, directed to the qualified voters of Crawford Township, in Crawford County, that the first election was held within the present limits of Wyandot County. Crawford Township then comprised the present townships of Crawford, Tymochtee and Sycamore. In pursuance of the

HISTORY OF WYANDOT COUNTY.   313

order of court, the electors assembled at the house of Henry Lish (who then operated a ferry over Tymochtee Creek in the present township of Tymochtee), on the 1st day of April, 1821. After the appointment of a Chairman, and the election *viva voce* of Ira Arnold and Seth Crocker as Clerks for the day, John Gordon, James Richards and James Whitehead as Judges, the legal voters present, thirteen in number, proceeded to elect by ballot the following named township officers: Ira Arnold, Clerk; John Gordon, James Richards and Ichabod Merriman, Trustees; Elijah Brayton and Rufus Merriman, Appraisers; Elijah Brayton, Listor; Thomas Leeper, Treasurer; Philip Peer and Henry Lish, Supervisors; Myron Merriman and James Whitehead, Fence Viewers; Isaac Walker, Constable, and Ciprian Stevens, Justice of the Peace.

The county of Crawford remained under the jurisdiction of Delaware until by the passage of a legislative act of date December 15, 1823, to take effect May 1, 1824, Marion County was organized and Crawford was ordered to be attached to it for judicial purposes. During the same session, however, by an act approved February 17, 1824, it was further ordered "that so much of the county of Crawford as lies north of the Wyandot Reservation, including one tier of townships lying east and west, be, and the same is hereby, from and after the passage of this act, attached to the county of Seneca for judicial purposes, until the county of Crawford shall be organized." During subsequent years a few other changes in jurisdiction took place from time to time, but no alterations in boundary lines occurred (where Crawford, Marion, Hardin and Hancock Counties joined each other), until the erection of Wyandot County.

FORMATION, ORGANIZATION, ETC., OF WYANDOT COUNTY.

By the provisions of an act of the State Legislature approved February 3, 1845, entitled "An act to erect the new county of Wyandott,* and alter the boundaries of the county of Crawford," Wyandot was formed from parts of Crawford, Marion, Hardin and Hancock Counties. The sections of the act which have an especial reference to this (Wyandot) county read as follows:

SECTION 1. Be it enacted by the General Assembly of the State of Ohio, That such parts of the counties of Crawford, Marion, Hardin and Hancock, as are embraced within the boundaries hereinafter described, be, and the same are hereby erected into a separate and distinct county, which shall be known by the name of Wyandott, and the seat of justice within and for said county shall be and is hereby fixed and established at, or in the immediate vicinity of Upper Sandusky to wit: Beginning at the southeast corner of Section 10, in Township 4 south, in Range 15, of the public survey of lands, in Marion County, and running thence north on the sectional lines, through Crawford County, to the north line thereof, between Sections 2 and 3, in Township 1 south, in Range 15, aforesaid; which line shall form the east boundary of said county of Wyandott, and the west line of Crawford County; thence west on the base line to the northwest corner of Section 2, in Township 1 south, of Range 12, in Hancock County; thence south on the sectional line to the northeast corner of Section 22, in the township and range last aforesaid; thence west on the sectional line to the northwest corner of said Section 22; thence south on the sectional line to the south line of said township as originally surveyed, between Sections 33 and 34; thence west on said township line to the northwest corner of Section 5 in Township 2 south, of the range last aforesaid; thence south on the sectional line through said Township 2, to the south line thereof, at the northwest corner of Section 5, in Township 3 south, of the range last aforesaid, in the county of Hardin; thence east to the northeast corner

---

* Before the organization of Wyandot County and the adoption of a county seal, this term had been written and printed in various ways as Wyandot, Wyandott and Wyandotte. Therefore, soon after the organization, the question of adopting a uniform style of spelling the county's title was considered by the first county officials, when at the suggestion of John D. Sears, Esq., the form of orthography still in use—WYANDOT—was approved and so entered upon the records.

of said Section 5; thence south on the sectional line to the southwest corner of Section 9, in Township 4 south, in the range last aforesaid; thence east, to the northwest corner of Section 13, in the township and range last aforesaid; thence south to the southwest corner of said Section 13; thence east on the sectional line to the southeast corner of Section 13, in Township 4 south of Range 13; thence north to the northeast corner of said last-mentioned Section 13; thence east, on the sectional line to the place of beginning: *Provided*, That the passage of this act shall not prevent the Mad River & Lake Erie Railroad Company from extending an arm from the main track of said railroad to the town of Findlay in the county of Hancock, as was secured to said company in the original act of incorporation.

* * * * * * * * * *

SEC. 4. That all Justices of the Peace, within those parts of the counties of Crawford, Marion, Hardin and Hancock, which by this act are erected into the county of Wyandott, and also within those parts of the counties of Richland and Marion, which by this act, are attached to the county of Crawford, shall continue to exercise the functions and discharge the duties of their respective offices, until their time of service shall expire, and their successors be elected and qualified, in the same manner as if they had been commissioned for the counties of Wyandott and Crawford respectively. * * *

SEC. 5. That the legal voters residing within the limits of the county of Wyandott, shall on the 1st Monday in April, in the year 1845, assemble in their respective townships, at the usual place of holding elections (where the usual places of holding elections are within the limits of the county of Wyandott, and in cases of fractional townships, where the usual places of holding elections are not included within the limits of the county aforesaid, the voters residing in each of such fractional townships, shall assemble in the township immediately adjoining such fractional township, and lying toward the center of said county), and proceed to elect the different county officers in the manner prescribed in the act to regulate elections, who shall hold their offices until the next annual election, and until their successors are chosen and qualified.

SEC. 6. It shall be the duty of the Commissioners of Wyandott County when elected and qualified, to make the most favorable contract or contracts with the Government of the United States, or with any person or persons for donations of land, town lots, moneys. or other property, for the erection of county buildings, either in the town of Upper Sandusky, or on land adjoining the same, as they may think most advantageous to the county of Wyandott; *provided* that the county buildings of Wyandott County shall not be erected at a greater distance than one-fourth of a mile from the State road leading from Columbus through Delaware, Marion and Upper Sandusky to Lower Sandusky. * * * * * * * * *

SEC. 8. The Commissioners of the respective counties from which territory is hereby taken, shall have power immediately upon the passage of this act, to attach fractional townships to other townships in their respective counties, or to organize such fractional townships into separate townships, as they may deem expedient, which power shall extend to the counties of Crawford and Wyandott, for the purpose of disposing of fractions coming within the limits of said counties made by this act.

* * * * * * * * * *

Thus, by a scrutiny of Section 1 of the act just quoted, it is ascertained that Wyandot County was formed from Townships No. 1, 2 and 3 south, in Ranges 13 and 14 east, and the fractional or western two-thirds of Townships 1, 2 and 3 south, in Range 15 east, of Crawford County; from fractional parts of Townships 1 and 2 south, in. Range 12 east, of Hancock County; from fractional parts of Townships 3 and 4 south, in the range last mentioned, of Hardin County, and from fractional Townships 4 south, in Ranges 13, 14 and 15 east, of Marion County.

In accordance with the provisions of Section 5 of the act above quoted, on Monday, April 7, 1845, the legal voters of the county assembled in their respective townships, at the several places designated for holding elections, and proceeded to the exercise of their rights as American freemen by voting for the various persons nominated to fill the county offices. In the aggregate, 1,289 ballots were deposited, and as a result the following officers were in due time declared elected: William Griffith, Stephen Fowler and Ethan Terry, County Commissioners; Abner Jurey, Treasurer; Samuel M. Worth, Auditor; Lorin A. Pease, Sheriff; John A. Morrison, Recorder; Albert Bixby, Coroner; Azariah Root, Surveyor; and Chester R. Mott, Prosecuting Attorney.

HISTORY OF WYANDOT COUNTY. 317

Concerning the political complexion of the officers first elected we learn that Griffith, Jurey, Pease and Root were Whigs, while Fowler, Terry, Worth, Morrison, Bixby and Mott were Democrats. These gentlemen at once attached their signatures to the required oath of office, filed their bonds of indemnity, etc., and within two weeks after their election were prepared for the transaction of public business in such apartments in and about the new and straggling built-up town as were found most convenient. In describing the initial proceedings, which took place in their respective departments, we turn to the records for the following items.

On the 16th day of April, 1845 (nine days after their election), Stephen Fowler, William Griffith and Ethan Terry, Commissioners-elect of the County of Wyandot (the same having taken the required oath of office before Abner Jurey, Esq.), first convened (the minutes fail to state where) for the transaction of business. Thereupon the bond of Samuel M. Worth, the Auditor-elect, was presented and approved, with Zuriel Fowler, Joseph Shorb and Guy C. Worth as his sureties. The Commissioners then authorized Guy C. Worth (who was then officiating as Clerk of the courts, by appointment) to contract for the purchase of the necessary books and stationery for the use of the different county offices; also to purchase an "iron press" for the Clerk's office, "if, in his opinion, it be advisable to obtain the same." On the same day the following resolutions were considered and approved:

Resolved, That the proposition of Moses H. Kirby to transfer his possessory right to the Indian Council House at Upper Sandusky to the county of Wyandot be accepted, and the Auditor authorized to issue an order in favor of Col. Kirby for $30 in full payment of his interest in said house.

Resolved, That the different officers of Wyandot County be authorized to obtain the necessary cheap furniture for the use of their respective offices, and present their bill to the Board of Commissioners at the June session.

Resolved, That the Auditor of Wyandot County is hereby authorized to procure the necessary abstracts from the tax duplicates of Crawford, Marion, Hardin and Hancock Counties, and that he procure, if need be, the services of the Auditors of the said counties respectively to assist him in obtaining the same.

Resolved, That the Auditor cause such repairs to be made upon the upper part of the Council House as will be required for the accommodation of the county officers."

The Commissioners then approved of the bond of Abner Jurey, Treasurer-elect, with John Jurey, Benjamin S. Welch, Christian Hoover and Jacob S. Staley as his sureties, and adjourned to meet in special session on the 28th day of April following.

As determined, the Commissioners again met on Monday, April 28, 1845, when it was ordered that the area of Jackson Township be increased, and Marseilles Township be erected. On the following day, their proceedings were far more important, and as follows:

UPPER SANDUSKY, Wyandot County, Ohio, April 29, 1845.

The Commissioners of Wyandot County this day met, and after a due consideration of the proposition for the establishment of the seat of justice of Wyandot County at the town of Upper Sandusky, adopted the following preamble and resolutions:

WHEREAS the Congress of the United States by an act[*] approved the 26th day of

---

[*] COPY OF THE ACT OF CONGRESS.

CHAPTER 23.—An act vesting in the County Commissioners of the county of Wyandot the right to certain town lots and outlots in the town of Upper Sandusky in the State of Ohio.

SECTION 1. Be it enacted by the Senate and House of Representatives of the United States of America in Congress assembled, That the right to one-third part of the unsold town lots in the town of Upper Sandusky by the act entitled " An Act providing for the sale of certain lands in the States of Ohio and Michigan ceded by the Wyandot tribe of Indians, and for other purposes," passed March 3, 1843, directed to be laid out and surveyed, and to one-third part of the outlots of said town, be and hereby is vested in the County Commissioners of the county of Wyandot, in the said State of Ohio ; on condition, nevertheless, that said Commissioners, or other competent authorities of said State of Ohio, shall permanently locate and fix the seat of justice of the county at said town, and that the net proceeds of the sales of said town and out-

7

February, A. D. 1845, have granted to the Commissioners of Wyandot County, one-third part of the inlots and outlots of the said town of Upper Sandusky, upon the condition that the said Commissioners should permanently locate and fix the seat of justice of said county at the said town of Upper Sandusky.

Be it therefore Resolved, That the seat of justice of said county of Wyandot be and hereby is permanently located and fixed at the town of Upper Sandusky.

Resolved, That the Register and Receiver of the Land Office at Upper Sandusky be requested to advise the Board of Commissioners of Wyandot County what lot or lots in the town of Upper Sandusky embrace valuable improvements made by this Indian agency at Upper Sandusky.

(COPY.)
LAND OFFICE UPPER SANDUSKY, April 29, 1845.
TO THE COMMISSIONERS OF WYANDOT COUNTY:

GENTLEMEN: The following resolutions passed by your board have this day been duly placed in our hands, to wit: "*Resolved,* that the Register and Receiver of the Land Office at Upper Sandusky be requested to advise the Board of Commissioners what lot or lots in the town of Upper Sandusky embrace valuable improvements made by the Indian Agency at Upper Sandusky." In reply to which we have to state that Outlot No. 49†, embraces all the valuable improvements made at Upper Sandusky for the use of the Indian Agency. Very respectfully,

ALBUR ROOT, *Register,*
MOSES H. KIRBY, *Receiver.*

Thereupon the following communication was prepared by the Commissioners, and at once sent forward, by mail, to the Secretary of the Treasury of the United States:

UPPER SANDUSKY, April 29, 1845.
TO THE HONORABLE SECRETARY OF THE TREASURY OF THE UNITED STATES:

SIR: We herewith transmit to you official information of the permanent location of the seat of justice for Wyandot County at the town of Upper Sandusky; and we are advised by the acompanying communication from the Register and Receiver of the Land Office at Upper Sandusky that Outlot No. 49 is the only one contained in the said town which embraces valuable improvements made by the Indian Agency at Upper Sandusky. And as it appears that this lot would not fall to the county by a selection of every third lot in alternate and progressive numbers in pursuance of the second section of the act of Congress of the 26th of February, A. D. 1845, entitled "An act vesting in the County Commissioners of the county of Wyandot the right to certain town lots and outlots in the town of Upper Sandusky in the State of Ohio, no substitution will, therefore, have to be made.

We would respectfully request the Honorable Secretary of the Treasury to make the selection in pursuance to the said law as soon as practicable and transmit the same to us.

We remain very respectfully your obedient servants,
STEPHEN FOWLER,
WILLIAM GRIFFITH,
ETHAN TERRY,
Commissioners of Wyandot County.

Communication from the Commissioner of the General Land Office in reply to the foregoing:

GENERAL LAND OFFICE, July 28, 1845.

I, James Shields,‡ Commissioner of the General Land Office, do hereby certify, that the annexed is a true and literal exemplification of the original on file in this office, approved by the Secretary of the Treasury, on the 12th day of July, 1845.

In testimony whereof, I hereunto subscribed my name and caused the seal of this office to be affixed, at the city of Washington, on the day and year above written.

JAMES SHIELDS, *Commissioner of the General Land Office.*

---

lots be applied by said County Commissioners, or other proper authorities, to the erection of public buildings, and the improvement of public squares and public grounds in said town.

SEC. 2. And be it further enacted, That the town lots and outlots of said town of Upper Sandusky, so to be granted and applied, shall be selected by alternate and progressive numbers (every third town lot and every third outlot according to their numbers respectively, being granted and applied as aforesaid) under the direction and subject to the control of the Secretary of the Treasury; Provided, that nothing herein contained shall be so construed as to grant to and vest in said County Commissioners any lot or lots heretofore appropriated to and used by the Indian agency at Upper Sandusky, and upon which there may remain any valuable buildings, orchard, or other valuable improvement belonging to the United States, and if any such town lot or outlot, so by its progressive number selected, should be found to comprise and include any such valuable building, orchard or other valuable improvement then the said Secretary of the Treasury is hereby authorized and directed to substitute some other lot or lots, of a fair and proportionate value.

Approved, February 26, 1845.
†The site of Fort Ferree.
‡Afterward known (during the Mexican war, and the war of the rebellion) as Gen. Shields.

HISTORY OF WYANDOT COUNTY. 319

List of town lots and outlots in the town of Upper Sandusky, Ohio, selected under the provisions of the act of Congress entitled "An act vesting in the Commissioners of the county of Wyandot the right to certain town lots and outlots in the town of Upper Sandusky, in the State of Ohio, approved 26th of February, 1845."

Town Lots numbered 3, 6, 9, 12, 15, 18, 21, 24, 27, 30, 33, 36, 39, 42, 45, 48, 51, 54, 57, 60, 63, 66, 69, 72, 75, 78, 81, 84, 87, 90, 93, 96, 99, 102, 105, 108, 111, 114, 117, 120, 123, 126, 129, 132, 135, 138, 141, 144, 147, 150, 153, 156, 159, 162, 165, 168, 171, 174, 177, 180, 183, 186, 189, 192, 195, 198, 201, 204, 207, 210, 213, 216, 219, 222, 225, 228, 231, 234, 237, 240, 243, 246, 249, 252, 255, 258, 261, 264, 267, 270, 273, 276, 279, 282, 285, 288, 291, 294, 297, 300, 303, 306, 309, 312, 315, 318, 321, 324, 327, 330, 333, 336, 339, 342, 345, 348, 351, 354, 357, 360, 363, 366, 369, 372, 375, 378.

Out Lots numbered 3, 6, 9, 12, 15, 18, 21, 24, 27, 30, 33, 36, 39, 42, 45, 48, 51, 54, 57, 60, 63, 66, 69, 72, 75, 78, 81, 84, 87, 90, 93, 96, 99, 102, 105, 108, 111, 114, 117, 120, 123, 126, 129, 132, 135, 138, 141, 144, 147, 150, 153, 156, 159, 162, 165, 168, 171, 174, 177, 180, 183, 186, 189, 192, 195, 198, 201, 204, 207, 210, 213, 216.

At a subsequent meeting of the County Commissioners, held on the 2d day of June, 1845, the boundaries of Pit, Crane and Antrim Townships were defined, and Eden, Ridge, Richland and Sycamore Townships were organized as separate townships. During the same session, it was further ordered that a tax of $1 be assessed upon each lawyer and physician practicing in the county. That a tax of four and one half mills on a dollar be levied for county purposes, also a tax of one and one-half mills on a dollar be levied for road purposes, and that the Auditor "be authorized to serve a notice upon John Shrenk* to leave the council house forthwith."

The Commissioners again met for the transaction of business on Saturday, July 26, 1845, and as the result of their deliberations, the following orders, etc., were made a matter of record:

Ordered, That the lots vested in their hands by the act of Congress, approved February 26, 1845, be exposed at public sale on the 20th, 21st and 22d days of August, 1845.

Ordered, That 200 copies of sale bills be printed, and that the same be published in the *Ohio Statesman, Ohio State Journal* and Wyandot *Telegraph*.

Ordered, That the Auditor procure a sufficient number of blank title bonds for such sale.

Ordered, That the lots be sold for one-fourth of the purchase money in hand, one-fourth in one year, one-fourth in two years, and the remaining one-fourth in three years; the payments to be secured with notes bearing interest.

Ordered, That Inlot No. 147 be reserved from sale, and that Lots No. 145 and 146 be procured for the use of the county to erect public buildings upon.

Ordered, That Mr. Joseph McCutchen be authorized to engage the services of Mr. Bishop, of Seneca County, as crier on the days of sale.

Ordered, That Peter B. Beidler be employed to copy from the records of the counties from which Wyandot County was taken, such records, surveys and field notes as may be strictly necessary to have in this county, also to make a plat of the county of Wyandot.

The following is a copy of the "sale bill" above mentioned:

PUBLIC SALE OF TOWN LOTS AT UPPER SANDUSKY.

The Commissioners of Wyandot County will offer the following valuable town property for sale at Upper Sandusky, Ohio, upon the 20th, 21st and 22d days of August next, to wit: The in and out lots in the town of Upper Sandusky vested in the said Commissioners by act of Congress approved February 26, 1845, being every third of the in and out lots selected by alternate and progressive numbers, amounting to 126 inlots and seventy-two outlots.

Upper Sandusky, a town laid out by the General Government, is delightfully situated on the Sandusky River, near the center of the Wyandot Reserve, and the seat of justice of the new county of Wyandot has been permanently fixed at said town.

Terms of Sale: One-fourth of the purchase money required in hand, the balance in three equal annual installments, secured by notes bearing interest.

STEPHEN FOWLER,
WILLIAM GRIFFITH,
ETHAN TERRY,
[ATTEST] *Commissioners of Wyandot County.*
SAMUEL M. NORTH, *Auditor.*

---

*Shrenk was the publisher of the Wyandot *Telegraph*, the first newspaper published in the county, and had occupied the council house as his printing house, from the middle of February, 1845.

The Commissioners then adjourned to the 11th of August following, for the purpose of appraising the lots. At the time designated, August 11, 1845, the members composing the Board of Commissioners met, and made an appraisement of the value of each lot, varying from $25 for the lowest, to $500 for the highest. They again met on the 19th day of August, 1845, and agreed upon the following terms of sale for the lots advertised to be sold:

One-fourth of the purchase money to be paid in hand, the residue in three equal annual payments, with interest, to be secured by promissory notes.

The terms of sale to be complied with on the day thereof. A title bond to be given, conditioned for the making of a deed to the purchaser upon the payment of the notes. Delinquent bidders to be held subject to the liabilities and restrictions usual in such cases.

Commissioners further order that Wyandot County orders and current bank papers of the Ohio banks be receivable in payment of the first installment.

That the crops growing upon the outlots be reserved to the occupants putting them in, who are required to remove them by the 10th day of October next.

Chester R. Mott, Esq., was employed as assistant clerk during the sales, and David Bishop, of Seneca County, as crier. The sale commenced at 10:30 o'clock A. M., on the 20th day of August, 1845, and continued three days. The following is a list of the lots sold, the names of purchasers, and the amount paid for each lot:

In Lot No. 3, Joseph McCutchen	$ 26
In Lot No. 9, George Yenner	30
In Lot No. 12, Joseph Chaffee	37
In Lot No. 15, James McConnell	25
In Lot No. 21, Stephen H. Sherwood	32
In Lot No. 24, James McConnell	38
In Lot No. 30, Guy C. Worth	26
In Lot No. 33, Guy C. Worth	25
In Lot No. 36, John N. Reed	25
In Lot No. 39, Jacob Sell	55
In Lot No. 42, Lorin A. Pease	54
In Lot No. 48, Guy C. Worth	43
In Lot No. 51, Victor M. Griswold	34
In Lot No, 57, Samuel M. Worth	57
In Lot No. 60, Upton Flenner	141
In Lot No. 63, John Vandenburg	81
In Lot No. 66, Christian Huber	50
In Lot No. 69, James McConnell	48
In Lot No. 72, Abner Jury	30
In Lot No. 75, Sanders A. Reed	46
In Lot No. 78, David Little	185
In Lot No. 81, Upton Flenner	26
In Lot No. 84, Andrew Dumm	42
In Lot No. 87, Samuel Miller	100
In Lot No. 93, Jacob Ronk	60
In Lot No. 96, Purdy McElvain	202
In Lot No. 99, Isaac C. Drum	29
In Lot No. 105, Isaac Ayers	125
In Lot No. 108, Chester R. Mott	35
In Lot No. 111, John Mackey	115
In Lot No. 114, John Shrenk	67
In Lot No. 120, John W. Senseny	262
In Lot No. 129, N. P. Robbins	550
In Lot No. 132, David Ayers	31
In Lot No. 138, Henry Houpt	48
In Lot No. 141, David Ayers	200
In Lot No. 144, David Ayers	650
In Lot No. 150, David Ayers	252
In Lot No. 153, Joseph McCutchen	154
In Lot No. 156, Joseph McCutchen	134
In Lot No. 159, Jeremiah Miner	418
In Lot No. 162, Jeremiah Miner	159

HISTORY OF WYANDOT COUNTY. 321

In Lot No. 165, David Watson and John D. Sears	230
In Lot No. 174, Joseph McCutchen	300
In Lot No. 180, David Epler	61
In Lot No. 186, James H. Drum	32
In Lot No 189, Henry Mattocks	167
In Lot No. 192, Lemar Walton	64
In Lot No. 195, Robert Taggart	95
In Lot No. 198, Daniel Tuttle	46
In Lot No. 201, Samuel Roth	32
In Lot No. 204, Jerusha West	27
In Lot No. 207, Anthony Bowsher	84
In Lot No. 210, Archibald Allen	76
In Lot No. 216, Christian Huber	200
In Lot No. 219, William Corbin	113
In Lot No. 228, Jackson B. Detray	46
In Lot No. 131, Henry Mattocks	155
In Lot No. 234, Robert Taggart	39
In Lot No. 237, Christian Huber	120
In Lot No. 240, John Tripp	26
In Lot No. 243, Abner Jury	92
In Lot No. 246, Michael Barnhart	40
In Lot No. 249, John Owens	52
In Lot No. 252, Thomas Hughes	33
In Lot No. 255, John W. Mavis	31
In Lot No. 261, David Watson	27
In Lot No. 264, John Buckingham	21
In Lot No. 267, John S. Rappe	35
In Lot No. 270, John S. Rappe	28
In Lot No. 276, Robert Lambert	23
In Lot No. 285, James R. Remington	25
In Lot No. 288, William B. Stokely	44
In Lot No. 291, John S. Rappe	24
In Lot No. 294, John Stewart	20
In Lot No. 300, George Hayman	26
In Lot No. 303, Purdy and Andrew McElvain	32
In Lot No. 306, A. M. Anderson, J. B. Alden and G. C. Worth	57
In Lot No. 309, Robert Cuppals	22
In Lot No. 315, William Shaffer	61
In Lot No. 318, Purdy and Andrew McElvain	24
In Lot No. 330, William Hill	23
In Lot No. 333, Enoch B. Elkins	31
In Lot No. 336, John Tripp	25
In Lot No. 342, Daniel Wright	54
In Lot No. 345, Antoine Christian	30
In Lot No. 348, John Tripp	27
In Lot No. 251, Joseph B. Fraser	26
In Lot No. 357, Chester R. Mott	20
In Lot No. 360, Antoine Christian	26
In Lot No. 363, George Orth	43
In Lot No. 369, William Myers	21
In Lot No. 375, Robert Taggart	24
In Lot No. 378, William Ayers	20
Out Lot No. 3, Stephen H. Sherwood	57
Out Lot No. 6, James McConnell	79
Out Lot No. 9, James B. Alden	134
Out Lot No. 12, David Wilson	306
Out Lot No. 15, Eli P. Quaintance	200
Out Lot No. 27, George Robinson	58
Out Lot No. 30, Chester R. Mott	58
Out Lot No. 33, Jeremiah Miner	63
Out Lot No. 36, James McConnell	51
Out Lot No. 39, Anthony Bowsher	12
Out Lot No. 42, R. W. Kinkead	56
Out Lot No. 45, David Ayres	50
Out Lot No. 48, Christian Huber	115
Out Lot No. 51, John S. Rappe	53
Out Lot No. 54, James McConnell	56
Out Lot No. 69, Thomas B. Ferguson	52
Out Lot No. 84, David Ayers (forfeited)	

322   HISTORY OF WYANDOT COUNTY.

Out Lot No 87, Jacob Ronk.......................................	37
Out Lot No. 90, Joseph McCutchen.............................	32
Out Lot No. 93, Chester R. Mott................................	35
Out Lot No. 96, Chester R. Mott................................	36
Out Lot No. 99, Joseph McCutchen.............................	43
Out Lot No. 102, Joseph E. Fouke...............................	35
Out Lot No. 105, William Bear...................................	37
Out Lot No. 108, William Ayers (forfeited)	
Out Lot No. 111, Henry Kirby....................................	36
Out Lot No. 114, James B. Alden................................	43
Out Lot No. 129, Amos Culver...................................	33
Out Lot No. 156, David Epler.....................................	30
Out Lot No. 168, Hiram Flack....................................	35
Out Lot No. 171, Purdy McElvain................................	105
Out Lot No. 174, John Kays.......................................	61
Out Lot No. 177, Anthony Bowsher.............................	25
Out Lot No. 183, John Kays.......................................	65
Out Lot No. 186, Joseph Mason..................................	116
Out Lot No. 189, Chester R. Mott...............................	30
Out Lot No. 201, Joseph Chaffee.................................	30
Out Lot No. 204, John W. Vandenburg........................	36
Out Lot No. 210, Prudy McElvain...............................	75
Out Lot No. 213, Abraham Trego................................	45
Out Lot No. 216, Joseph Chaffee.................................	40
Out Lot No. 207, Andrew Drum.................................	30

The total value of the lots sold during the three days amounted to $10,176.50, upon which cash or its equivalent was paid to the amount of $2,626.87½.

On the 27th of August, 1845, the Commissioners again met, as per adjournment, when it was ordered, "That the lots remaining unsold shall be open for entry until the 23d day of September next, with 50 per cent added to the appraisement heretofore put upon them by the Commissioners.

Ordered, That Samuel M. Worth be authorized to receive applications and make sales of such lots.

The following bills were allowed, as expenses arising from the sales of the town lots, viz.:

John Shrenk, printing...	$6 31
David Bishop, crier of sale.......................................	43 00
Chester R. Mott, clerk during sales............................	12 00
Stephen Fowler, Commissioner.................................	20 00
William Griffith, Commissioner................................	22 00
Ethan Terry, Commissioner.....................................	20 00
Samuel M. Worth, fees as Auditor.............................	30 00
	$153 31

*   *   *   *   *   *   *   *   *   *   *   *

On Tuesday, September 23, 1845 (as per order of the Commissioners), another public sale of town lots took place. The number of the lots, the names of purchasers, etc., being as follows:

In Lot No. 6, Amos Colver.......................................	$51 00
In Lot No. 27, A. Montee...	25 00
In Lot No. 45, Robert Bowsher.................................	34 50
In Lot No. 54, Benjamin Chambers............................	30 00
In Lot No. 102, John S. Rappe..................................	63 00
In Lot No. 168, Jesse Swan and Ezekiel Ervin..............	378 00
In Lot No. 177, William Axt.....................................	131 00
In Lot No. 183, Peter Ricker....................................	33 00
In Lot No. 225, Angelina Tannehill............................	26 00
In Lot No. 258, George W. Cox.................................	162 00
In Lot No. 297, Michael Vangundy............................	22 00
In Lot No. 324, A. Montee.......................................	24 00
In Lot No. 372, Samuel W. McDowell........................	37 50
Out Lot No. 21, John March....................................	32 00
Out Lot No. 81, Michael Vangundy............................	51 00
Out Lot No. 84, David Ayers....................................	31 00

Out Lot No. 108, Susannah Berry............................ 33 00
Out Lot No. 117, Christian Widman........................ 43 00
Out Lot No. 120, Hiram Pool................................ 60 00
Out Lot No. 180, Henry Backenstose........................ 32 00
Out Lot No. 192, Nathaniel C. Manley...................... 21 50
Out Lot No. 198, William Henry McRuff.................... 35 50

On the 2d of October, 1845, it was ordered by the Commissioners "that four hundred and ten dollars be appropriated out of the moneys received from the sale of lots to pay for In Lots numbered 145 and 146," which, with Lot No. 147, were set aside and designated as the site for the court house and county jail. The following day (October 3), additional lots were sold, as follows:

In Lot No. 18, A. Montee... $25
In Lot No. 126, Daniel G. Weddle and A. Rice................... 105
In Lot No. 171, John Lupfer....................................... 280
In Lot No. 222, William W. Bates................................. 229
In Lot No. 273, Hugh Robertson................................... 21
In Lot No. 282, A. Montee... 20
In Lot No. 321, Alfred Randall................................... 20
Out Lot No. 18, Joseph McCutchen................................ 31
Out Lot No. 24, Chester R. Mott.................................. 40

A number of the lots first sold were declared forfeited to the purchasers and reverted back to the county by reason of the non-payment of purchase money according to the terms of sale, and were afterward resold to other parties as late as 1853.

To June 11, 1853, the officials of the county had received in cash, for lots sold in the town of Upper Sandusky, the sum of $15,224.24, or in other words, the Government of the United States had *donated to the county of Wyandot an amount sufficient to purchase sites, and to construct the present court house and jail building.*

TOWNSHIPS.

Antrim—Was first organized as a township in Crawford County in 1822. It contains thirty-two sections, and was formed as it now exists June 2, 1845, when the first Board of Wyandot County Commissioners ordered that the fraction (eight sections) detached from Township 4 south, of Range 15 east, or Grand Prairie, in Marion County, be attached to it.

Crawford—Was organized as a township in Crawford County in the year 1821 Its nominal boundaries then included all, or at least nearly all, of that part of the former county now forming part of the county of Wyandot.

The organization of Crawford County took place we believe, in the year 1825, when Crawford Township was reduced to its present area—a full surveyed subdivision of thirty-six sections, known otherwise as Township No. 1 south, of Range No. 13 east.

Crane—We have not been able to ascertain when this township was so designated, though probably it was just prior to the formation of Wyandot County. On the 2d of June, 1845, the Wyandot County Commissioners ordered that " the progressive numbers from Section 1 to 9 inclusive in Pitt Township be attached to Crane Township," and on the same day they likewise ordered, that "Sections 1, 12, 13, 24, 25 and 36 of the original surveyed Township No. 2 south, of Range 14 east [Crane Township] be attached to Township No. 2 south, of Range 15 east." The same boundary lines prevail to-day, and thus Crane (it should be Tarhe) Township contains thirty-nine sections.

Eden—The greater portion of this township was formerly part of Leith, a township which was formed by order of the Commissioners of

Crawford County, in March, 1838. On the 2d of June, 1845, Stephen Fowler, William Griffith and Ethan Terry, the first Commissioners of Wyandot County, ordered that Sections 1, 12, 13, 24, 25 and 36, of the original surveyed Township No. 2 south, of Range 14 east, be attached to Township No. 2 south, of Range 15 east, and called *Eden* Township." The same boundaries have continued to the present time. It contains thirty sections.

Jackson—Was organized as a township in Hardin County prior to 1840. By the organization of Wyandot County in 1845, the major part of the township became a portion of the new county, and for that reason, perhaps, it retained its original name. At a special meeting of the Commissioners of Wyandot County, held April 28, 1845, it was ordered "that Sections 3, 4 and 9, in Township No. 4 south, of Range 12 east [Goshen Township] be attached to Jackson Township." The same boundary lines are still maintained, and the township contains twenty-seven sections.

Marseilles—At a special meeting of the Commissioners of Wyandot County, held on the 28th day of April, 1845, it was ordered "that Sections 1, 2, 10, 11, 12 and 13, in the aforesaid township and range [meaning Township No. 4 south, of Range 12 east], be attached to that portion of Township No. 4 south, of Range 13 east, taken from Grand Township, Marion County, and that the two fractional townships hereby attached shall constitute one township, and be called Marseilles." It will thus be observed that the present township consists of eighteen sections, or the northern half of the original township of Grand, Marion County, and six sections (1, 2, 10, 11, 12 and 13) taken from Goshen Township in Hardin County.

Mifflin—Although this township lay mostly within the Wyandot Reservation, it was so named and organized as a township in Crawford County prior to 1840. We have not been able to ascertain the precise date of its organization. It is a full surveyed township of thirty-six sections, and is designated in the United States surveys as Township No. 3 south, of Range No. 13 east.

Pitt—This township also lay mostly within the Wyandot Reservation, but it was known as a township in Crawford County before the beginning of the year 1840. Soon after the organization of Wyandot County, or on the 2d of June, 1845, the County Commissioners ordered "that the fractional part of Salt Rock Township [—— Sections 1 to 12 inclusive, of Township No. 4 south, of Range 14 east, formerly part of Marion County] be attached to Pitt Township, and that the progressive numbers from Section 1 up to 9 inclusive, in Pitt Township, be attached to Crane Township. These boundaries are still maintained, and the township thus contains thirty-nine sections.

Richland—Now comprising thirty sections of surveyed Township No. 2 south, of Range No. 12 east, was organized as one of the divisions of Hancock County in 1835. Ten years later, the same township, with the exception of the western tier of sections, became part of the then new county of Wyandot. On the 2d of June, 1845, the Commissioners of the last-mentioned county directed " that Richland fraction be organized into a separate township and called Richland."

Ridge—A fractional township of only fifteen sections, was detached from Amanda Township in Hancock County by the erection of the county of Wyandot. On the 2d of June, 1845, the first Board of Wyandot County Commissioners, ordered that " Amanda fraction be organized as a separate township, and called Ridge."

HISTORY OF WYANDOT COUNTY.   325

Salem—This township comprises thirty-six sections, or the whole of surveyed Township No. 2 south, of Range 13 east. It was largely embraced by the Wyandot Reservation and probably, was not organized and so named until just prior to the erection of Wyandot County.

Sycamore—Containing twenty-four sections of surveyed Township No. 1 south, of Range No. 15 east, was organized as a township in Crawford County in 1825. On the 2d of June, 1845, the first Board of Wyandot County Commissioners ordered "that the fractional township of Sycamore be organized into a separate township."

Tymochtee—Embraces the whole of surveyed Township No. 1 south, of Range No. 14 east. Formerly attached to Crawford Township, it was organized as a township in Crawford County, 1825. It was settled at an early day by an enterprising set of pioneers, and for a number of years was the most populous district in either Crawford or Wyandot Counties.

PUBLIC BUILDINGS, ETC.

The present court house and jail of the county stand upon grounds designated in the original plat of the town of Upper Sandusky as lots No. 145, 146 and 147. How these lots were acquired has already been shown. For several years the Indian council house was utilized for holding courts, etc., while the small block-house, known as the Indian Jail, answered for the incarceration of malefactors awaiting trial for or convicted of minor infractions against law and order.

However, early in the autumn of 1845, it was determined to build a county jail. Thereupon, contractors and builders, through the public press, were invited to send in sealed proposals for the construction of the proposed building. On the 30th of October of that year, the Commissioners met, opened and examined the proposals sent in. It was then ascertained that eight proposals had been made as follows: Adam Bear, $3,800; Speelman & Donnell, $2,890; Vincent G. Bell, $4,000; John McCurdy, $2,740; Henry Ebersoll, $4,475; Sylvester Alger, $3,435; Kerr, Rambo & Osborn, $4,250; Jacob Ronk, $4,150. As McCurdy's bid was the lowest, the contract was awarded to him and he at once entered into an agreement, by which it was stipulated that he should complete the jail (the building still in use) on or before the 1st day of November, 1846. It appears that McCurdy's contract was not a very good one—for him; for on the 9th day of March, 1848, he was allowed, by the Commissioners, "$500 over and above the contract price for building the jail." On the same day, too, that is, March 9, 1848, the following was made a matter of record: "Ordered, That the north bed-room in the back part of the jail, up-stairs, be appropriated for the use of the Recorder for an office. That the Auditor be authorized to purchase stove and pipe for the use of the same, and that he engage Judge McCurdy to finish the room in a suitable manner for said purpose."

On the 4th day of June, 1846, the first step was taken for the erection of the present court house. The County Commissioners then authorized the Auditor to cause a notice to be published in the *Democratic Pioneer*, *Ohio Statesman*, and *Ohio State Journal*, offering $50 for the best draft and specifications for a court house building, to cost from $6,000 to $9,000. "The draft and specifications to be forwarded to the Commissioners by the first Monday of August next, and the contract for building to be awarded on the 10th day of September following." On the 11th day of September, 1846, an agreement was entered into between the County Commissioners and

William Young, by the terms of which the latter agreed to build and complete a court house, on or before October 1, 1848 (according, to "a plan and specifications") for the sum of $7,000. Young's sureties for the faithful performance of his contract were Andrew McElvain, David Ayres, John A. Morrison, Daniel Tuttle and T. Baird. However, in July, 1847, another agreement was made, relative to building a court house, between the County Commissioners and John W. Kennedy and John H. Junkins, which, after reciting that Young had assigned his contract to his sureties, who in turn had re-assigned it to Kennedy & Junkins, stipulated that Kennedy & Junkins should complete the structure according to the original contract, and for the original consideration of $7,000, less the amount already paid Young. Notwithstanding two separate agreements had already been made for the completion of the court house, and that nearly three years had passed since the work was commenced, the spring of 1849 found the last-named contractors still struggling under a non-paying, disheartening contract. The Commissioners then entered into a third agreement, and therein agreed to pay John H. Junkins for the completion of the building the sum of $9,800, less the amount already paid to Young, and Kennedy & Junkins. It is probable that the structure was finished during the last days of 1849, for on the 16th day of January, 1850, the Commissioners authorized the Auditor to sell the Council House (which to that time had served for holding courts, etc.). "for the sum of $250, and that the same time be given on the payments as other county lots." In October, 1851, John H. Junkins was allowed an extra compensation of $2,200 for work on the court house, thus making the total cost of the building, complete, $12,000.

In October, 1870, A. H. Vanorsdall, to serve for three years; Tilman Balliet, to serve for two years, and George Harper, to serve for one year, were elected as the first Infirmary Directors of the county of Wyandot. Soon afterward, the present Wyandot County Infirmary was established on the Carey road, four miles north of Upper Sandusky. To that time the poor were "farmed out," a most wretched and heartless mode of procedure, which had been abandoned in many localities for at least half a century before. The farm consists of 200 acres, being in part the property once owned by Noah Eby. It occupies a beautiful and healthful location, and is amply supplied with water by a branch of the Tymochtee Creek. In the rear of the buildings are a few large apple trees, said to have been planted by the Wyandot Indians. The principal building is constructed of brick, with a length of eighty feet and a width of forty-five feet. It contains two large halls—one on the first and the other on the second floor—on each side of which are the dormitories occupied by the inmates. On the first floor are the large and well-arranged dining room and kitchen. Generally speaking, all of the rooms are spacious and well lighted, and during the winter are made comfortable by the use of steam. In summer, cozy porticos afford pleasant resting places for those who find here their only home on earth. Since its establishment, the infirmary has been well managed, and its farm and garden products, always of the best, largely supply the wants of its occupants.

A FEW NOTABLE PROCEEDINGS OF COURTS.

The first court held within the county of Wyandot was a special term of the Court of Common Pleas. Its members—Abel Renick, William Brown and George W. Leith, Associate Judges—convened at the office of Moses H. Kirby, Esq., in Upper Sandusky, on Tuesday, April 8, 1845, or the day following the first election for county officers, and after having appointed Guy C. Worth Clerk of Courts, *pro tempore*, adjourned without day.

The same Judges again met in special session on the 14th day of the same month and year, when a considerable and varied amount of business was transacted. Thus, the last will and testament of Adam Weininger was admitted to probate; Jacob Smith, Aaron Welch and Charles H. Dewitt were appointed appraisers of the estate of Tobias Kneagel, deceased; Moses H. Kirby, Esq., Dr. Joseph Mason and John D. Sears, Esq., were appointed School Examiners* within and for the county of Wyandot, to serve for the term of three years; the bonds of Lorin A. Pease, Sheriff-elect, to the amount of $3,000, with William Griffith, Ransom Wilcox and Benjamin Knapp as his sureties, were approved; Chester R. Mott, Esq., Prosecuting Attorney-elect, was sworn into office, and the bond of Albert Bixby, Coroner-elect, was also approved.

However, the first regular term of the Court of Common Pleas, beginning July 1, 1845, was held in the old Indian council house, which stood on the grounds now occupied by the old public school buildings, near the bluff, in the eastern part of Upper Sandusky. There was then present as officers of the court Hon. Ozias Bowen, Presiding Judge; Abel Renick, William Brown and George W. Leith, Associate Judges; Lorin A. Pease, Sheriff, and Guy C. Worth, Clerk, *pro tempore*. The court ordered that a "special venire be issued, commanding the Sheriff to summon forthwith fifteen good, true and lawful men, to serve the present term as grand jurors. Thereupon, the Sheriff returned into court the following panel:" Orrin Ferris, Enoch Thomas, Alvin J. Russell, Benjamin Knapp, Rodney Pool, John C. Dewitt, George W. Sampson, John Stokes, Hugh Welch, Andrew M. Anderson, H. Montee, Joseph E. Fouke, William J. Clugston, John Gormley and William Jones. Subsequently, Daniel Tuttle was granted a license as auctioneer by the payment of $3.

The first case brought before this court was entitled "Peter B. Beidler *vs.* Azariah Root, contested election of Surveyor for Wyandot County." The court decided that Beidler was entitled to the office, and that the contestor should pay the costs. During the same term, the grand jury found true bills against some ten or twelve persons for keeping tavern without license, gaming houses, nine-pin alleys, assaults, etc. Before final adjournment, Samuel Kenan, William J. Clugston, Daniel Straw, Moses H. Kirby, John Houck, Reuben Savage and Andrew McElvain were granted permission to retail liquors, etc., by the payment of $2 each.

Turning to the "Journal of the Supreme Court for the State of Ohio and County of Wyandot," we find the following as the first entries:

The undersigned Judges of the Supreme Court, of the State of Ohio, do by these presents constitute and appoint Guy C. Worth,† Esq., of Wyandot County, Ohio, Clerk of the Supreme Court, for said county, until the first day of the next term of said Supreme Court, and no longer. Before entering on the duties of his office under this appointment he is required to take the oath required by law, to give bonds in the sum of $10,000, conditioned as the statute requires, to the satisfaction of the County Auditor, with two good and sufficient sureties, and deposit the same with the County Treasurer and record this appointment on the journal of said court.

Given under our hands in open court this 30th day of July, A. D. 1845. at Findlay, Hancock County, Ohio.
[Signed.]
REUBEN WOOD,
M. BIRCHARD.

It was proposed to hold a term of the Supreme Court at Upper Sandusky,

---
*The same gentlemen served as School Examiners through several terms.
†Worth was re-appointed Clerk of Courts from time to time, until July 22, 1847, when he was appointed Clerk for the full constitutional term of seven years.

commencing Monday, July 6, 1846, but when the time arrived it was ascertained that a quorum would not be present. Thereupon, the Clerk was directed by Hon. Matthew Birchard, one of the Judges present, to make an entry of the fact herein stated, and "that the said court stands adjourned without day."

During the July term in 1847, the first case was acted upon in this court. It is made a matter of record, as follows:

ELIZABETH WHALEY
   vs.   } In Chancery—Petition for Divorce.
THOMAS WHALEY.

"On motion of the petitioner by Mr. Mott, her solicitor, the petition herein is dismissed without prejudice."

A glance at the records on file in the office of the Clerk of courts clearly indicates that during the nearly forty years which have passed by since the county was organized, a vast amount of business has been performed; that Wyandot has possessed its full share of those who apparently delight to indulge in litigation; yet to their credit be it said, the percentage of violently vicious inhabitants seems to have been remarkably small. But a trivial number, comparatively speaking, have been placed upon trial charged with murder, manslaughter, or assault with intent to kill, and its residents have yet to witness the first public execution within the county limits.

Among those, however, whose trial for murder excited much public interest, we cite the cases of Henry Gammell, Mrs. Bowsher, and James Wilson. It appears that during the year 1849, Henry Gammell and another man named McMullen (both of whom lived in or near Crawfordsville), drank whisky and played cards together. Finally they quarreled, and in the hand to hand struggle between them which followed, McMullen received a knife wound from the effects of which he died. Gammell was at once arrested and confined in the county jail. His case was continued through several terms, but finally he was tried and acquitted on the plea of self-defense.

At the February term in 1868, Mary L. Bowsher, a resident of Upper Sandusky, was indicted for the murder of William, Olive and Frances Bowsher, her children. Upon being arraigned, she pleaded not guilty. Thereupon it was ordered by the court that Robert McKelly and John Berry, Esqs., be appointed to assist the Prosecuting Attorney in the prosecution of the case. During the May term, she was tried and acquitted on the first indictment—charging her with the murder of William Bowsher; but on the second indictment, charging her with the murder of Frances Bowsher, she was held to bail to the amount of $4,000, and on the third indictment, charging her with the murder of Olive Bowsher, she was also held to bail in the sum of $4,000. Finally, however, at the September term, 1868, a nolle prosequi was entered respecting the last indictments, and she was discharged "to go hence without day." It was supposed that she hastened the death of her children by administering poison. Her own death occurred recently.

The murder of George W. Hite on the night of August 28, 1879, and the arrest, trial, conviction, and suicide of his murderer—Thomas McNurty, alias Patsey King, alias James Wilson—are events yet vividly impressed upon the minds of all present residents of the county. According to his confession, McNurty (he was tried and convicted under the name of Wilson), was a fair representation of a class so largely produced in the chief cities of our country—a class, usually direct descendants of foreign-born citizens, which takes to petty thieving, jockeying, gambling, drunkenness, prize-fighting, burglary and murder as naturally as a duck takes to water.

He was born in the city of New York in 1853. Ten years later, he was left to his own resources, and then began his career as a vender of newspapers, oranges, etc., in the city of his birth. His associations were of the vilest from the beginning, and it is probable that he could be termed a thief from the time he began to perambulate the streets of the great city. Next, he was known as a prize-package boy, on the lines of the Hudson River boats and railroad, then as a jockey rider at races, a brakesman on the New York Central Railroad, and a hack driver at Niagara Falls. From thence he moved westward. Failing to get such positions as he wished, yet always stealing and fighting, he passed up and down the Mississippi Valley; thence to Omaha, and in the winter of 1873 and 1874, to San Francisco, Cal. Returning from the last-named place to Cheyenne, not many days elapsed ere he was at the Black Hills, and from that time until the spring of 1879 his life was passed on the frontier, or at various points from the Missouri River westward to Pike's Peak, Leadville, etc. Meanwhile, he had continued his career of thieving and fighting, and had assisted in killing two or three men for their money, besides others out of mere revenge.

Early in 1879, he returned to Chicago, and at that place engaged to work as a laborer on the Pittsburgh, Fort Wayne & Chicago Railroad. With some others, he was sent to Upper Sandusky, but, after a few weeks, railroad work became irksome, and he abandoned it to engage in farm work for John Sell, who resided some distance to the eastward of Upper Sandusky. On the morning of August 28, Wilson and Sell effected a settlement. The farmer endeavored to "drive a close bargain" with his late assistant. The latter knew that Sell had money in his house, and out of revenge determined to return the same night and secure it, even if murder were committed. However, Wilson took the pittance due him, proceeded to the town of Upper Sandusky, and with other companions indulged in drinking whisky throughout the day. During that time, he met George W. Hite, a farmer, who resided about two miles south of the town of Nevada, and the two men partook of refreshments together. The result of Wilson's visit to town and his casual acquaintance with Hite are told in his confession, as follows:

"I did see Hite several times that afternoon, and ate some crackers and cheese with him, when he blowed about his wealth. I led him out to talk about his money, but made up my mind before we parted that it was all wind. I had no intention of injuring Hite or attempting to find any money about him. I had seen Sell put some money away in his house, and I thought that there was a pretty good roll of it, and in the absence of something better, I concluded to call on Mr. Sell that night. I got rid of Cawthorn in the evening, and this was as I desired. I then went west on the railroad to see whether my pistol would refuse. The first trial was a success, and that one satisfied me.

"At Julian's saloon I had talked trade, in the hope that it would enable me to test it then, but that failed. When I came in from trying my pistol on the railroad, I stopped at O'Donnell's saloon, and I think took a glass of beer and sat down, and while there Hite went west, but I don't recollect the talk related by the Agent Holdridge. My mind was engaged with John Sell, his family and his money. I thought that Sell and his family would not refuse me shelter for the night, and when once peaceably in the house, I felt sure that I could secure the money quietly some time in the night, but if I failed in this I intended to crowd matters, and if necessary, get away with the whole Sell family in order to get the money.

"I wanted then to get to Sell about 9 o'clock, so as to avoid suspicion, for I wanted them to receive me. So I was about O'Donnell's and along the railroad until about dark, when I took a big drink of whisky and went down to Main street, and when I passed Hunt's stable Hite had his horse out ready to start, but I paid very little attention to this, and went straight ahead to the next street, on which I turned east. My object then in leaving Main street was to avoid Cawthorn, or any one else who would likely want to detain me. I got out of town without being noticed, and got somewhere near the river bridge when Hite overtook me, and at once drew up and commenced his gab. I was annoyed at this, and in view of what might take place at Sell's, I wanted no truck with anybody else on the road. I thought he was riding a livery horse, and told him so, and this seemed to nettle him, and he wanted me to understand that he had a lot of horses, and good ones, too. I inquired about the size of his farm and the quantity of his stock and of his business generally, and he gave me such good, square rich answers that I thought my first opinion of him was wrong. He volunteered to tell me about turning off stock, I think that day, and collecting bills that day, so that I made up my mind soon after we turned into the Nevada road to investigate the matter. I walked along by his side to keep him company, and tried to interest him, and gave him my coat to carry for me, because it was too warm to wear it with comfort, and I knew that he would not run away and leave me while he had it. We then talked no more about money matters, but confined our talk principally to fast walking, fast horses, etc., until we got down to the woods beyond Sell's, when I took his horse by the bit and stopped him. I presented my revolver and demanded his money. He had not dreamed of any trouble, and this sudden turn in affairs completely unstrung him.

"We were both pretty drunk at the time. He trembled so that he could hardly get out his pocket-book, but he made no resistance, but handed it out at once, and spoke not a word. His purse was small, and I could tell from the feel of it that there was little or nothing in it. I was disappointed and vexed. Still holding the horse, I opened the purse to assure myself of about the amount, and when I saw so small a sum to reward me for all this trouble, I was mad. Of course this work was all done in a hurry. The moment I looked into the pocket-book, I said to Hite: 'You son of a b—h, is this all the money you've got?' and he faintly said 'Yes.' Then I said: 'You son of a b—h, take that,' and fired.

"I held the horse by the bridle when I shot. I did not intend to kill him, and did not think of trying to avoid killing him. I fired without thinking of where I would hit him, and caring as little. I blame my drunken condition for this dreadful piece of foolishness. The instant I shot, it struck me that I had hit him too hard. He tried to speak after I fired, and could not or did not. I slapped the horse under the belly and started him myself, and then jumped over into the woods and walked several rods, when I recollected that I had forgot my coat. Hite was still on the horse, and I began to hope that his injuries were not serious, but I dare not then attempt to recover my coat. He was nearing a house, and I withdrew deeper into the dense woods, and laid down. I had got a half pint of whisky in the evening, I think at Julian's, and I had about half of this left, which I drank, and threw the bottle away. I emptied the contents of the purse into my pocket and threw it away. I was not in sight of the house at this time, but I soon heard confusion over there, and I concluded that it was time to pull out. So I started I know not in what direction, but I reached an open field and came to the railroad, where I got the direction all right again, and started east at a five-mile gait. Before reaching the railroad, I heard a farm bell ringing back in the neighborhood of the trouble, and took it for the alarm."

It appears that Hite was shot through the heart, at a point on the Nevada road about two miles east of the Upper Sandusky. He kept his seat in the saddle until near the residence of Henry Keller, where, from appearances, he fell to the ground and at once expired. At 10 o'clock A. M. on the following day — Saturday, August 29 — two suspicious-looking characters were arrested in Nevada, taken to the county seat and lodged in jail. One of them proved to be McNulty *alias* Wilson. At September term of that year, the grand jury found a true bill against him, charging him with the murder of George W. Hite. He pleaded not guilty, whereupon Hons. Chester R. Mott and Curtis Berry, Jr., were assigned as counsel for his defense. The trial came on at February term, 1880, before Judge Beer and a jury of twelve men, and at its conclusion Wilson was found guilty of murder in the first degree. The judge then delivered his sentence, and ordered that he be hanged by the neck until dead, on the 18th of June following. The death warrant was duly issued by the State Executive, and all preparations were completed for the execution of the decree of court. But the condemned prisoner cheated the gallows and saved the county a little additional expense by committing suicide on the night of June 2, 1880. Cyanide of pottassi was found to have been the poison used, and a small vial containing some of the drug was found on the stand in Wilson's cell. His body was buried in the southeast corner of the Old Mission Cemetery, but ghouls — those who delight in grave-robbery on the plea of science — carried it away before the dawn of the next day.

RESULT OF ELECTIONS.

Under this head will be found a *resume* of nearly all general elections which have taken place in the county since it was organized. When the county started out upon a separate state of existence, there were among its early inhabitants many who cherished fond anticipations that it would prove to be a Whig district. The first newspaper—Shrenk's—was an able exponent of Whig principles, and the times seemed quite propitious for an organization which could boast of such leaders as Webster, Clay, Corwin and a brilliant host of others; but, as it proved, too many of the "original" inhabitants had already been rallied under the lead of "Old Hickory;" they were fresh from Democratic victories under Polk and Dallas, a hickory cudgel was yet the symbol of true Democracy, and when the smoke from the first political battle-field in the county uplifted, young Wyandot was found in alignment with the Democratic counties of the State. She has ever remained a Democratic stronghold, although occasionally a popular candidate from the ranks of the Republican party manages to secure an election to a county office.

ELECTION APRIL 7, 1845.

Commissioner—Charles Merriman, Whig, 635; Jonathan Kear, Whig, 638; William Griffith, Whig, 643; Robert Stokely, Democrat, 567; Stephen Fowler, Democrat, 669; Ethan Terry, Democrat, 678. Griffith, Fowler and Terry were elected.

Treasurer—Abner Jurey, Whig, 662; David Ellis, Democrat, 588; Jurey's majority, 74.

Auditor—Andrew M. Anderson, Whig, 618; Samuel M. Worth, Democrat, 668; Worth's majority, 50.

Sheriff—Lorin A. Pease, Whig, 639; John Kiser, Democrat, 629; Anthony Bowsher, Whig, 9; Pease's majority, 10.

Recorder—Joseph Chaffee, Whig, 578; John A. Morrison, Democrat, 662; Samuel M. Worth, Democrat, 1; Morrison's majority, 84.

Coroner—Albert Bixby, Democrat, 657; William Bevington, Whig, 624; John Ragon, Whig, 1; Bixby's majority, 33.

Surveyor—Azariah Root, Whig, 638; Peter B. Beidler, Democrat, 616; Root's majority, 22.

Prosecuting Attorney—Chester R. Mott, Democrat, 656; John D. Sears, Whig, 630; Peter B. Beidler, Democrat, 1; Mott's majority, 26.

ELECTION OCTOBER 14, 1845.

Commissioner—Silas Burson, Whig, 650; William Carey, Whig, 645; Jonathan Kear, Whig, 650; Stephen Fowler, Democrat, 678; Ethan Terry, Democrat, 693; William Bland, Democrat, 648. Terry, Fowler and Kear* were elected.

Auditor—Moses H. Kirby, Whig, 614; Samuel M. Worth, Democrat, 692; scattering, 14; Worth's majority, 78.

Treasurer—Abner Jurey, Whig, 660; George Harper, Democrat, 678; Harper's majority, 18.

Sheriff—Lorin A. Pease, Whig, 658; Thomas Baird, Democrat, 660; Baird's majority, 2.

Recorder—Joseph E. Fouke, Whig, 617; John A. Morrison, Democrat, 683; Joseph Fouke, 1; Morrison's majority, 66.

Surveyor—William Kiskadden, Whig, 640; Peter B. Beidler, Democrat, 695; Beidler's majority, 55.

Prosecuting Attorney—John D. Sears, Whig, 641; Chester R. Mott, Democrat, 680; Mott's majority, 39.

Coroner—Peter Houk, Whig, 633; Albert Bixby, Democrat, 693; Bixby's majority, 60.

ELECTION OCTOBER 13, 1846, FOR GOVERNOR.

TOWNSHIPS.	William Bebb.	David Tod.	Samuel Lewis.
Crane....†			
Marseilles	35	23	5
Mifflin	11	45	8
Pitt	96	32	1
Antrim	54	14	
Eden	25	23	
Sycamore†			
Tymochtee	89	167	
Crawford	90	97	
Jackson		33	
Ridge	7	41	
Richland	18	38	
Salem	21	10	
Totals	446	522	9
Majority for Tod		76	

* Kear and Burson had the highest and an equal number of votes; it was decided by lot in favor of Kear.
†The vote in this township was not reported.

Congressman—Ely Dresbach, Whig, 428; Rodolphus Dickinson, Democrat, 516; Joseph Jackson, 4; John K. Miller, 7; Dickinson's majority, 88.
Senator—John L. Green, Whig, 238; Henry Cronise, Democrat, 343; Cronise's majority, 105.
Representative—James McCracken, Whig, 237; George Donenwirth, Democrat, 247; John M. Mahan, 37; Donenwirth's majority, 10.

ELECTION OCTOBER 12, 1847.

Representative—Joseph E. Fouke, Whig, 696; Michael Brackley, Democrat, 741; Emery D Potter, 20; Brackley's majority, 45.
Commissioner—Rodney Poole, Whig, 684; John Welch, Democrat, 757; Welch's majority, 73.
Auditor—Abner Jurey, Whig, 660; Samuel M. Worth, Democrat, 767; Worth's majority, 107.
Treasurer—John Ragon, Whig, 642; George Harper, Democrat, 778; Harper's majority, 136.
Sheriff—Simeon E. Tuttle, Whig, 661; Thomas Baird, Democrat, 762; Baird's majority, 101.
Prosecuting Attorney—Moses H. Kirby, Whig, 664; Aaron Lyle, Democrat, 767; scattering, 2; Lyle's majority, 103.
Coroner—Stephen Whinery, Democrat, 668; Albert Bixby, Whig, 760; Bixby's majority, 92.

ELECTION OCTOBER 10, 1848.

Governor—Seabury Ford, Whig, 833; John B. Weller, Democrat, 939; Weller's majority, 106.
Congressman—Cooper K. Watson, Whig, 832; Rodolphus Dickinson, Democrat, 934; Dickinson's majority, 102.
Senator—Charles O'Neal, Whig, 835; Joel W. Wilson, Democrat, 933; Wilson's majority, 98.
Representative—William Griffith, Whig, 824; Machias C. Whitely, Democrat, 937; Whitely's majority, 113.
Commissioner—James M. Chemberlin, Whig, 818; Ethan Terry, Democrat, 951; Terry's majority, 133.
Recorder—Ernest M. Krakau, Whig, 819; John A. Morrison, Democrat, 943; Morrison's majority, 124.
Surveyor—Azariah Root, Whig, 812; Peter B. Beidler, Democrat, 951; Beidler's majority, 139.

ELECTION OCTOBER 9, 1849.

Congressman—Amos E. Wood, Democrat, 847; Daniel B. White, Whig, 180; scattering, 43; Wood's majority, 667.
Representative—Silas Burson, Whig, 720; Machias C. Whitely, Democrat, 828; Whitely's majority, 108.
Commissioner—Rodney Poole, Whig, 776; Isaac Wohlgamuth, Democrat, 823; Wohlgamuth's majority, 47.
Auditor—George W. Beery, Whig, 712; Chester R. Mott, Democrat, 864; Mott's majority, 152.
Treasurer—John Ragon, Whig, 687; George Harper, Democrat, 904; Harper's majority, 217.
Sheriff—William H. Renick, Whig, 678; Curtis Berry, Jr., Democrat, 906; Berry's majority, 228.
Prosecuting Attorney—Moses H. Kirby, Whig, 792; S. R. McBane, Democrat, 783; Kirby's majority, 9.

Coroner--Saunders A. Reed, Whig, 677; John N. Reed, Democrat, 908; Reed's majority, 231.
Convention—For, 916; against, 190; majority for, 726.

ELECTION APRIL 1, 1850.

Senatorial Delegate to Convention—John Ewing, Democrat, 764.
Representative Delegate to Convention—John Carey, Whig, 809; Benjamin P. Smith, 689; Peter B. Beidler, 8; Carey's majority, 120.

ELECTION OCTOBER 8, 1850.

Governor—William Johnston, Whig, 797; Reuben Wood, Democrat, 1,002; Edward Smith, 2; Wood's majority, ——.
Congressman—John C. Spink, Whig, 566; Frederick W. Green, Democrat, 999; Green's majority, 233.
Senator—Abel Rawson, Whig, 553; Michael Brackley, Democrat, 991; Brackley's majority, 438.
Representative—Wilson Vance, Whig, 570; Henry Bishop, Democrat, 996; Bishop's majority, 426.
Commissioner—Rodney Poole, Whig, 576; John Welch, Democrat, 982; Welch's majority, 406.

ELECTION ALOPTING THE NEW CONSTITUTION.

June 17, 1851, the State adopted the new constitution by 125,564 votes against 102,976 in opposition, and at the same time gave 104,255 votes for license, and 113,239 against it. In this contest Wyandot County gave 836 for the constitution, 567 against it; and, 958 in favor of license, and 487 against it. The aggregate votes on the new constitution do not contain the vote of Sycamore Township, the poll books of that township having never been returned.

ELECTION OCTOBER 14, 1851.

Governor—Samuel F. Vinton, Whig, 781; Reuben Wood, Democrat, 987; Samuel Lewis, Abolitionist, 1; Wood's majority, 206.
Supreme Judge—Allen G. Thurman, Democrat, 989; William B. Caldwell, Whig, 986.
Common Pleas Judge—Cooper K. Watson, Whig, 777; Lawrence W. Hall, Democrat, 959; Hall's majority, 182.
Senator—Abel Rawson, Whig, 781; Joel W. Wilson, Democrat, 968; Wilson's majority, 187.
Representative—Ushler P. Leighton, Whig, 790; David Snodgrass, Democrat, 979; Snodgrass's majority, 189.
Auditor—John Vanorsdall, Whig, 634; Chester R. Mott, Democrat, 873; Joseph E. Fouke, Whig, 209; Mott's majority, 239.
Commissioners—Jonathan Kear, Whig, 856; William Irvine, Democrat, 872; Irvine's majority, 16.
Probate Judge*—Joseph Kinney, Whig, 840; Robert McKelly, Democrat, 840.
Sheriff—William H. Renick, Whig, 791; Curtis Berry, Jr., Democrat, 949; Berry's majority, 158.
Treasurer—John Ragon, Whig, 566; George Harper, Democrat, 894; Joseph McCutchen, Democrat, 275; Harper's majority, 328.

---

*Each candidate having an equal number of votes, it was decided by lot in favor of Kinney.

Clerk of the Court—Guy C. Worth, Whig, 895; John A. Morrison, Democrat, 810; Worth's majority, 85.

Recorder—Clark Glenn, Whig, 659; William B. Hitchcock, Democrat, 1,088; Hitchcock's majority, 429.

Surveyor—Ernest M. Krakau, Whig, 797; James Williams, Democrat, 931; Williams' majority, 134.

Prosecuting Attorney—Moses H. Kirby, Whig, 893; Henry Maddux, Democrat, 796; Kirby's majority, 97.

Coroner—John W. Senseney, Whig, 726; John N. Reed, Democrat, 991; Reed's majority, 265.

ELECTION, OCTOBER 12, 1852.

Supreme Judge—Daniel A. Haynes, Whig, 784; William B. Caldwell, Democrat, 917; Caldwell's majority, 233.

Congressman—George W. Sampson, Whig, 768; Frederick W. Green, Democrat, 909; Green's majority, 141.

Probate Judge—Joseph Kinney, Whig, 940; Robert McKelly, Democrat, 753; Kinney's majority, 187.

Commissioner—Jonathan Kear, Whig, 979; David Miller, Whig, 988; John Myers, Democrat, 765; Clark R. Fowler, Democrat, 651; Henry Peters, Whig, 1; Kear and Miller were elected.

ELECTION OCTOBER 11, 1853.

Governor—William Medill, Democrat, 1,218; Nelson Barrere, Whig, 774; Samuel Lewis, Free Soil, 58; Medill's majority, 444.

Supreme Judge—Thomas W. Bartley, Democrat, 1,207; Franklin T. Backus, Whig, 806; Reuben Hitchcock, Whig, 28; Bartley's majority, 401.

Senator—Robert Lee, Democrat, 1,219; George W. Leith Whig, 763; B. Kerr, ———, 1; J. W. Vance, ———, 2; Lee's majority, 456.

Representative—Peter A. Tyler, Democrat, 1,019; John Carey, Whig, 939; John Halstead, ———, 2; Tyler's majority, 80.

Auditor—James V. S. Hoyt, Democrat, 1,079; Joseph McCutchen, Democrat, 738; John Vanorsdall, Independent Democrat, 145; Hoyt's majority, 341.

Sheriff—George P. Nelson, Democrat, 1,175; Joel Bland, Whig, 659; Thomas Gatchell, Whig, 137; Nelson's majority, 516.

Clerk of Court—Curtis Berry, Jr., Democrat, 1,082; James McLane, Whig, 816; Robert Reed, Democrat, 116; Berry's majority, 266.

Treasurer—William W. Bates, Democrat, 1,099; Henry I. Flack, Whig, 805; David Watson, Whig, 133; Bates' majority, 294.

Commissioner—John Welch, Democrat, 1,086; Isaac Bryant, Whig, 772; John R. Lupton, Whig, 160; Welch's majority, 314.

Prosecuting Attorney—Nelson W. Dennison, Democrat, 1,078; Moses H. Kirby, Whig, 878; George W. Beery, Whig, 1; Harmon Bower, 1; Dennison's majority, 200.

Coroner—Thomas Baird, Democrat, 1,068; Jonathan Hare, Democrat, 751; Clark Glenn, Whig, 160; Baird's majority, 317.

ELECTION OCTOBER 10, 1854.

Supreme Judge—Shepherd F. Norris, Whig, 724; Joseph R. Swann, Democract, 1,101; Swann's majority, 377.

Congressman—Josiah S. Plants, Democrat, 694; Cooper K. Watson, Whig, 1,129; Watson's majority, 435.

Clerk of Court—Curtis Berry, Jr., Democrat, 767; Thomas E. Grisell, Whig, 1,065; Grissell's majority, 298.

Recorder—William B. Hitchcock, Democrat, 814; Henry J. Flack, Whig, 1,019; Flack's majority, 205.

Surveyor—James H. Williams, Democrat, 702; E. M. Krakau, Whig, 540; Andrew Reynolds, Democrat, 9; Williams' majority, 162.

Commissioner—Samuel Kenan, Whig, 633; Jonathan Kear, Democrat, 1,191; Kear's majority, 558.

ELECTION OCTOBER 9, 1855.

Governor—Salmon P. Chase, Republican, 1,143; William Medill, Democrat, 1,045; Allen Trimble, Free Soil, 61; Chase's majority, 98.

Supreme Judge—(full term), Jacob Brinkerhoff, Republican, 1,202; William Kennon, Democrat, 1,048; Brinkerhoff's majority, 154.

Senator—James Lewis, Republican, 1,188; Warren P. Noble, Democrat, 1,047; Lewis' majority, 147.

Representative—Elias G. Spelman, Republican, 1,183; Samuel M. Worth, Democrat, 1,061; Spelman's majority, 122.

Auditor—Joseph McCutchen, Republican, 1,127; James V. S. Hoyt, Democrat, 1,064; McCutchen's majority, 63.

Treasurer—James C. Pease, Republican, 1,097; William W. Bates, Democrat, 1,137; Bates' majority, 40.

Probate Judge—Joseph Kinney, Republican. 1,199; Jonathan Maffett, Democrat, 1,045; Kinney's majority, 154.

Sheriff—Daniel Hoffman, Republican, 1,088; George P. Nelson, Democrat 1,139; Nelson's majority, 51.

Commissioner—Hiram H. Holdredge, Republican, 1,180; Clark R. Fowler, Democrat, 1,056; Holdredge's majority, 124.

Prosecuting Attorney—Moses H. Kirby, Republican, 1,178; Nelson W. Dennison, Democrat, 1,042; Kirby's majority, 136.

Coroner—Albert Mears, Republican. 1,178; D. S. McAlmon, Democrat, 1,060; Mear's majority, 118.

ELECTION OCTOBER 14, 1856.

Supreme Judge (long term)—Josiah Scott, Republican, 1,188; Rufus P. Ranney, Democrat, 1,174; Daniel Peck, American, 102; Scott's majority, 14.

Supreme Judge (short term)—Ozias Bowen, Republican, 1,167; C. W. Searle, Democrat, 1,175; Samuel Brush, American, 113; Searle's majority, 8.

Congressman—Cooper K. Watson, Republican, 1,164; Lawrence W. Hall, Democrat, 1,176; W. T. Wilson, American, 113; Hall's majority, 12.

Common Pleas Judge—Daniel W. Swigart, Republican, 1,195; Machias C. Whitely, Democrat, 1,213; scattering, 4; Whitely's majority, 18.

Commissioner—Milton Morral, Republican, 1,200; John Welch, Democrat, 1,136; Jacob Juvinall, American, 135; Morral's majority, 54.

Bank Charter—For, 1,114; against, 418; neutral, 70; majority for, 696.

ELECTION OCTOBER 13, 1857.

Governor—Salmon P. Chase, Republican, 1,136; Henry B. Payne, Democrat, 1,257; P. Van Lump, 64; Payne's majority, 121.

Supreme Judge—Milton Sutliff, Republican, 1,127; Henry C. Whitman, Democrat, 1,264; John Davenport, 66; Whitman's majority, 137.

HISTORY OF WYANDOT COUNTY. 339

Common Pleas Judge—John C. Lee, Republican, 1,141; George E. Seney, Democrat, 1,288; Seney's majority, 147.
Senator—George W. Sampson, Republican, 48; Guy C. Worth, Republican, 1,140; Robert McKelly, Democrat, 1,241; McKelly's majority, 101.
Representative—David Ayres, Republican, 1,067; Chester R. Mott, Democrat, 1,305; P. C. Barlow, 41; A. C. Clemens, 2; Mott's majority, 238.
Probate Judge—William A. Knibloe, Republican, 1,152; Jonathan Maffett, Democrat, 1,281; Maffett's majority, 129.
Auditor—F. W. Martin, Republican, 1,179; James V. S. Hoyt, Democrat, 1,271; Hoyt's majority, 92.
Treasurer—John Ragon, Republican, 1,174; James H. Freet, Democrat, 1,264; Freet's majority, 90.
Sheriff—Joseph McCutchen, Republican, 1,170; Curtis Berry, Sr., Democrat, 1,212; Berry's majority, 42.
Clerk of Court—T. E. Grisell, Republican, 1,140; Curtis Berry, Jr., Democrat, 1,294; Berry's majority, 154.
Recorder—Henry J. Flack, Republican, 1,229; William B. Hitchcock, Democrat, 1,194; Flack's majority, 35.
Surveyor—Aaron Bradshaw, Republican, 1,103; Peter B. Beidler, Democrat, 1,346; Beidler's majority, 243.
Commissioner—Sheldon Beebe, Republican, 1,126; John Baker, Democrat, 1,310; Baker's majority, 184.
Prosecuting Attorney—Moses H. Kirby, Republican, 1,211; George Crawford, Democrat, 1,229; Crawford's majority, 18.
Coroner—Albert Mears, Republican, 1,178; Benjamin Williams, Democrat, 1,252; Williams' majority, 74.

ELECTION OCTOBER 12, 1858.

Supreme Judge—W. V. Peck, Republican, 1,288; T. W. Bartley, Democrat, 1,141; Peck's majority, 147.
Congressman—John Carey, Republican, 1,414; L. W. Hall, Democrat, 962.
Common Pleas Judge—J. D. Sears, Republican, 1,342; J. S. Plants, Democrat, 1,080; Sears' majority, 262.
Probate Judge—Moses H. Kirby, Republican, 1,369; Jonathan Maffett, Democrat, 1,044; Kirby's majority, 325.
Commissioner—H. H. Holdridge, Republican, 1,250; D. H. Curlis, Democrat, 1,110; Holdridge's majority, 140.

ELECTION OCTOBER 13, 1859.

Governor—Rufus P. Ranney, Democrat, 1,390; William Dennison, Republican, 1,295; Ranney's majority, 95.
Supreme Judge—— Whitman, Democrat, 1,386; Gholson, Republican, 1,281; Whitman's majority, 105.
Senator—Thomas J. Orr, Democrat, 1,368; J. M. Stevens, Republican, 1,296; Orr's majority, 72.
Representative—J. M. White, Democrat, 1,396; J. F. Henkle, Republican, 1,287; White's majority, 109.
Auditor—Peter B. Beidler, Democrat, 1,344; Samuel Kirby, Republican, 1,308; Beidler's majority, 36.
Treasurer—James H. Freet, Democrat, 1,463; Charles Norton, Republican, 1,204; Freet's majority, 259.

Sheriff—James Culbertson, Jr., Independent, 1,401; Alex Watson, Democrat, 1,243; Culbertson's majority, 158.

Prosecuting Attorney—Henry Maddux, Republican, 1,384; George Crawford, Democrat, 1,279; Maddux's majority, 105.

Commissioner—Milton Morral, Republican, 1,394; John Kisor, Democrat, 1,284; Morral's majority, 112.

Coroner—Benjamin Williams, Democrat, 1,381; Alex Shoemaker, Republican, 1,283; Williams' majority, 98.

ELECTION OCTOBER, 9, 1860.

Supreme Judge—Thomas J. S. Smith, Democrat, 1,624; Jacob Brinkerhoff, Republican, 1,569; Smith's majority, 55.

Congressman—Warren P. Noble, Democrat, 1,461; John Carey, Republican, 1,738; Carey's majority, 277.

Clerk of Court—Curtis Berry, Jr., Democrat, 1,642; Joseph A. Maxwell, Republican, 1,544; Berry's majority, 98.

Recorder—Henry Miller, Democrat, 1,681; C. D. V. Worley, Republican, 1,504; Miller's majority, 177.

Commissioner—John Baker, Democrat, 1,616; Isaac Lundy, Republican, 1,570; Baker's majority, 46.

Surveyor—Andrew Reynolds, Democrat, 1,635; Aaron Bradshaw, Republican, 1,550; Reynolds' majority, 85.

ELECTION NOVEMBER, 6, 1860.

President—A. Lincoln, Republican, 1,531; Stephen A. Douglas, Democrat, 1,617; Douglas' majority, 86.

ELECTION OCTOBER, 8, 1861.

Governor—David Tod, Republican, 1,384; Hugh J. Jewett, Democrat, 1,562; Jewett's majority, 178.

Supreme Judge—Josiah Scott, Republican, 1,379; T. J. S. Smith, Democrat, 1,568; Smith's majority, 189.

Senator—W. C. Parsons, Republican, 1,364; William Lang, Democrat, 1,545; Lang's majority, 181.

Representative—F. F. Fowler, Republican, 1,354; Jonathan Maffett, Democrat, 1,549; Maffett's majority, 195.

Auditor—George Crawford, Republican, 1,330; Peter B. Beidler, Democrat, 1,607; Beidler's majority, 277.

Treasurer—J. L. Cooke, Republican, 1,333; D. C. Murray, Democrat, 1,588; Murray's majority, 255.

Sheriff—C. P. Shurr, Republican, 1,327; William Marlow, Democrat, 1,609; Marlow's majority, 282.

Probate Judge—M. H. Kirby, Republican, 1,550; John A. Morrison, Democrat, 1,345; Kirby's majority, 205.

Prosecuting Attorney——— Harrison, Republican, 1,349; John Berry, Democrat, 1,585; Berry's majority, 236.

Commissioner—J. Edgington, Republican, 1,361; C. R. Fowler, Democrat, 1,586; Fowler's majority, 225.

Coroner—William Irvine, Republican, 1,369; Benjamin Williams, Democrat, 1,559; William's majority, 190.

ELECTION OCTOBER 13, 1863.

Governor—John Brough, Republican, 1,666; C. L. Vallandigham, Democrat, 1,679; Vallandigham's majority, 13.

HISTORY OF WYANDOT COUNTY. 341

Representative—Jonathan Maffett, Democrat, 1,719; Samuel H. White, Republican, 1,651; Maffett's majority, 68.
Auditor—J. V. S. Hoyt, Democrat, 1,724; Frank W. Martin, Republican, 1,647; Hoyt's majority, 77.
Sheriff—Andrew W. Ingerson, Republican, 1,617; William Marlow, Democrat, 1,742; Marlow's majority, 125.
Commissioner—John Kisor, Democrat, 1,730; Jesse Edgington, Republican, 1,642; Kisor's majority, 88.
Surveyor—Andrew Reynolds, Democrat, 1,725; James L. Cook, Republican, 1,646; Reynolds' majority, 79.
Treasurer—D. C. Murray, Democrat, 1,741; Addison E. Gibbs, Republican, 1,641; Murray's majority, 100.
Clerk of Court—Frederick Agerter, Democrat, 1,730; Henry Miller, Republican, 1,644; Agerter's majority, 86.
Prosecuting Attorney—John Berry, Democrat, 1,726; Thomas E. Grisell, Republican, 1,641; Berry's majority, 85.
Recorder—Simeon Inman, Democrat, 1,730; James K. Agnew, Republican, 1,636; Inman's majority, 94.
Coroner—Benjamin Williams, Democrat, 1,718; John Holloway, Republican, 1,646; Williams' majority, 72.

ELECTION OCTOBER 9, 1866.

Congressman—William Mungen, Democrat, 1,925; —— Walker, Republican, 1,734; Mungen's majority, 191.
Common Pleas Judge—C. R. Mott, Democrat, 1,915; Cooper K. Watson, Republican, 1,722; Mott's majority, 193.
Clerk of Court—Fred Agerter, Democrat, 1,932; S. S. Pettit, Republican, 1,720; Agerter's majority, 212.
Commissioner—John Kisor, Democrat, 1,927; Roderick McKenzie, Republican, 1,731; Kisor's majority, 196.
Recorder—Simeon Inman, Democrat, 1,943; —— Thompson, Republican, 1,718; Inman's majority, 225.

ELECTION OCTOBER 8, 1867.

Governor—A. G. Thurman, Democrat, 2,183; R. B. Hayes, Republican, 1,609; Thurman's majority, 574.
Senator—C. Berry, Jr., Democrat, 2,188; John C. Leith, Republican, 1,590; Berry's majority, 598.
Representative—Samuel M. Worth, Democrat, 2,190; M. C. Gibson, Republican, 1,598; Worth's majority, 592.
Auditor—Jonathan Maffett, Democrat, 2,198; J. K. Agnew, Republican, 1,590; Maffett's majority, 608.
Treasurer—W. F. Goodbread, Democrat, 2,187; L. R. Seaman, Republican, 1,596; Goodbread's majority, 591.
Sheriff—William Michaels, Democrat, 2,192; D. Fishel, Republican, 1,600; Michaels' majority, 592.
Probate Judge—Peter B. Beidler, Democrat, 2,175; J. L. Cook, Republican, 1,617; Beidler's majority, 558.
Commissioner—J. Hollenshead, Democrat, 2,185; Isaac Mann, Republican, 1,604; Hollenshead's majority, 581.
Prosecuting Attorney—M. H. Kirby, Democrat, 2,170; Thomas E. Grisell, Republican, 1,597; Kirby's majority, 573.
Coroner—L. Gipson, Democrat, 2,192; J. Holloway, Republican, 1,597; Gipson's majority, 595.

Convention to Amend the Constitution—For, 1,487; against, 2,258; Majority against, 771.

ELECTION OCTOBER 13, 1868.

Congressman—William Mungen, Democrat, 2,138; Thomas E. Grisell, Republican, 1,620; Mungen's majority, 518.
Commissioner—D. C. Murray, Democrat, 2,157; Isaac Walton, Republican, 1,609; Murray's majority, 548.
Surveyor—John Agerter, Democrat, 2,131. (No opposition.)
Coroner—Levi Shultz, Democrat, 2,138; D. Fishel, Republican, 1,630; Shultz's majority, 508.

ELECTION OCTOBER 12, 1869.

George H. Pendleton, Democrat, 2,069; R. B. Hayes, Republican, 1,561; Pendleton's majority, 508.
Senator—A. S. Jenner, Democrat, 2,060; S. R. Harris, Republican, 1,572; Jenner's majority, 488.
Representative—John Kisor, Democrat, 2,002; R. A. Henderson, Republican, 1,604; Kisor's majority, 398.
Clerk of Court—William B. Hitchcock, Democrat, 2,060; — Brown, Republican, 1,515; Hitchcock's majority, 545.
Prosecuting Attorney—M. H. Kirby, Democrat, 2,047; Adam Kail, Republican, 1,563; Kirby's majority, 484.
Sheriff—Henry Myers, Democrat, 2,005; — Rieser, Republican, 1,518; Myers' majority, 487.
Auditor—Jonathan Maffett, Democrat, 2,031; J. L. Cook, Republican, 1,583; Maffett's majority, 448.
Treasurer—J. S. Hare, Democrat, 2,059; John Greer, Republican, 1,479; Hare's majority, 580.
Recorder—Adam Stutz, Democrat, 1,905; — Pool, Republican, 1,626; Stutz's majority, 279.
Commissioner—William Beam, Democrat, 1,983; S. Watson, Repubcan, 1,594; Beam's majority, 389.

ELECTION OCTOBER 11, 1870.

Supreme Judge—Richard A. Harrison, Democrat, 1,649; George W. McElvaine, Republican, 1,211; Harrison's majority, 438.
Congressman—Charles N. Lamison; Democrat, 1,650; I. D. Clark, Republican, 1,214; Lamison's majority, 436.
Probate Judge—Peter B. Beidler, Democrat, 1,373; Michael Brackley, Independent, 1,253; Beidler's majority, 120.
Commissioner—Thomas McClain, Independent, 1,639; Jacob Hollenshead, Democrat, 1,180; McClain's majority, 459.
Infirmary Directors—A. H. Vanorsdall (3 years), 1,638; Tilman Balliet (2 years), 1,636; George Harper (1 year), 1,637.
Coroner—Levi Shultz, Democrat, 1,628; Daniel Fishel, Independent, 27.

ELECTION OCTOBER 10, 1871.

Governor—George W. McCook, Democrat, 1,915; Edward F. Noyes, Republican, 1,580; McCook's majority, 335.
Senator—A. S. Jenner, Democrat, 1,912, U. F. Cramer, Republican, 1,576.

HISTORY OF WYANDOT COUNTY. 343

Representative—John Kisor, Democrat, 1,893 ; no opposition.
Common Pleas Judge—C. R. Mott, Democrat, 2,634 ; A. M. Jackson, Republican, 762 ; Mott's majority, 1,872.
Sheriff—Henry Myers, Democrat, 1,917 ; John F. Rieser, Republican, 1,573 ; Myers' majority, 344.
Commissioner—Henry Parker, Republican, 1,671 ; Milton Morral, Democrat, 1,811 ; Morral's majority, 140.
Surveyor—John Agerter, Democrat, 1,800; James K. Agnew, Republican, 1,659 ; Agerter's majority, 141.
Infirmary Director—Michael Depler, Democrat, 1,897 ; Henry Davis, Sr., Republican, 1,562 ; Depler's majority, 335.
Constitutional Convention*—For, 2,009 ; against, 1,346 ; majority for, 663.

ELECTION OCTOBER 8, 1872.

Supreme Judge—Isaac B. Riley, Democrat, 2,105 ; Richard R. Porter, Republican, 1,776 ; Riley's majority, 329.
Common Pleas Judge—James Pillars, Democrat, 2,101. No opposition.
Auditor—Robert A. McKelly, Democrat, 2,034 ; Henry Miller, Republican, 1,841 ; McKelly's majority, 193.
Clerk of Court—William B. Hitchcock, Democrat, 2,130; Samuel Lutz, Republican, 1,755; Hitchcock's majority, 375.
Recorder—Adam Stutz, Democrat, 2,095; Daniel Hartsough, Republican, 1,771; Stutz's majority, 324.
Commissioner—William Beam, Democrat, 2,096.
Coroner—Edward Christen, Democrat, 2,104; Moses Waggoner, Republican, 1,779; Christen's majority, 325.
Infirmary Director—Tilman Balliet, Democrat, 2,099; John McBeth, Republican, 1,789; Balliet's majority, 310.

ELECTION OCTOBER 14, 1873.

Governor—William Allen, Democrat, 2,039; Edward F. Noyes, Republican, 1,364; Allen's majority, 675.
Senator—John Seitz, Democrat, 2,052; David Harpster, Republican, 1,345; Seitz's majority, 707.
Representative—L. A. Brunner, Democrat, 1,934; John Markley, Republican, 1,250; Brunner's majority, 684.
Probate Judge—Joel W. Gibson, Democrat, 1,985; William R. De Jean, Republican, 1,404; Gibson's majority, 581.
Prosecuting Attorney—M. H. Kirby, Democrat, 2,071; Henry Maddux, Republican, 1,347; Kirby's majority, 724.
Sheriff—Jacob Schaefer, Democrat, 1,934; H. P. Marshall, Republican, 1,462; Schaefer's majority, 472.
Treasurer—William Smalley, Democrat, 3,261.
Commissioners—Thomas McClain, 1,949; Samuel M. Worth, 1,864; Benjamin F. Kennedy, 1,470; Michael Bretz, 1,456; McClain's majority over Kennedy, 479; Worth's majority over Bretz, 408.
Infirmary Director—Abram H. Vanorsdall, Democrat, 2,052; Moses Kirby, Republican, 1,362; Vanorsdall's majority; 690.

ELECTION OCTOBER 13, 1874.

Congressman—J. P. Cowan, Democrat, 1,687; W. Armstrong, Republican, 1,173; Cowan's majority, 514.

---
* For a full reconstruction of the Constitution of the State.

Common Pleas Judge—Thomas Beer, Democrat, 1,703; Josiah Scott, Republican, 1,164; Beer's majority, 539.

Auditor—R. A. McKelly, Democrat, 1,732; J. D. Foucht, Temperance, 930; McKelly's majority, 802.

Commissioner—J. Yentzer, Democrat, 1,359; R. Bennett, Temperance, 438; M. Morral, Independent, 1,055; Yentzer's majority, 304.

Surveyor—J. Greek, Democrat, 1,705; James L. Cook, Temperance, 959; Greek's majority, 746.

Coroner—Edward Christian, Democrat, 1,704; D. L. Kentfield, Temperance, 956; Christian's majority, 748.

Infirmary Director—R. McBeth, Democrat, 1,764; H. Peters, Temperance, 934; McBeth's majority, 830.

Election October 13, 1875.

Governor—William Allen, Democrat, 2,305; R. B. Hayes, Republican, 1,735; Allen's majority, 570.

"For the Commission"—For, 1,998; against, 444; Majority for, 554.

Senator—E. T. Stickney, Democrat, 2,287; William Monnett, Republican, 1,734; Stickney's majority, 553.

Representative—L. A. Brunner, Democrat, 2,256; Moses Gibson, Republican, 1,724; Brunner's majority, 532.

Clerk of Court—R. D. Dumm, Democrat, 2,238; R. M. Stewart, Republican, 1,766; Dumm's majority, 473.

Prosecuting Attorney—M. H. Kirby, Democrat, 2,279; Adam Kail, Republican, 1,715; Kirby's majority, 564.

Sheriff—Jacob Schaefer, Democrat, 2,187; —— Lime, Republican, 1,778; Schaefer's majority, 409.

Treasurer—William Smalley, Democrat, 2,306; J. R. Swann, Republican, 1,704; Smalley's majority, 602.

Recorder—Simeon Inman, Democrat, 2,236; John E. Goodrich, Republican, 1,727; Inman's majority, 509.

Commissioner—William Ayres, Democrat, 2,192; O. K. Brown, Republican, 1,802; Ayres' majority, 390.

Infirmary Director—Michael Depler, Democrat, 2,301; D. L. Kentfield, Republican, 1,743; Depler's majority, 558.

Election October 10, 1876.

Secretary of State—William Bell, Jr., Democrat, 2,483; Milton Barnes, Republican, 1,902; Bell's majority, 581.

Supreme Judge—William E. Finck, Democrat, 2,489; Washington W. Boynton, Republican, 1,900; Finck's majority, 589.

Congressman—Ebenezer B. Finley, Democrat, 2,490; Peter S. Grosscup, Republican, 1,897; Finley's majority, 593.

Common Pleas Judge—Thomas Beer, Democrat, 2,491; no opposition.

Probate Judge—Joel W. Gibson, Democrat, 2,475; David Harpster, Jr., Republican, 1872; Gibson's majority, 603.

Auditor—John Agerter, Democrat, 2,332; Henry Miller, Republican, 2,019; Agerter's majority, 313.

Treasurer—George W. Biles, Democrat, 2,515; Edwin A. Gordon, Republican, 1,869; Biles' majority, 646.

Commissioner—Peter Beam, Democrat, 2,519; Quincy A. Rowse, Republican, 1,841; Beam's majority, 678.

Infirmary Director—Jacob Swartz, Democrat, 2,492; James C. Andrews, Republican, 1,907; Swartz's majority, 585.

HISTORY OF WYANDOT COUNTY. 345

Coroner—Jacob Tribolet, Democrat, 2,459; Samuel Shepard, Republican, 1,875; Tribolet's majority, 584.

ELECTION OCTOBER 9, 1877.

Governor—William H. West, Republican, 1,722; Richard M. Bishop, Democrat, 2,405; Bishop's majority, 879.

Supreme Judge—William W. Johnson, Republican, 1,734; John W. Okey, Democrat, 2,391; Okey's majority, 657.

Senator—Lovell B. Harris, Republican, 1,711; John Seitz, Democrat, 2,391; Seitz's majority, 680.

Representative—Isaac M. Kirby, Republican, 1,775; Willard D. Tyler, Democrat, 2,350; Tyler's majority, 575.

Common Pleas Judge—Jacob F. ———, Republican, 1,735; Henry H. Dodge, Democrat 2,395; Dodge's majority, 660.

Prosecuting Attorney—Miller B. Smith, Republican, 1,736; Moses H. Kirby, Democrat, 2,373; Kirby's majority, 637.

Sheriff—John M. Houston, Democrat, 2,125; Joseph Hutter, Republican, 1,819; Houston's majority, 306.

Commissioner—Hiram J. Starr, Republican, 1,794; Jacob Yentzer, Democrat, 2,228; Yentzer's majority, 494.

Surveyor—William McDowell, Republican, 1,745; Jacob Greek, Democrat, 2,383; Greek's majority, 638.

Infirmary Director—James H. Lindsey, Republican, 1,738; Robert McBeth, Democrat, 2,396; McBeth's majority, 658.

Free Banking Act—For, 605; against, 1,826; majority against, 1,221.

ELECTION OCTOBER 8, 1878.

Secretary of State—Milton Barnes, Republican, 1,907; David R. Paige, Democrat, 2,448; Paige's majority, 541.

Supreme Judge—William White, Republican, 1,903; Alexander F. Hume, Democrat, 2,452; Hume's majority, 549.

Congressman—E. B. Finley, Democrat, 2,354; Charles Foster, Republican, 1,944; Finley's majority, 410.

Clerk of Court—Robert D. Dumm, Democrat, 2,565; W. E. Benton, Republican, 1,787; Dumm's majority, 778.

Auditor—John Agerter, Democrat, 2,119; Landline Smith, Republican, 2,201; Smith's majority, 82.

Treasurer—George W. Bates, Democrat, 2,525; Robert W. Pool, Republican, 1,831; Bate's majority, 694.

Recorder—Simeon Inman, Democrat, 2,581; John E. Goodrich, Republican, 1,766; Inman's majority, 815.

Commissioner—William Ayres, Democrat, 2,042; Benjamin F. Kennedy, Republican, 1,992; N. Willoughby, Independent, 200; Ayres' majority, 50.

Infirmary Director—Elias Streby, Democrat, 2,450; James H. Lindsay, Republican, 1,899; Streby's majority, 551.

Coroner—Jacob Tribolet, Democrat, 2,408; George W. Kenan, Republic, 1,899; Tribolet's majority, 509.

ELECTION OCTOBER 14, 1879.

Governor—Charles Foster, Republican, 2,282; Thomas Ewing, Democrat, 2,812; Ewing's majority, 530.

Supreme Judge—William W. Johnson, Republican, 2,261; William J. Gilmore, Democrat, 2,830; Gilmore's majority, 569.

Senator—Stephen R. Harris, Republican, 2,240; Moses H. Kirby, Democrat, 2,825; Kirby's majority, 585.
Probate Judge—William R. De Jean, Republican, 2,206; Joel W. Gibson, Democrat, 2,849; Gibson's majority, 643.
Prosecuting Attorney—William F. Pool, Republican, 2,213; George G. White, Democrat, 2,860; White's majority, 647.
Sheriff—John M. Houston, Democrat, 2,820; Henry Myers, Republican, 2,156; Myers' majority, 664.
Commissioner—Benjamin F. Kennedy, Republican, 2,446; William M. Baldwin, Democrat, 2,604; Baldwin's majority, 158.
Infirmary Director—John Greer, Republican, 2,260; John Swartz, Democrat, 2,822; Swartz's majority, 562.

ELECTION OCTOBER 12, 1880.

Secretary of State — Charles Townsend, Republican, 2,316; William Lang, Democrat, 2,920; Lang's majority, 604.
Supreme Judge—George W. McIlvaine, Republican, 2,316; Martin D. Follett, Democrat, 2,921; Follett's majority, 605.
Congressman — S. E. Fink, Republican, 2,315; George W. Geddes, Democrat, 2,925,
Commissioner— John Greer, Republican, 2,412; Abraham Bope, Republican, 2,125; Henry Herring, Democrat, 2,791; George Harper, Democrat, 3,012.
Treasurer—John L. Lewis, Republican, 2,314; George W. Freet, Democrat, 2,913; Freet's majority, 599.
Surveyor—Isaac M. Kirby, Republican, 2,568; Jacob Greek, Democrat, 2,596; Greek's majority, 28.
Infirmary Director—David S. Bretz, Republican, 2,306; Reuben Lowmaster, Democrat, 2,865.

ELECTION NOVEMBER, 1880.

President—James A. Garfield, Republican, 2,398; Winfield S. Hancock, Democrat, 2,983; Hancock's majority, 585.

ELECTION OCTOBER 11, 1881.

Governor — Charles Foster, Republican, 1,963; John W. Bookwalter, Democrat, 2,644; Abraham R. Ludlow, 184; John Seitz, 1; Bookwalter's majority, 681.
Supreme Judge—Nicholas Longworth, Republican, 1,979; Edward F. Bingham, Democrat, 264; Gideon T. Stewart, 174; Longworth's majority, 1,715.
Senator — Moses H. Kirby, Democrat, 2,628; Martin Deal, 9; Kirby's majority, 2,619.
Representative—L. A. Brunner, Democrat, 2,574; Samuel Lutz, Republican, 2,144; Brunner's majority, 430.
Common Pleas Judge— Thomas Beer, Democrat, 2,631. No opponent.
Clerk of Court—Hiram H. Hitchcock, Democrat, 2,140; Avery Henderson, Republican, 2,540; Henderson's majority, 400.
Prosecuting Attorney—Robert McKelly, Democrat, 2,516; Robert Carey, Republican, 2,149; McKelly's majority, 367.
Sheriff—Charles F. Schuler, Democrat, 2,545; V. O. Tuttle, Republican 2,521; Schuler's majority, 24.

HISTORY OF WYANDOT COUNTY. 347

Auditor—John Agerter, Democrat, 2,175; Landline Smith, Republican, 2,521; Smith's majority, 346.
Recorder—Simeon Inman, Democrat, 2,854; Hazard P. Tracy, Republican 1,893; Inman's majority, 961.
Commissioner—John K. Hare, Democrat, 2,623; Cyrus Griffith, Republican, 2,096; Hare's majority, 527.
Infirmary Director—Elias Streby, Democrat, 2,627; David L. Kentfield, Republican, 2,108; Streby's majority, 519.

ELECTION OCTOBER 10, 1882.

Secretary of State—Charles Townsend, Republican, 1,850; James W. Newman, Democrat, 2,347; Fred Schumaker, ———, 20; George L. Hafer, ———, 1; Newman's majority, 497.
Supreme Judge—John H. Doyle, Republican, 1,844; John W. Okey, Democrat, 2,356; John W. Roseborough, 21; Lloyd G. Tuttle, 1; Okey's majority, 512.
Congressman—Lovell B. Harris, Republican, 1,844; George E. Seney, Democrat, 2,336; scattering, 13; Seney's majority, 492.
Probate Judge—John L. Lewis, Republican, 1,826; Darius D. Clayton, Democrat, 2,356; Clayton's majority, 530.
Treasurer—Henry Kear, Republican, 1,821; George W. Freet, Democrat, 2,393; Freet's majority, 572.
Commissioner—Isaac Norton, Republican, 1,811; A. H. Vanorsdall, Democrat, 2,386; Vanorsdall's majority, 575.
Infirmary Director—Joseph Ellis, Republican, 1,849; Jacob C. Wentz, Democrat, 2,352; Wentz's majority, 503.
Coroner—I. B. Gibbs, Republican, 1,844; James N. Nelson, Democrat, 2,370; Nelson's majority, 526.

ELECTION OCTOBER 9, 1883.

Governor—Joseph B. Foraker, Republican, 2,241; George Hoadley, Democrat, 3,056; Ferdinand Shumacher, ———, 21; Hoadley's majority, 815.
Supreme Judge (short term)—William H. Upson, Republican, 2,233; Martin D. Follett, Democrat, 3,068; Follett's majority, 835.
Supreme Judge (long and unexpired term)—John H. Doyle, Republican, 2,234; Selwyn N. Owen, Democrat, 3,068; Owen's majority, 834.
Senator—John H. Williston, Democrat, 3,062. No opposition.
Representative—L. A. Brunner, Democrat, 2,984; Joseph A. Maxwell, Republican, 2,290; Brunner's majority, 694.
Sheriff—Charles F. Schuler, Democrat, 3,137; Irvin Bacon, Republican, 2,139; Schuler's majority, 998.
Commissioner—George Harper, Democrat, 2,849; Benjamin Morris, Republican, 2,416; Harper's majority, 433.
Surveyor—William C. Gear, Democrat, 3,130; O. E. Reynolds, Republican, 2,158; Gear's majority, 972.
Infirmary Director—Reuben Lowmaster, Democrat, 2,992; Milton Kear, ———, 2,262; Lowmaster's majority, 730.

CONSTITUTIONAL AMENDMENTS.

Judicial Amendment—For, 2,064; against, 1,357; majority for, 707.
Regulation and taxation of the liquor traffic—For, 771; against, 2,351; majority against, 1,580.

HISTORY OF WYANDOT COUNTY.

Prohibition of intoxicating liquors—For, 2,674; against, 1802; majority for, 872.

The following table shows the total vote in each township as cast at the October election of 1883:

Antrim	135	Pitt	313
Nevada Village	432	Richland	361
Crane	351	Ridge	127
Upper Sandusky	870	Salem	278
Crawford	581	Sycamore	325
Eden	251	Tymochtee	386
Jackson	469		
Marseilles	201	Total	5,336
Mifflin	256		

OFFICERS ELECTED.

The following is a summary of those who have represented Wyandot County as United States, State and County officers.

CONGRESSMEN.

John Carey, 1859–61; John Berry, 1873–1875.

STATE SENATORS.

NAMES.	YEARS.	NAMES.	YEARS.
Amos E. Wood	1845–46	William Lang	1862–64
Henry Cronise	1846–48	Thomas J. Orr	1864–66
Joel W. Wilson	1848–50	Curtis Berry, Jr	1866–70
Michael Brackley	1850–51	Alexander E. Jenner	1870–74
Joel W. Wilson	1852–54	John Seitz	1874–76
Robert Lee	1854–56	E. T. Stickney	1876–78
James Lewis	1856–58	John Seitz	1878–80
Robert McKelly	1858–60	Moses H. Kirby	1880–84
Thomas J. Orr	1860–62	John H. Williston	1884–86

STATE REPRESENTATIVES.

NAMES.	YEARS.	NAMES.	YEARS.
Michael Brackley	1845–46	James M. White	1860–62
George Donnenworth	1846–47	Jonathan Maffett*	1862–64
Michael Brackley	1847–48	Parlee Carlin	1864–66
M. C. Whitely	1848–50	Samuel M. Worth	1866–70
Henry Bishop	1850–51	John Kisor	1870–74
David Snodgrass	1852–54	L. A. Brunner	1874–78
Peter A. Tyler	1854–56	Willard D. Tyler	1878–82
Elias G. Spelman	1656–58	L. A. Brunner	1882–86
Chester R. Mott	1858–60		

COUNTY COMMISSIONERS.

NAMES.	YEARS.	NAMES.	YEARS.
William Griffith	Spring, 1845	Jonathan Kear	1852
Stephen Fowler	Spring, 1845	John Welch	1853
Ethan Terry	Spring, 1845	Jonathan Kear	1854
Jonathan Kear	Fall, 1845	Hiram H. Holdridge	1855
Ethan Terry	Fall, 1845	Milton Morral	1856
Stephen Fowler	Fall, 1845	John Baker	1857
Isaac Wohlgamuth	1846	H. H. Holdridge	1858
John Welch	1847	Milton Morral	1859
Ethan Terry	1848	John Baker	1860
Isaac Wohlgamuth	1849	C. R. Fowler	1861
John Welch	1850	John Kisor	1863
William Irvine	1851	John Kisor	1866
David Miller	1852	J. Hollenshead	1867

*Re-elected in 1864, but was contested and his seat given to Parlee Carlin.

HISTORY OF WYANDOT COUNTY. 349

NAMES.	YEARS.	NAMES.	YEARS.
D. C. Murray	1868	Peter Beam	1876
William Beam	1869	Jacob Yentzer	1877
Thomas McClain	1870	William Ayers	1878
Milton Morral	1871	William M. Baldwin	1879
William Beam	1872	Henry Herring	1880
Thomas McClain	1873	George Harper	1880
Samuel M. Worth	1873	John K. Hare	1881
J. Yentzer	1874	A. H. Vanorsdall	1882
William Ayers	1875	George Harper	1883

AUDITORS.

NAMES.	YEARS.	NAMES.	YEARS.
Samuel M. Worth	1845–49	J. V. S. Hoyt	1863–65
Chester R. Mott	1849–53	Jonathan Maffett	1867–72
James V. S. Hoyt	1853–55	Robert A. McKelly	1872–76
Joseph McCutchen	1855–57	John Agerter	1876–78
James V. S. Hoyt	1857–59	Landline Smith	1878–84
Peter B. Beidler	1859–63		

TREASURERS.

NAMES.	YEARS.	NAMES.	YEARS.
Abner Jurey	1845–	J. S. Hare	1869–74
George Harper	1845–53	William Smalley*	1874–76
William W. Bates	1853–57	George W. Biles	1876–78
James H. Freet	1857–61	George W. Bates	1878–80
D. C. Murray	1861–66	George W. Freet	1880–84
W. F. Goodbread	1866–69		

RECORDERS.

NAMES.	YEARS.	NAMES.	YEARS.
John A. Morrison	1845–51	Simeon Inman	1864–70
William B. Hitchcock	1851–55	Adam Stutz	1870–76
Henry J. Flack	1855–61	Simeon Inman	1876–85
Henry Miller	1861–64		

CLERKS OF THE COURTS.

NAMES.	YEARS.	NAMES.	YEARS.
Guy C. Worth	1845–54	Fred Agerter	1864–70
Curtis Berry, Jr.	1854–55	William B. Hitchcock	1870–76
Thomas E. Grisell	1855–58	R. D. Dumm	1876–82
Curtis Berry, Jr.	1858–64	Avery Henderson	1882–85

PROBATE JUDGES.

NAMES.	YEARS.	NAMES.	YEARS.
Joseph Kinney	1852–58	Peter B. Beidler	1868–74
Jonathan Maffett	1857–58	Joel W. Gibson	1874–82
Moses H. Kirby	1858–68	Darius D. Clayton	1882–86

SURVEYORS.

NAMES.	YEARS.	NAMES.	YEARS.
Azariah Root	1845–46	J. H. Williams	1867–69
Peter B. Beidler	1846–52	John Agerter	1869–75
James Williams	1852–58	Jacob Greek	1875–83
Peter B. Beidler	1858–61	William C. Gear	1883–86
Andrew Reynolds	1861–67		

PROSECUTING ATTORNEYS.

NAMES.	YEARS.	NAMES.	YEARS.
Chester R. Mott†	1845–47	Henry Maddux	1860–62
Aaron Lyle	1848–50	John Berry	1862–68
Moses H. Kirby	1850–54	Moses H. Kirby	1868–80
Nelson W. Dennison	1854–58	George G. White	1880–82
George Crawford	1858–60	Robert McKelly	1882–84

*Died and was succeeded in office by J. S. Hale.
†Moses H. Kirby was appointed May 22, 1847, vice Mott, resigned.

SHERIFFS.

NAMES	YEARS	NAMES	YEARS
Lorin A. Pease	1845–46	William Marlow	1862–66
Thomas Baird	1846–50	William Michaels	1866–70
Curtis Berry Sr	1850–54	Henry Myers	1870–74
George P. Nelson	1854–58	Jacob Schaefer	1874–78
Curtis Berry	1858–60	John M. Houston	1878–82
James Culbertson, Jr	1860–62	Charles F. Schuler	1882–86

CORONERS.

NAMES	YEARS	NAMES	YEARS
Albert Bixby	1845–50	Levi Shultz	1868–72
John N. Reed	1850–54	Edward Christen	1872–76
Thomas Baird	1854–56	Jacob Tribolet	1876–80
Albert Mears	1856–58	—— Heym	1880–82
Benjamin Williams	1858–68	James N. Nelson	1882–84
L. Gipson	1868–72		

CHAPTER VII.

THE BENCH AND BAR.

INTRODUCTORY—EARLY JUDICIAL PROCEEDINGS IN THE TERRITORY—THE FIRST STATE CONSTITUTION—ARTICLE IV, CONSTITUTION OF 1851—SUPREME COURTS—DISTRICT COURTS—COURTS OF COMMON PLEAS—THE JUDGES OF THE SAME—LENGTH OF THEIR TERMS OF OFFICE—BIOGRAPHICAL SKETCHES —RESIDENT MEMBERS OF THE BAR—BRIEF MENTION OF MANY OF THEM.

INTRODUCTORY.

THE part played by law in the organization of human society is that of an everacting force, a force essential to its very existence, and upon which human happiness and well-being are unceasingly dependent. Without law, mankind would long ere this have perished, as no organization is possible without it. Upon the wise interpretation as well as the judicious framing of the laws, the well-being of a community is established as upon a rock-like foundation, whence it naturally flows as a consequence that the history of those upon whom this duty devolves must form no unimportant portion of a work of this character. The whole superstructure of law is founded upon a few principles of natural justice, and, therefore, at its base, in its essential principles, "in its inmost bosom's core," law is the exponent of right and truth and justice; and, notwithstanding the efforts of the cunning and unscrupulous, it will still be found that on the whole law is on the side of right, and the popular prejudice against lawyers has its basis chiefly in ignorance of the true nature of a lawyer's functions, which are, to see that every one has the benefit of the privileges accorded him by the laws of the land, and that the forms of law are rigidly preserved, as upon their strict enforcement of these the stability of society depends.

As the business of the lawyer is to deal with the daily affairs of men, and as these are becoming more and more complex and artificial, it is clear that where so many complex interests and counter-interests are to be protected and adjusted, to the Judge and the advocate are presented problems that require the deepest research and the most trained intellects. As change follows change in modern society, without intermission. It is also evident that the laws and institutions of the past will not answer the requirements of the present. The blue laws of Connecticut would burst from the limbs of the modern Samson like the cords from the hero of old, and the gigantic Afrites that Aladdin saw from his lamp could not be returned to their narrow prison house. The discoveries in the arts and sciences, the invention of new labor-saving contrivances, the enlargement of industrial pursuits, the unprecedented development of commerce, the founding of new communities into cities and States, require that the science of law should advance *pari passu*, in order to subserve the wants and provide for the necessities of these new conditions. The true lawyer is the man of the hour, and upon his ability and integrity society is largely dependent. One of the profession has wisely said:

"In the American State the great and good lawyer must always be prominent, for he is one of the forces which move and control society. Public confidence has generally been reposed in the legal profession. It has ever been the defender of popular rights, the champion of freedom regulated by law, the firm support of good government. In times of danger, it has stood like a rock and beaten the mad passions of the hour and firmly resisted tumult and faction. No political preferment, no mere place can add to the power or increase the honor which belongs to the pure and educated lawyer. The fame of Mansfield and Marshall and Story can never die. 'Time's iron feet can print no ruin trace' upon their character. Their learning and luminous expositions of our jurisprudence will always light our pathway. * * * Lord Bacon has said, 'Every man is a debtor to his profession;' and assuredly this is true of every lawyer. If worthy, it gives him an honorable character and high position. The lawyer should prize and honor his profession. He should value its past renown and cherish the memory of great men, whose gigantic shadows walk by us still. He should love it for the intrinsic worth and innate glory of the fundamental truths which adorn it."

The paucity of material at the service of the historian as to those who have exerted so important an influence upon the county's welfare and progress, is indeed a matter of surprise. We, however, present our readers with that which the corroding hand of time has left untouched. The greater portion of the story might, however, be unlocked to him who would patiently study the strata of society, as the geologist studies the stony records of the earth's past history.

Before entering upon the specific portion of our story, we can truthfully premise that the bench and bar of Wyandot County has ever been distinguished, and has ever stood prominently forward in comparison with the profession in the sister counties of the grand commonwealth of Ohio. Wyandot has had names connected with her bar which have adorned the pages of our country's history; names of soldiers who did not shrink from taking up the sword in defense of their country; names that have adorned the halls of Legislation of the State; names that have adorned men not merely of learning and culture, superadded to native ability, but which also have united with these gifts and graces the proud title of honest men, the noblest work of God.

THE BENCH.

The earliest judicial government for the territory now constituting Ohio was vested in a general court composed of three Judges, provided by the ordinance of 1787. The first Judges were Samuel Holden Parsons, James Mitchell Varnum and John Cleves Symmes, the latter being appointed in place of John Armstrong, who declined to serve. They were to adopt only such portions of the laws of the original States as were deemed suitable to the condition and wants of the people, and were not empowered to enact new laws. In the autumn of 1787, the Governor and Judges Varnum and Parsons met at Marietta and began the duty of legislating for the Territory, continuing in session until December. Contrary to the provisions of the ordinance, they enacted a number of laws on different subjects and submitted them to Congress, as required. That body, however, did not approve them from their manifest illegality under the terms of the ordinance. After the assembling of Congress in 1789, under the new constitution, the appointments made under the articles of confederation being deemed to have expired, the following new Judges were appointed for the Northwest Territory. Samuel Holden Parsons, John Cleves Symmes and William Barton. The latter declined to serve and George Turner was appointed to fill the vacancy. Judge Parsons soon afterward died, and in March, 1790, Rufus Putnam was appointed to fill the vacancy caused by his death. Putnam resigned in 1796, to enable him to accept the office of Surveyor General, and Joseph Gilman, of Point Harmar, was chosen to fill the vacancy. Judge Turner left the Territory in the spring of 1796, and during his absence resigned his seat on the bench, which was filled by the appointment of Return Jonathan Meigs, in February, 1798. The Judges then in commission continued to hold their seats until the adoption of a State Constitution.

Between 1790 and 1795, numerous acts were passed which did not receive the sanction of Congress, as they were enacted rather than adopted, and finally in the summer of 1795, at a legislative session held at Cincinnati, a code of laws was adopted from the statutes of the original States, which superseded the chief part of those previously enacted, that had remained in force in the Territory, regardless of their doubtful constitutionality. This code of laws as adopted was printed at Cincinnati in 1795, by William Maxwell, and became known as the Maxwell Code; that was the first job of printing executed in the Northwestern Territory. But very little change was made therefrom until the first session of the General Assembly, held under the second grade of government, September 16, 1799.

"The ordinance and the compact," says Judge Burnet, "which was the constitution of the Territory, contained but little specific legislation. It prescribed the rule of descents; the mode of transferring real estate, by deed of lease and release, and of devising or bequeathing it by will. It regulated the right of dower and authorized the transfer of personal property by delivery; saving always to the French and Canadian inhabitants, and other settlers who had before professed themselves citizens of Virginia, their laws and customs then in force among them, relative to the descent and conveyance of property. In addition to these provisions, the compact ordained that no person demeaning himself in a peaceable manner should be molested on account of his mode of worship or religious opinions. It also secured to the inhabitants forever the benefits of the writ of habeas corpus, of trial by jury, of a proportionate representation of the people in the Legislature, and of judicial proceedings, according to the course of the Common Law."

The courts of Common Law in the Territory assumed chancery powers as a necessity, as there was no tribunal in said Territory vested with such powers. Several necessary laws were passed at the first session of the Territorial Legislature at Cincinnati, but matters regarding courts and their powers were not satisfactorily settled until the adoption of the first State Constitution in 1802. The General Court provided for by the ordinance of 1787 consisted, as before stated, of three Judges, "appointed by the President with the advice and consent of the Senate, each of whom received a salary of $800 from the Treasury of the United States. It was the highest judicial tribunal in the Territory, and was vested with original and appellate jurisdiction in all civil and criminal cases, and of capital cases; and on questions of divorce and alimony its jurisdiction was exclusive. It was, however, a common law court, merely without chancery powers, and it was the court of *dernier ressort*. It had power to revise and reverse the decisions of all other tribunals in the Territory, yet its own proceedings could not be reversed or set aside, even by the Supreme Court of the United States. It was held at Cincinnati in March, at Marietta in October, at Detroit and in the western counties at such time in each year as the Judges saw proper to designate."

The travels of the Judges and members of the bar in those early years, to and from the places of holding courts—Cincinnati, Marietta and Detroit—were attended with difficulties of the most serious nature. The distances were always great, settlements were scarce and the way was rough. Their journeys were made on horseback, and it was exceedingly necessary that the horses they rode should be good swimmers, for it was in the days before bridges had been thought of, and only the best fording places along the numerous streams were sought out by the tired travelers. Judge Burnet, who knew from experience all the trials of the times, wrote of them as follows:

"The journeys of the court and bar to those remote places through a country in its primitive state, were unavoidably attended with fatigue and exposure. They generally traveled with five or six in company, and with a pack-horse to transport such necessaries as their own horses could not conveniently carry, because no dependence could be placed on obtaining supplies on the route; although they frequently passed through Indian camps and villages, it was not safe to rely on them for asssistance. Occasionally small quantities of corn could be purchased for horse feed, but even that relief was precarious and not to be relied on. In consequence of the unimproved condition of the country, the routes followed by travelers were necessarily circuitous and their progress slow. In passing from one county seat to another, they were generally from six to eight, and sometimes ten days in the wilderness, and, at all seasons of the year, were compelled to swim every water-course in their way which was too deep to be forded; the country being wholly destitute of bridges and ferries, travelers had, therefore, to rely on their horses as the only substitute for those conveniences. That fact made it common, when purchasing a horse, to ask if he were a good swimmer, which was considered one of the most valuable qualities of a saddle horse."

Lynch law was liable to be adopted by the men of the border settlements, and one or two instances of its execution in the form of public whippings are known to have occurred; but in August, 1788, a law was published in Marietta, establishing a "General Court of Quarter Sessions of the Peace, and County Courts of Common Pleas," and these superseded the Lynch code before it had been in operation a year. Mr. McMillan was appointed the Presiding Judge of those courts in the county of Hamilton.

The first Constitution of the State of Ohio, adopted November 29, 1802, contained in its third article the following provisions for the judicial government of the State:

SECTION 1. The judicial power of this State, both as to matters of law and equity, shall be vested in a Supreme Court, in Courts of Common Pleas for each county, in Justices of the Peace, and in such other courts as the Legislature may from time to time establish.

SEC. 2. The Supreme Court shall consist of three Judges, any two of whom shall be a quorum. They shall have original and appellate jurisdiction, both in common law and chancery in such cases as shall be directed by law; *Provided*, That nothing herein contained shall prevent the General Assembly from adding another Judge to the Supreme Court after the term of five years, in which case the Judges may divide the State into two circuits, within which any two of the Judges may hold a court.

SEC. 3. The several Courts of Common Pleas shall consist of a President and Associate Judges. The State shall be divided by law into three circuits; there shall be appointed in each circuit a President of the Courts, who, during his continuance in office, shall reside therein. There shall be appointed in each county not more than three nor less than two Associate Judges, who, during their continuance in office, shall reside therein. The President and Associate Judges in their respective counties, any three of whom shall be a quorum, shall compose the Court of Common Pleas, which

HISTORY OF WYANDOT COUNTY. 357

court shall have common law and chancery jurisdiction in all such cases as shall be directed by law; *Provided*, That nothing herein contained shall be construed to prevent the Legislature from increasing the number of circuits and Presidents after the term of five years.

SEC. 4. The Judges of the Supreme Court and Courts of Common Pleas shall have complete criminal jurisdiction in such cases and in such manner as may be pointed out by law.

SEC. 5. The Court of Common Pleas in each county shall have jurisdiction of all probate and testamentary matters, granting administration, the appointment of guardians, and such other cases as shall be prescribed by law.

SEC. 6. The Judges of the Court of Common Pleas shall, within their respective counties, have the same powers with the Judges of the Supreme Court, to issue writs of certiorari to the Justices of the Peace, and to cause their proceedings to be brought before them, and the like right and justice to be done.

SEC. 7. The Judges of the Supreme Court shall, by virtue of their offices, be conservators of the peace throughout the State. The Presidents of the Courts of Common Pleas shall, by virtue of their offices, be conservators of the peace in their respective circuits; and the Judges of the Court of Common Pleas shall, by virtue of their offices, be conservators of the peace in their respective counties.

SEC. 8. The Judges of the Supreme Courts, the Presidents and the Associate Judges of the Courts of Common Pleas, shall be appointed by a joint ballot of both Houses of the General Assembly, and shall hold their offices for the term of seven years, if so long they behave well. The Judges of the Supreme Court and the Presidents of the Courts of Common Pleas shall, at stated times, receive for their services an adequate compensation, to be fixed by law, which shall not be diminished during their continuance in office; but they shall receive no fees or perquisites of office, nor hold any other office of profit or trust under the authority of this State or the United States.

SEC. 9. Each court shall appoint its own Clerk for the term of seven years; but no person shall be appointed Clerk, except *pro tempore*, who shall not produce to the court appointing him a certificate from the majority of the Judges of the Supreme Court that they judge him to be well qualified to execute the duties of the office of Clerk to any court of the same dignity with that for which he offers himself. They shall be removable for breach of good behavior at any time by the Judges of the respective courts.

SEC. 10. The Supreme Court shall be held once a year in each county, and the Courts of Common Pleas shall be holden in each county at such times and places as shall be prescribed by law.

SEC. 11. A competent number of Justices of the Peace shall be elected by the qualified electors in each township in the several counties, and shall continue in office three years, whose powers and duties shall, from time to time, be regulated and defined by law.

SEC. 12. The style of all processes shall be "The State of Ohio;" all prosecutions shall be carried on in the name and by the authority of the State of Ohio, and all indictments shall conclude against the peace and dignity of the same.

The new constitution of Ohio, adopted June 17, 1851, made various changes in the courts, and Article 4, providing for judicial matters in the State, is as follows:

SECTION 1. The judicial power of the State shall be vested in a Supreme Court, in District Courts, Courts of Common Pleas, Courts of Probate, Justices of the Peace, and in such other courts, inferior to the Supreme Court, as the General Assembly may from time to time establish.

SEC. 2. The Supreme Court shall consist of five Judges, a majority of whom shall be necessary to form a quorum or pronounce a decision. It shall have original jurisdiction in quo warranto, mandamus, habeas corpus and procedendo, and such appellate jurisdiction as may be provided by law. It shall hold at least one term in each year at the seat of government, and such other terms at the seat of government or elsewhere as may be provided by law. The Judges of the Supreme Court shall be elected by the electors of the State at large.

SEC. 3. The State shall be divided into nine Common Pleas districts, of which the county of Hamilton shall constitute one, of compact territory and bounded by county lines; and each of said districts, consisting of three or more counties, shall be subdivided into three parts of compact territory, bounded by county lines, and as nearly equal in population as practicable, in each of which one Judge of Common Pleas for said district, and residing therein, shall be elected by the electors of said subdivision. Courts of Common Pleas shall be held by one or more of these Judges in every county in the district as often as may be provided by law; and more than one court or sitting thereof may be held at the same time in each district.

SEC. 4. The jurisdiction of the Courts of Common Pleas and of the Judges thereof shall be fixed by law.

SEC. 5. District Courts shall be composed of the Judges of the Courts of Common Pleas of the respective districts, and one of the Judges of the Supreme Court, any three of whom shall be a quorum, and shall be held in each county therein at least once in each year; but if it shall be found inexpedient to hold such court annually in each county of any district, the General Assembly may, for such district, provide that said court shall be holden at three annual sessions therein, in not less than three places; *Provided*, that the General Assembly may, by law, authorize the Judges of each district to fix the times of holding the courts therein.

SEC. 6. The District Court shall have like original jurisdiction with the Supreme Court, and such appellate jurisdiction as may be provided by law.

SEC. 7. There shall be established in each county a Probate Court, which shall be a court of record, open at all times, and holden by one Judge, elected by the voters of the county, who shall hold his office for the term of three years, and shall receive such compensation, payable out of the county treasury, or by fees, or both, as shall be provided by law.

SEC. 8. The Probate Court shall have jurisdiction in probate and testamentary matters, the appointment of administrators and guardians, the settlement of the accounts of executors, administrators and guardians, and such jurisdiction in *habeas corpus*, the issuing of marriage licenses, and for the sale of land by executors, administrators and guardians, and such other jurisdiction in any county or counties as may be provided by law.

SEC. 9. A competent number of Justices of the Peace shall be elected by the electors in each township in the several counties. Their term of office shall be three years, and their powers and duties shall be regulated by law.

SEC. 10. All Judges other than those provided for in the constitution, shall be elected by the electors of the judicial district for which they may be created, but not for a longer term of office than five years.

SEC. 11. The Judges of the Supreme Court shall, immediately after the first election under this constitution, be classified by lot, so that one shall hold for the term of one year, one for two years, one for three years, one for four years and one for five years; and at all subsequent elections, the term of each of said Judges shall be for five years.

SEC. 12. The Judges of the Courts of Common Pleas shall, while in office, reside in the district for which they are elected; and their term of office shall be for five years.

SEC. 13. In case the office of any Judge shall become vacant before the expiration of the regular term for which he was elected, the vacancy shall be filled by appointment by the Governor, until a successor is elected and qualified ; and such successor shall be elected for the unexpired term at the first annual election that occurs more than thirty days after the vacancy shall have happened.

SEC. 14. The Judges of the Supreme Court and of the Court of Common Pleas shall, at stated times, receive for their services such compensation as may be provided by law, which shall not be diminished or increased during their term of office; but they shall receive no fees or perquisites, nor hold any other office of profit or trust under the authority of this State or the United States. All votes for either of them, for any elective office, except a judicial office, under the authority of this State, given by the General Assembly, or the people, shall be void.

SEC. 15. The General Assembly may increase or diminish the number of the Judges of the Supreme Court, the number of the districts of the Court of Common Pleas, the number of Judges in any district, change the districts or the subdivisions thereof, or establish other courts, whenever two-thirds of the members elected to each House shall concur therein; but no change, addition or diminution shall vacate the office of any Judge.

SEC. 16. There shall be elected in each county, by the electors thereof, one Clerk of the Court of Common Pleas, who shall hold his office for the term of three years, and until his successor shall be elected and qualified. He shall, by virtue of his office, be Clerk of all other courts of record held therein ; but the General Assembly may provide by law for the election of a Clerk, with a like term of office, for each or any other of the courts of record, and may authorize the Judge of the Probate Court to perform the duties of Clerk for his court, under such regulations as may be directed by law. Clerks of courts shall be removable for such cause and in such manner as shall be prescribed by law.

SEC. 17. Judges may be removed from office by concurrent resolution of both Houses of the General Assembly, if two-thirds of the members elected to each House concur therein ; but no such removal shall be made except upon complaint, the substance of which shall be entered upon the journal, nor until the party charged shall have had notice thereof, and an opportunity to be heard.

SEC. 18. The several Judges of the Supreme Court of the Common Pleas and of such other courts as may be created, shall respectively have and exercise such power and jurisdiction, at chambers or otherwise, as may be directed by law.

SEC. 19. The General Assembly may establish Courts of Conciliation, and prescribe their powers and duties ; but such courts shall not render final judgment in any case, except upon submission by the parties, of the matter in dispute, and their agreement to abide such judgment.

SEC. 20. The style of all process shall be, "The State of Ohio ;" all prosecutions shall be carried on in the name and by the authority of the State of Ohio, and all indictments shall conclude, "against the peace and dignity of the State of Ohio."

SUPREME COURTS.

From 1845, until the close of June term, 1851, the higher courts held at Upper Sandusky were designated the Supreme Courts of the State of Ohio, and Judges Reuben Wood, Matthew Birchard, Edward Avery, Nathaniel C. Reed, Peter Hitchcock, William B. Caldwell and Rufus P. Spalding, officiated here at various times in the order named. Then, by a change of the organic law—the adoption of the State Constitution of 1851—district courts were established, and the phrase first mentioned (as applied in Sec. X. Art. 3, of the Constitution of 1802) was abandoned.

DISTRICT COURTS.

The first District Court (a special term) held in Wyandot County, convened for the first time at Upper Sandusky, October 5, 1852. There were present Hon. John A. Corwin, Judge of the Supreme Court, and Lawrence W. Hall and John M. Palmer, Judges of the Court of Common Pleas. The district was then denominated the Third Common Pleas District. Subsequent terms of this court have been held at Upper Sandusky, as follows:

1853—August term, Allen G. Thurman, Supreme Judge; Lawrence W. Hall and Benjamin Metcalf, Judges Court of Common Pleas.

1854—September term, John A. Corwin, Supreme Judge; Lawrence W. Hall and Benjamin Metcalf, Judges Court of Common Pleas.

1855—September term, Lawrence W. Hall, John M. Palmer and Benjamin Metcalf, Judges Court of Common Pleas.

1856—September term, Jacob Brinkerhoff, Supreme Judge; Benjamin Metcalf and Lawrence W. Hall, Judges Court of Common Pleas.

1857—September term, A. Sankey Latta, Machias C. Whitely and William Lawrence, Judges Court of Common Pleas.

1858—September term, T. W. Bartley, Chief Justice of the Supreme Court; A. S. Latta and William Lawrence, Judges Court of Common Pleas.

1859—Third Subdivision of Tenth Judicial District, August term, Milton Sutliff, Supreme Judge; Machias C. Whitely, George E. Seney and Josiah S. Plants, Judges Court of Common Pleas.

1860—Same division and district, June term, William Y. Gholson, Supreme Judge; Machias C. Whitely, George E. Seney and Josiah S. Plants, Judges Court of Common Pleas.

1861—Same division and district, June term, Josiah S. Plants, Machias C. Whitely and George E. Seney, Judges Court Common Pleas.

1862—Same division and district, July term, Josiah Scott, Supreme Judge; Machias C. Whitely and Josiah S. Plants, Judges Court of Common Pleas.

1863—Third Judicial District, June term, Josiah S. Plants, Benjamin Metcalf and Machias C. Whitely, Judges Court of Common Pleas.

1864—Same district, August term, Jacob Brinkerhoff, Judge Supreme Court; William Lawrence, A. S. Latta and Machias C. Whitely, Judges Court of Common Pleas.

1865—Same district, August term, Jacob Brinkerhoff, Judge Supreme Court; A. S. Latta and O. W. Rose, Judges Court of Common Pleas.

1866—Same distrist, August term, Jacob S. Conklin, A. S. Latta and James McKenzie, Judges Court of Common Pleas.

1867—Same district, August term, Josiah Scott, Judge Supreme Court; Jacob S. Conklin, A. S. Latta, James McKenzie and Chester R. Mott, Judges Court of Common Pleas.

1868—Same district, September term, John Welch, Judge Supreme Court; Jacob S. Conklin, James Pillars and Chester R. Mott, Judges Court of Common Pleas.

1869—Same district, September term, William White, Judge Supreme Court; Jacob S. Conklin, James Pillars and Chester R. Mott, Judges Court of Common Pleas.

1870—No term.

1871—Third Judicial District, April term, A. S. Latta, James Pillars and Chester R. Mott, Judges Court of Common Pleas.

1872—No term.

1873—Third Judicial District, March term, James Pillars, A. S. Latta and Abner M. Jackson, Judges Court of Common Pleas.

1874—Same district, April term, James Pillars, A. S. Latta and Abner M. Jackson, Judges Court Common Pleas.

1875—Same district, March term, A. S. Latta, James Pillars and Thomas Beer, Judges Court of Common pleas.

1876—Same district, April term, same Judges as above.

1877—Same district, April term, Thomas Beer, James Pillars and Selwyn N. Owen, Judges Court of Common Pleas.

1878—Same district, March term, same Judges as above.

1879—Same district, March term, same Judges.

1880—Tenth Judicial District, April term, John McCauley, John L. Porter and Henry H. Dodge, Judges Court of Common Pleas.

1881—Same district, March term, Henry H. Dodge, John McCauley and John L. Porter, Judges Court of Common Pleas.

1882—Same district, March term, Henry H. Dodge, John L. Porter and John McCauley, Judges Court of Common Pleas.

1883—Same district, April term, Thomas Beer, Henry H. Dodge and John McCauley, Judges Court of Common Pleas.

1884—Same district, March term, Thomas Beer, Henry H. Dodge and George F. Pendleton, Judges Court of Common Pleas.

COURT OF COMMON PLEAS.

Judge Ozias Bowens, of Marion, presided over the Common Pleas Courts of Wyandot County from July 1, 1845 (the date the first term of court began), until the close of November, 1851, when, by a change of the organic law of the State, his services as the presiding officer of the circuit, as then formed, were brought to a close. On the 28th of November, 1851, the following proceedings took place at Upper Sandusky at a meeting of the members of the bar of the old Second Judicial Circuit of the State of Ohio:

"This day Moses H. Kirby, Esq., on behalf of the members of the bar, appeared in open court and read the following proceedings of a meeting held by said members, which, on motion, is ordered to be entered upon the journal of the court, to wit:

"At a meeting of the members of the bar of the Second Judicial Circuit of the State of Ohio, in attendance upon the court of Common Pleas of the November term 1851, sitting in Wyandot County. On motion, Moses H. Kirby was chosen Chairman, and R. G. Pennington, Secretary. On motion of C. K. Watson, a committee of five was appointed by the chair to draft and submit to the meeting resolutions expressive of the esteem in which the members of the bar of the circuit hold the judicial services and character of the Hon. Ozias Bowen, Presiding Judge of said circuit, upon his retirement from the bench which he has occupied for the term of fourteen years, and also an expression toward the services of the associates who with him occupy the bench. C. K. Watson, J. P. Pillars, J. Plants, J. D. Sears and R. McKelly were appointed such committee, and who reported to the meeting, and which were unanimously adopted, the following preamble and resolutions:

WHEREAS, By a change of the organic law of this State, the official services and duties of the Hon. Ozias Bowen, as President Judge of this judicial circuit are about to close. Therefore, for the purpose of perpetuating the estimation which his judicial services have justly merited and received for a period of fourteen years from the members of the bar of his circuit.

Resolved, That in the discharge of all his official duties, we recognize the character of an able, upright and impartial Judge.

Resolved, That upon a survey of his judicial career, we find nothing to condemn, and in reluctantly parting with him, we indulge the hope that those who succeed him may successfully emulate so fair an example of judicial integrity and ability.

Resolved, That the Hons. Abel Renick, George W. Leith and Hugh Welch, Associate Judges of this county, have conscientiously and faithfully discharged the duties of an honorable office, and will in their retirement bear with them the assurance of the respect and esteem of the community which has enjoyed the benefit of their services.

Resolved, That the proceedings of this meeting be presented to the court with the request that the same be entered upon the journal, and also, that they be published in the several papers in this judicial circuit.   MOSES H. KIRBY,
ROBERT G. PENNINGTON, *Secretary.*   *Chairman.*

Judge Lawrence W. Hall, the successor of Judge Bowen, began his first term of court in Wyandot County March 15, 1852, and continuing through a full constitutional term of five years, terminated his labors here as a Judge at the close of November term, 1856. Hon. William Lawrence, of Bellefontaine, held the next Court of Common Pleas, beginning April 21, 1857. Then came Hon. Machias C. Whitely, of Findlay, who, elected for a term of five years, in October, 1856, presided over the July session, in 1857, and thereafter until the close of April term, 1858. Subsequently, during the remainder of Judge Whitelys' term, Judges George E. Seney (the present member of Congress from this district) and Josiah S. Plants, of Bucyrus, alternately presided over courts held at Upper Sandusky. Judge Plants, however, appears to have performed more work here than either Whitely or Seney, and occupied the bench almost uninterruptedly from the latter part of 1858, until his death in August, 1863, when Judge Whitely again appeared as the presiding officer, and continued until the close of 1864. Then came Hon. Jacob S. Conklin, of Sidney, in May, 1865, succeeded by Judge Whitely, who presided for one year, beginning with October term, 1865.

Judge Chester R. Mott, of Upper Sandusky, was elected in October, 1866, and served a term of five years. Meanwhile, during the same term, Judges James McKenzie, James Pillars and E. M. Phelps, also presided at various Courts of Common Pleas held at Upper Sandusky. Judge Mott's successor, Hon. Abner M. Jackson, of Bucyrus, was elected in October, 1871. He served until the summer of 1874, when he resigned and removed to Cleveland, and afterward to Colorado. To fill out his unexpired term, the Governor appointed the present incumbent, Hon. Thomas Beer, also a resident of Bucyrus.

Of some of the Judges of the Court of Common Pleas mentioned in the foregoing paragraphs, we append the following biographical sketches.

Hon. Ozias Bowen, who died September 26, 1871, was one of the giants of the Marion County bar. Born July 23, 1805, in Oneida County, N. Y.; not much is known of his early career, but sufficient has been preserved to establish the fact that he was reared amid a community of outspoken, heroic, high-principled people, and these early surroundings gave a permanent basis for his moral character. When a youth of eighteen, he appeared in Ashtabula County, Ohio, where he studied law and was admitted to the bar, and where he also published a weekly newspaper. In 1828, he became a resident of Marion, Ohio, and after engaging in teaching and merchandizing for a brief period, he resumed the practice of his profession, rising to the positions of Prosecuting Attorney, and Judge of the Court of Common Pleas, which last-named position he held with credit to himself and benefit to the community for fourteen years, his circuit extending at one time as far northward as Lake Erie. A seat on the bench of the Supreme Court of Ohio was also awarded to him. In whatever tended to advance the welfare of the people, he took a deep interest; education found in him its warm advocate; all churches alike shared his bounty, although the Presbyterian community claimed him as its especial member. The cause of the slave found in Judge Bowen an ardent advocate, and his associations were ever with the Republican party. He was the friend and coadjutor of such men as Salmon P. Chase, Columbus Delano and the like. His fine residence in the southern part of the town of Marion attested that his labors had met with their due pecuniary reward. In physique, he was five feet and eleven inches in height, while his weight was nearly two hundred pounds, thus attesting that a vigorous body is ever the basis of a vigorous mind.

Judge Bowen's profession and the practice of it made him a prominent and noticeable character, not only in the town and county where he lived, but throughout the State, and to him, as a lawyer, more attention should be given than to any other phase of his character. He was a leading lawyer, eminent and successful, the peer of any with whom he came in contact professionally. He was not a fluent or eloquent speaker, and brought to his aid none of the graces or tricks of voice or action of the trained elocutionist. As an advocate he was reasonable, logical, plain, fair, direct and powerful, and although he could not sway or control a court or jury by bursts of eloquence, yet he had immense influence as a shrewd, argumentative reasoner. He was a good judge of men and character, and had what has always been the element or secret of success in every department of man's work—a vast amount of good, solid common sense.

In his practice, he was fair, bold, fearless and dignified, always commanding and securing the attention and respect of the court.

He was exceedingly careful in giving advice and counseling in litigation, always desiring to avoid and keep out of bad cases; but when he had determined to go on he entered upon the work of the preparation and trial of his cases with the determination to succeed, and no client could ever charge him with neglect or want of zeal. His many years of practice and his long experience as a judge made him exceedingly familiar with the law and especially rules of court and of practice. Yet even in his later years, he never went into court, in even the smallest of cases, without a brief, both of facts and of law. With good natural qualifications and long experience, he put no especial dependence in either, but did depend on the results of special preparation and labor in every case. His secret of success was indomitable energy and unremitting labor. He kept a common-place book, in which were noted the results of his investigations, and always ready and at hand; he had a brief when any subject came before him a second time. Every trial in which he was engaged found him with a full and especially prepared brief, and every one was tried with a view of taking it to a higher court if he did not secure on the first trial what he thought he ought to have, and his cases will show that even where he was beaten below, he was most likely to be successful in the end. He was a bold, hard fighter, and like every strong, uncompromising character, made some enemies, but the profession will always recognize him as one of the strongest men at the bar in Northern Ohio in his day. His thoroughness was remarkable and his attention to details equally so. His students will always remember one direction which he gave as to the conduct of trials, viz., "Never omit to make *every* point in your case, no matter how trifling or small it may seem to you, for although it may look trifling, yet it may be the decisive point in the mind of the court or jury to which you are trying the case." This notice of Judge Bowen's professional character and career would not be complete if we failed to note one beautiful trait in that character, and that is his uniform kindness and courtesy to the young men of his profession. All who were so fortunate as to practice with him will remember this. No young man ever appealed to him for professional assistance in vain, when he was free and could give it. He gave the benefit of his experience and counsel willingly and joyfully, and always had a kind and encouraging word to those who felt the embarrassment of inexperience. The young lawyers who were about him remember him gratefully. To do the life and professional character of Judge Bowen justice, we cannot, probably, better sum up the whole matter than by saying, "He was a great lawyer." *

Hon. William Lawrence resided at Bellefontaine, Logan County. He was a well-read lawyer, possessed remarkable industry and energy, and was a satisfactory Judge. Morally, he was religious and without blemish. He was always pleasant and affable, and was popular both with the people and the bar. He was a former resident of Morgan County, this State. At the opening of the court in May, 1861, when the people were excited about the war, he ordered the Sheriff to raise the national flag over the cupola of the court house in Marion, which order the Sheriff refused to obey. The latter was therefore brought into court and fined for contempt. He then hoisted the flag according to the original order. In 1862, Judge Lawrence went to the front as Colonel in command of a regiment of volunteers. While in the service his salary as Judge continued, which he drew and distributed to the school districts throughout his circuit. In the fall of 1864, he was elected to a seat in Congress, and resigned his position upon the bench to enter upon his new round of duties. Near the close of the term of President Hayes he was appointed First Comptroller of the United States Treasury, which position he now occupies.

Hon. Josiah S. Plants, of Bucyrus, was a gentleman of sterling worth and popular with all classes. In August, 1863, while hunting in Indiana, he was accidentally wounded by his own piece from the effects of which he died. He was then serving a second term as Judge of the Common Pleas Court of his district.

Hon. Chester R. Mott, of Upper Sandusky, is mentioned in the article entitled "The Bar" of this volume, also in the history of the town of Upper Sandusky, to which readers are referred.

---
* From an article prepared by J. F. McNeal, Esq.

Hon. Thomas Beer, of Bucyrus, was born in Wayne County, Ohio, September 7, 1832. His literary course of studies was completed at the Vermilion Institute, Hayesville, Ashland County, Ohio, and in 1848 he began teaching school. Having chosen law as a profession, he commenced its study with John C. Tidball, Esq., of Coshocton, in 1851, teaching school meanwhile to defray expenses, and remained with him until 1853. From 1854 to 1858, he served as postmaster at Alliance, Ohio. In the latter year he became editor of the *Stark County Democrat* at Canton, Ohio, and in 1862, editor of the *Crawford County Forum*. He was admitted to the bar in 1862, and began to practice at Bucyrus, Ohio. In 1863, he was elected to represent Crawford County in the State Legislature, and was re-elected, thus serving through the sessions of 1864–66, 1866–68. He also served as a member of the Constitutional Convention held at Columbus and Cincinnati in 1873–4. On the 15th of August, 1874, he was appointed by the Governor, Judge of the Common Pleas Court, for the Fourth Subdivision of the Third Judicial District of Ohio, then comprising the counties of Wood, Hancock, Seneca, Wyandot, Crawford and Marion. In October, 1874, he was elected to fill the unexpired term of Judge Jackson, who had resigned. In 1876, he was re-elected for the full term of five years, and in 1881, was again re-elected to serve until February 9, 1887. As a practitioner Judge Beer was fair and honorable. On the bench he is not rapid in his decisions, but takes time to fortify himself with precedents, which practice leads the people to regard him as a careful, impartial and upright Judge.

Wyandot County is now, with Crawford and Marion, in the Second Subdivision of the Tenth Judicial District of the State.

Prior to the adoption of the State Constitution of 1851, those who, as residents of Wyandot County, sat on the bench as Associate Judges, were Abel Renick, William Brown, George W. Leith, Joseph Chaffee, A. M. Anderson and Hugh Welch, all of whom were Whigs.

THE BAR.

Respecting those who, as resident attorneys, have practiced at the Wyandot County bar during the past forty years, the results of many hours of labor, passed in patient, diligent research, are placed before the reader as follows: It is first explained, however, that the names of those now practicing in the county, are marked by an asterisk, and that more extended sketches concerning many will be found in the biographical notes attached to the history of the town of Upper Sandusky.

Jude Hall, Esq., who is mentioned as the first resident attorney at Upper Sandusky, established an office here for the transaction of legal business as early as the year 1843, and remained some three or four years thereafter. He is remembered and spoken of by the oldest inhabitants as a rather eccentric character, a hard worker in the cause of his clients, a ready debater, and could, when he deemed the occasion fitting, pour forth into the ears of lenient Judges, and wondering, almost awe-stricken jurors, stilted, grandiloquent rhetoric without stint. The following amusing reminiscences respecting Mr. Hall have been furnished us by his early cotemporary, John D. Sears, Esq.

"The reminiscent first saw Jude Hall in 1844, during a term of the Common Pleas of Crawford County, where he defended a client, from the western part of the county who had been indicted for perjury in swearing to an answer in chancery. His principal ground of defense, and which was urged with great vehemence and much iteration, was, that there had been no intentional perjury, but that the unlucky falsehood was "a mere discrepancy of the pen." The defendant was acquitted. At another term of the same court, held in the same year, our learned advocate was trying an action of trespass for hog-stealing, brought into court by appeal from Crawford Township. Among the adverse witnesses was the pettifogger who had been pitted against Jude before the Justice, and whom, in his argument to the jury, he demolished in the words and figures of speech following: 'Gentlemen of the jury, you may put one foot upon Hercules, and the other upon Jupiter, and lay your telescope, astraddle of the sun, and gaze over this wide creation, and you can't find as mean a man as John Smith." At another time, when trying a case in a Justice's court at Bucyrus, he attacked and overwhelmed the opposing counsel, with this pondrous climax: "Why, your honor! He's a mere circumstance, a fabric, a ruta baga." The writer was present at a trial in the high court of Osceola, then presided over by Bishop Tuttle, when Hall was counsel for the defendant, and Col., afterward, Judge Scott, represented the plaintiff. At the close of the plaintiff's testimony, the usual motion for a non-suit was made and argued, and Jude began his closing speech, in this crushing and magniloquent style: "The gentleman may roar like a salamander, but my positions are adamantine, and must prevail." With these few specimen bricks, we dismiss this erratic genius, whose stay with us was as brief as it was brilliant. We never shall see his like again, nor know we whence he came or whither went. Peace to his metaphors, his climaxes and his allegories."

Hon. Chester R. Mott* was born in Susquehanna County, Penn., July 15, 1813. Having obtained an excellent common school and academic education, he engaged for a brief period in teaching at Erie, Penn. Subsequently he studied law under the instructions of J. W. Riddle and William Lyon, of Erie, and in 1837 was admitted to practice. He continued at Erie until the spring of 1844, when he removed to the town of Upper Sandusky. He assisted in the organization of Wyandot County, and in the spring of 1845, was elected its first Prosecuting Attorney. He was elected County Auditor in 1849, and re-elected to the same position in 1851. In 1857, he was chosen to represent the counties of Hardin and Wyandot in the State Legislature. He was again elected Prosecuting Attorney of Wyandot in 1865. The following year he was elected Judge of the Court of Common Pleas for the Fourth Subdivision of the Third Judicial District, composed of Crawford, Hancock, Seneca and Wyandot Counties, for the full constitutional term of five years. He has also served as Mayor of the town of Upper Sandusky, and as an efficient member of the Board of Education.

Hon. Moses H. Kirby,* who for many years has enjoyed the distinction of being the oldest member of the Wyandot County bar, was born in Halifax County, Va., May 21, 1798. He graduated from the University of North Carolina in 1820, and returning to Hillsboro, Highland Co., Ohio (to which place his widowed mother had removed from Virginia, in 1815), at once began the study of law under Richard Collins, Esq. Three years later he was admitted to practice, and the same year (1823) was appointed Prosecuting Attorney for Highland County, which office he held for seven years. In 1826, he was elected to represent Highland County in the State Legislature, and being re-elected from time to time served in the same position until 1831, when by a joint ballot of the Senate and House of Representatives, he was elected Secretary of the State for a term of three years.

At the expiration of his term as State Secretary he resumed the practice of law at Columbus, Ohio. Subsequently he was elected and served as Prosecuting Attorney for Franklin County, Ohio. In 1842, he was appointed by President Tyler Receiver of the United States Land Office at Lima, Ohio, where he remained until the summer of 1843, when the office was removed to Upper Sandusky. After the expiration of his term of service as Land Receiver, he once more resumed the practice of his profession in the town which has since been his continuous place of residence—Upper Sandusky. He was appointed Prosecuting Attorney of Wyandot County in 1847, to fill a vacancy caused by the resignation of Mr. Mott, and, in an alternate manner, has since served in the same capacity for a period of twenty years. In 1858, he was elected Probate Judge, serving two terms, and in 1879, the people of his district chose him as their Representative in the State Senate. He was re-elected to the same office in 1881, and concluded the term to the entire satisfaction of his constituents.

Hon. John D. Sears,* a leading member of the Wyandot County bar since the county's organization, was born in Delaware County, N. Y., February 2, 1821. He became a resident of Crawford County, Ohio, in 1836, and soon after entered the Ohio University at Athens, where his literary studies as a student were completed. Afterward he studied law at Bucyrus, with Hon. Josiah Scott (since Chief Justice), and in 1844 was admitted to the bar. On the 3d of March, 1845, he settled in the town of Upper Sandusky, then a hamlet of less than a dozen buildings of all classes, and has ever since taken an active part in promoting its prosperity, as well as that of the whole county. He has not been an office-seeker, but has given his attention to the practice of his profession, in which he occupies a conspicuous place, being regarded as an able and sound attorney. However, in 1873, he was elected and served as a member of the Third State Constitutional Convention which assembled at Columbus, Ohio. He served on the judiciary and other important committees, and was recognized as one of the ablest and most accomplished members of that body. He has also served as Mayor, and for many years as School Examiner, member of the Board of Education, etc., of the thriving town which has entirely grown up under his personal observation.

Hon. Robert McKelly* is another whose name stands out conspicuously in the history of Wyandot County. He was born in Lancaster County, Penn., April 8, 1815. He became a resident of Ohio in 1834, and after reading law under Henry B. Curtis, Esq., and Col. John K. Miller, was admitted to the bar in 1842. The same year, he began to practice his profession at Bucyrus, where he remained until the summer of 1845, when he removed to Upper Sandusky, and assumed the duties of Register of the United States Land Office, a position to which he had been appointed by President Polk, and which he held for three years. He became the first Probate Judge of Wyandot County under the constitution adopted in 1851. In 1857, he was elected to represent the Thirty-first District, composed of Crawford, Seneca and Wyandot Counties, in the State Senate. He also served as Director and President of the Ohio & Indiana Railroad before its consolidation with other lines, under the title of the Pittsburgh, Fort Wayne & Chicago Railroad. He is the present Prosecuting Attorney of this (Wyandot) County.

Capt. Peter A. Tyler was a resident of McCutchenville long before the organization of Wyandot County. About 1852, he removed to Upper Sandusky, where he continued to reside until his death. In April, 1861, he recruited a company of Wyandot County men and joined the Fifteenth Regiment of Ohio Volunteer Infantry, serving with that command as Captain for a term of three months. Subsequently, he led into the field another company of Wyandot County Volunteers. (See Military Record in this work). Some time after the war he became involved in a personal difficulty at Bucyrus, Ohio, which resulted in his being wounded by a pistol shot, of which injury he died soon after at Upper Sandusky.

William K. Wear, who is mentioned as an attorney at Upper Sandusky as early as the spring of 1845, came here from Highland County, Ohio. Possessing neither transcendent abilities nor good looks (he had a stiff neck, carrying his head to one side, and was deaf in one ear), and prone to indulge in transactions not altogether reputable, he did not prove to be a success in this field. After tarrying here for a year or so, he left one day or night in a rather hurried manner, proceeding southerly, and breathing maledictions against John D. Sears, Esq., which are best repeated by the "Judge" himself. Wear was last heard from in California.

Hon. George W. Beery, Sr., President of the Wyandot County Bank, was born in Fairfield County, Ohio, July 22, 1822. In June, 1847, he became a resident of Upper Sandusky, and, with Aaron Lyle as a partner, engaged in the practice of law under the title of Beery & Lyle. This partnership continued for two years, when Col. Lyle started for California, dying en route. Mr. Beery, however, kept on in the practice of his profession until the inauguration of the internal revenue system, during the late civil war, when he was appointed by President Lincoln Internal Revenue Assessor for the (then) Fifth Congressional District of the State of Ohio. After being relieved from the duties of that office by Andrew Johnson, he organized the Wyandot County Bank, of which flourishing institution he has been President since April 1, 1867, the date of its organization. Mr. Beery has ever been known as a man of great positiveness and strength of character—a most worthy and honorable citizen, and a public-spirited, noble-hearted gentleman.

Col. Aaron Lyle, already mentioned as the law partner, for a brief period, of George W. Beery, Esq., also came to Upper Sandusky from Fairfield County, Ohio, in the summer of 1847. Soon after, he was elected Prosecuting Attorney, but he did not continue long in that position, for in April, 1849, accompanied by Col. A. McElvain and Editor William T. Giles, he started overland for the California gold fields. He died en route, and was buried far from the haunts of civilization.

S. R. McBane, an attorney at law, came to Upper Sandusky about the year 1848, but remained only a short time. Of his subsequent career we have derived no information.

Hon. B. P. Smith was for some years a resident at Carey. He was an able attorney, and during his residence in this county served as a member of the State Constitutional Convention of 1850–51. He removed from Carey to Huron County, Ohio.

B. F. Ogle and A. F. Anderson, attorneys at law, also resided at Carey years ago.

Henry Maddux, a native of Somerset County, Md., was born July 7, 1819. He became a resident of Marion County, Ohio, in the spring of 1836. In 1846, he came to Wyandot County. Subsequently he studied law, and at June term, 1851, was admitted to the bar. He was appointed School Examiner in 1853, which position he held until 1868, when he resigned and removed to Springfield. Ohio. In the spring of 1870, he returned to Upper Sandusky, and soon after was elected Prosecuting Attorney. Mr. Maddux was quite successful in the accumulation of worldly wealth, and during the last years of his life served as a Director of the First National Bank of Upper Sandusky. His death occurred during recent years.

Nelson W. Dennison, known to early residents of Upper Sandusky as an attorney at law, also as the publisher and editor of the *Democratic Vindicator* for a brief period, removed to Boonesboro, Boone Co., Iowa, in the summer of 1857.

Col. Cyrus Sears, a brother of Hon. John D. Sears, was admitted to the bar in September, 1856. During the late civil war he rendered efficient service as Lieutenant of a battery of light artillery, and as Colonel of a colored regiment. (See his biography, also Chapter 12, of this work). For about three years after the close of the war of the rebellion he practiced law with his brother before mentioned. He is now engaged in various business pursuits in this county, having abandoned the legal profession.

Hon. John Berry was born in the region now embraced by Wyandot County April 26, 1833. After completing his literary studies at the Wesleyan University, Delaware, Ohio, he began the study of law at Upper Sandusky with Hon. Robert McKelly. Subsequently he attended the Cincinnati Law School, graduated therefrom with honor, and was admitted to the bar in April, 1857. He then became identified with the interests of Upper Sandusky and resided here until his death. Although he was a gentleman possessed of much ability and widely esteemed, yet it appears that he preferred the practice of his profession rather than office-holding. However, he served as Mayor of Upper Sandusky, and as Prosecuting Attorney for the county, and in 1872 was elected to represent the Fourteenth Ohio District in the United States House of Representatives, 1873–75.

Hon. Curtis Berry, Jr.,* a brother of Hon. John Berry, was also "to the manor born," a native of the territory now known as Wyandot County. Having completed his literary course of studies at the Ohio Wesleyan University, Delaware, Ohio, he read law at Upper Sandusky under the instructions of his talented brother, and at June term, 1860, of the Wyandot County Court, was admitted to the bar. He has since served three terms as Clerk of Courts for Wyandot County. He also represented the Thirty-first District, consisting of Seneca, Crawford and Wyandot Counties, in the State Senate, during the years 1866–68 and 1868–70. Mr. Berry, now an invalid, resides in the eastern part of the town of Upper Sandusky, on grounds rendered historic, as the place where Col. Crawford's men stopped to quench their thirst, at a spring, on their outward march in June, 1782; as the site of Fort Ferree, war of 1812–15, and as the place where William Walker, of Wyandot Indian memory, resided. He has been known as a firm Democrat, a good attorney, and a forcible speaker.

D. A. Harrison, who was chiefly employed while here as Superintendent of the Public Schools, at Upper Sandusky, now resides in the town of Springfield, Ohio.

Henry A. Hoyt, who was associated with Hon. Robert McKelly for a brief period, is a present resident of the State of Iowa.

George Crawford, Esq., known years ago as a young attorney at Upper Sandusky, also as a gallant soldier during the war of the rebellion, is the present publisher and editor of the *Independent*, at Marion, Ohio.

George G. White,* Esq., now and for a number of years past known as a resident attorney in active practice, was admitted to the bar in August, 1867.

Western Biogl. Pub Co

*Yours truly
R. M. Kelly*

Thomas E. Grisell,* Esq., a native of Columbiana County, Ohio, came to Upper Sandusky in 1852. In 1854, he was elected Clerk of Courts of Wyandot County, and served a term of three years. Besides attending to his law practice, he has found time to engage in other business pursuits, which have been conducted in a very successful manner. He is an able lawyer and highly respected as a citizen.

Elza Carter,* a member of the present Wyandot County bar, is a partner of the gentleman above mentioned (Grisell).

Hon. Darius D. Hare,* the present Mayor of the town of Upper Sandusky, was born in Seneca County, Ohio, January 9, 1843. He completed his literary studies at the Wesleyan University, Delaware, Ohio, in 1863. In 1864, he enlisted in the Signal Corps of the United States Army, in which service he continued till the close of hostilities. Subsequently he was detailed, in the same service, as Clerk at the headquarters of Gen. Sheridan at New Orleans, till discharged by Special Order of the War Department in 1866. He then entered the Law Department of the Michigan University at Ann Arbor, and after a thorough course of studies, was admitted to the bar by the District Court of Wyandot County, in September, 1867. He practiced at Carey for a brief period, but in 1868 located in Upper Sandusky, which has since been his place of residence. He has served as City Solicitor, as Mayor, and as a member of the Board of School Examiners for this county through several terms. Although one of the youngest members of the present bar, Mr. Hare has built up an extensive and lucrative practice, and is known as one of the ablest expounders of the law in Wyandot County.

Allen Smalley,* Esq., was born December 26, 1841, in Ashland County, Ohio. With his father's family he became a resident of Wyandot County in 1854. In the spring of 1862, he enlisted in the Forty-ninth Ohio Infantry, in which command he served nearly one year, or until discharged for disability. After recovering his health, he attended the Ohio Wesleyan University at Delaware, through two terms. In the spring of 1864, he again entered the service of the United States as a member of the Signal Corps. He was with Commodore Farragut's fleet at Mobile, Ala. After the close of the war he entered the Law Department of the Michigan University, and graduated from that institution in 1868. Soon after, he was admitted to the bar at Olney, Ill., where he practiced until 1870. Subsequently he passed some months in the South. Next he taught school in Posey County, Ind., for five months. Then he returned to Wyandot County. Since 1874, besides practicing his profession, he has served as Justice of the Peace, and as an active member and officer of the County Agricultural Society.

Hon. Peter B. Beidler,* was born in Berks County, Penn., December 23, 1818. He became a resident of this region in 1842, was elected County Surveyor of Crawford County in 1843, assisted in the organization of Wyandot County in 1845, and after a close contest with Azariah Root, was by order of court awarded the same position in the new county of Wyandot. Since that time he has served as County Surveyor through several terms. Also as Probate Judge for nine consecutive years, and as Mayor of the town of Upper Sandusky. He was admitted to the bar in 1874.

George G. Bowman, Esq., now a successful attorney in the State of Nebraska, was a member of the Wyandot bar some ten years ago.

Adam Kail, Esq., a resident of the county from early boyhood, and who had served as a volunteer during the war of the rebellion, was also an attorney of considerable ability. He died of consumption in Florida in December, 1881.

Hon. Willard D. Tyler, a son of Capt. Peter A. Tyler, now resides in the State of Texas. He served one term as prosecuting attorney for Wyandot County, and represented the same county in the State Legislature during the sessions of 1878–80, and 1880–82.

William F. Pool,* Esq., was born in Richland County, Ohio, July 23, 1848. Having obtained a good English education, he began teaching at the age of nineteen, and continued in that occupation until 1872, when he began the study of law under the preceptorship of Henry Maddux, Esq., of Upper Sandusky. He was admitted to the bar in 1875, and at once began to practice in the Wyandot County courts. He was for a time associated with George G. Bowman, and subsequently with Adam Kail until the death of the latter.

Judge Joel W. Gibson* was born in that part of Crawford County, Ohio, now known as Wyandot, December 19, 1842. His education was chiefly acquired in the public schools. In 1862, he enlisted in the One Hundred and Twenty-third Ohio Infantry, and with that gallant command participoted in numerous actions fought in the Valley of Virginia. He was severely wounded in the right leg in the battle of Winchester, June 15, 1863, and fell into the enemy's hands. A few days later, an amputation of the wounded member was successfully performed. He was honorably discharged, and for a few years was engaged in various occupations. He has served as Revenue Collector, Justice of the Peace, and Probate Judge. In 1875, he was admitted to the bar. After retiring from the office of Probate Judge, in February, 1883, he formed a partnership for the practice of law with Hon. Robert McKelly. This firm still continues.

Enoch D. Bare,* Esq., was born in Richland County, Ohio, September 16, 1848. His education was obtained in the public schools, supplemented by a course of studies at the Northwestern Normal School of Ohio. He began teaching at the age of eighteen, and continued that occupation during the major portion of his time until 1874, when he commenced the study of law in the office of Hons. John and Curtis Berry, Jr., of Upper Sandusky. He was admitted to the bar in April, 1876, and at once entered upon the practice of his profession at Upper Sandusky, his present place of residence.

Darius D. Clayton,* Esq., the present Probate Judge of this county, was born in Pitt Township, Wyandot County, Ohio, February 19, 1850. His literary studies were completed in the Wesleyan University at Delaware, Ohio, and the Oberlin College of same State. He graduated from the last-named institution in 1876. In 1877, he began the-study of law under the instruction of Darius D. Hare, Esq., and November 8, 1878, was admitted to the bar at Columbus, Ohio. His term as Probate Judge began February 12, 1883.

Robert Carey,* Esq., was born in Ontario, Canada, February 17, 1845. Having completed his studies in the Toronto Provincial Normal School, he early engaged in the occupation of teaching, and continued as an instructor in Canada and the United States, until 1877 when he began the study of law with D. W. Brooks, Esq., of Detroit, Mich. Subsequently he attended the Law Department of the Michigan (Ann Arbor) University, for one year. Then returning to Upper Sandusky, he still further pursued his law studies, under the instruction of Judge Mott, until May 5, 1880, when he was admitted to practice in the various courts of the State.

Milton B. Smith * and W. T. Dickerson,* attorneys at law, are present residents of the town of Carey, where they have been established for a number of years.

James T. Close,* Esq., the youngest member of the present Wyandot County bar, was born in Alexandria City, Va., October 27, 1856. He was educated at Alexandria, Va., Washington, D. C., and Whitestown Seminary, N. Y. In 1874, he began the study of law with Judge Michael Thompson, of Washington, D. C., at the same time attending lectures at the National Law University, and concluding a three years' course in the office of David L. Smoot, of Alexandria, Va. In 1877, he was admltted to practice in the courts of Virginia and the District of Columbia. In 1878, he came to Wyandot County, Ohio, and opened a law office in the town of Nevada. Subsequently he visited the South, and was also employed in the War Department at Washington, D. C. In September, 1882, he became a resident of Upper Sandusky, and in 1883, was appointed official stenographer of the county of Wyandot for a term of three years.

CHAPTER VIII.

THE MEDICAL PROFESSION.

A Writer Confronted by Difficulties—Medical Makeshifts of the Early Settlers—One of the Oldest Describes the Ague—The Physicians of the County in 1845—Early and Present Physicians at Upper Sandusky—A Sketch of Dr. Fowler—Of Dr. Sampson, and of Dr. McConnell.

UNDER this caption, it would be a pleasurable task to mention the names, locations, characteristics, etc., of all regularly educated physicians who have lived and practiced medicine in the region now known as Wyandot County; but from the fact that, as a class, the gentlemen of the medical profession lead a life more nomadic than their brothers of legal accomplishments, that no reminiscences of Wyandot's early medical practitioners have ever been compiled, and that no medical association has ever been formed and perpetuated in the county, the work, at this late day, of compiling a chapter in any respect complete, and within the time placed at our disposal, is wholly impracticable.

The early settlers of this and adjoining counties were great sufferers from "fever and ague," and, occasionally, from another form of disease termed the "milk-sickness." But few of the people being acquainted with the last-mentioned disease, its effects, cure, or prevention, and having but few physicians among them, and those when they first came here were mostly unacquainted with the disease, a large percentage of these cases proved fatal. Some heads of families would obtain from distant towns supplies of jalap, calomel, "tartar mattix," etc., and dose their families and neighbors; others would boil a kettle full of butternut bark, and make a supply of butternut pills, or dig up a quantity of blue-flag, culver, may-apple and blood-root, pulverize and swallow them, or take them in pills or decoctions, just as might suit the fancy of the prescriber or patient. But, as an old resident has said, "We soon had plenty of doctors traversing the highways and byways so much, that any one who wished to be doctored could be so treated to his heart's content."

Another early settler, in describing the fever now termed malarial, writes as follows: "One of the greatest obstacles to the early settlement and prosperity of the West, was the ague, 'fever and ague,' or 'chills and fever,' as it was variously termed. In the fall almost everybody was afflicted with it. It was no respecter of persons. Everybody looked pale and sallow, as though he were frost-bitten. It was not contagious, but was derived from impure water and malaria, such as is abundant in a new country. The impurities from them, combined with those which come from bad dietetics, engorged the liver and deranged the whole vital machinery. By and by, the shock would come, and come in the form of a 'shake,' followed by a fever. These would be regular on certain hours every alternate day, sometimes every day, or every third day. When you had the chill you couldn't get warm, and when you had the fever you couldn't get cool. It was exceedingly awkward in this respect, indeed it was! Nor would it stop for any sort of contingency; not even a wedding in the family would stop it. It was tyranical. When the appointed time came around, everything else had to be stopped to attend to its demands. It didn't have even any Sundays or holidays."

After the fever went down, you still did not feel much better; you felt as though you had gone through some sort of collision, or threshing machine, or jarring machine, and came out, not killed, but you some times wish you had been. You felt weak, as though you had run too far after something, and then didn't catch it. You felt languid, stupid and sore, and was down in the mouth and heel, and partially raveled out. Your back was out of fix; your head ached, and your appetite was crazy. Your eyes had too much white in them; your ears, especially after taking quinine, had too much roar in them, and your whole body and soul were entirely woe-begone, disconsolate, sad, poor and good-for-nothing. You didn't think much of yourself, and didn't believe that other people did, either; and you didn't care. You didn't make up your mind to commit suicide, but sometimes wished some accident would happen to knock either the malady or yourself out of existence. You imagined that even the dogs looked at you with a kind of self-complacency. You felt that even the sun had a sickly shine about it.

About this time you came to the conclusion that you would not accept the whole State of Ohio as a gift; and if you had the strength and means, you picked up Hannah and the baby and your traps and went back "yander to Ole Virginny," "Pennsylvany," Maryland, New York or the "Jarseys." You didn't sing, but you felt the following :

> "And to-day the swallows flitting
> Round my cabin, see me sitting
> Moodily within the sunshine,
> Just inside my silent door.

> "Waiting for the 'ager,' seeming
> Like a man forever dreaming;
> And the sunlight on me streaming
> Throws no shadow on the floor;
> For I'm too thin and sallow
> To make shadows on the floor—
> Nary shadow any more!"

The above is not a mere picture of the imagination. It is simply recounting, in quaint phrase, what actually occurred in thousands of cases. Whole families would sometimes be sick at one time, and not one member scarcely able to wait upon another. Labor or exercise always aggravated the malady, and it took Gen. Laziness a long time to thrash the enemy out. And those were the days for swallowing all sorts of "roots and yarbs," and whisky, etc., with a faint hope of relief. And finally, when the case wore out, the last remedy taken got the credit of the cure.

We have not learned who could justly claim the honor of being the first resident physician in the territory now known as Wyandot County, but it is altogether probable that Tymochtee Township could boast of the continued presence of one of these disciples of Esculapius as early as 1825. In 1845, however, when the first Board of County Commissioners ordered that a special tax of $1 be levied upon each attorney and physician in the county, the physicians mentioned upon the tax lists were as follows : Crane Township, Joseph Mason and David Watson ; Ridge Township, Noah Wilson ; Richland Township, David Adams ; Jackson Township, William Cope ; Marseilles Township,* Wells Chisney and Orrin Ferris; Crawford

---

* Dr. Westbrook, the first physician to locate at Marseilles Village, was there in 1835, also Dr. Hall.

Township, Howard Clark and John Foster ; Tymochtee Township, Alvin Bingham, John Free, Ziba A. Letson, Erastus Ranger, George W. Sampson, and Dr. Dunn; Antrim Township, Augustus W. Munson ; Pitt Township, James H. Drum, Stephen Fowler and James B. McGill.

Among other early physicians at Upper Sandusky, besides Joseph Mason, who died in 1852, and David Watson, were James McConnell, who came in the summer of 1845 ; Madison Fletcher, who located here in 1846 ; Orrin Ferris and William Kiskadden, druggists and physicians, in 1848, and George T. McDonald, also in 1848.

In the list of later and present physicians, we find the names of R. A. Henderson,* William Irwin, Dr. Ramsey, I. H. Williams, J. W. Smalley, Dr. Thompson, Dr. Sigler, Dr. Kilmer, J. W. Barnes, J. W. White,* N. Hardy,* F. J. Schug, R. N, McConnell,* D. W. Byron,* Rudolph Heym, J. W. Rosenberger, Isaac N. Bowman,* W. K. Byron,* G. O. Masky,* L. P. Walter* and J. W. Davis.*

Dr. Stephen Fowler, one of the first physicians to locate within the limits of the present county of Wyandot, and who also served as one of Wyandot's first County Commissioners, died near Little Sandusky December 26, 1847, in the fifty-ninth year of his age.

He was born in Berkshire County, Mass., October 4, 1789. When quite young, his father removed his family to Rutland County, Vt., where the sons were trained as farmers. After attaining his majority, Stephen began the study of medicine. Having completed a thorough course of medical studies, he first began to practice, near the close of the war of 1812-15, in a United States army hospital at Burlington, Vt. He there gained great credit for his skill and success in treating patients suffering with an epidemic fever then prevailing.

Soon after the close of the war referred to, he determined to go South, and, in accordance with his plans, began a journey on horseback from Vermont toward New Orleans ; but when he had reached a point in Bradford County, Penn., he became quite ill. The settlers there, who were chiefly natives of New York and the New England States, then persuaded him to remain with them. He there married Miss Leefe Stevens, raised a large family of children, and obtained a large practice. Indeed, it has been related that his ride was so extensive in Pennsylvania that, during the prevalence of an epidemic disease, he was compelled to keep relays of horses posted upon his circuit. In Pennsylvania, he accumulated quite a handsome competency, and remained there until 1827, when he removed to the "Sandusky Plains," and purchased the beautiful property which he occupied until his death.

He had thought to abandon his profession when settling in Ohio, but he found the country new and unhealthful, and, more with the intention of endeavoring to alleviate the distress of his neighbors than the hope of pecuniary reward, he again engaged in the practice of medicine and followed it in connection with farming with untiring energy until attacked by a dyspeptic disease which finally terminated his signally industrious and useful life. He represented the district composed of Crawford, Marion and Union Counties in the State Legislature during the sessions of 1837-38 and 1838-39. When Wyandot County was organized in 1845, he was elected as one of its first County Commissioners, and was re-elected to the same office and served until October, 1847, when he positively declined another nomination. Dr. Fowler was ever courteous, affable, and unassuming to all men, and

---

* Physicians now in practice.

was highly respected throughout this quarter of the State. His widow still survives, and now resides in the town of Upper Sandusky.

Dr. George W. Sampson settled in Tymochtee Township in the spring of 1828, and at once commenced the practice of medicine. In January, 1830, he removed to and settled at McCutchenville, where he has resided ever since. At the time of his arrival, the road from Upper Sandusky to Tiffin was the only one laid out in this part of the county. All traveling was accomplished by following the Indian trails. His practice extended to Melmore on the east, Little Sandusky on the south, ten miles beyond Find lay on the west, and to Tiffin on the north. Owing to the absence of bridges, he was compelled to ford or swim all streams, and often rode seventy and seventy-five miles in a day and night during the sickly seasons. There are now more than fifty physicians in the same territory.

His first patient was a Mr. Crane, who then lived upon lands now occupied by the town of Carey. A son, about eighteen years of age, came for him on foot, bareheaded, barefooted, and with only enough clothing to cover about one-half of his person. He led the way to where they lived, and it required fast riding, the doctor says, to keep in sight of him.

He practiced a great deal among the Indians, and still has the books on which are the accounts of Hicks, Summundewat, Sarrahos, Warpole, Mononcue, Squindecta, Peacock, Washington and Coon, chiefs among the Wyandots, and Steele, Wiping-stick, Half-John and Comstock among the Senecas. He had long experience and great success in treating "milk sickness," or "trembles." This disease prevailed on the prairies and along the streams, but says he never knew a case below the mouth of Tymochtee Creek.

The Doctor is still engaged in the practice of medicine, and possesses considerable physical vigor and energy, although having performed bodily toil and endured mental anxiety sufficient to have worn out any ordinary man.*

Dr. James McConnell was born in Huntingdon County, Penn., March 8, 1802. As the name indicates, he was of Scotch-Irish origin, a descendant of a class of intelligent, hardy pioneers, who settled the central counties of Pennsylvania prior to the beginning of the Revolutionary war. During that war they were to a man known as stanch patriots, and as determined, successful Indian fighters. After completing a thorough course of literary and medical studies, Dr. McConnell began the practice of his profession at Lewistown, Penn., where he remained for a number of years. In the summer of 1845, he became a resident of Upper Sandusky. Here he resumed practice, and for about a quarter of a century thereafter, stood at the head of his profession. His professional services were in great demand, and though known as a genial, honest, large-hearted man, he accumulated a handsome competency. He retired from the toils and anxieties of his calling in 1868, yet until within a very recent period his tall, lithe form, was daily one of the most familiar objects to be seen upon the streets of Upper Sandusky. Pleasant in his manners and a fluent conversationalist, he was a gentleman well calculated to win and retain the esteem of the public. He died Saturday, April 12, 1884, after an illness of but seven or eight days' duration.

Sketches of other gentlemen of the medical profession will be found in the respective town and township histories of this work.

---

*From a sketch written in 1879.

CHAPTER IX.

THE PRESS.

THE WYANDOTT TELEGRAPH—EXTRACTS FROM ITS COLUMNS—THE PIONEER—
VARIOUS COMMENTS AND EXTRACTS—THE TRIBUNE—THE VINDICATOR—
THE HERALD—THE PIONEER CHANGED TO THE REPUBLICAN—THE CHIEF—
BIOGRAPHICAL—SKETCHES OF WILLIAM T. GILES, ROBERT D. DUMM, LOUIS
A. BRUNNER, PIETRO CUNEO, HENRY A. TRACHT, FRANK T. TRIPP—CAREY
PUBLICATIONS—THE NEVADA ENTERPRISE—THE SYCAMORE NEWS.

UPPER SANDUSKY'S JOURNALS AND JOURNALISTS.

THE following historical account of the newspapers of Upper Sandusky to 1871, are copied almost verbatim from a series of articles which, prepared by Hon. John D. Sears, of Upper Sandusky, were published in The *Wyandot Democratic Union* during the spring of the year above indicated:

It is not designed to make an apology for the order or want of order in these notes; yet, if an excuse is needed for giving precedence to the subject of this chapter, it may be found in the well-known fact that one of the principal objects of the division of the State into counties is to afford an adequate supply of county printing. Our laws have in effect taken care that there shall be no county without its newspaper.

The Act creating the county of Wyandot was passed February 3, 1845, and within two weeks thereafter the *Wyandott Telegraph*, our first newspaper, was established at Upper Sandusky, the new county seat. The date of its first issue is not known to the writer, as his earliest copy is No. 4, Vol. I, dated March 8, 1845. The editor and proprietor was John Shrenk, who had previously published a paper at Bucyrus, and more recently at Kenton, from which latter place he removed to Upper Sandusky.

The politics of this first publication were Whig. "Terms of subscription, one dollar and fifty cents per annum, if paid in four weeks from the time of subscription; otherwise, two dollars will be charged." "Advertisements will be inserted at the following rates: One dollar for three insertions of each square, of twelve lines or less, and twenty-five cents for each subsequent insertion." It was a five-column folio, size, $20\frac{3}{4} \times 27\frac{3}{4}$ inches, and pretty well printed.

Our earliest number of the *Telegraph* contains the proceedings of the first Whig county convention, held at Upper Sandusky on the 5th of March, 1845, and a call signed "Many Democrats," for a meeting of the Democracy on the 15th of March, to make nominations for county officers. There was also an announcement of Maj. Anthony Bowsher as an Independent candidate for Sheriff, and a communication from "A True Democrat," with some unfavorable criticisms of the Major's qualifications for the office, in the course of which the indignant writer says: "When such persons become fit for office, we may look for the end of time." Doubtless we may look for it, but we have elected many worse men, and still Gabriel forbears to blow.

In the editorial columns appeared the following: "We have just received the important news from Washington that Congress has passed a law making a donation of town lots to the county of Wyandot. * * * * It donates one third of the inlots and one-third of the outlots to the county of Wyandot, provided the county seat is established here, for the purpose of putting up public buildings, and improving the streets, public squares and public grounds. * * * * The donation is a noble one, and, if rightly managed and justly appropriated, our citizens will never be subjected to an onerous tax for public buildings. Few new counties have been so highly favored as Wyandot, and we predict for her an unexampled tide of prosperity. * * * * The number of lots which the county will get by the provisions of this law will be 126 inlots and 72 outlots. The outlots contain two acres each. * * * "

The only thing in this number of the *Telegraph* which looks like a local item, is a line at the foot of a column in which it is said, "The Sandusky River is still raising"—and that was not true according to our recollection.

The advertising portion fills a little more than half a column, and is made up of a notice by Moses Dudley & William W. Norton, warning the public against purchasing certain notes made by them, payable to Thomas C. Theaker, and which they say they are determined never to pay, as they were obtained by deception and fraud; the professional card of Benjamin M. Penn, attorney at law, Kenton, Ohio; M. H. Kirby, attorney at law, Upper Sandusky, Ohio; Chester R. Mott, attorney at law, Upper Sandusky, Ohio; J. Lawrence & William K. Wear, attorneys at law, Kenton and Upper Sandusky; Scott (Josiah) & Sears (John D.), attorneys at law, Bucyrus and Upper Sandusky, and Thomas Spybey's advertisement of "Tailoring at Kirby's Hotel, shop upstairs." There were, besides, several prospectuses and a complimentary notice of Wistar's Balsam of Wild Cherry, which in the dearth of other matter, was duplicated and appears on both outside and inside of the paper.

Among the news is an abstract of legislative proceedings as late as March 1, and a statement of the manner in which the new cabinet was to be composed, information of which was said to have been received by the Baltimore *American*, through the magnetic telegraph.

There is also the following credited to the Urbana *Citizen*: "The way hungry expectants are crowding into Washington is a caution to honest people. On Wednesday morning last, sixteen stages, averaging nine passengers each, left Wheeling for the East, and the *Times* says that the number leaving daily for some time past, has varied from five to fifteen, all bound for Washington to see Polk inaugurated and gather up the crumbs that fall from his table."

That would not be thought much of a shower in these modern days, when our great railroad facilities are scarce sufficient to accommodate the crusade of patriots seeking to serve the country for pay.

The *Telegraph* was published in the Indian Council House until that building was taken possession of for county purposes, at which time Shrenk moved to the lot now occupied by the Methodist Church, and while his new office was getting ready for occupation worked off one number of his paper in the open air under an apple tree.

Besides the number already described, our files contain No. 11, for May 10, No. 12, May 17, No. 16, June 14, No. 23, August 9, and No. 29, for October 10, 1845. The missing numbers will probably never be found.

Numbers 11 and 16 do not contain a paragraph of local news or a scrap of editorial. There is very little original matter in either of the other numbers; the last being pretty well filled with that choice literature supposed to be so effective upon a pending election, and which is intended to remedy all deficiencies in the voter's qualifications to exercise the elective franchise. No. 23 contains an original poem, written for the *Telegraph*, by A. W. B. However, excepting of course the poetry, the most interesting and valuable portions of these old papers are the advertising columns.

On the 10th of May, there are two road notices, an administrator's notice, a Sheriff's sale, on an execution from Marion County. Harvey & Fouké's advertisement of wool-carding at Little Sandusky, the card of David Watson, physician and surgeon, and timely warning by Samuel M. Worth, Auditor, of the action taken by the County Commissioners in reference to the act to improve the breed of sheep. On the 17th of May, there is a notice in chancery, by Robert McKelly, solicitor for the petitioner. On the 14th of June, Alexander Valentine calls attention to his new establishment for the manufacture of coffins and other cabinet ware; Joseph McCutchen announces that his new store is now opening in Upper Sandusky; Dr. A. W. Munson gives notice of his permanent location at Wyandot, for the purpose of attending all calls in the line of his profession; and Rowe & Tyler (Peter A.) attorneys at law. Marion and McCutchenville, advertise their readiness to attend to business in Wyandot and surrounding counties.

On the 9th of August, John Rummell advertises his fulling mill, in Tymochtee Township, operated by steam and water power. There is an estray notice from the estray book of Abraham Myers, J. P. of Crawford Township; an attachment notice from Richland Township; a tax notice by Abner Jurey, County Treasurer, giving the levy for 1845, in which the highest rate in any township is 19 mills on the dollar valuation, and a special notice in reference to road taxes, from Samuel M. Worth, County Auditor. This number of the *Telegraph* also contains a notice by Stephen Fowler, William Griffith and Ethan Terry, County Commissioners, of a public sale of town lots at Upper Sandusky, on the 20th, 21st and 22d days of August, 1845, at which time they will offer the in and outlots in said town, vested in the said Commissioners by Act of Congress approved February 26, 1845, being every third of the in and outlots selected by alternate and progressive numbers, amounting to 126 inlots, and 72 outlots. Terms of sale, one-fourth of the purchase money required in hand, the balance in three annual installments, secured by notes bearing interest. Daniel Walker also announces to the public that he has commenced the tailoring business in Upper Sandusky, at the hotel of Col. A. McElvain.

The last number of the *Telegraph* contains another Sheriff's sale; the Sheriff's proclamation of the forthcoming election; J. Duly's offer of 23 cents, and no thanks, for the return of a runaway apprentice; a notice signed "Many Carpenters," requesting the carpenters and joiners of Upper Sandusky and vicinity to meet at the court house, to consult on matters of importance to the trade, and a notice from Samuel M. Worth, Auditor, that sealed proposals will be received until the 30th of October, for the erection of a jail in Upper Sandusky. The latter announcement affords indisputable evidence of our rapid advance and great progress in civilization.

We linger lovingly over this number, and part from it with regret, for it was the last issue of the Wyandott *Telegraph* which ever saw the light. Without warning, it was cut off in the flower of its youth. The Whigs didn't rally strong enough; the Democrats elected their entire county ticket, except one County Commissioner, in the autumn of 1845, and there was no hope of sustenance from the county printing. These misfortunes and the effort of spelling Wyandot with two t's were too much for it, and it went out.

Shrenk, the publisher and editor, was an industrious, energetic man, who did most of his own work. The mental labor, however, of getting up the paper was not excessive.

In the *Democratic Pioneer* of November 7, 1845, we find this paragraph, which, with a courtesy belonging to the country editor of the old school, refers to its lately defunct contemporary, and which we insert as the obituary notice and epitaph of the Wyandott *Telegraph*:

"The thing that decamped from this place, and took up his abode in Napoleon, Henry County, and is issuing a little filthy sheet, is said to be doing great service to the Democracy of that county, and the Democrats are returning their thanks to him. Good. We hope our friends in those regions will give him plenty of rope, and the consequence will be seen."

The successful rival of the *Telegraph* was the *Democratic Pioneer*, the publication of which was commenced by William T. Giles on the 29th of August, 1845. This was a six-column folio, substantially of the same size as the *Telegraph*, but with narrower columns and less margin, printed on type that had seen much service, and edited by its publisher, a journeyman printer recently out of his apprinticeship. Giles was a young man of excellent habits, industrious, persevering and frugal; in fact, very much like the late Benjamin Franklin, who made himself famous a hundred years ago by the exercise of qualities which, however common they have since become, were then something of a rarity.

In mechanical execution the *Pioneer* suffered by contrast with its predecessor, and in literary excellence it had nothing to boast of; yet its editorial columns, filled with awkward English and bad grammar, were launched against the enormities of Whiggery with the courage if not the skill of veterans. There was, withal, a spice of independence of party dictation, as well as the rules of grammar, both of which find illustration in a single paragraph which we quote literally from the prospectus for the *Pioneer:*

"It is the intention of the editor to be perfectly free and uncontrolled by any man or set of men, and always willing to receive the counsel of such as are desirous of promoting the good cause, for which it is published to vindicate, as the advice of many is likely to be more correct than the few."

We wish also to copy another short article which is not only a fair specimen of the editorial style of the early *Pioneer*, but will recall to our older readers a state of things very characteristic of Upper Sandusky in the fall of 1845.

"REMOVING OUR OFFICE.

"While our office is rolling along the streets in Upper Sandusky to its future place of destination, we are sticking up these lines. Hereafter we may be found a little west of Mr. McCutchen's store, occupying a spot in the orchard, where at all times we will be happy to see and accommodate our friends. Our situation will be on the Wyandot avenue, in our opinion a very beautiful spot.

"We can, with much truth, say Democracy is progressing, for we are now progressing up street at a pretty fair rate. We would be glad to have all the coons in christendom here who deny that Democracy is progressing, for certainly when they would see us progressing they would have to admit the fact."

In the first number of the *Pioneer*, Robert McKelly announces himself as an attorney at law and solicitor in chancery, and D. Ayres & Co. advertise their new store, new goods and new prices, and inform the public that "their store may be found obliquely opposite Mr. Kirby's hotel." On the

12th of September, John Sell notifies the public of his location in Upper Sandusky, where he will hereafter practice as an attorney at law and solicitor in chancery, and J. & J. Myers announce the opening of a new grocery and bakery.

The *Pioneer* continued under the management of its original proprietor until February, 1849. On the 16th of that month, the publisher announced the prospective winding up of his connection with the paper, and on the 23d he published his valedictory, and announced the sale of the establishment to Josiah Smith and Elijah Giles. William T. Giles soon afterward started for California, and the *Pioneer* was conducted by the new publishers, under the name of J. Smith & E. Giles, and with no other very obvious change. Some time in 1850, Mr. Smith withdrew from the editorial chair, and the paper remained under the sole control of Elijah Giles, until the return of William T. Giles from California in 1853.

It was during the eventful railroad campaign in the fall of 1850 that the memorable attack upon the liberty of the press in the person of the then editor of the *Pioneer* occurred. This event, though discreditable to the county, ought to be held in remembrance as a warning to all who may be disposed to imitate the outrage. For that purpose we reproduce, from perhaps the only copy in existence, Mr. Giles' own account of the transaction:

"AN ATTEMPT TO MOB US.

"On the second Tuesday of October,—that ever-memorable day, when Ohioans exercise the rights of suffrage—the first and best of all blessings that freemen are endowed with—gained and given to us by our worthy and patriotic forefathers, whose names have been signed to the Declaration of Independence—thus preserving to us our liberties and the privileges that the God of Nature intended for us. On this great day, many of our fellow-citizens went to the different polls in the county; and we among the rest, not dreaming that our country was infested with a cowardly mob of villains, went to Jackson Township. While there, six or seven bullies from Marseilles came for the purpose above named. One of them was sent into the house to meet and greet us as a friend, while the others were kept out, fearing mistrust of what was going on; and he had the audacity to carry it out with the impudence of old Satan. He approached us and spoke in the most friendly terms—'How do you do, friend Giles?' We spoke in return. He then said he wanted to talk privately, and asked us to walk out with him, which we unhesitatingly did.

"Before getting off the porch, he said he had 'a crow to pick with us, to walk some distance with him;' all understood by his companions, that after getting us out from the house, they would surround us, so that we could not get to the house in such an emergency as this. When we were led to the spot selected—distant from the house, so that our friends could not hear us in the hour of distress, or come to our relief—they all jumped around us, as if to say—'We've got you now.'

"Their countenances bore the most corrupt design; their fiendish eyes gave expression that led us to believe that their hearts were so tickled with the 'old boy' as to place our life in their brutal hands. At this moment our heart was full of agony, and almost bleeding to think there were men in the country who would thus take a lone stranger, and use him thus barbarously.

"Directly after we were surrounded, the *big* little bully, McGavern, threw off his coat and declared he would whip us. What a great little brave fellow he was, when he had five or six bullies to back him—swearing they would have a kick at us as we would fall! McGavern struck us several blows in the breast, swearing by all that was good and bad we had weapons, for he was told so at Brownstown. Did he suppose, if we had, that we would have stood and let such insults be heaped upon us? If we would have had weapons he would not have struck us so often, for if we ever in our life could have been or was aggravated to use anything of the kind, it was at that time.

"While we were in this position, asking for quarter, one of our very special friends in the house heard us, and ran to our rescue. When he found we were being abused, he stepped between us and the man that was striking us, and told us to go to the house. When we started, up stepped Mr. Lewis Merriman (a man of notoriety, by the way), begging of our friend to let us be whipped, as, he said, we so richly deserved it. But our friend, a true-hearted man, would not swerve from the integrity and friendship existing between us, but said: 'Never shall he be hurt as long as I am here.' A true friend in the time of need is really a true one; and his name and the names of those that befriended us in that hour shall be sacred in our bosom the longest day we live.

"Had we been surrounded by Indians of the most savage character, and made the appeals that we did to those white savages, they would have shrunk from the scene, and not treated us half so bad. Could we tell our feelings, or describe the scene as it actually took place, it would be as an imaginary picture, untold of in the history of mankind.

"It is not necessary for us to make a long preface to this story at this time, as we expect to be called upon to notice it again, and make the names and characters of the individuals conspicuous."

It need not be said that the sympathies of the entire press of the country were aroused concerning this outrage, or that the expression of them was loud, frequent, and finally overpowering.

In the spring of 1853, William T. Giles, having returned from California, resumed the control of the *Democratic Pioneer*, and soon after changed its name to the *Wyandot Pioneer*.

Having thus hastily sketched the fortunes of the *Democratic Pioneer*, until the return of its founder and its change of name, we must now retrace our steps to notice other luminaries which from time to time arose and shone and went out.

On the 18th of July, 1848, at Upper Sandusky, James S. Fouke & Co.* issued the first number of the *Wyandot Tribune*, a sheet of the same size as that on which the *Pioneer* was printed, but with only five columns to the page. The *Tribune* was like all other tribunes in those days—a Whig paper. It was well printed, was conducted with moderate ability, and assisted materially in the election of Taylor and Fillmore.

However, on the 17th of February, 1849, Fouke published his valedictory, in which, while declining to enumerate the reasons for his withdrawal, he gives one which is tolerably satisfactory, for he says: "The patronage of the office is not sufficient to meet our engagements, and hence the necessity of our leaving." At the same time, he announces the transfer of the paper to Mr. A. C. Hulburd, who is introduced as "a young man deserving the encouragement and patronage of the Whig party."

On the 1st of December, 1849, Hulburd formed a partnership with M. R.

---

*G. L. Wharton was Fouke's partner when the *Tribune* was established. He sold out to the latter in December, 1848.

Gould, and the *Tribune* was thenceforward conducted by Hulburd & Gould, until January 25, 1851, when it had reached the twenty-eighth number of the second volume. At the date last named, the publishers announced that they had found it necessary to suspend the publication of their paper for a time, in order to collect their outstanding accounts. As might have been inferred, this was the last appearance of the *Wyandot Tribune*.

As before stated, William T. Giles, having assumed the publication of the *Democratic Pioneer*, changed its name to the *Wyandot Pioneer*, which was issued on the 23d of June, 1853, on an enlarged sheet, as a seven-column paper, and printed on new type. With his increased experience, Giles produced a paper which held a very respectable rank among the country press, and which, although Democratic, was at the same time liberal and conciliatory. He continued to publish it until September 2, 1854, when he sold out the establishment to one William Appleton, who ran it about a year. Under Appleton's management the paper was frequently referred to as a Know-Nothing organ.

In January, 1855, Giles brought suit for an unpaid balance of the purchase money due for the newspaper, and swore out an attachment against Appleton as a non-resident. The press, types and fixtures were attached and appraised at $800. Shortly afterward, some gentlemen of this place (Upper Sandusky) paid off Giles' judgment, and the *Pioneer* passed under the editorial control of Col. William T. Wilson, and became an exponent of the principles of the then new Republican party.

The next change was in July, 1856, when the *Pioneer* was sold to George W. Keen and Horatio N. Lewis,* who, the next year, July 2, 1857, transferred the establishment to Charles G. Mugg, who, to use the language of his salutatory in the number for July 9, 1857, thenceforth became "editor, publisher and proprietor in his *propria persona*."

On the 29th of October, 1857, Mugg reduced the size of the *Pioneer*, making it once more a six-column paper, and on the 11th of February, 1858, having sold out to Col. Wilson, he retired from the "tripod" with something of a flourish. It may be said that nothing in his editorial career became him like the leaving it, as witness this specimen brick from his valedictory:

"Since we have been in the business, we have filled all sorts of positions —we have at the same time been editor, foreman, pressman, jour. and devil (by the way, the devilship suited tolerably well, as we were somewhat devilishly inclined before we went into the business), and have been compelled to labor day and night to get out our paper, and if any of our patrons think they could have done better than we have done, just let them invest $800 in a 'one-horse' printing office, and try the experiment. There are various reasons why we have not succeeded any better as a newspaper political editor; we were too honest to be a politician—too poor to be independent—too proud to beg—worth too much property to get our work done for nothing —drank too much lager for a temperance man—too little 'rotgut' for the 'rummies'—too much of a moral man for the b'hoys— too much of a rowdy for the pharisaical part of the community—in fine, we had all the disadvantages, and but few of the advantages of our exalted position."

Again we must go back to gather up the broken threads of our narrative.

---

*Horatio N. Lewis, then twenty-five years of age, died at Chicago, Ill, in September, 1857, from injuries received on the cars of the Pittsburgh, Fort Wayne & Chicago Railroad, near Alliance, Ohio, in July 1857.

By the transfer of the *Pioneer* to William Appleton in 1854, the Democratic party was left without an organ, a tolerable state of affairs, though not to be of long continuance, for on the 3d of November, 1854, Robert D. Dumm commenced the publication of the *Democratic Vindicator*, a handsomely printed seven-column folio, of the same sized sheet then used by the *Pioneer*. About the close of the first volume, the new paper passed under the editorial control of N. W. Dennison, who conducted it until July 3, 1857, at which date he bade the public farewell, and informed them that he was about to pitch his tent in the West. He soon after went to Boonsboro, Iowa, taking press and types with him, and thus did the *Vindicator* cease to vindicate.

The gap was soon filled, however, for there was no lack of valiant men ready to spread buckets full of printer's ink on the least provocation or smallest chances of remuneration, and on the 20th of August, 1857, Nathan Jones and J. W. Wheaton issued the first number of the *Democratic Union*. As early as December 24, following, Mr. Jones had become sole editor and publisher, and on the 18th of February, 1858, he published to the world his farewell address, and Robert D. Dumm took control of the *Union*. As first issued by Jones & Wheaton it was a six-column folio. The office was partially destroyed by fire just before it passed into the hands of Jones.

When Col. Wilson took charge of the *Pioneer* the second time, it was conducted for awhile as a neutral paper. It soon manifested Republican proclivities, and erelong became a decided political and party organ.

NOTE.—With the most scrupulous investigation into the lives and deaths of the ephemeral newspapers of Wyandot County, we have omitted in its proper place to mention the short-lived Wyandot *Herald*. This paper was started after Elijah Giles had ceased to publish the *Pioneer*. It was conducted by "Charles Warner, editor and publisher," and its first number was issued April 19, 1853. It survived long enough to reach its sixth number, when it passed into the hands of William T. Giles, and No. 7 was issued by him on the 23d of June, 1853, as the Wyandot *Pioneer*. It was Democratic in politics, and not otherwise remarkable.

The *Democratic Union*, under the control of Robert D. Dumm,* and the Wyandot *Pioneer*, in charge of Col. William T. Wilson, were respectively the organs of the Democratic and Republican parties for a number of years, following the party banners and playing the party tunes with a faithfulness and devotion which, however undesirable in a newspaper, are indispensable qualifications for a party organ.

On the 3d of May, 1861, Colonel, then Capt. William T. Wilson, left for the seat of war in Western Virginia, in command of a company of Wyandot County volunteers, then known as the "Wyandot Guards," and his estimable wife, Mrs. L. A. Wilson, was left in charge of the *Pioneer*. The newly-installed lady editor published three numbers, which were fully equal to those which preceeded and followed them under other management. The *Pioneer* then passed into the hands of Louis A. Brunner, a former resident of Maryland. On the 16th of September, 1864, Otho J. Powell became a joint proprietor of the paper, and the *Pioneer* was published by Brunner & Powell until August 23, 1865, when Mr. Brunner again became sole proprietor. A few months later, however, or on the 31st of January, 1866, the *Pioneer* again passed under the control of Col. Wilson, who on the 27th of September, 1866, was succeeded by Pietro Cuneo,

---
* In 1865, Mr. Dumm introduced the first cylinder press run in this part of Ohio; several years, indeed, before such a press was used in Tiffin, Lima or Mansfield.

the present editor and proprietor of that paper. On the 7th of January, 1869, Mr. Cuneo changed the name of the Wyandot *Pioneer*, which since that time has been known as the "*Wyandot County Republican.*" He was the first Upper Sandusky publisher to introduce steam power.

On the 12th of November, 1868, Robert D. Dumm took leave of the *Union*, and was succeeded by E. Zimmerman, who on the 1st of November, 1870, was in turn succeeded by Louis A. Brunner. The latter continued as sole editor and proprietor of the paper until during the month of August, 1873, when Mr. Dumm (who, as the senior member of the firm of R. D. Dumm & Co., had been editing and publishing the Ft. Wayne, Ind., *Sentinel*, a daily and weekly newspaper, from November, 1868), returned and purchased a one-half interest in the *Union*. The firm of Dumm & Brunner then continued until October, 1874, when they sold out to Charles L. Zahm. The last named individual continued in control until about the 1st of November, 1877, when he transferred his interests to D. J. Stalter and R. D. Webster. The firm of Stalter & Webster only continued some six or eight months, when the junior member retired, leaving Mr. Stalter in sole control until November 27, 1879, when the *Union* again passed into the hands of Messrs. Dumm & Brunner, its present editors and proprietors, who erected for it the building on the corner of Main and Railroad streets, and put in steam power to run its presses.

The old, and it may be added trite saying, that "tall oaks from little acorns grow," is quite applicable when reference is made to The *Weekly Chief*, Upper Sandusky's latest acquisition in the journalistic field. It appears that in August, 1876, H. A. Tracht, then a youth of but fourteen years of age, purchased $6 worth of material and began printing cards. As his business increased he added more stock to his office, which was then located in the back part of his father's shoe store, and in May, 1878, began the publication of a small monthly sheet, styled the *Wyandot Chief*, which was continued for one year. After the discontinuance of this paper, the youthful editor again increased his facilities for doing job work and secured the assistance of practical mechanics.

On the 16th of August, 1879, he issued the first number of *The Weekly Chief*, which in size was a folio of 13x20 inches. In January, 1880, it was made a six-column folio. Prosperity rendered another enlargement necessary, and on the 21st of May, 1881, it appeared as a seven-column folio, and in April, 1882, as an eight-column folio. In September, 1883, it was changed to its present dimensions and style—a well-printed six-column quarto.

BIOGRAPHICAL.

It is a pleasing task to write of those connected with the early history of Wyandot, and certainly no one occupies a more prominent place in the recollection of our people than William T. Giles, our first Democratic editor.

The subject of this sketch was born in New Lisbon, Columbiana County, Ohio, July 18, 1823. He attended the schools of that then quaint old town until he was about fifteen years old, when he went into the printing office of the *Ohio Patriot* to learn the business. The *Patriot* was then owned by Hetzell & Gregg, and young Giles remained with them until the office was sold to William Duane Morgan, brother of Gen. Morgan, and the last Democratic Auditor of State, prior to the election of Mr. Kissewitter last October. He continued in the office with Mr. Morgan until 1843,

HISTORY OF WYANDOT COUNTY. 389

when he went to Bucyrus, holding a position on the *Crawford County Democrat*, then published and edited by T. J. Orr. Printing offices in Bucyrus those days were not the bonanzas they are now, and Giles could not get enough money from handsome Tom Orr to pay his board, which was $1.25 per week. Mr. Orr would rather sit on a store box all day than dun a subscriber, and consequently Tom's bank book was always a few loads of wood behind. Tom was an able writer, but could do nothing with more ease than any other man in America. The *Crawford County Democrat* was started some time early in 1845, but in Orr's hands it was a failure, the paper collapsed, and he urged Giles, his only employe, to buy the material and remove it to Upper Sandusky and commence the publication of a Democratic paper. Giles insisted that he neither had money nor experience as a writer, and did not feel like embarking in the enterprise. Orr, however, insisted, giving Giles to understand that unless some arrangement could be made, he could not pay him for labor due, and that he might be compelled to count imaginary railway ties on his way back to New Lisbon. After a good deal of persuasion, Giles, in company with a personal friend, the late lamented William M. Scroggs, visited Upper Sandusky, which at that time was a very small place. The Democrats, Capt. S. M. Worth, R. McKelly, Col. A. McElvain, Col. Joseph McCutchen, Peter B. Beidler, C. R. Mott, George Harper, and in fact, all the Democrats urged the establishment of a Democratic paper, while the Whigs put in their words of discouragement, saying it could not live in so new a county; but Giles thought it was a case of necessity; he was like the fellow after the ground hog—he must have meat—and there was mighty little prospect of getting any out of Tom Orr; so he said, "Sink or swim, survive or perish, here goes." He returned to Bucyrus, informed Orr of his decision, in case they could agree upon terms. Orr wanted to know what proposition Giles had to make. Giles said, "If you sell me the material on eight months' time, taking a note for the amount over what is due me, and agree to take the material back in case payment is not made when due, and will then agree to pay me my wages, deducting ten per cent for use of materials, it is a go—otherwise not." Orr agreed to the proposition. Col. Scott, a very fine lawyer, drew up the contract and note, which were properly signed.

Giles then returned to Upper Sandusky to seek shelter for his press and material, but could not secure a place, without buying a building—a small chair shop—that stood in the middle of Fourth street, in the vicinity of the present African Church. Now came the question, "How can I buy?" Giles related the condition of things to some Democratic friends, and the result was, the money was raised, the house bought and held for payment. The next move was to get the material from Bucyrus to Upper Sandusky. Giles borrowed Col. McKelly's horse, took an early morning start, rode over to Bucyrus, employed Frederick Fireing, loaded his wagon, and returned to Upper Sandusky the same day, without eating a bite until arriving at McElvain's old log hotel, located where the brewery now stands.

The publication of the *Democratic Pioneer* was begun under these embarrassing circumstances, and all the difficulties did not stop here. Giles had to buy a lot to put his building on, as there was some law or restriction compelling the removal of all houses from the streets. At the time of the removal of the building by Mr. Russel, Giles stood at the case, set up the notice of the removal, and headed it "Progressive Democracy," as can be seen by reference to the old files of the *Pioneer*, which have only been fully preserved in the county by Hon. J. D. Sears.

Pay day came, and Giles owed more than he did at the start, so he at once wrote T. J. Orr the following lines:

UPPER SANDUSKY, ———, 1846.

T. J. Orr, Esq., Bucyrus, Ohio:

DEAR SIR—Unable to make the payment—ready to comply with the article.

Respectfully yours, W. T. GILES.

Mr. Orr was in the same condition—he could not pay—and in a long letter urged Giles to go on and pay when and as he could. Giles took his advice and worked away. One evening, as Giles was passing Col. Mc Cutchen's store, he heard his name mentioned, and naturally felt inclined to hear what was being said, and to see who were in the store. He quietly approached the door, and in the dim candle light, saw Cols. Chaffee, McCutchen and others, and heard them lamenting the condition of the young editor. They were "really sorry that the country was so thinly settled and the town so small, that the *Pioneer* could not survive; that Giles was industrious, energetic, etc., but the fates were against him." After hearing their remarks, Giles said, "By the Eternal, if I burst it will not be my fault." He went home but did not sleep much that night. In the morning, he rose and resolved to board himself, and did for about sixteen months, on an average cost of 48 cents per week, earning and saving sufficient to pay all his debts. After free from debt, he boarded at Zimmerman's Blue Ball Hotel till 1849.

During his struggle for existence, Giles was urged to "take the post office as it would help him to stem the tide." He refused for a long while, but finally consented. A petition was put in circulation, and Col. McElvain, who was then Postmaster, and had urged Giles to take the office, refused to sign the petition, remarking that "Giles could not get the office without he had other signers." This raised the Irish in Giles, and he "made a vow that he would have the office with just those names and none other, or not have it at all." He then wrote to the Hon. Henry St. John, who was then the Member of Congress from this district, giving a statement of facts, and sent forward the petition. Col. McElvain called upon Giles and wanted him to call a meeting, and let the meeting decide between them. Giles said: "No, I have done everything I am going to do in this matter, and you may call all the meetings you want." No meeting was called, but Giles became Postmaster, but only held the office long enough to see that it would not pay him, when he resigned, and had John A. Morrison appointed before any one knew of his resignation, excepting Mr. Morrison and a few friends.

During the time Giles held the office, some malicious party sent a report to Washington that the mail matter was turned upon the counter and every one who came in was Postmaster. This was false, as Giles never had a counter in his office, and would not let people in while changing the mail. A secret agent came along one cool morning, jumped from the coach (for this was the time of old stage coaches), and was going to rush into the office, when he was informed by Giles "that he couldn't come in," but that he could go into the printing-office.

The agent did as ordered, and when the mail was overhauled, reported to Giles his mission, and said, "I am glad to find the report about your office false. I will report you all right when I return." Giles said, "So far as the report goes, it is all false, but when you get back to Washington, you can tell them if they do not like the way this office is managed, they can take it and go to the devil with it." What report was made is not known, but Mr. Giles kept the office till he resigned.

Giles often relates his mode of living, and laughs over early days at

Upper Sandusky, and tells of the time several parties procured a license for an old couple, on conditions that they would mount some boxes in front of a store, and get married. Col. Kirby was then Justice of the Peace, and tied the knot.

The *Democratic Pioneer*, in the face of all trials and tribulations, prospered in the hands of W. T. Giles up and until the spring of 1849, when he sold a part of the office to Josiah Smith, and gave the other half to Elijah Giles, his brother. Mr. Smith paid but a small amount down, and W. T. Giles gave the notes to Elijah, who bought Smith's interest, paying him with his own notes. When Giles started for California with Col. Lyle, one of God's own noblemen, Col. A. McElvain, his sons William and Purdy, Messrs. Jones and Walker, he left the *Pioneer* well supplied with ink, paper, etc. At the time of the departure, Col. Lyle and Giles were in poor health, and it was not supposed that either would live to get to St. Joseph, Mo. Their friends tried to persuade them to give up the trip, but it was a useless effort. We well remember the morning they took teams and started for Carey, no railway running to Upper Sandusky at that time. At Carey they took the cars for Cincinnati, and a steamer thence to St. Louis, where a change of steamers had to be made for St. Joseph. Col. McElvain and his son, Purdy, took horses and money and went overland to St. Joseph to buy up cattle, with which to cross the plains. They bought seven yokes, or two teams. Giles, having some ready money, got more than his share in this purchase, but never got it out of the teams, for all the cattle died. On the way up the Missouri River, Mr. Walker, father-in-law of Henry Miller, took the cholera and died at St. Joseph, destitute, excepting what he received from Giles. Buck Kirby, a colored man, whom all the old settlers well remember, concluded to go to California with this party. Mr. Giles provided him with boots and some clothing for the trip, and paid his bills at St. Joseph for some weeks till the teams arrived, and just before starting out of this city Giles was seized with cholera, and had to be taken from his horse and placed in a wagon. His recovery was very doubtful, but having lots of determination, had his party hitch up the cattle and drive on, saying, "If I die, I will die as far out as I can get." The result was Giles got well, and soon Col. McElvain was taken with the same disease, and all thought would die, but he also recovered.

In crossing the plains at that time it was necessary to go in large bodies, and a train of about thirty or forty teams formed a company and elected Col. McElvain Captain. The front team had to take the rear the following day. One day Buck Kirby, as he was called, was driving one of the teams, the last team in the train. Buck crawled into the wagon and went to sleep. One of the oxen became unyoked and strayed off, and the train traveled two or more miles before the discovery was made, and when Capt. McElvain heard of the lost ox, it is unnecessary to tell those who knew him, that he swore a blue streak. He threatened to shoot Buck if he should ever do such a trick again. The ox was found grazing, drove up, put in place, and the train moved on. Giles had been out hunting, and when he returned to the train he found Buck greatly alarmed, wanting to leave and go into a train, mostly from Marion, Ohio. Giles tried to persuade him out of the notion, but Buck insisted on going for fear that McElvain might shoot him in the absence of Giles. It was agreed that Buck might take the boots and clothes bought for him and go, which he did, and it was reported got through to California and died. No member of the party ever saw Buck after he went into the Marion train.

A sad event took place at Fort Laramie to the party from Upper Sandusky. They arrived there and concluded to rest the teams and sun their clothes. Here they found Maj. Sanderson, of the regular army, in command. Major was an "Ohio man," and acquainted with Capt. McElvain, who had boarded with him in Columbus, so he invited McElvain and his friends to dinner. Col. Aaron Lyle and Giles were great friends—always together at home, and never broke friendship on the plains. They slept together in a wagon. While lying at the fort they sunned their clothes, and that evening Colonel said he was very hungry, and Giles said, "Buck, Col. Lyle is hungry; get up a good supper." Colonel ate heartily, but he coughed severely. At night Giles had to go out on guard duty till 1 o'clock, and did so, riding about two or three miles. When he returned to camp he was surprised to find Col. Lyle sitting up in the wagon. Colonel said, "Giles, will you bring me a canteen of water?" The reply was, "Yes." Giles went to the Laramie River, brought the water; Colonel drank and lay down; Giles got into the wagon—put down the curtains, when Colonel remarked, "Please put it up, it seems so close." In the morning when Giles was called, he found the Colonel lying by his side dead! The shock given Giles can better be imagined than expressed. In fact, although the death was daily expected, yet all were surprised. He passed away easily, for his arms were resting across his breast as if he passed from earth without a struggle. After making a coffin, and burying Col. Lyle in the burying-ground belonging to the fort, the party left for California. They took in Salt Lake; heard Brigham Young preach three sermons. Here Giles, McElvain and one or two others boarded for several days with a prophet who had two wives. One of the wives wanted to go with the train to California, but it was not a safe thing at that time to meddle with the wives of Mormons. While at this city, Giles traded horses and bought one, and in company with seven other men, packed through to California, leaving the teams with McElvain and son and a Mr. Jones, whom they were taking through. Jones was a merchant in Upper Sandusky at an early day. What became of him after arriving in California, the writer does not know. Giles, on horse, and with his pack animal, arrived in California several weeks before McElvain and son, for it will be remembered William McElvain died at Independence, Mo., before going on the plains. Giles and his comrades who packed through bought a rocker, and made several hundred dollars each in the mines, in that many weeks. They sold their claim for a mule, for which Giles paid $85. This claim panned out about $100,000. Giles bought a few more animals at Sacramento City, packed them with provisions, and went up the Sacramento Valley to Lawson's ranch, where he found McElvain and son, nearly destitute. After some days' rest, Giles got some cattle, and the party hitched to a wagon and worked their way to Yuba City, where they opened a trading-post, and soon another at Shasta City. Shortly after Giles returned from Shasta City he was taken sick; and just at a time it was not certain whether he would live or die, McElvain took the money on hand and left for Ohio. Giles recovered, went to work, put up a large amount of hay, several thousand dollars' worth, and most of this was set on fire and burned. Then he had two teams and about $300 in money left. What was to be done he did not know, but it would not do to sit down and waste what little he had, so he loaned a mule to a friend who had also been a sufferer by fire, and the two went to the mountains to seek fortunes, but found nothing to suit them, and after spending some weeks in the mountains, returned to Yuba

City, and Giles went over to Marysville, and here he found his friend, Hon. J. W. McCorkle, the Member of Congress from that district, and also an "Ohio man." Mac said to Giles, "Where have you been? I sent over to your town for you, but got no information of your whereabouts. Col. Rust was here—wants a partner to start a Democratic paper, and I referred him to you." Giles said, "Send Rust word I am here; come to Marysville, and I will meet him." Mac did as requested, and in a few days Rust came to Marysville, and arrangements were made to start the paper. Giles borrowed some money on his teams, and with Rust went to San Francisco, where they found a Mr. Gee, got him interested in the paper, and in a few weeks their presses and types were packed and shipped to Marysville, where on November 3, 1851, the *California Express* came out, published by Gee, Giles & Co., and edited by Col. Richard Rust. It was not long till Gee became discontented, and sold his third of the office to W. T. Giles, and the paper ran in the firm name of William T. Giles & Co. until about the 15th of July, 1852, when, through Col. Rust, Giles consented to take in other partners, and sold a portion of his interest, retaining one-fourth. Soon Giles found his mistake, hired John L. Mitchell to run his interest and went to San Francisco, bought presses and types, and went to Downieville, Sierra County, Cal., where on the 10th day of June, 1852, he put out the first issue of the *Mountain Echo*. He sold this paper after publishing it for some time, went back to Marysville, and ran his own interest for a short time in the *California Express*, and in the spring of 1853, sold the entire interest in the establishment and returned to Ohio.

After looking about and visiting for some time, Giles settled down, and resumed publication of the *Wyandot County Pioneer*. Soon after taking hold of the paper he went to Cincinnati, bought new types, press, etc., enlarged the paper, and made it one of the neatest as well as one of the best country papers in the state. Mr. Giles felt disappointed after he started this paper, for the promises made to him were not fulfilled as he thought, and he sold out, and in company with Irey Quaintance, went to Iowa, bought land and lots, returned here and wintered over 1854, and in the spring of 1855 he bought some teams, took Elijah Giles and family, Henry Giles and another young man to Newtown, Jasper County, Iowa. In the fall of 1855 Irey Quaintance and W. T. Giles returned to Upper Sandusky and wintered. In the spring both married, Mr. Giles taking Miss Mary E. Scroggs, and Mr. Quaintance Livonia Trager. In the spring of 1856, the four returned together to Newton, Iowa, but W. T. Giles could not remain long out of the editorial harness. He sold out in Iowa; went to Freeport, Ill., bought the *Bulletin* and published it for many years. He sold the *Bulletin* to his brother-in-law, J. R Scroggs, in 1864, and in that spring went by team to Virginia City, Montana Territory. Here he broke a leg, and spent two years and some money, and returned to Illinois; sold out there and removed his family to Council Bluffs, Iowa, where he owned and published the *Bugle*, and a German paper for a time. During the time Giles was in Council Bluffs, J. R. Scroggs died at Freeport, Ill., and this left the *Bulletin* without an editor, and Giles returned and resumed charge of the paper. In a short time after this, he started the *Lee County Democrat* at Dixon, Ill., but soon sold that paper, and continued in the *Bulletin* for a long time, and sold it. Since then he started the *Illinois Monitor*, in Freeport, and published it over three years. He edited the *Dakota Herald*, at Yankton, Dakota Territory, for several months, and is now publishing the Freeport *Democrat*.

During Giles' early days in Upper Sandusky, we remember one incident that occurred to him and our friend J. G. Roberts. It was when Giles was keeping bachelor's hall. A show came along, and Giles being the only editor in this section, got a family ticket, so Roberts and Giles agreed to go, and each take two ladies. This was done; Giles sending all the family in first, and then passing the ticket, followed. The doorkeeper surprised, muttered out, "That fellow has a h—l of a family to keep bachelor's hall."*

Robert D. Dumm, the senior member of the firm of Dumm & Brunner, editors and proprietors of The Wyandot *Union*, was born in the city of Pittsburgh, Penn., July 3, 1835, being the fourth son of Andrew and Mary (Shall) Dumm. His father served in the American Army during the war of 1812-15, and his paternal grandfather, who was a native of Baden, Germany, served as a soldier during the Revolutionary struggle. His grandparents upon his mother's side were of English origin. In 1842, with his parents, he came to this part of Ohio, and settled at McCutchenville. Three years later he became a resident of the town of Upper Sandusky, and at the age of ten years entered the *Pioneer* printing-office as an apprentice under William T. Giles. He served with Mr. Giles four years, receiving during that time six months' schooling as per contract. During the year 1849, in connection with J. Zimmerman, he published the *Pioneer*, with Elijah Giles as editor. In 1852, he published the paper alone, Elijah Giles still remaining as editor, and continued to be employed in that capacity until 1853, when he entered the Ohio Wesleyan University as a student. In 1854, however, he was induced to leave school and start a new Democratic newspaper at Upper Sandusky, termed the *Vindicator*, of which he was editor and publisher. This proceding was deemed necessary on the part of the Democratic leaders of the county, by reason of the fact that the old *Pioneer* had degenerated into a Know-Nothing organ. Mr. Dumm continued to publish the *Vindicator* about eighteen months, when he sold out to N. W. Dennison, and began the study of law with Hon. Chester R. Mott. In the winter of 1856-57, he attended the Cincinnati Law School, where he graduated with honor and was admitted to the bar. Soon after he located at Freeport, Ill., where he remained nearly one year. He then returned to Upper Sandusky, married, and in February, 1858, purchased the then recently established *Union*, a journal which he conducted in a very successful manner for a period of eleven years. Having sold out the *Union* to E. Zimmerman, he removed to Fort Wayne, Ind., in November, 1868, and during the succeeding five years edited and published the Fort Wayne *Sentinel*,—a daily and weekly newspaper—with unwearied and, we may add, marked ability. In August, 1873, he again returned to Upper Sandusky, purchased a one-half interest in his old paper, the *Union* (yet still retaining his share in the *Sentinel*), and with, L. A. Brunner as his partner, published the *Union* for a little more than one year, when Charles L. Zahm, by purchase, became the owner of the *Union* office. Subsequently Mr. Dumm disposed of his disastrous investment at Fort Wayne, and in the fall of 1875 was elected by a very flattering majority to the office of Clerk of Wyandot County. In 1878, he was re-elected to the same position, and thus served for a continuous period of six years. On the 27th of November, 1879, the *Union* again passed into the hands of its present proprietors—Messrs. Dumm & Brunner. On the 1st of September, 1882, this firm purchased one-half of the Marion *Mirror* office, and during the political

---

*Copied from an article which was published in the *Wyandot Union* in December, 1883.

campaign of 1883 Mr. Dumm edited that paper with a vigor and ability not easily surpassed.

We have thus briefly outlined the active business career of a gentleman who has been closely identified with the interests of Wyandot County since its establishment. One who, although a strict party man, and a zealous worker for the success of the Democratic party, has ever been consistent, and has so demeaned himself as to challenge the admiration of even the most bitter of his political opponents. His untiring efforts for the promotion of the material interests, and the general prosperity of his town and county, have also secured for him the gratitude and respect of Wyandot County residents in general, and to-day none stand higher in their estimate of character and true worth than Robert D. Dumm. As already shown, he has grown up, and has been educated in the printing office, and, probably, has done more to bring Wyandot County journalism up to its present proud position than all others combined. As an editorial writer he has acquired a reputation truly enviable, and which, indeed, is not confined by State limits. Ever careful, vigorous, versatile, brilliant and facetious, his readers are never disappointed in the perusal of an article prepared by him.

He was married on the 29th day of December, 1857, to Miss Sarah J., only daughter of Dr. R. A. Henderson, of Upper Sandusky. The results of this union are two sons, both of whom are young gentlemen of notable qualifications—William G., the present efficient Deputy County Clerk, and Frank E., who is now employed in the *Union* office.

Hon. Louis A. Brunner is of German ancestry, and was born in Frederick City, Frederick Co., Md. He fully availed himself of the advantages of an elementary and classical education, and after a thorough course of theological study was licensed, in the summer of 1846, to preach at Columbus, Ohio. Subsequently, he entered upon the duties of the ministry, and served several Presbyterian congregations. In the spring of 1852, he was elected by the Presbytery of Marion, Ohio, Commissioner to the General Assembly, and attended the sittings of that body in Philadelphia, Penn., in May following. In 1860, his nervous centers gave way, prostrating him to such an extent as to force him to relinquish his chosen profession. However, having from a young boy dabbled in printer's ink, and being compelled to labor for a livelihood, he purchased a printing office, and took charge of the editorial department, and, while not engaged in the duties of the tripod, worked at the case sticking type. He has performed editorial work on the *Odd Fellow*, published at Boonsboro, Washington Co., Md.; the *Pioneer* and the *Union* of Upper Sandusky, and the Ft. Wayne *Daily Sentinel*, an interest of which he owned in 1868 and 1869. He has resided in Wyandot County since 1849, excepting four years passed in Maryland, from 1856 to 1861. He has served on the Board of School Examiners of Wyandot County, as a member of the Village Council, and was elected a member of the Sixty-first, Sixty-second, Sixty-fifth and Sixty-sixth General Assemblies of the State of Ohio, occupying, during the session of 1883–84, the honored position of Speaker pro tem. In the Sixty-fourth General Assembly, he served as Clerk of the House, and his large experiences as a law-maker, and his peculiar fitness for clerical duties—the result of early training—made him one of the best clerks the Assembly ever had, and it was so acknowledged by the members of both parties. Hence, as a mark of recognition, embodying the admiration of members, he was presented at the close of the session with a costly gold watch and chain, which he still carries with pardonable pride. Mr. Brunner's first year in the General

Assembly was marked with ability and true statesmanship, and although it is seldom the lot of a new member to take prominence at the beginning, his experience was an exception, for before the close of the session he was the recognized leader of his side of the House, and this position he has ably and gracefully maintained during every term of his legislative career. His superior qualifications as a presiding officer attracted attention from all parts of the State, and in the Sixty-sixth General Assembly he was the almost unanimous choice of his party for Speaker, yet his usefulness upon the floor, and his own inclinations for activity amid conflict, induced him to decline the honor, and to accept at the demands of his party the position of Speaker pro tem. He is perhaps the finest parliamentarian in the State, and we cannot better express this opinion than to give an extract from a letter written by a newspaper correspondent during the session of 1883-84: "The Wyandot Sachem, Brunner, as speaker pro tem., has demonstrated himself to be a superior presiding officer, fit to have held the gavel of the Long Parliament of Cromwell's days, and whose legislative career has given his solid little Gibraltar (Wyandot County) a cameo-like prominence in the State's councils."

In 1879, Mr. Brunner, in connection with Robert D. Dumm, purchased the Wyandot *Union* of D. J. Stalter, and by their united labors again made the old *Union* one of the best county newspapers in the State. It now enjoys a large circulation, and an enviable, widespread reputation. As an editor, Mr. Brunner has few superiors. He is logical, clear and very effective, and has gained many admirers from his humorous touches of local incidents; but his great force and efficiency is as a campaigner, filling his well-rounded and emphatic periods in that direct and forcible manner, which leaves no room for effective reply. While a ready, spicy and able writer, he is equally as ready and effective as a speaker, which his prominence in the House, on all the important questions of state policy, has fully made clear. His polish as a gentleman, and his great tact in winning and retaining the admiration and esteem of his fellow-citizens is due to some extent to his genial nature, thorough education and wide range of information gained through the avenues of an extensive and careful study of books and men. In September, 1882, he, with his old partner, Mr. Dumm, bought a half interest in the *Mirror*, at Marion, Ohio, and although it proved to be a profitable investment, and their connection with the Democracy of Marion County highly acceptable and pleasant, after eighteen months they sold their interest to their partner, Col. J. H. Vaughan. A part of this time Mr. Brunner was editor of the paper, and in the memorable campaign of 1883 gained a host of admirers for his efficient editorial work.

Since the close of the legislative session of 1883-84, he has assumed a controlling interest and editorial charge of the Seneca *Advertiser*, one of the oldest and best newspapers published in Ohio, and he has fully made up his mind to make that city his future home. He still holds his connection with the Wyandot *Union* with Mr. Dumm, but undoubtedly in the near future will sever that relation and give his whole attention to the *Advertiser*, which will advance under his influence and enterprise, and rapidly become the leading county paper of the State.

He was married in 1850 to Miss Jane Sherman, of Delaware, Ohio, who was a native of Watertown, N. Y. Their three children are Mary, now the wife of John W. Geiger, of Tiffin, Ohio; Addie, now Mrs. B. W. Holman, of Washington, D. C., and Grace.

Pietro Cuneo, the present editor and proprietor of the *Wyandot County*

Republican, is a native of Pian de Cuni (a small village in Italy, which is situated about twenty-five miles southeast of Genoa, and five miles east of Chiavari), where he was born September 29, 1837. His early life was passed amid scenes common to the peasant class of his native country, and which are vividly portrayed by himself in his highly interesting lecture entitled, "Recollections of Italy." On the 6th of March, 1849, accompanied by his father, he bade adieu to his mother, sisters and brother, and en route to America set out on foot for the seaport town of Genoa. About the 10th of March, the ship upon which the father and son had secured passage sailed and on the 10th of May, 1849, it safely landed its passengers at the city of New York.

"When I arrived in New York," says Mr. Cuneo, "I could not understand a solitary word of the English language, had no trade, and could not read nor write my own name in any language. I was, therefore, compelled to labor for very low wages, and I soon abandoned the hope of amassing a fortune. In about two years, in consequence of sickness, my father was compelled to return to Italy, and left me alone, with the expectation that I would also return in about two years more." After various discouraging trials and vicissitudes, young Cuneo obtained employment in the fall of 1852* with Josiah Starn, a farmer, who lived three miles from Camden, N. J. At that time he purchased a spelling book and endeavored to master the English alphabet, but after a few evenings he became utterly discouraged and gave the book away. However, during the following winter he effected an arrangement with John Hinchman, who lived one mile east of Gloster, N. J., to work for his board and attend the district school. About the 1st of December, 1853, he started to school and took his first lesson in learning the alphabet. "I tried hard to learn," says he, "and the teacher and pupils took particular pains to assist me. By the 1st of March, when I again commenced to work, I had progressed so far as to be able to read and write a little."

The year 1854 found him in Chester County, Penn., where, after a long search for work, he met William Martin, who lived between Coatesville and Parkesburg, and who gave him employment through the winter of 1854–55, and an opportunity to attend the Rockdale School. The next winter he became an inmate of William Hamill's house, situated two miles south of Parkesburg, where he also worked for his board and attended the public school. In September, 1856, he arrived at Canton, Ohio, almost penniless, and after a vain attempt to find work among the farmers in that vicinity, by mere chance, C. Aultman, of the firm of Aultman & Co., hired him to work as a laborer at 77 cents per day, board not included. Subsequently he arranged to pass the winter with Christian Neisz, who resided near Canton, and there worked for his board and attended school. The following spring he returned to the shops of Messrs. Aultman & Co., where he remained the major portion of the time for nine years, being promoted from time to time until his wages rose to $2.50 per day. He continued to study and work, frequently fourteen hours out of the twenty-four, and so improved that in the winter of 1858–59 he was able to teach school where he had formerly attended as a pupil.

In 1865, he purchased a half interest in the Medina (Ohio) *Gazette*, but at the expiration of nine months sold out. He then removed to his present home—Upper Sandusky—where he purchased the *Pioneer*. He afterward

---

*In the spring of 1852, he began to work with John Cordray, near Milford, Del., at the rate of $3 per month and continued with the latter six months.

changed its name to the *Republican*, and is still its proprietor and editor. Appointed and re-appointed by his firm, personal friend, Gen. U. S. Grant,* he served as Postmaster at Upper Sandusky, from May 10, 1869, to July 1, 1877. As may be inferred, Mr. Cuneo is a stanch Republican, a Stalwart among Stalwarts, and a warm friend and admirer of Grant, Conkling, and their friends.

He was married, December 24, 1861, to Miss Myra V. Miller, of Canton, Ohio, who, born in Sandyville, Ohio, in March, 1842, died at Upper Sandusky December 27, 1883. Of ten children born to them, four of whom were twins, five are still living—Laura T., Sherman A., Edward Noyes, Eva and Roscoe Conkling.

Henry Albert Tracht, the founder and present editor and proprietor of the *Weekly Chief*, was born in Upper Sandusky, Ohio, August 26, 1862. His parents, Philip and Lucinda (Keil) Tracht, though of German descent, were both born in Crawford County, of this State. His education was acquired in the public schools of his native town, and at an early period in life too, for when only fourteen years of age he was compelled to give up his studies, by reason of an annoying and painful affection of his eyes. Some months later he established a small job printing-office, which proved to be a successful business venture, and from that modest beginning has grown up by degrees the present very creditable and successfully managed sheet, known throughout a wide region as the *Chief*. Mr. Tracht is still unmarried, and apparently has a bright future before him.

Frank T. Tripp, eldest son of Franklin and Elizabeth (Bowsher) Tripp, was born in Upper Sandusky, Ohio, September 26, 1850. He obtained a common school education, and at the age of thirteen years began learning the printing business in the Wyandot *Pioneer* office, with Col. W. T. Wilson, who shortly after sold the paper to Pietro Cuneo. He remained with Mr. Cuneo six years, assisting him in the post office for the term of two years. He was married, October 26, 1871, to Miss Irene M. Stevenson, youngest daughter of James N. and Susanna Stevenson, now deceased. By this union four children were born, viz., Harry J., May 20, 1872; Susan Edith, April 12, 1874; Anna Grace, November 28, 1880, and Sarah Maria, August 2, 1882. The first-born, Harry, died April 30, 1879, and Anna Grace, August 26, 1881.

During the winter of 1872–73, he purchased a one-third interest in the Wyandot *Democratic Union*, and was associated with L. A. Brunner and D. F. Druckemiller. He disposed of his interest three months later, and removing to Carey, Wyandot Co., Ohio, established the Carey *Weekly Times*. He conducted the business there for nearly four years, and then sold the same to Hon. L. A. Brunner. When he became a resident of Carey he was elected Corporation Clerk, and served in that capacity until his removal back to Upper Sandusky in the fall of 1876. He was then employed by Charles L. Zahm, who was then publishing the *Union*, as foreman and local editor.

Since that time, Mr. Tripp has been connected with the press of Upper Sandusky, more or less, as local editor. Since November 27, 1879, he has been with the *Union*, foreman of its job rooms and assistant editor. He is a brilliant young journalist, and has a bright future before him. As a local writer of incidents and happenings he has few superiors. His style is fine and effective, losing none of the little details around which throngs the in-

---

*Some two years ago, Gen. Grant sent a large photograph of himself to Mr. Cuneo, which is probably one of the best pictures of the great General in existence.

terest of a recital. He is always ready, and gifted with a literary turn of mind which frequently sparkles in his graceful and well-rounded periods. He is a young man, yet his care and faithfulness in his profession has all the marks of experience and native thought. He rarely takes to the humorous, but when he does his writings are sure to contain a dash of the irresistible. His social qualities, though never pretentious nor obtrusive, are none the less of a high order, and few in our midst have more or warmer friends. Mr. Tripp has been a correspondent for the Cincinnati and Eastern papers for several years, and his articles have attracted wide attention.

CAREY PUBLICATIONS.

The *Carey Blade*, Carey's first newspaper, was established by Franklin Dame, a young man only fifteen years of age, in December, 1872. It was a small four-column folio. After getting out four numbers, its publication was suspended, but young Dame conducted a job printing-office for several months thereafter.

The *Carey Weekly Times* was established by Frank T. Tripp, Jr., of Upper Sandusky, now foreman of the Wyandot *Democratic Union* office, on the 8th of May, 1873. He continued its publication until August. 1876, when it passed under the control of Louie A. Brunner, of Upper Sandusky. In 1878, Mr. Brunner transferred his interests to Samuel M. Gillingham, who conducted the paper until January 1, 1880, when it was purchased by its present editors and publishers, George H. Tallman & Co., consisting of George H. Tallman and A. H. Balsley, editor of the *Jeffersonian*, of Findlay, Ohio. This paper, known since it passed under the control of Gillingham as the *Wyandot County Times*, is a seven-column folio, has a circulation of 700 copies, and is neutral in political matters.

George H. Tallman, the present editor of the *Wyandot County Times*, was born at Canal Winchester, Ohio, May 2, 1851. His parents, Hinton and Amanda (Thompson) Tallman, were natives of the State of Virginia, and his maternal grandfather was born in Scotland. When he was ten years of age, the parents of George H. removed to Delaware, Ohio, where he remained ten years, meantime passing two years as a student of the Ohio Wesleyan University at Delaware. In the spring of 1871, he proceeded to Fremont, Ohio, where he was engaged until 1873, as a salesman in a boot and shoe store. In July of that year he became a resident of Port Clinton, Ohio, where he remained until April, 1875, when he located at Findlay, Ohio, and soon after entered the office of A. H. Balsley, editor of the Findlay *Jeffersonian*, for the purpose of learning the printer's trade. There he remained until January 1, 1880, when he entered into a partnership with his former employer, Mr. Balsley, and with him purchased the *Wyandot County Times*, which paper he has since conducted in a very successful manner.

His wife, Molly, a daughter of A. H. Balsley, was born in Pittsburgh, Penn., October 10, 1853, and came to Ohio with her parents when two years of age. They have one daughter, named Neta. Mr. Tallman is a member of the organization known as the Knights of Honor.

THE NEVADA-ENTERPRISE.

This publication, issued by Rev. A. B. Kirtland, made its first appearance under date of January 1, 1872. Mr. Kirtland continued in contro until May 1, 1876, when Messrs. T. H. & J. H. Harter became its owners On the 1st of January, 1879, J. H. Harter sold his interest to J. M. Wilcox

Harter (T. H.) & Wilcox then conducted the paper until November 1, 1882, when Mr. Wilcox purchased Harter's interest and remained sole editor and proprietor until November 1, 1883, when the present firm of Wilcox & Holmes was formed, by Frank Holmes purchasing a one-half interest. This paper is neutral in politics, has a circulation of eight hundred copies, and its annual gross receipts are from $2,500 to $3,000.

Joseph M. Wilcox, editor of the Nevada *Enterprise*, was born in Mifflin County, Penn., January 1, 1855. His parents were Christian and Sarah (Miller), Huffnagle, but his father dying when our subject was a mere child and his mother soon after marrying H. S. Wilcox, the latter name was adopted and has since been retained. His father was born in Pennsylvania and died in that State January 18, 1861. His mother was a daughter of Thomas and Susan (Dorman) Miller, and was born in Union County, Penn., in 1823. Being left a widow in 1861, she moved to Ohio the same year and located at Bellevue, where she was married to H. S. Wilcox in 1863, and where she resided about two and one-half years. She then moved with her husband to Tiffin, and one year later to Millmore; two years after this, they located at Benton, Crawford County, and five years later at the present point of residence, Nevada. Our subject spent the first nineteen years of his life attending school, acquiring a good education. In 1874, he entered the Normal School at Ada, Ohio, and passed a thorough course in the art of book-keeping, after which he spent one year in the wholesale millinery establishment of A. & E. Thompson, beginning January 1, 1875. May 1, 1876, he entered the office of the Nevada *Enterprise* to learn the trade of printing, and January 1, 1879, he purchased a half interest in the office, where he has since been engaged. He is well versed in the "mysteries" of his calling, and publishes a spicy and newsy country paper. Mr. Wilcox was married, January 1, 1879, to Miss Celia Gillan, who was born in Petersburg, this county, December 23, 1856. Her parents are William K. and Eliza (Betzer) Gillan, and both reside in Nevada. Mr. and Mrs. Wilcox have one child, Harry, born October 8, 1879. Mr. Wilcox is a member of the F. & A. M., and favors Republicanism in things political. His work is performed with ability and in all respects he is highly esteemed in his community.

Frank Holmes, a son of Dr. Samuel W. and Sarah E. (Ensminger) Holmes, was born in the town of Upper Sandusky, Ohio, August 4, 1862. Until seventeen years of age he attended the public schools of his native town. He then worked one year in the *Union* office, and subsequently was engaged for six months in the office of the Marion *Independent*. On the 29th of May, 1880, he assisted in getting out the first number of the Sycamore *Star*, under the firm name of S. W. Holmes & Son. He continued to be interested as editor and proprietor of the *Star* until May 29, 1883, when it was sold to the News Publishing Company. On the 1st of November, 1883, he purchased a one-half interest in the *Nevada Enterprise*, of which he still continues as part owner. He was married, December 25, 1883, to Ella, daughter of John and Ellen (McGlen) Turner, of Sycamore, Ohio. She was born in the city of Harrisburg, Penn., August 16, 1866.

THE SYCAMORE NEWS.

This weekly journal was founded as the Sycamore *Star* May 29, 1880, by S. W. Holmes & Son. It started as a five-column quarto, and was managed by its founders until May 29, 1883, when the News Publishing Company, consisting of William Corfman (who had been local editor from

October 1, 1882), C. C. Clark, R. J. Plummer and J. E. Goodrich (with C. C. Clark as manager, and Corfman and Plummer as editors) became its owners. On the 1st of July, 1883, Corfman and I. E. Beery purchased the paper and managed it together until January 1, 1884, when Mr. Corfman retired, leaving Mr. Beery in sole control. On the 31st day of January, 1884, the latter changed the size of the paper to an eight-column folio. The present title was adopted on the 29th day of May, 1883. The *News* is an independent family newspaper, and has a wide circulation.

CHAPTER X.

EDUCATIONAL INTERESTS—CLERICAL PROFESSION.

THE DAYS OF LOG SCHOOLHOUSES—OLDEN TIMES MANNER OF TEACHING—SPELLING SCHOOLS—ITEMS FROM THE SCHOOL REPORT OF 1882—PRESENT EXAMINERS—THE FIRST MEETING OF THE WYANDOT TEACHERS' ASSOCIATION—TEACHERS' INSTITUTE OF 1882—EARLY MODES OF RELIGIOUS WORSHIP—MINISTERS OF THE GOSPEL, 1845 TO 1851 INCLUSIVE—EARLY POETS AND POETRY.

EDUCATIONAL INTERESTS.

AS a sort of prelude to a topic which, treated at its best, possesses but little interest for the general readers, we insert the following pen-picture of the primitive log schoolhouse, and the manner of teaching school twenty-five and thirty years ago in this county, and, indeed, throughout all of the northern portion of the United States (with the exception of the large towns and cities), before the advent of teachers' institutes, the graded school system, uniform text books, and costly high school buildings. The truthfulness of this description will be recognized by the old and the middle-aged readers at a glance.

The primitive log schoolhouse was erected in every neighborhood as soon as there were a dozen children to attend school. The general architecture of this original academy of the wilderness was the same as that already described for the cabin; the difference being that the furniture of the schoolhouse consisted exclusively of benches for seats and a desk fastened to the wall on two sides of the room, behind the principal row of benches, on which the pupils did their writing and laid articles not used for the time being. These writing desks were simply rough slabs, resting upon pins driven inclined into the wall, and they extended nearly the whole length and width of the building. The fire-place averaged larger than those in dwellings.

Imagine such a house, with the children seated around, the teacher on one end of a bench or in a chair, with no desk, and you have a view of the whole scene. The "schoolmaster" has just called "Books! books!" at the door, and the scholars have just run in, almost out of breath from vigorous play, taken their seats, and are, for the moment, hurriedly "saying over their lessons" in a loud whisper, preparatory to recitation. While they are thus engaged, the teacher is, perhaps, sharpening a few quill pens for the pupils, for no other kind of writing pen had been thought of as yet. In a few minutes, he calls up an urchin to say his A B C's. The little boy stands beside the teacher, perhaps leaning against him The teacher, with his pen-knife (urchin wishes he owned such a knife), points to the first letter, and asks what it is. The little fellow remains silent, for he does not know what to say. "A," says the teacher; "A," echoes the urchin. Teacher then points to the next, when the same programme is carried out, and so on, with three or four letters a day, and day after day until the "boy has got all his A B C's by heart." At the conclusion of these exercises, the teacher bids the "Major" to go to his seat and study his letters, and when he comes to a letter he doesn't know to come to him and he will tell him.

Accordingly, he returns to his seat, looks on his book a little while, and then goes trudging across the floor to his master, pointing to a letter outside of his lesson, and holds it up awkwardly in front of the teacher's face. He is told that that letter is not in his lesson, and he needn't study it now, and he trudges, smilingly as he catches the eye of some one, back to his seat again; but why he smiled he has no definite idea.

To prevent wearing the books out at the lower corner, every pupil was expected to keep a "thumb-paper" under his thumb as he held the book in his hand, which was then the custom, there being no desks in front of the scholars. Even then the books were soiled and worn through at this place in a few weeks, so that a part of many lessons were gone. Consequently, the request was often made, "Master, may I borrow Jimmy's book, to git my lesson in? Mine hain't in my book; it's tore out." It was also customary to use book pointers, to point out the letters or words in study as well as in recitation. The black stem of the maiden-hair fern was a favorite material from which pointers were made.

The a-b, ab, scholars through with, perhaps the second or third reader class would be called up, who would stand in a row in front of the teacher, "toeing the mark," which was actually a chalk or charcoal mark, or a crack, and, commencing at one end of the class, one would read the first "verse," the next the second, and so on round and round, Sunday school fashion, taking the paragraphs in the order they occur. Whenever a pupil hesitated at a word, the teacher would pronounce it for him. And this was all there was of the reading exercise.

Those studying arithmetic were but little classified, and they were, therefore, generally called forward singly and interviewed, or the teacher would visit them at their seats. A lesson, comprising several "sums," would be given for the next day to those in classes, while others would press forward without any regard to quantity. Whenever the learner came to a "sum he couldn't do," he would go to the teacher with it—unless he was a drone—and the teacher would do it for him.

In geography, no wall maps were used, no drawing required, and the studying and recitation comprised only the "getting-by-heart" names and places. The recitation proceeded like this: "Where is Norfolk?" "In the southenstern part of Virginia." "What bay between Maryland and Virginia?" "Chesapeake." "What is the capital of Pennsylvania?" "Harrisburg." "Where does the Susquehanna River rise?" "In New York."

When the hour for writing arrived, the time was announced by the master, and every pupil learning the art would throw his feet over and around under the writing desk, facing the greased paper or glass window, and proceed to "follow copy," which was invariably set by the teacher at his leisure moments, not by rule, but by as nice a stroke of the pen as he could make. Blue ink and blue paper were both common, and a "blue time," the learner often had of it.

About half past 10 o'clock, the master would announce, "School may go out," which meant, "little play-time," in the children's parlance, called in modern times "recess" or "intermission." Sometimes the boys and girls were allowed to have this intermission separately. Between playtimes, the request, "Master, may I go out?" was often iterated, to the annoyance of the teacher and the disturbance of the school.

At about half past 11 o'clock, or a little later, the teacher would announce, "Scholars may now get their spelling lessons," and then, in prospect of "big play-time" being near at hand, they would, with the characteristic loud whisper, "say over" to themselves the lesson a given number of times. "Master, I've said my lesson over four times," would sometimes be heard. A few minutes before twelve, the "little spelling class" would recite, and then the "big spelling class." The latter would comprise the larger scholars and the greater part of the school. They would stand in a row, toeing the mark in the midst of the floor, or standing with their backs against an unoccupied portion of the wall. One end of the class was the "head," the other the "foot," and when the pupil spelled a missed word correctly he would "go up," "turning down" all those who had missed it. The recitation done, the class would number, the head pupil numbering as at the foot, where he or she would take station next time, to have another opportunity of turning them all down. Before taking their seats, the teacher would say, "School's dismissed," which was the signal for every child rushing for his dinner, and enjoying the "big play-time." The same programme would also be followed on closing school in the afternoon.

"Past the Pictures." This phrase had its origin in the practice of pioneer schools which used Webster's Elementary Spelling Book, toward the back part of which were a few reading lessons illustrated with pictures—as the mastiff, the stag, the squirrel, the boy stealing apples, the partial lawyers, the milk-maid's day dream, and poor Tray. Succeeding this illustrated portion of the book were a few more spelling exercises, of a peculiar kind; and when a scholar succeeded in reaching these he was said to be "past the pictures," and was looked up to as being smarter and more learned than most other youths expected to be. Hence the application of this phrase came to be extended to other affairs in life, especially where scholarship was involved.

Spelling and singing schools were held at night, at the schoolhouse, when a general frolic was had, and sometimes mischief was done by the "rowdies." On assembling for the spelling match, two youths would volunteer as "captains," to "choose sides" and have a contest. Various methods were adopted, even in the same neighborhood, for conducting this exciting exercise. Sometimes "tally" would be kept; at other times a system of cross-spelling would be followed, commencing at the head or at the foot, or they would spell straight around, or have a "word-catcher" appointed for each side, or would "turn down," etc. After an hour's contest, an intermission was had, which was indeed a lively time for conversation. After recess, the practice was to have a regular spelling-down, sometimes the sides chosen at the first taking their places so as to carry on a sort of double contest, and sometimes taking all the assembly promiscuously. The audience dismissed, the next thing was to "go home," very often by a round-about way, "a-sleighing with the girls," which, with many, was the most interesting part of the evening's performance.

The singing school was of later introduction, but afforded equal advantage for a jubilee. These occasions were looked forward to with great anticipation, even by the older folks.

From the published reports are gathered the following items regarding the educational interests of Wyandot County, for the year ending August 31, 1882, the report for 1883 having not yet been made public:

Amount of school moneys received within the year: Balance on hand September 1, 1881, $49,918.13; State tax, $11,175; irreducible school fund, $3,681.28; local tax for school and schoolhouse purposes, $45,258.73; received on sale of bonds, $1,745; fines, licences, etc., $350.35; total receipts, $112,128.49.

HISTORY OF WYANDOT COUNTY. 407

Expenditures: Paid primary teachers, $29,822.77; paid high school teachers, $2,370.25; for managing and superintending, $1,050; for sites and buildings, $22,703.19; for interest on or redemption of bonds, $509.11; for fuel and other contingent expenses, $6,386.42; total expenditures, $62,841.74; balance on hand September 1, 1882, $49,286.75.

Amount received by the county from the State Common School Fund, $11,175; amount paid by the county into the State Common School Fund, $10,935,81; excess of receipts over payments from this fund, $239.19; number of youth between six and twenty-one years of age in the county, 7,616 amount received by the county as interest from the Section 16 school fund, $4,124.53.

Number of unmarried youth in the county between the ages of six and twenty-one years: White boys, 3,991; white girls, 3,583; total, 7,574; colored boys, 25; colored girls, 17; total, 42; whole number between six and twenty-one years, 7,616; number between sixteen and twenty-one, 1,937; population of the county in 1880, 22,401.

Number of townships in the county, 13; number of subdistricts, 107; number of separate districts, 4; number of primary schoolhouses erected within the year, 5; cost of the same, $6,955.

Whole number of primary schoolhouses in the county, 107; number of primary schoolhouses in separate districts, 5; total, 112; value of schoolhouses and grounds, $123,050.

Number of school rooms, exclusive of rooms used only for recitation, 127; number of teachers necessary to supply the schools, 133.

Number of different teachers employed: Gentlemen in township primary schools, 95; ladies in township primary schools, 113; gentlemen in separate district primary schools, 4; ladies in separate district primary schools, 16; gentlemen in high schools, 5; ladies in high schools, 1; grand total of teachers employed for the year ending August 31, 1882, 234. Number of teachers who taught the entire time the schools were in session, 40.

Average wages of teachers per month: Gentlemen in township primary schools, $35; ladies, same, $22; gentlemen in separate district schools, $46; ladies, same, $33; gentlemen in high schools, $60; average number of weeks the schools were in session within the year: Townships, 26; separate districts, 32; high schools, 35; rate of local tax, in townships, 3.6; in separate districts, 6.5.

·Different pupils enrolled: Boys in township primary schools, 2,402; girls in township primary schools, 2,019; boys in separate districts, 602; girls in separate districts, 647; boys in high schools, 42; girls in high schools, 71; grand total, 5,783. Average daily attendance in all schools, 3,868.

High School Statistics: Total receipts for school purposes within the year, at Upper Sandusky, $31,014.21; at Carey, $5,210.54; at Nevada, $6,414.17; total expenditures at Upper Sandusky, $15,073.80; at Carey, $2,358.60; at Nevada, $5,575.13. Number of schoolhouses at Upper Sandusky, 3; at Carey 1; at Nevada, 1. Number of schoolrooms at Upper Sandusky, 11; at Carey, 4; at Nevada, 6 Value of school property at Upper Sandusky, $18,000; * at Carey, $7,000; at Nevada, $14,000. Number of teachers employed at Upper Sandusky, gentlemen, 2; ladies, 10; at Nevada, gentlemen, 3; ladies, 4; at Carey, gentlemen, 1; ladies, 4. Average wages per month paid, at Upper Sandusky, gentlemen, $80; ladies, $35; at Carey, gentlemen, $75; ladies, $35; at Nevada, gentlemen, $57; ladies, $31. Superintendent at Upper Sandusky, W. A. Baker; salary,

---

* Does not include the elegant new school building which, at that time, was not commenced.

$900; Superintendent at Carey, J. S. Lewis; salary, $750; Superintendent at Nevada, D. E. Niver; salary, $600. Superintendents for the year 1882–83, J. A. Pittsford, at Carey; D. E. Niver, at Nevada, and W. A. Baker, at Upper Sandusky.

The present County Examiners are D. D. Clayton, whose term expires August 31, 1884; M. M. Hollanshead, whose term expires August 31, 1884, and W. C. Gear, whose term expires August 31, 1885.

The first meeting of the Wyandot Teachers' Association was held in the court house at Upper Sandusky—in the old Indian Council House—on Friday, August 25, 1848. At this meeting, Rev. Charles Thayer served as Chairman, and C. P. Culver as Secretary. After adopting various resolutions, those assembled adjourned to meet at the same place on Saturday, September 5, 1848, at 1 o'clock, P. M. Since that date the teachers of the county have kept abreast of the times, and have almost annually met at the county seat, seeking by professional contact, to widen their sphere of knowledge and usefulness.

At the Wyandot Teachers' Institute, held at Upper Sandusky, for five days, commencing August 28, 1882, eight lecturers and instructors, and seventy male and female teachers were present. Of the $192.16 received from the County Treasurer, from members and from other sources, to meet the expenditures of the occasion, $60 were paid lecturers and instructors, and $39.35 were paid for other expenses, leaving a balance on hand of $92.81. The cost of the institute per day was $19.87, and per member, $1.42. The lecturers and instructors present at this session of the institute were W. A. Baker, Robert Carey and D. D. Clayton, of Upper Sandusky; W. W. Hobbs, of Nevada; J. L. Lewis, of Pitt; M. Manley, of Galion; J. A. Pittsford, of Carey, and H. M. Perkins, of Delaware. Of the $60 paid to lecturers, Manley received $50, and Perkins $10.

CLERICAL.

EARLY MODES OF RELIGIOUS WORSHIP.

Although matters relating to church organizations—the date of their establishment, building of houses of worship, change of pastors, etc.—are treated at length in the separate township histories, yet we cannot forbear adding a paragraph or two in this connection, for the purpose of showing the manner of conducting religious worship at an early day, and also to mention the names of some of the early divines of the county.

Says a writer, in speaking of early religious worship in this part of Ohio, "The Methodists were generally first on the ground in pioneer settlements, and at that early day were more demonstrative in their devotions than at the present time. Pulpit oratory was more full of action, and fraught with soaring flights, while the grammatical dress was thought of but little. Family worship, especially among the pioneer Methodists and United Brethren, partook of the zealous fervency of their more public devotions. We then had a most emphatic American edition of that pious old Scotch practice so eloquently described in Burns' 'Cotter's Saturday Night:'

"The cheerfu' supper done, wi' serious face
They round the ingle formed a circle wide;
The sire turns o'er wi' patriarchal grace,
The big ha' Bible, once his father's pride.
His bonnet rev'rently is laid aside,
His lyart hafferts wearing thin and bare,
Those strains that ance did sweet in Zion glide,
He wales a portion wi' judicious care,
And 'Let us worship God,' he says wi' solemn air.

> "They chant their artless notes in simple guise;
> They tune their hearts—by far the noblest aim;
> Perhaps 'Dundee's' wild warbling measures rise,
> Or plaintive 'Martyrs,' worthy of the name;
> Or noble 'Elgin' beats the heavenward flame,
> The sweetest far of Scotia's hallowed lays.
> Compared wi' these, Italian trills are tame;
> The tickled ear nae heartfelt raptures raise;
> Nae unison hae they wi' our Creator's praise.
>
> "The priest-like father reads the sacred page—
> How Abraham was the friend of God on high, etc.
>
> "Then kneeling down to Heaven's Eternal King,
> The saint, the father and the husband prays;
> Hope 'springs exulting on triumphant wing,'
> That thus they a' shall meet in future days;
> There ever bask in uncreated rays,
> No more to sigh or shed the bitter tear,
> Together hymning their Creator's praise,
> In such society, yet still more dear,
> While circling time moves round in an eternal sphere."

The familiar tunes of pioneer worship were mostly in the minor key, and very pensive and solemnly inspiring, in striking contrast with the worldly sound of nearly all modern church music. As they are named in the old "Missouri Harmony" (who has seen this music book within the last thirty years?), the characteristic standard tunes were such as Bourbon, Consolation, China, Canaan, Conquering Soldier, Condescension, Devotion, Davis, Fiducia, Funeral Thought, Florida, Golden Hill, Ganges, Greenfields, Greenville, Idumea, Imandra, Kentucky, Lenox, Leander, Mear, New Orleans, Northfield, New Salem, New Durham, Olney, Primrose, Pisgah, Pleyel's Hymn, Rockbridge, Rockingham, Reflection, Supplication, Salvation, St. Thomas, Salem, Tender Thought, Windham, etc., besides a great number known only by the first lines of the words, as "O, how happy are they," "Come, thou fount of every blessing," "O, for a glance of heavenly day," "Jesus my all, to heaven is gone," etc.

Once or twice a day—in the morning just before or after breakfast, and in the evening just before retiring to rest—the head of the family would call to order, read a chapter in the Bible, announce the hymn and time by commencing to sing, when others would join, then he would deliver a most fervent prayer. If a pious guest was present, he would be called upon to take the lead in the religious exercises; and if, in those days, a person who prayed either in the family or in public, did not pray as if it were his very last on earth, his piety was thought to be defective.

Numbers of other orthodox denominations also had their family prayers, in which, however, the phraseology was somewhat different from that of the Methodists, and the voices kept low and calm.

EARLY MINISTERS OF THE GOSPEL.

The following list embraces the names, denominations, etc., of the ministers of the Gospel who were licensed by the Court of Common Pleas during the years from 1845 to 1851, inclusive, to solemnize marriages in Wyandot County:

Benjamin Sager, Christian, April, 1846; Charles Thayer, Presbyterian, October, 1846; Nathan Evans, German Reformed, October, 1846; George Turk, Lutheran, November, 1847; Silas DeBolt, Predestinarian Baptist, May, 1848; James Milligan, Methodist Episcopal, November, 1848; Augustus Price, Baptist, November, 1848; Jacob Schaner, Evangelical Lutheran,

April, 1849; John Casper Christian Voight, German Lutheran, July, 1849; Louis A. Brunner, Presbyterian, November, 1849; Robert Weeks, United Brethren, April, 1850; Philip Cole, Methodist Episcopal, July, 1850; James B. Oliver, Evangelical Lutheran, November, 1850; Frederick Dolmetsk, Lutheran, November, 1850; James P. Hastings, Bible Christian, July, 1851; Samuel Kelso, United Brethren, November, 1851.

EARLY POETS AND POETRY.

Wyandot County is better adapted to grass and corn than to poetry, consequently but little attention has been paid to the culture of the Parnassian crop.

The only specimen of aboriginal Wyandot poetry known to the writer is a hymn, of which a few verses are given, by Rev. James B. Finley, in his "Life Among the Indians." The first couplet reads as follows:

> "Yar-ro tawsa shre-wan daros
> Du-saw shaw-taw tra-war-ta."

The rest will be forthcoming when called for.

The genial and simple-hearted Count Coffinberry, in his "Forest Rangers," has sung of the Sandusky Plains, and told how—

> "Crawford proved more fortunate,
> For he escaped the public hate
> By being captured there and dying,
> When from the field his hosts were flying."

He has also portrayed the gathering of Indian warriors, when—

> "Along Sandusky's verdant shore
> Did hosts of dusky natives pour."

In a note to the passage first quoted, he informs his readers that the locality of Col. Crawford's torture is on the Tyamoherty, about four miles above its junction with the Sandusky River, and probably about ten miles in a straight line from his battle-ground on the Sandusky Plains.

But we are keeping our readers too long from the earliest poem, which is justly entitled to consideration, as a product of Wyandot County, and which was written during our first summer for our first newspaper, and published in the *Wyandott Telegraph* on the 9th of August, 1845. We transcribe carefully from the only copy now known to be in existence:

AMERICA.

> Land where the Indians love to roam—
> Where true patriots' blood has flown;
> Where freedom's sun has brightly shone
> 'Tis thee I love.
> There's beauty in thy naked soil,
> Bespeaking smiles of love;
> Thy rocks and blooming wilds proclaim
> Protection from above.
>
> Land where the Pilgrim fathers rest,
> Where no foe from us can freedom wrest;
> Of the bright and growing West
> 'Tis thee I love.
> Where the eagle soars on pinions free,
> O'er the towering mountain's top;
> Thus proudly boasting of the liberty
> That bears her onward—up.

Land where the people's voice is heard;
Where on none are kingly powers confer'd;
Where freedom is the boasted word;
   'Tis thee I love.
Here no aristocratic lords
Have power to bind us down,
But freedom grants—that sacred word—
Power to each and every one.

Land of the patriot Washington;
Of the lamented Harrison;
Of the Statesman Jefferson
   'Tis thee I love.
Thou art as a brightly shining star,
That is from every country seen;
Whose rays shine brighter every year,
Though clouded thou at times hast been.

Land that is lashed by Atlantic's wave;
Where monarchy soon found a grave;
That our fathers fought to save;
   'Tis thee I love.
Thy cities great with crowded streets,
Tell of a nation prosperous, free!
Where every stranger kindness meets,
While in this land of liberty.

Land where the wrung soul may rest;
Where each may alike be blest;
Where the laborer is ne'er oppressed;
   'Tis thee I love.
Yes, thou art the land I prize above
All others known to me,
Thou art the land so dearly loved,
   Sweet land of liberty!   —A. W. B.
McCutchenville, July 26, 1845.

Of this poet all the other works have perished, and of his name nothing remains but the initials. The poem itself will doubtless suggest to some of our readers a rather clear imitation of an ode which is sometimes sung in the churches.

Next in order of time, is the remarkable poem which was published for the first and only time in the *Democratic Pioneer* for January 9, 1847, and which, with the editorial note that preceded it, we give entire.

The following lines some may suppose to be borrowed, but Mr. Harris informed us that they are wholly original, no portion being selected. These lines contain something sublime and beautiful, as every one will admit upon a perusal. It is altogether in the author's own style, and without alteration or amendment:

THE PRESENT AT PARTING.

Ellan dear, here is a book,
To pick one for you great pains I took.
And if I never do return,
My heart for you will always burn.

Ellan dear, do not take it amiss,
But take it with a parting kiss,
And wherever you may be,
When you look at this you will think of me.

Ellan dear, thou art a friend.
On whom a person may depend,
And with you and your good heart,
I am sorrow that I have to part.

> Ellan dear, I must now go,
> I bear good will to friend and foe,
> The time has come, I now must I,
> Bid you, my dear, a long good by.
>
> —*By J. A. Harris.*

Notwithstanding the doubts suggested in the preliminary note, we unhesitatingly pronounce the foregoing poem to be wholly original. There is no question but that Mr. Harris made it entirely out of his own head, and had plenty of chips and blocks left.

The rare and authentic specimen of original indigenous poetry appeared in the *Pioneer* of January 19, 1849. The author, Robert Taggart, was an Elder in the Presbyterian Church, whose pious aversion to the sinful amusement of dancing found or forced an utterance in the following song. The introductory note, and the song itself—with the exception of one verse, which, containing more truth than poetry, is especially liable to misconstruction—are copied literally.

At the request of a friend, and in compliance with a resolution passed by a number of persons, we publish the following lines as written by Mr. Taggart:

ORIGINAL SONG.

> You countries and cities, I pray you draw near,
> A comical ditty you quickly shall hear,
> The boys about here they think to advance,
> By courting the girls and learning to dance,
>   And its O shame for them.
>
> The boys about here they think theirs the plan,
> You'll not say one word but you'll have it again;
> And more they'll put to it, they will if they can,
> And many a boy sits up for a man.
>   And its O shame for them.
>
> Their jackets is short as e're they can be,
> And in their bosoms they'll wear a gold key;
> Their pantaloons they must have up to their chin,
> And they're buckled and strapped like a horse in a sling.
>   And its O shame for them.
>
> But now we leave off these sporting young lads,
> And go to the girls, they're ten times as bad;
> They'll powder their hair and rowlers they'll wear.
> And just like an owl in the bush they'll appear,
>   And its fine fun for them.
>
> They'll go to the church and down they will sit,
> They'll laugh and they'll not know at what,
> They'll laugh and they'll point and they'll think themselves wise,
> And they can't get a man if they would lay down their lives,
>   And its fine fun for them.
>
> Oh, when they go there, their box they'll pull out;
> They hit it a crack to make you look about;
> They'll hand it to one, they'll hand it to two,
> Saying, Sir, won't you take it, or Madam won't you?
>   And its fine fun for them.
>
> With ribbands and lace they toss off their head,
> And with a gauze veil they'll cover their face;
> Their top-locks and lug-locks look wonderful queer,
> And they hold up their head like a stiff-bridled mare.
>   And its fine fun for them.

The following lines, which have a somewhat familiar sound, purport to have been "written for the *Wyandot Tribune*," and were published in that paper on June 30, 1849. That the greater portion of them had been written before for some other purpose is quite probable:

NIGHT.

I love the dark and gloomy night,
When moon and stars are hid from sight;
When deafening thunders awful roll,
And lightnings flash from pole to pole.

When Nature rests in silent awe,
As if to scan some secret flaw,
Amid her vast and ponderous wheels,
While all creation trembling reels.

Thus when the elements contend,
And lightnings with the darkness blend,
I'd have some fair one by me then,
To watch the tempest's gathering might.

How grand the scene! how blest the choice
Of such an one in such an hour!
The dismal heavens would form our bower,
As blackning clouds around us lower.

UPPER SANDUSKY, June 30, 1849. —*C. G. F.*

For a few years afterward Wyandot County struggled along as best it could, without a sacred or other poet, until C. G. Mugg took charge of the *Wyandot Pioneer*, and in the omniverous spirit which marked his control of that paper, became his own poet. As a fair example of his best style, we give the general reflections with which he concluded a lengthy poem on the subject of Col. Crawford's rather well-known mishap, published in the *Pioneer* of October 29, 1857, and entitled "Battle Island." After portraying the varying fortunes and final result of the fight, our poet continues:

Long years have passed, and many a morn and eve,
Time's changes on the face of nature weave;
Where once the wigwam of the savage stood,
Or where unseen in pathless solitude,
Roamed the wild deer and beast of prey alone,
By marshy fen, by reeds and grass o'ergrown,
All these have passed away and in their place,
Are dwellings of a nobler, better race.

Where once the Indian village decked the plain,
Bright summer shows her fields of waving grain,
Which in the spring and early summer bloom,
Blossom alike o'er white and red—man's tomb.
To thee, thou Battle Isle, changes but few have come,
Since erst the Wyandot thy shade his home
Had made. Now wave thy oaks as green as when
Thou shelteredst in their need brave Crawford and his men.

Though near an hundred years have fled,
Thy shade still reaches o'er the slumbering dead,
That sleep in one huge grave, by midnight fires
Dug, for our murdered Anglo-Saxon sires.
God rest them! May their children ever keep
Sacred the spot where their forefathers sleep,
And may they make that mound, in years to come,
A sacred shrine—a proud mausoleum.

The same poet editor produced "A Lay of the Heart," which was given to the public in the *Pioneer* of January 14, 1858. The first of the four verses composing this lay is quoted as a fair example of its author's sentimental poetry:

> Fairest of earth's bright-eyed daughters,
>   Milder thou than breath of morn
> Gladsome as the chime of waters,
>   O'er the wold at twilight borne.
> List the lay of one who loves thee,
>   One but who lives in thy smile—
> Dearer far to him than any,
>   Gem that gleams on Eastern isle.

"The Upper Sandusky Bard," whose lengthy productions in poetry were published in several numbers of the *Democratic Union*, beginning with January, 1858, was another whose poetic efforts, perhaps, entitle him to some recognition in these pages, but as before intimated, his articles all verge upon the extreme of prolixity, and as space and time with us are valuable, we will cordially delegate the task of their reproduction to those possessing more appreciation and more leisure.

Again turning to the last article contributed by Mr. Sears, we find him commenting upon the only poetess Wyandot County has produced as follows:

"Though we disclaim any credit for so ordinary an act of politeness, we trust our readers will not overlook the fact, that the places of honor in these sketches have been reserved for our only poetess, the sweet and sentimental songtress, who gave to the world the gushings of her gentle heart. in a small 16mo volume, bound in muslin and modestly labeled, 'Lute's Poems.'"

Turning to the title page, we are introduced with somewhat more formality to "Poems by Lute, respectfully dedicated to M. C. H:"

> O let us seek some friendly isle,
>   Far o'er the deep blue sea,
> Where none save nature's own sweet smile,
>   Will rest on you and me;
> Where frowns we've met in other years,
>   Will sink in Lethe's streams,
> Where pa-sing smiles and bitter tears,
>   Will never haunt our dreams.

"Printed for the author at the establishment of the United Brethren, at Dayton, Ohio, 1858."

While the opening lines of the dedicatory strains above quoted remind us somewhat forcibly of the fate of that unfortunate colt which was drowned in attempting to cross the river to get a drink, and although there are many other passages in the book where impulsive genius has set the rules of composition and grammar at defiance; yet it is our only printed volume of poetry—it may be the only one we shall ever have—and we are determined to make the most of it. Consider for a moment, in a proper spirit of thankfulness, and without exulting over our less fortunate neighbors, how few of the eighty odd counties in Ohio have a printed volume of their own homemade poetry.

"Lute's Poems" are the unassisted work of a young lady who was brought up in Wyandot County, whose intellectual training was the work of our common and other schools, and whose heart here received that education of love, hope and disappointment which finds full expression in the volume before us.

Such selections as our space permits will be given for the benefit of our readers, the most of whom will never see ought more of the contents of this privately printed and already very scarce book. There are many religious poems, notable among which are *Kedron, Jesus Wept, Jerusalem and The*

Reconciliation. The last-named is Miltonic, both in style and subject, and treats of Adam and Eve's criminations, recriminations and final reconciliation after the ejectment from Eden. There are many pieces devoted to the perpetuation of the very laudable affections of the author as a sister and daughter, some obituary feeling offerings to departed friends, a few fancy sketches such as *The Fairy's Tale* and *The Aborigines,* and also something philosophic, and didactic in reference to Homer and Napoleon; yet, among them all, we prefer those pieces which treat of the gentle passion, those outpourings of the heart, whose intensity might almost compensate the lack of genius. Our few extracts, which will be confined to this class, can have no more fitting introduction than the hymn to the god with plump cheeks, who with bow and quiver, and without trowsers, is worshiped openly or in secret, by all sentimental young ladies under the name of

CUPID.

Little, flying gleam of fancy,
 Little ray
Chasing peace away,
Every day, and every hour,
Proves more absolute his power,—
Habitant of every nation,
Handed down through all creation,
 Here, there, everywhere,
Making mischief where he can,
In the heart of man.

Little flying gleam of fancy,
 Little ray,
Chasing peace away,
Styled by some a gift from heaven,
Others say, whence unforgiven—
Spirits dwell in blackest night,
He has 'scaped and come to light.

Loved by some, and scorned by others;
Still their hatred never smothers
The bright fires which he starts,
On the altar of our hearts.

Another poem is addressed to some faithless swain, and entitled:

YOU CANNOT QUITE FORGET ME.

You cannot quite forget me—
 Go leave me if you will—
But lingering memories of me
 Will haunt your pathway still.

The tears when we have parted,
 The smiles when we have met,
The kindly words we've spoken,
 You never can forget.

You cannot quite forget me,
 Although another shrine
May claim your priceless favor,
 You'll often think of mine.

The smiles from some one fairer,
 Awhile may drown regret,
But still our sunny mornings
 You never can forget.

And then in a spirit of despondency, doubtless caused by that fellow's persistent efforts to forget her, the fair songstress declared:

I'LL NEVER LOVE AGAIN.

Yes, yes, the happy dream is past,
 To retain it I was fain;
But 'twas delusion now I know,
 And I'll never love again.

O! may the past, the dreamy past,
 As the summer rose depart;
And again I'll mingle with the gay,
 But with a heavier heart.

For still fond memories of the past,
 I ever will retain,
Remembering him I used to love,
 I'll never love again.

Yet, despite the disappointment and deception, faithlessness and broken vows, true to the promptings and the destiny of the female heart, she continues to love under all disadvantages, as evidence of which we cite the concluding poem in this volume, and with it close our sketch of the early poets and poetry of Wyandot County:

TO ———.

They tell me, love, they tell me,
 That thou art sadly changed,
That from the one that lived for thee
 Thy heart is now estranged.

They tell me of thy baseness,
 To send a sickening dart,
In thoughtless ease and trifling mood,
 Into a trusting heart.

But this heart will never cherish
 One bitter thought of you,
But live to love thy memory,
 Of time when thou was't true

Thou was't not false—O! no,
 Not ever false as now,
Once truth was pictured in thine eye,
 And stamped upon thy brow.

And though thou'st proved, basely false,
 And played a traitor's part,
Methinks that still an honor's gleam
 Must nestle in thine heart.

They tell me to forget thee,
 And that at pleasure's shrine
I may lose in oblivion,
 The love which still is thine.

The following beautiful and expressive poem was written by Frank E. Dumm, who has gained considerable distinction as an elocutionist, and a very brilliant writer for one of his years. He was born in Upper Sandusky August 22, 1862, and is a son of R. D. Dumm, editor of the Wyandot *Union*:

LENA'S MOTHER.

DECLAMATION.

Where is your mother? Come, Lena dear,
Stand close by my side, first wipe off that tear.
In a land far away—beautiful land—
A maiden there lived—child, give me your hand—
A blithe, happy maid, who played all day long,
So sweet was her smile and bright was her song,
That the boatmen who passed on the river below
Would silence their oars e'er turning to go.
The easel-bowed trav'ler would slacken his pace
To gaze on the gems that shone in her face;
And turn as he passed to imprint on his mind
The beauty and light he was leaving behind.

So fair was this maiden, my Lena, child,
So innocent, artless, so undefiled,
That the country lads with much emotion,
Spoke the burden of their heart's devotion;
But she loved one, and only one, and he!
Well, Lena, child, he was somewhat like me.

She used to sing a plaintive song, so sweet,
It mocked the river's rippling feet;
It was a mellow, mother's lullaby;
I'll sing it child, if you'll come nigh:

LULLABY.

Slumber as sweet as the breath of the roses,
  Close Lena's lids, protect Lena's sleep,
For man never knows what the morrow proposes,
  What snares on the land, what rocks in the deep;
    Sleep, Lena, sleep,
    Angels will keep
    Ever by thee,
    Ever nigh thee,
And lead you through dreamland's beautiful highways—
Mansions and bowers and woodlands and by-ways—
    Sleep, Lena, sleep.

DECLAMATION.

Sweet lullaby, how it brings back to me
The time, child, when you sat on my knee,
With your soft white hands clasped closely in mine—
A look on your face that was half divine;
And with tears in my eyes and drooping head,
I gazed on the patient face of the dead.

How sweet to my soul came that lullaby,
And lightened the grief of both you and I—
    Sleep, Lena, sleep,
    Angels will keep
    Ever nigh you,
    Ever by you;
The smile on her face, the light in her eye,
Spoke thro' the soul that ascended on high.

Come, child, we'll sing your mother's lullaby,
And softly, child, for her spirit is nigh;
Sweetly, too, and let a tear dim the eye—
Sweet, mellow, Lena's mother's lullaby.

    (*Repeat Lullaby.*)

Heard you not, Lena, child, the voice that long
Has been lost to our joys, echo the song?
Or heard you not flowers sighing to me
From a grassy mound, far over the sea?
Nor felt you the dread of silence that fell
On the mystic life, o'er the magic spell
That bears each token of life's fitful ways,
To the souls that revel in sun-lit days?
Heard you not a step so soft and light,
Falling as sweetly as rays of bright
Golden sunbeams, and then gliding away—
Leaving a shadow 'mid shadows to play?
That was your mother, Lena, watching nigh
So softly echoing our lullaby.

LULLABY.

Slumber as soft as the breath of the roses,
  Close Lena's lid's, protect Lena's sleep,
For man never knows what the morrow proposes,
  What snares on the land, what rocks in the deep.
      Sleep, Lena, sleep,
      Angels will keep
      Ever by thee,
      Ever nigh thee,
And lead you through dreamland's beautiful highways,
Mansions and bowers and woodlands and by-ways—
      Sleep, Lena, sleep.

CHAPTER XI.

MATERIAL PROGRESS.

POPULATION OF TOWNS AND TOWNSHIPS BY DECADES—THE STANDING OF TOWNSHIPS IN 1845—TRANSPORTATION FACILITIES—INDIAN TRAILS—WAGON ROADS—RAILROADS—POST OFFICES AND POSTMASTERS—AGRICULTURAL PRODUCTIONS—STATSITICS FOR THE YEAR 1882—COUNTY AGRICULTURAL SOCIETY.

IN the endeavor to show the gradual progress of the county of Wyandot during the past forty years (likewise its present resources), and for reasons which should be obvious to the general reader, we have here arranged under one general heading sundry topics, each of which, if treated independently, would not furnish sufficient material to form separate chapters.

POPULATION.

Wyandot County began its existence in the spring of 1845, with about 5,000 white inhabitants; that its progress has been rapid with respect to population, is clearly shown by the following tabulated statement, which has been compiled with much care from the United States census reports:

TOWNSHIPS AND VILLAGES.	YEARS.			
	1880.	1870.	1860.	1850.
Antrim Township, including the following villages	1928	1061	1245	766
Nevada* Village (part of). (See Eden Township.)	790			
Wyandot Village	130			
Crane Township, including the following villages	5082	3876	2877	1544
Upper Sandusky Village	3545	2564	1599	783
Mononcue Village	50			
Crawford Township, including the following villages	2213	1860	1626	1301
Carey Village	1148	692		
Crawfordsville Village	61			
Eden Township, including the following villages.	1793	1423	1247	643
Edenville Village	50			
Little York Village	50			
Nevada* Village (part of). (See Antrim Township)	246			
Jackson Township, including the village of Kirby	1331	771	603	395
Kirby Village	294			
Marseilles Township, including the village of Marseilles	840	603	693	539
Marseilles Village	273	251		
Mifflin Township	1455	866	870	570
Pitt Township, including the following villages	1268	991	957	886
Fowler City Village	126			
Little Sandusky Village	182			
Richland Township, including the village of Wharton	1676	1271	1014	599
Wharton Village	399			
Ridge Township	689	584	583	501
Salem Township	1548	1103	1070	738
Sycamore Township, including the following village	1058	850	937	880
Sycamore Village	272			
Tymochtee Township, including the following villages.	1620	1631	1874	1817
Belle Vernon Village	112			
McCutchenville Village	230			
Mexico Village	115			
Tymochtee Village	38			
Total population by decades	22401	18553	15596	11169

* Total population of the village of Nevada, in 1880, lying in Antrim and Eden Townships, 1,036.

THE STANDING OF TOWNSHIPS IN 1845.

Antrim—Number of tax-payers assessed for personal property, 75; acres of land, 8,603½; value of lands, including houses, mills, etc., $25,995; value of town lots, including buildings, $738; horses, in number, 134; value, $5,-360; cattle, in number, 238; value, $1,904; merchants capital, and money at interest, $501; pleasure carriages, in number, 1; value, $40; total amount of taxable property, $33,639; State tax, $335.47; county tax, $218.65; road tax, $50.45.

Crane—Number of inhabitants assessed for personal property, 57; horses in number, 85; value, $3,400; cattle, in number, 100; value, $800; merchant's capital, and money at interest, $1,950; pleasure carriages, in number, 2; value, $100; total amount of taxable property, $6,250; State tax, $43.75; county and school tax, $40.62; poor tax, $31.25; road tax, $9.37; total amount of taxes assessed, $125.

Crawford—Number of tax-payers assessed for personal property, 165; acres of land, 17,830; value of lands, including houses, mills, etc., $38,868; value of town lots, including buildings, $2,288; horses, in number, 252; value, $10,080; cattle, in number, 690; value, $5,520; merchant's capital and money at interest, $2,185; pleasure carriages, in number, 9; value, $480; total amount of taxable property, $59,421; State tax, $415.94; county and school tax, $386.23; road tax, $89.13; total amount of taxes assessed, $891.31.

Eden—Number of tax-payers assessed for personal property, 18; acres of land, 2,704; value of lands, including houses, mills, etc., $8,452; horses, in number, 26; value, $1,040; cattle, in number, 56; value, $448; pleasure carriages, in number, 2; value, $105; total amount of taxable property, $10,045; State tax, $70.31; county and school tax, $65.29; road tax, $15.06; total amount of taxes assessed, $150.67.

Jackson—Number of inhabitants assessed for personal property, 48; acres of land, 15,686; value of lands, including houses, mills, etc., $20,352; horses, in number, 65; value of same, $2,600; cattle, in number, 145; value of same, $1,160; total amount of taxable property, $24,112; State tax, $168.78; county and school tax, $156,72; road tax, $36.16; total amount of taxes levied, $361.68.

Mifflin—Number of inhabitants assessed for personal property, 60; acres of land, 6,162; value of lands, including houses, mills, etc., $12,392; horses, in number, 86; value, $3,440; cattle, in number, 169; value, $1,352; merchant's capital and money at interest, $114; total amount of taxable property, $17,298; State tax, $121.08; county and school tax, $112.43; road tax, $25.94.

Marseilles—Number of inhabitants assessed for personal property, 86; acres of land, 14,460; value of lands, including houses, mills, etc., $34,-496; value of town lots, including buildings, $2,889; horses, in number, 126; value, $5,040; cattle, in number, 304; value, $2,432; merchants' capital and money at interest, $7,925; pleasure carriages, in number, 2; value, $140; total amount of taxable property, $52,522; State tax, $367.65; county and school tax, $341.39; road tax, $78.78; total amount of taxes levied, $787.83.

Pitt.—Number of tax payers assessed for personal property, 121; acres of land, 9,936; value of lands, including houses, mills, etc., $28,694; value of town lots, including buildings, $2,110; horses in number, 200; value, $8,000; cattle in number, 425; value, $3,400; merchants' capital and money at interest, $4,490; pleasure carriages in number, 6; value, $450; total amount of taxable property, $47,144; State tax, $300; county and school tax, $306.43; road tax, $70.71; total amount of taxes assessed, $707.16.

Richland.—Number of inhabitants assessed for personal property, 62; acres of land, 17,279; value of lands, including houses, mills, etc., $30,959; value of town lots, including buildings, $36; horses in number, 79; value, $3,160; cattle in number, 165; value, $1,320; merchants' capital and money at interest, $139; total amount of taxable property, $35,614; State tax, $249.29; county and school tax, $231.49; township tax, $35.61; road tax, 124.64; total amount of taxes levied, $641.05.

Ridge.—Number of inhabitants assessed for personal property, 67; acres of land, 9,678; value of lands, including houses, mills, etc., $18,328; value of town lots, including buildings, $133; horses in number, 107; value of same, $4,280; cattle in number, 161; value of same. $1,288; pleasure carriages in number, 1; value $40; total amount of taxable property, $24,069; State tax, $168,48; county and school tax, $156.44; road tax, $36.10; total amount of taxes levied, $361.03.

Salem.—Number of inhabitants assessed for personal property, 34; acres of land, 5,114; value of lands, including houses, mills, etc., $9,420; horses in number, 53; value, $2,120; cattle in number, 131; value, $1,048; total amount of taxable property, $12,588; State tax, $88.11; county and school tax, $81.82; road tax, $18.88; total amount of taxes levied, $188.82.

Sycamore.—Number of tax payers assessed for personal property, 123; acres of land, 13,372; value of lands, including houses, mills, etc., $36,380; horses in number, 230; value, $9,200; cattle in number, 446; value, $3,568; merchants' capital and money at interest, $200; pleasure carriages in number, 10; value, $535; total amount of taxable property, $49,903; State tax, $349.32; county and school tax, $324.36; township tax, $49.90; road tax, $74.85; total amount of taxes assessed, $798.44.

Tymochtee.—Number of tax payers assessed for personal property, 260; acres of land, 17,180; value of lands, including houses, mills, etc., $47,518; value of town lots, including buildings, $8,272; horses in number, 387; value, $15,460; cattle in number, 636; value, $5,088; merchants' capital and money at interest, $7,919; pleasure carriages in number, 16; value, $873; total amount of taxable property, $85,150; State tax, $596.05; county and school tax, $553.47; township tax, $42.57; road tax, $127.72; total amount of taxes levied, $1,319.82½.

Grand Summary.—Number of inhabitants assessed for personal property, 1,176; acres of land, 138,005; value of lands, including houses, mills, etc., $310,954; value of town lots,* including buildings, $16,066; horses in number, 1,830; value of same, $73,200; cattle in number, 3,366; value of same, $29,328; merchants' capital and money at interest, $25,444; pleasure carriages in number, 49; value of same, $2,763; total amount of taxable property, $457,755; State tax, $3,204.28¼; county and school tax, $2,975.40; township tax, $128.09; poor tax, $31.25; road tax, $757.86; total amount of taxes levied in 1845, $7,096.89¼.

TRANSPORTATION FACILITIES.

Indian Trails.—The first white men to visit this region—the Indian traders, and the equally adventurous hunters and trappers—found their way from stream to stream, from prairie to prairie, and from one valley to another by following the trails or paths then in use by the Indians.

---

* This summary does not include the town lots, etc., in the town of Upper Sandusky, nor the lands and value thereof in Crane Township, which were not mentioned in the assessment of 1845.

The latter certainly displayed much astuteness, or, if we may use the term, engineering skill, in the choice of their routes of travel, for the same paths were pursued by the traders with their pack-horse trains. Next they were followed by the rude military roads hewed out by the axmen and pioneers attached to the American armies under Gen. Harrison and others during the war of 1812-15. Next came the highways, constructed under State authority. Then followed the ordinary wagon roads, and lastly, the railways of the present day.

At this late day, and with no authentic evidence as a guide, it is impossible to describe the route of the various trails which led through this immediate region during its occupation by the Indians. It is a well-authenticated fact, however, that, from time immemorial, the Wyandots and other Indians used a broad and well-defined trail, which in its course northward from the head-waters of the Scioto River to Sandusky Bay, led directly over the site of the present town of Upper Sandusky. Another favorite route with the aborigines, termed the "Old War Trace," intersected the trail just mentioned at Upper Sandusky, and thence led off in a southeasterly course through the present towns of Caledonia, Mount Gilead, Fredericktown and Mount Vernon, down Old Creek to White Woman River. Doubtless many other minor trails crossed and led into the broad paths above referred to, but, as before intimated, it is now an impracticable task to even attempt to describe them.

Wagon Roads, Ferries, etc.—Without a doubt, the first attempt at road-making by the whites in the territory now embraced by Wyandot County, took place during the year 1812. This route, called the "Old War Road," was cut out by Gen. Harrison's soldiers, and passed in a nearly north and south direction through Upper Sandusky and the central part of the present county. Some years after the close of the war of 1812-15, and by a treaty stipulation with the Wyandot Indians, a State road was marked out and somewhat improved, which led from Delaware to Upper Sandusky, and thence on to Lake Erie, *via* the towns now known as Tiffin, Fremont, etc. This road became well established, and for many years was the chief highway leading into this region. However, as the country settled up, public highways became indispensable, and they were slowly and gradually made, simultaneously with the building of the log cabin residences and the development of farms.

A number of roads were authorized to be laid out in this region by the authorities of Marion, Crawford, Hancock and Hardin Counties before the organization of Wyandot County. Since that time a large number of others have been opened, and a vast sum of money, in the aggregate, appropriated to improve them. Yet the county cannot yet boast of a mile of turnpike or macadamized road, and as a result of the peculiar character of the soil, the ordinary highways during certain seasons of the year are well-nigh impassable.

By turning to the court records it is ascertained that in 1847 Joseph T. Torrey was denied the right to maintain a ferry over the Tymochtee Creek, on the State road leading from Upper to Lower Sandusky. In July of that year, however, Jacob Bugh and Daniel F. Hodge, under the firm name of Bugh & Hodge, were granted the privilege of keeping and maintaining for one year "a ferry over the Sandusky River where the road crosses the said river, east of McCutchenville;" and at November term, 1848, Michael Noel and Cornelius Shaw were granted a license for one year to keep and maintain a ferry "at a point on the Tymochtee Creek, where the road leading from Upper Sandusky to McCutchenville crosses said creek."

Railroads.—*Indianapolis, Bloomington & Western Railway Company.*—The corporate history and the changes which have led to this title, are briefly stated as follows: By a special charter, granted January 5, 1832 (O. L. 15), the Mad River & Lake Erie Railroad Company was incorporated and vested with the right to construct a railway from Dayton via Springfield, Urbana, Bellefontaine, to or near Upper Sandusky, Tiffin and Lower Sandusky, to Sandusky, Huron County; also to construct branches to the seats of justice of any county through which the road may be located.

Thereafter the following legislation furthering the interests of the corporation was had on the several dates specified:

An act to authorize a loan of credit of the State of $200,000 to the said company, approved March 14, 1836 (34 O. L., 570).

An act to authorize the Commissioners of Logan County to subscribe for $25,000 of the capital stock of the company, approved December 19, 1836 (35, O. L., 7).

An act to authorize the Commissioners of Hardin County to subscribe $30,000 to the capital stock of the company, and, in case the railroad is located through the town of Kenton, to make a donation to the company of any lots owned by the county in or near Kenton; approved March 16, 1839 (37 O. L., 343).

An act to authorize the Commissioners of Hancock County to subscribe to the capital stock of the Mad River & Lake Erie Railroad Company the sum of $60,000, or such sum as shall be sufficient to construct a railway or branch from the main track of said railway to the town of Findlay, and to pay such subscription; authorizes the said Commissioners to issue the bonds of the said county, bearing interest at not over six per cent per annum, payable to said railroad company, or any other person or body corporate, no bond so issued to be for a less sum than $1,000; approved February 19, 1845 (43 O. L., 109).

Under the last-mentioned act, and the authority of the charter of the Mad River & Lake Erie Railroad Company, the Findlay Branch Railroad was built from Carey, Wyandot County, on the main line, to Findlay, the county seat of Hancock County, a distance of 15.54 miles, and has ever since been operated and held as a part of the Mad River & Lake Erie Railroad.

On the 6th of February, 1847 (45 O. L., 65), an act was passed authorizing the town of Springfield to subscribe $20,000 to the stock of the company, to be applied to construction between Springfield and Dayton; and two days later another act was passed (see 45 O. L., 87) authorizing the Commissioners of Clark County to subscribe, on behalf of said county, not exceeding $25,000 to the capital stock of the Mad River & Lake Erie Railroad Company, payment therefor to be made by transferring to it certificates to an equal amount of stock heretofore subscribed by said Commissioners in behalf of said county, to the capital stock of the Little Miami Railroad Company.

In the spring of 1847, an effort was made in Wyandot County to secure railway connections with the Mad River & Lake Erie Railroad. Thus on the 21st of April, 1847, at a railroad meeting held in Upper Sandusky, for the purpose of inaugurating a movement looking to the building of a branch railroad from Upper Sandusky to connect with the railroad above mentioned, Dr. James McConnell was elected President; David Ayres, Vice President; and Samuel M. Worth, Secretary. Robert McKelly, Esq., then stated the object of the meeting. Whereupon Henry Peters, Moses H. Kirby, Robert

McKelly, John McCurdy and Samuel M. Worth were appointed a committee to ascertain the terms by which a railroad could be constructed from Upper Sandusky to intersect the Mad River & Lake Erie Railroad. However, it appears that in view of certain difficulties attending the construction of the proposed branch railroad, and the fact that the building of an east and west trunk line to pass through Upper Sandusky was already being agitated, all further efforts regarding the branch road were abandoned.

The Mad River & Lake Erie Railroad Company located and constructed its road from Tiffin to Sandusky by way of Bellevue. In 1851, the Sandusky City & Indiana Railroad Company, which was chartered by act of February 28 of that year (49 O. L., 434), proceeded to build a road from Tiffin to Sandusky via Clyde, and this route being deemed more favorable than the other, on December 1, 1854, the last-named company leased this road for the term of ninety-nine years, renewable forever, to the Mad River & Lake Erie Railroad Company, which has since operated the same as a part of its line, ultimately abandoning the other route. The organization of the Sandusky City & Indiana Railroad Company is kept up for the purpose of perpetuating the lease, the interest of the companies being identical, and the road having been built in the interest of and with means furnished by the Mad River & Lake Erie Company, one person acting as President of both corporations.

On the 1st of June, 1854, the company leased the road of the Springfield & Columbus Railroad Company for the term of fifteen years, agreeing to stock and run the same out of the proceeds, paying first the operating expenses; second, the interest on the $150,000 outstanding bonds of the Springfield & Columbus Company, and the balance to the lessor.

Subsequently, by a decree of the Court of Common Pleas of Erie County, of date February 23, 1858, the name of the Mad River & Lake Erie Railroad Company was changed to Sandusky, Dayton & Cincinnati Railroad Company. See Record of Corporations, office of Secretary of State, No. 1, p. 446. At that time the road was in full operation on that part of the line passing through Wyandot County.

On the 4th of February, 1865, a bill was filed by the trustee of one of the mortgages, covering the entire property, in the Court of Common Pleas of Erie County, against the company for foreclosure of mortgage and sale of the property; and on the 13th of October following, O. Follett was appointed Receiver and Special Master Commissioner in the case, who operated the road under the orders of the court.

While the suit was pending, various parties interested entered into an agreement for a capitalization of the stock and debts of the company, a sale of the road, and a re-organization under the proceedings for foreclosure; and in pursuance of this arrangement an order was issued by the court to sell the entire property, including the rights and franchises of the company, which, accordingly, on the 5th of January, 1866, was sold by the Receiver and Master Commissioner to three Trustees, who purchased the same in trust for the benefit of the parties to the agreement of capitalization, which included nearly all the persons representing the stock and various classes of debt.

On the 2d of July, 1866, the certificate of re-organization, under the name of the Sandusky & Cincinnati Railroad Company, was filed in the office of the Secretary of State. See Record of Corporations No. 3, p. 518.

This company, on the 8th of October, 1866, leased its road and property for the term of ninety-nine years, renewable forever, to the Cincinnati,

Dayton & Eastern Railroad Company, but by mutual agreement of the two companies, January 9, 1868, the lease was surrendered to the Sandusky & Cincinnati Railroad Company. Two days later, on January 11, 1868, there was filed in the office of the Secretary of State (see Record of Corporation, No. 4, p. 64) a decree of the Court of Common Pleas of Erie County, changing the name of the Sandusky & Cincinnati Railroad Company to the Cincinnati, Sandusky & Cleveland Railroad Company. This last named company, on the 28th of June, 1870, leased for a period of ninety-nine years, from July 1, 1870, renewable forever, the road, property and rights of the Columbus, Springfield & Cincinnati Railroad Company (successor to the Springfield & Columbus Railroad Company, heretofore named as lessors to the Mad River & Lake Erie Company), the latter agreeing to complete its line of road from London to Columbus by September 1, 1871, and to keep and maintain its corporate existence and organization, the first party to have the privilege of issuing coupon bonds to the amount of $1,100,000, secured by mortgage or deed of trust on the property, and agreeing to maintain, use and operate the road from Columbus to Springfield, making such additions, etc., as the business may require, pay all running expenses, damages for loss or injury to property or persons, all taxes, etc., and to pay as rental, when in possession of the whole line between Springfield and Columbus, in equal quarterly payments, forty per centum of the gross earnings and income of the road between Springfield and Columbus; provided that when the aggregate thus to be paid shall exceed the sum of $120,000; the first-named company shall pay, and the latter be entitled to receive fifty per centum only of such excess in addition, the first party guaranteeing that the annual payment to the Columbus, Springfield & Cincinnati Railroad Company shall not be less than $80,000 each year.

The following in relation to the above lease is from the annual report of this company, June 30, 1872, to the Commissioner: "The lease has been modified so that this company, instead of paying forty per cent of the gross earnings of that road, guarantees the principal and interest of the bonds of the Columbus, Springfield & Cincinnati Railroad Company, and its stock, exchanged for stock of this company, share for share, is owned and held in trust by the Cincinnati, Sandusky & Cleveland Railroad Company."

The company has made a perpetual lease of that portion of its road extending from Springfield to Dayton, receiving therefor thirty-five per cent of the gross earnings, to the Cincinnati & Springfield Railway Company, by whom it was transferred, together with a lease in perpetuity of its own railway rights, privileges and franchises, to the Cleveland, Columbus, Cincinnati & Indianapolis Railway Company.

On the 8th of March 1881, this company, and the Columbus, Springfield & Cincinnati Railroad Company, leased their roads to the Indianapolis, Bloomington & Western Railway Company, for ninety-nine years, renewable forever.

This road affords excellent facilities to the residents of the western part of Wyandot County, and running in a general northeast and southwest course, traverses, with sidings, 19.85 miles within the county limits. Its chief stations in Wyandot are Carey and Whartonsburg.

Pittsburgh, Fort Wayne & Chicago Railway Company.—This company was organized in the summer of 1856, by the consolidation of the interests of the Ohio & Pennsylvania Railroad Company (which was incorporated

February 24, 1848, by the Legislature of Ohio, and April 11, 1848, by the Legislature of Pennsylvania), the Ohio & Indiana Railroad Company (which was incorporated March 20, 1850, by the Ohio Legislature, and ratified January 15, 1851, by the Indiana Legislature), and the Fort Wayne & Chicago Railroad Company, which was incorporated in Indiana September 22, 1852, by filing articles of association with the Secretary of State, and in Illinois by an act of the State Legislature dated February 5, 1853.

Turning to a report (dated at Pittsburgh, Penn., May 6, 1856), addressed to the stockholders of the three roads by George W. Cass, President of the Ohio & Pennsylvania Railroad Company; Robert McKelly, President pro tem. of the Ohio & Indiana Railroad Company, and Joseph K. Edgerton, President of the Fort Wayne & Chicago Railroad Company, we find the following facts concerning the early history of these roads.

The Ohio & Pennsylvania Railroad Company, as originally incorporated, was authorized to extend its road from Pittsburgh to the State line of Indiana, in the direction of Fort Wayne. The company did not, however, deem it expedient to exercise the full power of its charter, and the present town of Crestline, a point on the Cleveland, Columbus & Cincinnati Railroad, 187 miles west of the city of Pittsburgh, was established as the western terminus of the Ohio & Pennsylvania Railroad.

It was supposed in that early period in the history of the company, that the extension of the road westward from Crestline could be better carried on under the auspices of another and independent company. The road was, therefore, only constructed from Pittsburgh to Crestline, and was opened for business over its whole length on the 11th day of April, 1853.

Pending the progress of the Ohio & Pennsylvania Railroad, and with a view to its western extension to Fort Wayne, the Ohio & Indiana Railroad Company was chartered and organized under the laws of Ohio and Indiana, and empowered to construct its road from Crestline to Fort Wayne. Liberal subscriptions were obtained from the counties along the line of the road, and from private individuals, and in the spring of 1852 the work of construction was commenced. On the 1st of November, 1854, the road was opened from Crestline to Fort Wayne, a distance of 131¼ miles. The Pennsylvania and the Ohio & Pennsylvania Railroad Companies had also aided largely in its construction by their means and credit, and in 1856 owned about one-fourth of the road, its rolling stock, etc.

The successful commencement and progress of the Ohio & Indiana Railroad led to the organization in September, 1852, under the general railroad laws of Indiana, of the Fort Wayne & Chicago Railroad Company, with power to build a railroad from Fort Wayne, Ind., the western terminus of the Ohio & Indiana Railroad, to the city of Chicago, Ill. This organization was strongly encouraged by the officers of the road first mentioned in this paragraph. Indeed, the Ohio & Indiana and the Fort Wayne & Chicago Companies were regarded as so strongly identified in interests that both were placed under the care of the same President, and obtained station grounds in common at Fort Wayne.

The Ohio & Pennsylvania Railroad Company subscribed $100,000 of the stock of the Fort Wayne & Chicago Railroad, and the Ohio & Indiana Company made a similar subscription to the amount of $213,550.

The Fort Wayne & Chicago Railroad was commenced in the summer of 1853, and its completion by January, 1854, was confidently expected, but unavoidable delays, monetary depressions, etc., occurred, and at the time of the consolidation of the three roads in 1856, as the Pittsburgh, Fort Wayne

& Chicago Railroad, only 20 miles of the 147 miles from Fort Wayne to Chicago were finished.

The relative value of the stocks agreed upon at the time of consolidation were as follows: Ohio & Pennsylvania, 120; Ohio & Indiana, 100; Fort Wayne & Chicago, 106.

Length of each road: Pittsburgh to Crestline, 187 miles; Crestline to Fort Wayne, 131 miles; Fort Wayne to Chicago, 147 miles. Air line distances between the same points: Pittsburgh to Crestline, 146 miles; Crestline to Fort Wayne, 126 miles; Fort Wayne to Chicago, 136 miles.

Not deeming it pertinent to this work to follow further the history of the consolidated organization—to give an account of its litigations, transfers, leases, etc.—we invite the attention of the reader to a few matters of local interest connected with the history of this grand avenue of travel and commerce, now operated as a part of the great Pennsylvania Railroad system, which in passing through the central part of Wyandot from east to west, having the towns of Nevada, Upper Sandusky and Kirby as its principal stations, has 24.44 miles of road bed in this county, including 4.20 miles of sidings.

The first action taken by the people of Upper Sandusky to secure railway facilities, or rather the route of the then proposed Ohio & Pennsylvania Railroad through their town, resulted in a meeting being held in the court house on the night of December 30, 1848. At that time Robert Taggart was elected President, and William King, Secretary. Various speeches were made, and a number of resolutions were adopted to further the end in view, but other details of the doings of this assemblage have not been preserved.

In complying with the provisions of the thirteenth section of an act entitled "An act to incorporate the Ohio & Indiana Railroad Company," approved March 20, 1850, a majority of the votes polled at an election held in Wyandot County on the 8th day of October, 1850, were in favor of the proposition that the Commissioners of the county subscribe to the capital stock of the said company $50,000. Two days later, however, a writ was issued from the Court of Common Pleas of the county, which enjoined the Commissioners from subscribing to the capital stock of the road. Thereupon they (the Commissioners) refused to proceed in the matter, and retained Messrs. Berry, Sears, McKelly and Kirby, as attorneys in a suit in chancery brought by John Carey and others in the Common Pleas Court of Wyandot County. This case was continued until March term, 1854, when (considering the fact that the railroad in question was nearly completed without aid from Wyandot County*) the injunction, by the consent of both parties was made perpetual.

The railroad buildings at Upper Sandusky and the railroad bridge over the river at the same place were built in the summer of 1853. On Friday, November 11, 1853, the completion of the Ohio & Indiana Railroad to Upper Sandusky was celebrated at the latter place by the firing of cannon, with music, speeches, etc., and a grand supper at the Exchange Hotel. The first through passenger train from Pittsburgh reached Upper Sandusky on Friday, January 20, 1854. It here made connection with the Mad River & Lake Erie Railroad, which led to Sandusky and Cincinnati. Mr. Mills, in 1854, became the first telegraph operator at Upper Sandusky. At the same time E. P. Copeland was known as the first freight and ticket agent.

---

*The town of Upper Sandusky subscribed $15,000 to the capital stock of the Ohio & Indiana Railroad Company, which was paid.

However, the latter was succeeded in the course of a few weeks by Curtis Berry.

Columbus & Toledo Railroad Company.—This company was incorporated May 28, 1872, under the general act of May 1, 1852, the corporators being M. M. Greene, P. W. Huntington, B. E. Smith, W. G. Deshler, James A. Wilcox and John L. Gill, of Columbus, Ohio, who were empowered to construct a railroad from the city of Columbus to the city of Toledo, through the counties of Franklin, Delaware, Marion, Wyandot, Seneca, Wood and Lucas, a distance of 123.7 miles. The capital stock named in the certificate of incorporation is $2,500,000, which by law is divided into shares of $50 each. On the 1st of July, 1872, subscription books were opened in Columbus and Toledo. During the succeeding three months, $270,000 having been duly subscribed, the corporators called a meeting of the stockholders, which was held in the city of Columbus on the 13th day of November following, and nine Directors were duly elected. On the same day the Directors met and organized the company, by the election of the proper officers. One year later—October 15, 1873—the line of the road was permanently located through the towns of Delaware, Marion, Upper Sandusky, Carey and Fostoria. The bids for construction were opened August 4, 1875, and on the 16th of the same month a contract was concluded with Miller, Smith & Co. They commenced work the next day, and in November, 1876, the work upon the line from Marion to Columbus was sufficiently completed to justify the company in complying with the urgent solicitation of the stockholders and business men along the route to commence running trains. This was done at considerable cost in proportion to the amount of business, which was, necessarily, limited on so short a distance upon a new and incomplete road.

On the 9th of November, 1876, a contract was made with the Pennsylvania Railroad Company for joint use of the Toledo & Woodville road from Walbridge to Toledo, five and one-half miles, including the bridge of that road over the Maumee River at Toledo, and its depots and other terminal facilities in that city.

Early in January, 1877, the entire line was so far completed that through business was commenced, and regular trains were run between Columbus and Toledo, under an arrangement with the contractors, who were, however, occupied for some time after that in finishing up the road, so that it was not fully completed and accepted by the company until July following. This road—118.2 miles—was constructed, fully equipped and provided with all the necessary and proper terminal accommodations in Columbus* and Toledo, at a cost of $3,338,507.54.

In July, 1881, this road—the Columbus & Toledo Railroad—was sold to a syndicate, and the name was thereupon changed to the Columbus, Hocking Valley & Toledo Railroad.

In passing through the central part of Wyandot County, in a northwest and southeast course, 24.40 miles of road bed, including 2.26 miles of sidings are required. The principal stations in the county are Fowler, Upper Sandusky, where it crosses the Pittsburgh, Ft. Wayne & Chicago Railway, and Carey where it crosses the Indianapolis, Bloomington & Western Railway.

POST OFFICES.

Under this heading will be found a complete list of Wyandot County's

---

*In Columbus, on the 22d of February, 1877, an arrangement was effeted with the Columbus & Hocking Valley Railroad Company, for the joint use of its terminal property.

HISTORY OF WYANDOT COUNTY. 431

post offices and postmasters, which, through the courtesy of Hon. George E. Seney, the present Member of Congress from this district, and Hon. Louis A. Brunner, the present Speaker *pro tem.* of the Ohio House of Representatives, has been procured especially for this work from the books of the Post Office Department at Washington, D. C.

BELLE VERNON—(Late in Crawford County).

Jacob Curtis, May 10, 1842; Ezekiel Eckleberry, Jr., September 11, 1848; Ashford Stover, December 10, 1855; Seldon T. Payne, May 29, 1861; J. V. Stevenson, March 12, 1867; Jacob Staum, December 22, 1870; David Dubre, October 25, 1871; Daniel Pope, January 2, 1879; Daniel Bope, January 20, 1879; Marshal B. Snover, April 2, 1883.

BIG TURTLE.

Thomas Wolverton, May 29, 1854. Discontinued December 10, 1855.

BOWSHERVILLE—(Late in Crawford County).

William H. Hunt, October 31, 1839; Albert Mears, October 17, 1845; Barnet Hughes, September 19, 1863. Discontinued April 17, 1865.

CRAWFORD—(Late in Crawford County).

George Ames, November 15, 1844; Abraham Myers, July 29, 1845. Name changed to "Carey," June 5, 1848.

CAREY—(Late Crawford P. O.).

Abraham Myers, June 5, 1848; Samuel B. Turner, July 5, 1861; Roswell Perry, December 4, 1865; David Jay, March 2, 1868; Robert Gregg, February 22, 1869; James W. Herndon, June 24, 1881. Re-appointed (Pres.) April 2, 1883; (President and Senate), December 20, 1883.

CRAWFORD.

Joseph D. Baxter, June 5, 1848; George Unger, June 27, 1848; William Parker, June 11, 1849; Reuben Savidge, November 17, 1851; Solomon Hare, April 6, 1855. Discontinued November 12, 1860. Re-established January 15, 1877, and McDowell M. Carey appointed. McDonough M. Carey, January 31, 1877.

DEUNQUOT.

James Culver, June 3, 1880.

KIRBY.

James C. Culbertson, September 26, 1854; Franklin Hilliard, December 15, 1855; Hugh H. Long, May 14, 1857; James Warren, September 27, 1858; Perry Knox, July 26, 1861; Franklin Pope, February 22, 1864; Ormund W. Johnson, December 11, 1865; Silas S. DeBolt, October 4, 1869; Luzern E. Landon, May 2, 1872.

LITTLE SANDUSKY—(Late in Crawford County).

Joseph E. Fouke, July 10, 1841; John Q. A. Worth, October 9, 1846; Joseph E. Fouke, November 8, 1849; William E. Hurxthal, November 1, 1850; Joseph E. Fouke, February 16, 1852; John F. Myers, September 5, 1853; Robert W. Malone, March 14, 1855; John S. Fouke, July 22, 1856; Samuel M. Worth, April 25, 1861; Joseph Wilmith, December 31, 1864; James Whittaker, November 4, 1880.

LOVELL.

Jonathan Z. Walborn, January 10, 1877; John E. Kirby, December 23, 1878; Jonathan Z. Walborn, June 16, 1879; Jacob H. Foster, October 30, 1882.

McCUTCHENVILLE—(Late in Crawford County).

Michael Brackley, August 8, 1840; Roswell Perry, July 24, 1845; Henry Freet, February 28, 1849; James M. Chamberlin, November 13, 1849; Henry V. Brinkerhoff, May 1, 1851; John Myers, July 26, 1853; George W. Hoffman, December 9, 1856; David Hoffman. Jr., January 26, 1858.

MARSEILLES—(Late in Marion County).

Jasper Hunt, August 3, 1844; William M. Chesney, September 23, 1845; James P. Maddox, September 28, 1847; Charles Merriman, February 8, 1849; Lewis Merriman, December 30, 1851; John M. Chesney, July 29, 1853; Robert H. Mitchell, September 19, 1861; William M. Thompson, September 16, 1865; Charles W. Gates, June 21, 1866; J. O. Studebaker, April 3, 1876; George W. Davis, January 16, 1882; Josiah Smith, July 3, 1882; John W. Kennedy, March 30, 1883.

MEXICO—(Late in Crawford County).

Nicholas S. McCullough, November 14, 1843; William Nowell, April 7, 1846; Jacob H. Funk, September 24, 1851; Jared M. Hord, November 4, 1853; Edward P. Marble, January 18, 1856; Henry C. Bogard, March 29, 1859; Adam R. Ganter, May 4, 1863; B. A. Wright, February 22, 1864; John N. Biggs, March 21, 1864; Henry M. Nichols, June 24, 1867; William Carr, March 20, 1871; Levi Gault, March 8, 1876; Levi F. Gault. April 6, 1876.

NEVADA.

William McJunkin, July 18, 1854; Robert Dixon, June 1, 1857; William McJunkin, March 22, 1858; Emanuel Aurand, January 29, 1859; Thomas J. Hinkle, August 9, 1860; William McJunkin, October 13, 1862; John Sheehy, January 10, 1867; Cyrenus De Jean, April 13, 1869; Thomas C. De Jean, October 19, 1874; William B. Woolsey, June 20, 1881.

PITT.

Cyrus Sears, January 15, 1877.

PLEASANT DALE—(Late in Hardin County).

Thomas Scott, March 23, 1846. Discontinued May 18, 1850.

SEAL.

James F. Wadsworth, December 26, 1850; Andrew Giegg, October 13, 1857; Elkanah F. Elliott, April 16, 1859; Philip Perdew, November 5, 1864; Hugh McKibbin, April 13, 1866; Benjamin Ulrick, November 22, 1867; John M. Lee, May 21, 1869; Levin D. Johnson, September 6, 1872; James Culver, November 3, 1873; Arthur S. Andrews, June 18, 1877.

SYCAMORE—(Late in Crawford County).

Samuel Hudson, October 19, 1831; Luther L. Pease, November 13, 1849; Alexander W. Brinkerhoff, November, 5, 1851; John Harper, January 21, 1857; Pemberton C. Kitchen, June 28, 1861; Abram N. Gibbs, October 13, 1862; John W. Reynolds, April 5, 1865; A. Saffelt, November 23, 1870;

HISTORY OF WYANDOT COUNTY.   433

Abram N. Gibbs, January 5, 1871; Frank Babcock, November 9, 1875; Francis M. Babcock, November 24, 1875; Henry M. Byers, June 4, 1877; John E. Kitchim, April 23, 1879; Mrs. Mary King, May 9, 1881.

TYMOCHTEE—(Late in Crawford County).

William Irvine, May 17, 1844; Samuel Kenan, May 24, 1845; Spencer St. John, September 13, 1847; Samuel B. Turner, April 9, 1850. Discontinued September 26, 1850. Re-established January 23, 1851, and James H. Williams appointed. Alfred Enninger, November 17, 1851; Ellis Carter, June 23, 1854; John Ringeisen, July 24, 1855; Joseph Sanders, October 3, 1861; George W. Freet, April 24, 1865; John A. Roberts, August 8, 1866; George W. Freet, June 26, 1867; Philip Enders, April 18, 1875; Levi W. Spetler, May 6, 1875; Henry Long, December 3, 1878. Discontinued September 20, 1881.

UPPER SANDUSKY (c. h.)—(Late in Crawford County).

Andrew McElvain, October 12, 1844; Hiram Flack, August 12, 1845; William T. Giles, January 21, 1846; John A. Morrison, April 21, 1846; Josiah Smith, January 12, 1847; Austin C. Hubbard, June 12, 1849; James W. Brown, March 19, 1850; William McCandlish, March 12, 1857; Lewis R. Seaman, August 8, 1864; William A. Lovett, January 24, 1865; Moses H. Kirby, August 28, 1866; William B. Hitchcock (President and Senate), April 20, 1867; Pietro Cuneo, April 6, 1869. Re-appointed (President and Senate), March 20, 1873; re-appointed (President), May 24, 1877. William M. Thompson (President), June 25, 1877; (President and Senate), November 8, 1877 ; re-appointed (President and Senate), January 12, 1882; John F. Rieser, February 26, 1884.

WARPOLE.

Daniel Straw, February 25, 1852. Discontinued August 2, 1858. Re-established May 15, 1862, and Ephraim Stansberry appointed. Discontinued December 13, 1870. Re-established August 17, 1874, and Jeremiah O'Neal appointed. Discontinued February 10, 1882.

WHARTONSBURG.

James E. James, July 20, 1852; Ira Bristoll, March 3, 1855; Adam De Brough, January 31, 1866; Charles Hostler, September 23, 1867; Hiram P. Marshall, December 18, 1867; Adam B. Houck, January 11, 1869; Sylvanus R. Coats, August 9, 1869. Name changed to Wharton, July 21, 1879, and Sylvanus R. Coats re-appointed.

WYANDOT—(Late in Marion County).

John Kirby, June 10, 1837; Augustus W. Munson, January 14, 1846; Samuel Kirby, July 19, 1850; James H. Reicheneker, September 23, 1850; Henry Flock, June 3, 1854; Joseph Turney, December 4, 1860; Henry Flock, March 31, 1864; Daniel Flock, October 31, 1870; James G. Junkins, July 31, 1871. Discontinued September 23, 1872. Re-established July 11, 1873, and Daniel Flock appointed.

AGRICULTURAL PRODUCTIONS.

Wyandot County has ever been famed for the natural fertility of its soil and its varied agricultural productions, yet, notwithstanding these advantages, the cultivation of the ground and the raising of live stock was not the road to wealth for the pioneers of this region. The great embarrassment under which they labored was the difficulty of getting their products to market. Despite roots and stumps, sprouts and bushes, the newly-cleared land brought forth bountiful harvests; but the early wagon-roads were, at most seasons of the year, in an almost impassable condition; canals and railroads were entirely wanting, and the distance to large towns, and consequent markets was so great, and the route so difficult and hazardous, that the pioneer farmer had but little encouragement to burden himself with surplus productions. However, the completion of various railroad lines leading north, east, south and west, has wrought a wonderful change during the past twenty-five years. Values have rapidly increased, and many farmers are now termed wealthy.

The following facts concerning the farm products, live stock, etc., of Wyandot County for the year 1882, have been compiled from the reports of the Ohio State Board of Agriculture, published in 1883:

Acres wheat sown, 34,674; bushels wheat produced in 1882, 467,841; average yield per acre, 13.49; acres sown for 1883, 31,450; cost of commercial fertilizers bought for crop of 1883, $62; acres buckwheat sown, 43; bushels buckwheat produced, 648; acres corn planted in 1882, 31,433; bushels corn produced, 1,314,606; acres oats sown, 6,299; bushels oats produced, 193,998; average yield of same per acre, 30.79; acres rye sown, 142; bushels rye produced, 2,073; acres barley sown, 23; bushels barley produced, 472; acres of meadow lands cultivated, 14,157; tons of hay produced, 17,583; acres clover sown, 9,157; tons of clover produced, 7,872; bushels of clover seed produced, 4,328; acres clover plowed under, 1,184; acres of flax cultivated, 82; bushels of flax seed produced, 429; acres of potatoes cultivated, 1,104; bushels of potatoes produced, 92,850; gallons milk sold for family use, 56,589; pounds butter made in home dairies, 445,957; pounds butter made in factories and creameries, 24,600; pounds cheese made in factories, 77,000; acres tobacco cultivated, 4; pounds of tobacco produced, 9,610; number hives of bees, 1,238; pounds of honey produced, 22,763; acres sorghum cultivated, 8; pounds sugar manufactured, 145; gallons syrup manufactured, 2,800; pounds maple sugar manufactured, 6,255; gallons maple syrup manufactured, 4,477; dozens eggs produced, 363,029; dozens eggs shipped beyond the State, 107,625; acres in vineyards, 16; pounds of grapes gathered, 56,165; gallons wine pressed, 407; acres occupied by orchards, 3,160; bushels apples produced, 85,156; bushels peaches produced, 3,823; bushels pears produced, 714; bushels cherries produced, 208; bushels plums produced, 42; bushels sweet potatoes produced, 98; acres land cultivated, 119,359; acres of pasture, 52,384; acres of woodland, 49,334; acres lying waste, 2,430; total number of acres owned, 223,507; pounds wool shorn, 435,217; milch cows owned, 4,769; stallions owned, 28; total number of dogs, or *hydrophobic generators* owned, 1,663; sheep killed by dogs, 312; value of sheep thus killed, $1,299; sheep injured by dogs, 331; amount of damage to same, $738; domestic animals died of disease—hogs, 758; value of same, $5,118; sheep, 1,179; value of same, $3,820; cattle, 183; value of same, $4,499; horses, 132; value of same, $10,672; losses by flood—live stock, value, $626; grain, etc., value, $2,381; houses, etc., value, $170; fences, etc., value, $6,215.

The number of horses, cattle, sheep, hogs and mules owned in Wyandot County in 1883, according to the County Auditor's report to the State Auditor, was as follows: Horses, 6,888; cattle, 13,490; sheep, 84,244; hogs, 23,733; mules 157.

HISTORY OF WYANDOT COUNTY. 435

The following statement shows the inches of rainfall at Upper Sandusky, from January 1 to October 1, 1883: January, 1.14; February, 7.39; March, .48; April, 3.29; May, 6.58; June, 6.21; July, 4.94; August, 1.13; September, 1.44. Total rainfall during the nine months indicated, 32.60 inches.

COUNTY AGRICULTURAL SOCIETY.

The Wyandot County Agricultural Society was organized at a meeting held in the court house at Upper Sandusky on the 3d day of January, 1852. One hundred and twenty-nine members were then reported, and after the adoption of a constitution and by-laws, the following named gentlemen were elected as officers to serve for the first term of one year: President, Hugh Welch; Vice President, Abel Renick; Secretary, John D. Sears; Treasurer, Henry Peters; Managers, John Gormley, Samuel M. Worth, John Kisor, Francis Palmer and Jonathan Kear. Subsequently, at a meeting of the Board of Directors of the society, held at the Treasurer's office, May 29, 1852, George T. Frees, Henry Peters, A. J. Failor, Orrin Ferris and Robert McKelly, were appointed a committee "to consult upon the ways and means of getting up an agricultural fair, to ascertain whether suitable ground can be procured, to recommend a list of premiums, and to report thereon to the next meeting of this board." It was further ordered that the proceedings of the meeting be published in the *Democratic Pioneer*.

The next meeting of the Board of Directors was held at the court house, June 26 following, when the committee appointed at the last session reported that Chester R. Mott, Esq., had offered suitable grounds for the society's exhibition, and on motion this offer was unanimously accepted. At the same meeting, a premium list and various rules and regulations were adopted, and September 30 and October 1 following were named as the days for holding the first annual exhibition.

As proposed, the first annual fair of the Wyandot County Agricultural Society was held in the vicinity of the "old council house," at Upper Sandusky, during the days above mentioned. It was well attended, and afforded an indication of future success. The persons to whom premiums were then awarded were as follows:

HORSES.

Best blooded stallion, S. P. Fowler	$4 00
Second best blooded stallion, Teunis Ten Eyck	2 00
Best draught stallion, John Fehl	4 00
Best brood mare and colt, S. P. Fowler	4 00
Second best brood mare and colt, Isaac Jaqueth	2 00
Second best draught stallion, John Bope	2 00
Best three-year-old colt, Barnet Hughes	2 00
Second best three-year-old colt, W. B. Hitchcock	Diploma
Best two-year-old colt, Andrew Clingman	2 00
Second best two-year-old colt, Barnet Hughes	Diploma
Best yearling colt, Scott M. Fowler	2 00
Second best yearling colt, William Parker	Diploma
Best span of matched horses, Charles Merriman	2 00
Second best span of matched horses, Hugh Welch	Diploma
Best saddle horse, William E. Harxthol	Diploma
Best plow team, John Lupton	2 00
Second best plow team, D. H. Peterson	Diploma
Best horse for business, Dr. Orrin Ferris	Diploma

CATTLE.

Best yoke of oxen, Henry H. Honer	$3 00
Best two-year-old bull, Abel Renick	3 00

Second best two-year-old bull, Henry Peters	1 00
Best yearling bull, Howell Lundy	2 00
Best bull calf, Henry Peters	1 00
Best cow and calf, Abel Renick	3 00
Second best cow and calf, Teunis Ten Eyck	Diploma
Best two-year-old heifer, Henry Peters	2 00
Best yearling heifer, Henry Peters	1 00
Best fat cow, Abel Renick	2 00
Best three-year-old steer, Thomas V. Reber	2 00
Best two-year-old steer, Abel Renick	1 00
Best brood cow, William H. Renick	2 00

SHEEP.

Best short wool buck, Orrin Ferris	$2 00
Second best short wool buck, John S. Rappe	Diploma
Best six French Merino ewes, Alonzo Robbins	2 00
Second best six French merino ewes, Orrin Ferris	Diploma
Best French merino buck lambs, H. H. Holdridge	1 00
Second best French merino buck lambs, Alonzo Robbins	Diploma
Best French merino ewe lambs, H. H. Holdridge	1 00
Second Best French merino ewe lambs, A. J. Tailor	Diploma
Best Leicester buck, John S. Rappe	2 00
Second best Leicester buck, G. A. Cover	Diploma
Best Leicester buck lamb, G. A. Cover	1 00
Second best Leicester buck lamb, Robert McKelly	Diploma
Best Leicester ewes, McKelly & Sears	2 00
Second best Leicester ewes, John S. Rappe	Diploma
Best Leicester ewe lamb, John S. Rappe	1 00

SWINE.

Best boar, James G. Roberts	$2 00
Second best boar, G. R. Nelson	Diploma
Best sow, Virgil Kirby	2 00
Second best sow, Virgil Kirby	Diploma
Best sow and four pigs, Virgil Kirby	2 00
Best boar pig, James G. Roberts	Diploma

GRAIN AND FARM PRODUCTS.

Best two acres of wheat, Hugh Welch	$5 00
Best bushel of wheat, Hugh Welch	Diploma
Best bushel of corn, Thomas Baird	Diploma
Best three squashes, Joseph Kemp	Diploma
Best lot of onions, Joseph Kemp	Diploma
Best lot of potatoes, George T. Frees	Diploma

FARMING IMPLEMENTS, ETC.

Best wagon, John Kisor	$2 00
Best buggy, Charles Merriman	1 00
Best plow, Gerhart Shultz	2 00
Best cooking stoves, Anderson & McGill	Diploma
Best parlor stoves, Snyder & Waggoner	Diploma
Best hand cider mill, Solomon Hare	Diploma

FOWLS.

Best lot of chickens, F. R. Palmer	$1 00
Second best lot of chickens, John D. Sears	Diploma

FRUIT.

Best and greatest variety of apples, Hugh Welch	$2 00
Second best and greatest variety of apples, Gerhart Shultz	1 00
Best collection of grapes, Hugh Welch	1 00
Best specimen of quinces, Mrs. P. B. Beidler	Diploma
Second best specimen of quinces, Mrs. H. Peters	Diploma

DOMESTIC AND MISCELLANEOUS.

Best worked quilt, Mrs. John Holderman	$1 00
Second best worked quilt, Mrs. Solomon Hare	Diploma
Best hearth rug, Mrs. Leefe Fowler	1 00
Second best hearth rug, Mrs. Dr. McConnell	50

Best pair fringe mittens, Mrs. Hite........................ 25
Best lamp mat, Mrs. J. S. Rappe........................... 1 00
Best stand cover, Mrs. Leefe Fowler....................... Diploma
Best ottoman cover, Mrs. John S. Rappe.................... Diploma

The society's diploma was also awarded with each cash premium. In April, 1853, the society leased lands for exhibition purposes of Dr. Orrin Ferris, which were occupied until 1856, when grounds were purchased from George Saltsman by a stock company, mainly composed of members of the society. In the spring of 1861, the original plat was enlarged by the purchase of four acres from Col. Joseph McCutchen, for which the sum of $200 was paid. In the autumn of 1875, the grounds were still further enlarged by the purchase of fifteen acres from Peter B. Beidler. At the present writing the lands owned by the society (comprising thirty acres) are fenced and furnished with the necessary buildings, etc., for a successful exhibit of all articles, animals, etc., brought forward. During the late war, when agricultural exhibitions were of little moment to a people struggling to maintain the best form of government on earth, one or two years passed by without an annual fair being held. Other than that, fairs have been held each year since the organization of the society, and usually have proved fairly successful. In the fall of 1883, the sum of $1,188 was awarded in premiums. The present members of the society are 519 in number. Its Presidents, Vice Presidents, Secretaries and Treasurers are and have been as follows:

YEARS.	PRESIDENT.	VICE PRESIDENT.	SECRETARY.	TREASURER.
1852....	Hugh Welch.....	Abel Renick......	John D. Sears.....	Henry Peters.
1853....	Henry Peters....	Abel Renick......	John D. Sears.....	Orrin Ferris.
1854....	George W. Leith.	Findlay F. Fowler.	A. J. Failor.......	M. H. Gillett.
1855....	Henry Peters*...	....	James G. Roberts.	M. H. Gillett.
1856....	Gen. Myers......	A. J. Taylor......	George W. Beery..	M. H. Gillett.
1857....	Thomas V. Reber.	Findlay F. Fowler.	T. E. Grisell......	John D. Sears.
1858....	Thomas V. Reber.	W. H. Renick....	Curtis Berry, Jr...	A. J. Failor.
1859....	Thomas V. Reber.	W. H. Renick....	Curtis Berry, Jr...	A. J. Failor.
1860....	Thomas V. Reber.	H. J. Starr.......	Curtis Berry, Jr...	A. J. Failor.
1861....	Thomas V. Reber.	H. J. Starr.......	Curtis Berry, Jr...	A. J. Failor.
1862....	Thomas V. Reber.	H. J. Starr.......	Curtis Berry, Jr...	A. J. Failor.
1863....	Thomas V. Reber.	H. J. Starr.......	W. H. Jones......	Wesley Hedges.
1864....	Thomas V. Reber.	M. H. Gillett.....	W. H. Jones......	Wesley Hedges.
1865....	Thomas V. Reber.	....	W. H. Jones......	....
1866....	Thomas V. Reber.	William Gibson...	W. H. Jones......	J. A. Maxwell.
1867....	Thomas V. Reber.	J. Ayres..........	W. H. Jones......	J. G. Roberts.
1868....	John S. Rappe...	Curtis Berry, Jr...	H. A. Hoyt........	J. A. Maxwell.
1869....	John S. Rappe...	H. J. Starr.......	Adam Kail........	L. A. Brunner.
1870....	John S. Rappe...	Curtis Berry, Jr...	Adam Kail........	L. A. Brunner.
1871....	....	....	D. D. Hare........	Jacob Juvinall.
1872....	McD. M. Carey..	Curtis Berry, Jr...	D. D. Hare........	Jacob Juvinall.
1873....	J. S. Rappe......	S. H. White......	D. D. Hare........	Jacob Juvinall.
1874....	H. J. Starr.......	S. H. White......	D. D. Hare........	Jacob Juvinall.
1875....	H. J. Starr.......	S. H. White......	Allen Smalley.....	J. G. Roberts.
1876....	J. S. Hare.......	G. W. Kenan.....	Allen Smalley.....	J. G. Roberts.
1877....	S. H. White......	G. W. Kenan.....	Curtis B. Hare....	Ed A. Gordon.
1878....	L. B. Harris.....	Adam Kail........	Curtis B. Hare....	Ed A. Gordon.
1879....	L. B. Harris.....	B. Williams......	Curtis B. Hare....	Ed A. Gordon.
1880....	L. B. Harris.....	B. Williams......	Curtis B. Hare....	Ed A. Gordon.
1881....	L. B. Harris.....	B. Williams......	C. D. Hare........	Ed A. Gordon.
1882....	John F. Curlis...	Charles S. Bradley.	C. D. Hare........	Ed A. Gordon.
1883....	L. B. Harris†....	L. P. Walter......	C. D. Hare........	Ed A. Gordon.
1884....	L. B. Harris.....	J. A. Van Gundy..	C. D. Hare........	Ed A. Gordon.

* Resigned in April, 1856, and W. W. Bates elected to fill vacancy.
† Mr. L. B. Harris, for several years, has been one of the most active members of the State Board of Agriculture.

CHAPTER XII.

THE COUNTY'S MILITARY RECORD.

ALLUSION TO EARLY WARS—WAR OF 1812-15—MEXICAN WAR—WAR OF THE REBELLION—SKETCH OF THE FIFTEENTH INFANTRY—FORTY-NINTH INFANTRY—FIFTY-FIFTH INFANTRY—EIGHTY-FIRST INFANTRY—EIGHTY-SECOND INFANTRY—ONE HUNDRED AND FIRST INFANTRY—ONE HUNDRED AND TWENTY-THIRD INFANTRY—ONE HUNDRED AND FORTY-FOURTH INFANTRY—ELEVENTH OHIO BATTERY—MENTION OF MANY SOLDIERS BELONGING TO VARIOUS COMMANDS.

WHILE it is true that the "French and Indian War," the struggle for American independence, various desolating Indian wars, and the war of 1812-15 had all taken place long before the settlement, by the whites, of any portion of the territory now designated Wyandot County, yet many of the pioneers who located here were descendants of Revolutionary sires, while others among them had been active participants in wars of a later date. This region, too, had already gained prominence in history as the scene of Crawford's disastrous engagement with the Indians and their British allies in 1782, and as the point of concentration, during the war of 1812-15, of a considerable body of American riflemen. Crawford's expedition, however, has already been treated at considerable length in another place, hence this chapter begins with a brief account of the operations conducted here during the last war with Great Britain.

In October and November, 1812, several battalions of Pennsylvania Militia, mustered into the service of the United States for a term of six months, and under the command of Brig. Gen. Richard Crooks, marched from the southwestern counties of Pennsylvania—the region which had furnished men for Crawford's expedition thirty years before—towards what was then termed the "Northern" or "Canadian Frontier." Cutting out roads through the wilderness for the passage of their wagon trains and artillery, Gen. Crooks' command moved forward from Pittsburgh via the sites of the present towns of Canton and Mansfield to a point now occupied by the town of Upper Sandusky, intending to take part with the Kentucky volunteers in the reduction of British posts along the Great Lakes; but it appears that this body of Pennsylvanians proceeded no farther than this point—Upper Sandusky. Here they erected a work of defense termed Fort Ferree, and here they remained through the following winter, or until their terms of service had expired. The locality chosen had certain advantages in a military point of view, being at the junction of Gen. Harrison's military road leading southward to the Ohio River, and northward to Lower Sandusky; besides, it commanded an extended view of the surrounding country, had a fine spring of pure limpid water gushing from the foot of the low bluff near by, and was a central place in the country of the friendly Wyandots, whose principal town was about four miles distant in a northeasterly direction.

Fort Ferree occupied grounds on the east side of the present town, or near the bluff about fifty rods northeast of the court house. It was a square stockade work, inclosed an area of about two acres, and had very substantially constructed block-houses at each of the four corners, one of which was standing as late as 1850. The troops, while stationed at this place, were rather poorly supplied with camp and garrison equipage, provisions, and medical stores; a wilderness, hundreds of miles in extent, separated them from their base of supplies and their homes, and many sickened and died. The bodies of those who died here seem to have been buried where the present public buildings stand, and for some distance to the westward of the same; for street gradings, and various excavations made in the vicinity mentioned, have brought to the surface, bones of the human body, buttons bearing the letters U. S. stamped on their face, and rosettes of leather with the American eagle in brass fixed upon them.

During the same war, Gen. Harrison made this point his headquarters for a brief period. At the same time, a number of companies of "light horse" encamped on "Armstrong's Bottom," two miles south of the fort. One mile north of Fort Ferree, near the river, Gov. Meigs encamped in August, 1813, with several thousand of the Ohio militia, then on their way to the relief of Fort Meigs. The place was called "The Grand Encampment," and subsequently was chosen as the "Mission Farm." Receiving here the news of the raising of the siege of Fort Meigs, and the repulse of the British at Fort Stephenson, they prosecuted their march no farther, and were soon after permitted to return to their homes.

When the Mexican war began, Wyandot, as a county, had been in existence but a few months, yet many more men offered their services as volunteers than could be accepted. Thus, we learn, that during the last days of May, 1846, a body of volunteers known as the "Sandusky Rangers," and commanded by Capt. John Caldwell, marched from Upper Sandusky to Cincinnati, Ohio. They were stationed at "Camp Washington," near that city (where one of their number, W. L. Stearns, died of disease), until the 19th of June following, when, for some well-founded reason, they were mustered out of service. Immediately after their discharge, several of the "rangers" re-enlisted in commands which were retained in service. Among those who thus joined the company from Tiffin were H. Miller, Jr., A. W. Coleman, W. L. Beard, T. D. Shue, A. Potter, John Stouffer, D. Nichols and C. West.

At a war meeting, held in Upper Sandusky June 1, 1846, another company of volunteers was formed. Its officers were Andrew McElvain, Captain ; Moses H. Kirby, First Lieutenant ; Christian Huber, Second Lieutenant; Thomas Officer, Ensign; and Purdy McElvain, First Sergeant. But this company also failed to be accepted for a term of service, and from that time all organized efforts to recruit volunteers at this point ceased. Subsequently, Capt. John Caldwell was appointed Commissary of a regiment of Ohio volunteers, and proceeded to México in August, 1846. In June, 1847, Lieut. H. Miller, Jr., and other Wyandot County volunteers returned home from Mexico.

> " Ah ! never shall the land forget
> How gushed the life-blood of her brave—
> Gushed, warm with hope and courage yet,
> Upon the soil they fought to save." *

Immediately after the election of Abraham Lincoln as President of the United States, the rebel leaders of the South began making preparations

---

From Bryant's "Battle Field."

for secession and war. During the closing months of Buchanan's administration, State after State in the slave-holding portion of the Federal Union had passed ordinances of secession, officers were commissioned, companies and battalions were organized, and long before Lincoln's inauguration, all was in readiness to seize every vestige of Government property in their midst—navy-yards, forts, arsenals, mint, revenue cutters, and the thousands of stands of arms, cannon, ammunition, etc., so conveniently placed at their disposal by the traitor Floyd. They had erected batteries on Morris and James Islands, on Stono Inlet and Cumming's Point, all looking to the bombardment and capture of Fort Sumter and a repulse of all Federal attempts to re-enforce or retake it.

At last, after too long pursuing a halting policy, which looked much like connivance at treason, President Buchanan, aroused to a sense of duty by the murmur of the loyal people, decided to re-enforce and re-victual the threatened fort. Accordingly, on the 5th of January, 1861, the steamer Star of the West, chartered by the Government, left the city of New York with 250 troops, their ammunition and accoutrements, and started for Fort Sumter. On the morning of the 9th of January, as she slowly steamed up the bay, a masked battery on Morris Island, manned by rebels, opened fire upon her. There and then was fired the first gun in the fearful life and death struggle since known as the war of the rebellion. The "star-spangled banner" was floating over the steamer. She continued on her course some ten minutes, the batteries belching forth their shot, flame and smoke, when it was found impossible to execute the order, as it was necessary to pass close under the guns of the battery on the island; also near Fort Moultrie, ere she could make for Sumter. Capt. McGowan, the officer in charge, turned her down the channel and returned to New York. Fort Sumter was doomed.

Thus passed the hours until the 4th of March, 1861, when the Nation changed its rulers. James Buchanan retired and Abraham Lincoln assumed the administration of the National Government. The interest manifested by the people, both North and South, was painfully intense. The people of the North awaited with anxious solicitude the publication of his inaugural address, for in that they were to know the fate of the nation— whether its dignity, its rights and power would be upheld and vindicated or the Southern oligarchy be permitted to subjugate its power, humiliate its flag, and forever destroy the existence of the great American Republic.

President Lincoln's inaugural was received with joy by the mass of the people at the North. At the South it was accepted as a *declaration of war*, and they rejoiced that such a shallow pretense was afforded them. The policy of both sections now rapidly assumed shape, and preparations were made for war. The object which was to bring on the iron storm loomed up heavily in the Southern horizon. That object was Fort Sumter. Every day proved that the rebels of South Carolina intended to capture the fort. On the 11th of April, Gen. Beauregard demanded of Maj. Anderson its surrender. The Major replied that his sense of honor and his obligations to his country prevented his compliance with it. Other correspondence followed during the night of the 11th of April, but unsatisfactory to the rebel authorities. Maj. Anderson remained loyal to the "old flag," and evinced so strong a determination to maintain it, that it was resolved to reduce the fort. Hardly had the first gray of dawn, on the 12th day of April, revealed Sumter, ere a shell was thrown from a battery on James Island, which burst directly over the works. All Charleston people were

out on their housetops or high eminences to witness the terrible scene, and one young female rebel, in a letter written that morning at Charleston, to her mother in Columbia, S. C., began as follows: "Dear Mama— The cannons are now whizzing through the air. Cousin George thinks the Yankees will soon all be killed, or compelled to surrender. All of our friends are out to see the fun. It is just grand."*

The die was now cast. Civil war was now inaugurated. Fort Sumter fell on the 13th of April, after a terrific bombardment of thirty-four hours' duration. This was the commencement of the grand tragedy speedily to follow. On the 15th of April, 1861, President Lincoln called by proclamation for seventy-five thousand volunteers to suppress the insurrection. He also called an extra session of the National Congress, to convene on the coming 4th of July. The very next day the rebel government issued a call for thirty-two thousand volunteers, which, with their former force, equaled that of the National Government. These troops were rapidly equipped and put into the field. Departments were organized and Generals commissioned and assigned commands. Washington at once became the rallying point of the larger portion of the Northern volunteers.

Nowhere throughout the loyal North did the President's proclamation, calling for seventy-five thousand volunteers to serve for a period of three months, create more patriotic enthusiasm, or meet with a more cordial response in the immediate tender of men for service in the armies of the United States than in the county of Wyandot. For a brief period all business, apparently, was suspended, and naught was seen or heard in the streets of her towns but the display of National colors, groups of excited men in earnest discussion, small parties of volunteers marching in cadence step, or to the drum beat, and the voices of impassioned orators, who, though usually able and active workers—at home, were seldom to be seen or heard in the fore-front of battle. As a result, hardly had the wires ceased to click the call for men ere three full companies of Wyandot County volunteers, under the command of Capts. Wilson, Kirby and Tyler, were in readiness to move forward where ordered. From that hour until the close of the war, the loyal and patriotic people of the county never lagged when called upon for men, material, or money, and her sons, sufficient in number to form nearly two regiments, performed valiant service upon all the great battle-fields of the rebellion. As a means, therefore, of perpetuating their names and their deeds to the latest generations, the remainder of this chapter will be devoted to brief accounts of the various battles, marches, etc., in which they were conspicuous participants.

FIFTEENTH OHIO INFANTRY.

This regiment was among the first to respond to the President's call for 75,000 men for three months' service, and on the 4th of May, 1861, it was organized at Camp Jackson, Columbus, Ohio. Four days later it moved to Camp Goddard, near Zanesville, Ohio. Here it passed about ten days in preparing for active duty in the field. It was then ordered into West Virginia, and crossing the Ohio River at Bellaire, it was employed for some time in guard duty on the Baltimore & Ohio Railroad, advancing as far as Grafton. Subsequently it was engaged in the rout of the rebels under Gen. Porterfield, at Philippi—June 13—and afterward took part in the movements around Laurel Hill and Carrick's Ford. The Fifteenth performed a large amount of marching and guard duty and rendered valua-

---

* Extract from a letter picked up by the writer, near a deserted mansion, during Sherman's march through the Carolinas in 1865.

ble service to the Government in assisting to stay the progress of the enemy, who were endeavoring to carry the war into the North. Having served its term of enlistment, it returned to Columbus, Ohio, and was discharged about the 1st of August, having lost but two men—one killed and one died of disease. Three of its companies during the three months' service—C, G and I —commanded respectively by Capts. William T. Wilson, Peter A. Tyler and Isaac M. Kirby, were recruited in Wyandot County.

Immediately after the disbandment of the three months' organization, Col. Moses R. Dickey and Lieut. Col. William T. Wilson, assisted by Maj. William Wallace and Capts. Cummings, McClenahan, Miller, Kirby, Askew, Glover, Dawson, Cummins, Gilliland and Holloway, began the reorganization of the regiment for the three years' service. Recruiting progressed rapidly, many of the original members re-enlisted, and ere the lapse of many days at "Camp Mordecai Bartley," near Mansfield, Ohio, the ranks of the Fifteenth Regiment were again filled. Of its ten companies, D, Capt. Isaac M. Kirby in command, represented Wyandot County.

The regiment left Camp Bartley for Camp Dennison September 26, 1861, and after a few days detention at the latter place, in obtaining arms, equipments, etc., it proceeded to Lexington, Ky. A few days later it was transported by rail to Louisville, and from there to Nolins Station, where it was assigned to the Sixth Brigade (Gen. R. W. Johnson), Second Division (Gen. A. McD. McCook), of the Army of the Ohio, then commanded by Gen. William T. Sherman, subsequently by Gen. Buell. It thereafter participated in the movements of Buell's army, without sustaining any losses worthy of mention until in the second day's battle at Pittsburg Landing, where it lost six men killed and sixty-two wounded. With its division the regiment remained in the vicinity of Corinth, Miss., until the middle of June, when it marched away with Buell's army, and after moving from point to point in the States of Alabama, Tennessee and Kentucky, arrived at Nashville, Tenn., November 7, 1862, as part of Gen. Rosecrans' command, the latter having succeeded Gen. Buell on the march from Louisville to Nashville.

In the battle of Stone River the regiment was heavily engaged, losing eighteen killed, and eighty-nine wounded. Subsequently it took part in the advance movements which resulted in the occupation of Chattanooga. After crossing the Tennessee River the regiment remained on the extreme right flank of the army until the morning of the 19th of September, 1863, when it marched for the battle-field of Chickamauga, a distance of thirteen miles, and was engaged soon after its arrival. In that battle the regiment lost one officer and nine men killed, two officers and sixty-nine men wounded and forty men missing. The regiment bore its share in the arduous labors and privations of the siege of Chattanooga, and on the 25th of November participated in the brilliant assault of Mission Ridge, capturing a number of prisoners and some artillery. On the 28th of November the regiment, then belonging to the First Brigade, Third Division, Fourth Army Corps, marched with the corps to the relief of Burnside's troops at Knoxville, Tenn., arriving on the 8th of December.

On the 14th of January, 1864, the greater portion of the regiment having re-enlisted for another term of three years, it started for Columbus, Ohio, via Chattanooga, for veteran furlough. It arrived at Columbus with 350 veterans on the 10th of February, and on the 14th of March its members re-assembled at Camp Chase to return to the field, numbering, with recruits, more than 900 men. On returning to the front the train conveying the regiment was thrown from the track near Charleston, Tenn., by which accident twenty men were more or less injured. In the Atlanta campaign, which began the first week in May and terminated September 1, the Fifteenth Regiment, as part of the Fourth Army Corps, was an active participant. At Rocky Face Ridge, Resaca, Dallas, Kenesaw Mountain, Chattahoochie River and Atlanta the regiment won imperishable honors.

When Hood's rebel army began its march northward, the regiment formed a portion of the army under Gen. Thomas, which was sent to thwart the plans of the enemy. It did not participate in the battle at Franklin, Tenn., but at Nashville the gallantry of its members was conspicuous. The pursuit of Hood's defeated army was continued into Northern Alabama, where the regiment remained until the middle of March, 1865, when it was ordered to move into East Tennessee. After performing the duties assigned it in that region, the regiment was ordered to Nashville, and reached the last-named point about the 1st of May. On the 16th of June it was ordered to proceed to Texas.

With a good degree of cheerfulness the men turned their backs once more upon their homes, went to Johnstonville and thence by boats to New Orleans. Moving down a short distance below the city they bivouacked on the old Jackson battle grounds until July 5, when they embarked for Texas. The regiment arrived at Indianola July 9, disembarked, and in order to obtain a sufficient supply of water marched the same night to Green Lake, a distance of about twenty miles. Remaining there just one month, on the 10th of August it marched for San Antonio, a distance of 150 miles. The scarcity of water, the extreme heat, the want of suitable rations, together with inadequate transportation, all combined, made this one of the most severe marches the regiment ever endured. It reached the Salado, a small stream near San Antonio, on the 21st of August, and remained at that point until October 20, when it was designated to perform post duty in the city, and continued to act in that capacity until November 21, when it was mustered out of service and ordered to Columbus, Ohio, for final discharge. The regiment left San Antonio on the 24th of November, and marched to Indianola, proceeding thence by way of New Orleans and Cairo, to Columbus, Ohio, where it arrived December 25, and was finally discharged from the United States service December 27, 1865. Thus, as a regiment, the Fifteenth had been in service about four years and eight months. It was among the first to be mustered in and one of the last to be mustered out.

Following are the names of officers and men who served in the regiment from Wyandot County:

Three months' men—Field and Staff—Surgeon, Orrin J. Ferris; served full term.

Company C—Capt. W. T. Wilson.
First Lieut. F. W. Martin.
Second Lieut. H. C. Miner.
Orderly Sergt. D. S. Brown.

Privates, H. Aneshensley, I. L. Barger, Paul Berleen, D. P. Blaser, Thomas Boyle, J. W. Brandenburg, J. W. Brewer, O. K. Brown, Henry Carr, J. S. Chapin, George A. Clark, Thomas Clark, Jacob Clinger, D. Cover, George Crawford, Joseph DeLong, Samuel Dunn, John Ebersole, Peter Fernwalt, R. B. Ferris. Enos Goodman, J. Halstead, G. Hardin, W. Helsel, W. Holmes, J. Huey, John Keller, J. A. Kerr, John Keys, A. B.

Lindsay, W. P. Mahon, J. G. McClain, J. McClary, H. McLaughlin, A. T. Mitchell, Elias Morris, G. C. Myers, H. B. Nichols, Nicholas Ratz, M. Ragon, W. Reichman, O. Reed, D. Reynolds, Henry Reynolds, J. Reynolds, J. F. Rose, John Sahn, S. C. Sahn, Henry Schidigger, A. Smith, J. A. Smith, C. Stevens, F. A. Stevens, B. E. Stewart, J. Stewart, J. Stofer, Noah Stoker, J. H. Stoner, J. Straw, D. Swartz, J. H. Swinehart, D. S. Terry, A. P. Troup, H. D. Vroman, J. Wamus, J. A. White, J. D. Williams, C. Wilt, Levi Willoughby, W. H. Woodcock, H. Wuscher.

Company G—Capt. P. A. Tyler.
First Lieut. William H. Kilmer.
Second Lieut. Samuel Harper.
Orderly Sergt. R. W. Morris.
Privates, Fred Agerter, S. F. Anno, W. F. Atherton, George Babbitt, J. J. Basom, W. F. Basom, Isaac Blackburn, Conrad Bope, J. Boyer, F. Brobst, W. Bryant, Henry Campbell, Abraham Conger, John Conger, C. Copler, S. Cooper, A. Covill, M. Cowgill, H. Demming, J. Dipprey, W. Dipprey, J. L. Durbin, R. J. Earp, H. H. Eggleston, E. Ekleberry, E. P. Emerson, W. Eyestone, J. Frank, J. Grunditsch, O. Hall, D. Hartsough, G. W. Hawk, Lewis B. Henry, G. Howell, S. F. Hughes, J. R. Ingerson, A. J. King, J. C. Kitchen, T. Laux, M. B. Layton, E. Longabaugh, R. M. Lundy, D. Maloy, D. Mays, S. Mays, H. McCormick, Jacob Mellon, P. R. Moore, F. Myers, L. Peterson, W. Picket, R. W. Pool, J. E. Reed, J. F. Reidling, J. W. Reynolds, H. Rinebarger, J. G. Risterpher, W. Rummell, A. J. Shaner, F. Sneringer, S. Spalding, E. Spencer, William Spencer, J. Spoon, W. Spoon, J. Surplus, H. Trowbridge, W. D. Tyler, W. Vanchoik, T. A. Van Gundy, G. Waggoner, D. Walton, M. Walton, Levi White, B. F. Willoughby, M. Willoughby, I. Wood, H. Yager, J. Yeager.

Company I—Capt. I. M. Kirby.
First Lieut.—D. J. Culbertson.
Second Lieut.—Samuel Bachtell.
Orderly Sergt.—J. S. Start.
Privates, James R. Ahlefeld, Charles D. Allison, David Allison, Moses Allison, J. B. Bibby, P. Bloom, James Boroff, James Bowers, Hudson Breese, John Byers, A. J. Caldwell, B. F. Culver, Oscar David, S. DeJean, Martin A. Ditty, R. W. Druckmiller, E. P. Dumm, John Estle, John M. Ewing, Matthew Ewing, Fred Forney, Peter Forney, Wm. L. Foy, Mathias Free, David Galbraith, D. A. Geiger, J. B. Getchel, David Gilliland, W. Goodin, R. T. Gormam, A. M. Gunder, H. D. Gunder, Hugh Guthery, D. E. Hale, Leonard Hartle, W. H. Hefflebower, W. Hefflefinger. W. M. Hesser, Rush Holloway, Harrison Horick, James Irvin, David James, Henry Jaquett, Albert Jewell, J. R. Jurey, John A. Kerr, C. E. Livenspire, Marvin Lumbard, W. H. Maffett, W. H. Mulford, E. S. Munger, Stephen Murphy, Michael Myers, William O'Brien, George P. Price, Hugh, Reinhard, J. S. Renshaw, Lewis Ridling, G. W. Rockwell, Marion Rockwell, Dr. C. J. Rodig, Alonso N. Sawyer, D. J. Shay, Hiram Storm, T. M. Straw, John Warner, Harrison Washburn, Z. Welch, John Welk, James Weller, W. H. Welsh, J. B. White, W. S. White, David Whitmore, S. W. Wolf, Ephraim Yerk.

Recruits, W. H. Ashbrook, Edmund Basely, E. Blow, Peter Blow, John Burn, W. H. Cone, J. H. Corning, D. W. Doughty, W. S. Dumm, J. B. Graham, Richard Gwin, D. Hagerman, A. J. Hazen, M. Howell, Thomas Irvine, Wesley Kerr, W. J. Kuntz, West McClain, Ellis Quaintance, William Roberts, Benton Sell, A. D. Snider, George Spayth, John Spooner,

James Westenholm, John Whinnery, William Whipple, A. S, Wormley, —— Wood, William Young.

Three Years' Men—Field and Staff—Lieut. Col. William T. Wilson, commissioned August 7, 1861; resigned August 11, 1862.

Surgeon, Orrin Ferris, commissioned October 21, 1861; resigned March 15, 1862.

Company C—Corp. Julius Straw. Privates, Henry Carr, Jerome Kennedy, West McClain, N. McFarland, C. Stevens, George Spayth.

Company D, First Term—I. M. Kirby,* Captain; D. J. Culbertson, First Lieutenant; Samuel Bachtell, Second Lieutenant; S. S. Pettit, Orderly Sergeant; William H. Mulford, Second Sergeant; Robert T. Gorman, Third Sergeant; T. M. Straw, Fourth Sergeant; William Palmer, Fifth Sergeant; John Caldwell, First Corporal; Ambrose Norton, Second Corporal; Lowry Leith, Third Corporal; John Sheehy, Fourth Corporal; James Weller, Fifth Corporal; William O'Brien, Sixth Corporal; George Kirby, Seventh Corporal; George T. Renshaw, Eighth Corporal.

Privates, John S. Albert, O. C. Brown, John Burke, William H. Campbell, William Carr, Francis A. Carter, William H. Cavins, J. A. Clark, Thomas Coffaild, Myron Conger, Dennis Conroy, William Conroy, J. W. Corwine, John Crouse, Oscar Davis, Jerry Driscol, J. T. Duly, Nelson Ellis, E. G. Emptage, James M. Ewing, John M. Ewing, James Fowler, David Galbraith, Christopher Gay, James A. Gorman, O. E. Gravell, John Hahn, John H. Harder, Lorenzo D. Harkem, John Hart, Leonard Hartle, A. J. Hazen, Fred Hensel, John W. Hensel, John Hesser, J. D. Higginbotham, John Hollowell, Mathias Howell, Charles H. Huffman, John A. Inglehart, Silas Jones, James O. Keller, Newton Kennedy, Orville Kerr, A. B. Keyes, Edward Kightlinger, Emanuel Lambright, Adam Lautzenhiser, Moses B. Layton, Daniel Logan, Marvin Lumbard, John Martin, Wesley McCormick, A. S. Miller, George W. Myers, Christian Nafzgar, John Osborne, Eli Ragon, Thomas Ragon, Butler Reamy, Adam Reish, Cornelius Rex, Henry Schriver, T. L. Shaw, Royal Sherman, Joseph Sims, Joseph Snyder, Alexander Sproat, E. H. Stevens, George W. Tucker, Daniel Van Gundy, James Van Gundy, David, Vroman, J. N. Welsh, William R. White, Daniel D. Williams, John Williams, C. W. Williamson. Joseph Wilson, William Wolford, Jacob T. Wood, Nathan A. Worley, William Worley, Bela B. Zimmerman, John W. Zook.

Company D (at a later period)— Capts. David J. Culbertson, commission revoked; Samuel S. Pettit, resigned, April 28, 1864.

First Lieut. Samuel Bachtell, promoted to Captain April 7, 1863; resigned as First Lieutenant September 1, 1864; Charles J. Rodig, killed September 16, 1864.

Sergts. Ambrose Norton, John Sheehy, E. H. Stevens, Daniel Williams.

Corps. William H. Worley, J. C. Rasey, Daniel Van Gundy.

Privates, Charles Baldwin, J. A. Brewer, Henry Campbell, W. P. Carr, M. B. Conger, Oscar Davis, Edward Davis, L. D. Harkum, Nelson Ellis, J. M. Ewing, James M. Ewing, M. V. Ewing, J. A. Inglehart, Frederick Hensel, John W. Hensel, J. E. Hesser, James Keller, Newton Kennedy, Orvill Kerr, A. B. Keys, George Kirby, Henry C. Nagel, A. Lautzenheiser, William Mahon, E. Lambright, Henry Schnooer, Marvin Lumbard, Ed Kightlinger, Adam Risby, John Osborn, A. E. Miller, James Van Gundy, Leonard Hartle, T. R. Walker, Peter Worley, Royal Sherman.

---

*Resigned May 4, 1862.

Company G—Musician, T. A. Van Gundy.
Privates, Conrad Bope, William Cummings, Jacob Grunditsch, J. C. Kitchen, William Spencer.
Company H—Private, Thomas J. Finnell.
Company I—Privates, Alexander Ash, A. J. Hazen, William Ash, R. M. Druckemiller, J. L. Gilliland, Andrew Larick, Stephen Murphy, Hugh Rinehart, G. W. Rockwell.
Company K—Privates, Samuel Yencer, Gabriel Hardin.
Of companies not reported—Joseph Henderson, C. E. Livenspire, Richard Loder, E. S. B. Spencer, J. R. Jurey. Jessup Yencer, J. A. Simmons, Frank Simpson, William Soon, Charles Hoffman, Peter Hoffman, William Holden, E. P. Emerson, William Emptage.

FORTY-NINTH OHIO INFANTRY.

The Forty-ninth Ohio Infantry was recruited in the counties of Crawford, Hancock, Seneca, Sandusky and Wyandot during the summer of 1861. The latter county was represented in all of its companies, but more largely in Company D than any other. The regimental rendezvous was established at Camp Noble, near Tiffin, Ohio, where an organization was completed on the 5th of September. Five days later, the regiment left its rendezvous and arrived at Camp Dennison, Cincinnati, on the 11th of that month, where it received arms and equipments. On the 20th of September, it embarked on the cars for Western Virginia. After waiting an hour or so, this order was countermanded, and the regiment directed to report to Gen. Robert Anderson, at Louisville, Ky., where it arrived on the 21st of September, thus gaining the proud distinction of being the first Union Regiment to occupy Kentucky soil, other than Gen. Rousseau's small command of loyal Kentuckians, which organized on the Indiana side of the river, at the falls of the Ohio, had marched though Louisville three days before, and taken position at Muldraugh's Hill, thus foiling the rebel Buckner in his plan to seize and occupy Louisville.

The reception of the Forty-ninth in Louisville was cordial in the extreme. It was not known outside of military headquarters that the regiment was on its way from Ohio. Hence, as the two boats transporting the command, lashed together, neared the wharf (the regimental band performing national airs) and as the regiment landed, the people of the city—wrought up to a high state of excitement by the stirring events of the two or three days immediately preceding—received it with enthusiasm, formed in its rear and marched with it through the principal streets to the headquarters of Gen. Anderson. The hero of Sumter appeared on the balcony of the hotel and welcomed the regiment in a short address, to which Col. Gibson responded in his happiest vein. These ceremonies over, the people of Louisville turned out *en masse*, improvised a magnificent dinner at the Louisville Hotel, and the men of the regiment had a hilarious time, while the officers dined with Gen. Anderson. In the evening the regiment proceeded by rail to Shepardsville, and thence to the Rolling Fork, where it joined Gen. William T. Sherman's command—the "Louisville Legion," and detachments of other troops under the command of the chivalrous Col. Lovell H. Rousseau. The next morning (September 23), in company with Rousseau, the regiment moved forward, wading the Rolling Fork waist-deep, drove a small body of rebel troops from Elizabethtown, and then, supperless, bivouacked for the night. On the 11th of October, it moved to Nolin Creek, and established Camp Nevin, and in December following was here assigned to the Sixth Brigade (composed of the Fifteenth Ohio, Col. Moses R. Dickey; Forty-ninth Ohio, Col. William H. Gibson; Thirty-second Indiana, Col. August Willich; and Thirty-ninth Indiana, Col. Thomas J. Harrison) in command of Gen. Richard W. Johnson; Second Division, Gen. A. McD. McCook in command, Army of the Ohio.

On the 14th of February, 1862, the regiment, with its brigade and division, advanced toward Bowling Green. After some delay in crossing the river, it marched in the direction of Nashville, reaching that city on the 3d of March. On the 16th of the same month, it marched with Buell's army to join Grant's forces at Pittsburg Landing, arriving there in the evening of the first day's battle—April 6. It participated in the engagement of the 7th of April, and contributed its full share of work in driving the enemy from the field. Thereafter, as part of Buell's army, the Forty-ninth engaged in all the battles, marches, reverses, etc., which characterized Buell's command during the spring, summer and early autumn of 1862. Subsequently it fought with Rosecrans at Stone River, Liberty Gap and Chickamauga; under Thomas at Missouri Ridge, and with Sherman during the Atlanta campaign.

When Gen. Rosecrans, then in command of the Army of the Cumberland, commenced his movement on Murfreesboro on the 26th of December, 1862, the Forty-ninth moved out of Nashville on the Nolinsville Turnpike with the right wing under Gen. McCook, and after constant skirmishing found itself in line of battle on the extreme right of the Union army before Murfreesboro on the evening of the 30th. At 6 o'clock the next morning, Kirk's brigade, to the left and front, was furiously assailed, and, giving way, was thrown back on the Forty-ninth, which at once became engaged, and was borne back by overwhelming numbers a mile and a half to the Nashville Turnpike, which it reached after an incessant conflict of nine hours. On the following morning, the regiment was sent to reconnoiter on the right and rear of the main army. Rejoining its brigade, it operated during the remainder of the day on the extreme right of the army, in connection with Stanley's cavalry. On Friday, January 2, 1863, it was held in reserve until late in the afternoon, when, upon the repulse of Van Cleve's division on the left, it was ordered, with its brigade, to retrieve the fortunes of the day in that part of the field. It joined in a magnificent bayonet charge, which resulted in recovering the lost ground and a severe defeat to the enemy.

At Chickamauga, the Forty-ninth held a position in the morning of the first day, on the extreme right of the Union forces, forming part of Gen. Richard W. Johnson's division. Before being engaged, however, the division was shifted to the extreme left of the army and joined Thomas' corps. At 2 o'clock P. M., the regiment became engaged with the enemy's right, posted in a dense woods. A charge was made, the enemy driven, and two guns captured by the Forty-ninth. This charge occurred between 3 and 4 o'clock P. M. At dusk, the enemy having been re-enforced, made a charge. The enemy gained a point directly in front of the brigade, delivered a withering volley, and with their accustomed yell rushed forward with the bayonet. Although on the alert, the Union forces were staggered and gave some ground. They quickly rallied, however, and repulsed the rebels. During the second day at Chickamauga the regiment was constantly engaged in various parts of the field, and with the Fifteenth Ohio and Goodspeed's battery, accomplished a brilliant exploit. The enemy had broken through the Union left and were exultingly charging for the center, when the Forty-ninth faced to the rear and poured into the enemy a withering fire. From the other side of the circle, Goodspeed's battery and the Fifteenth Ohio poured a destructive, unceasing fire, and the rebels were checked and sent back flying to their main body. The brigade of which the Fifteenth and Forty-ninth Ohio formed part, was the last to leave the field of Chickamauga. It halted at Rossville one day, and the following night retired to Chattanooga.

By the consolidation of the orginal Twentieth and Twenty-first Army Corps in October, 1863, into the organization known during the remainder of the war as the Fourth Army Corps, the brigade* of which the Forty-ninth Ohio formed part, was transferred to the Third Division of the Fourth Corps. As part of the last mentioned command, the regiment fought on many other fields and always maintained the high reputation its gallant members had attained from the beginning of their service. At Mission Ridge, it was one of the first to plant its colors on the summit of that mountain. Immediately after this success, the regiment moved with Granger's corps to the relief of Burnside's forces at Knoxville. This campaign was one of the most severe that the regiment had ever been called upon to endure. The weather was intensely cold, with snow on the ground, the men almost naked and without shoes, and the rations exhausted. The march of the relieving army over the mountains of East Tennessee was literally marked by bloody foot-prints. Yet the soldiers of the West did not grumble, but were ever eager to be led against the foe. In the midst of this campaign the men of the Forty-ninth, in common with those of all other regiments, were called upon to re-enlist for another term of three years; a majority of them responded favorably to the summons, and at the conclusion of the march proceeded homeward on veteran furlough.

In the Atlanta campaign the regiment participated in the battles at Rocky Face Ridge, Resaca, Dallas, Kenesaw Mountain, Chattahoochie River, and the series of engagements around Atlanta. Also in the movements that resulted in the battles at Jonesboro and Lovejoy Station. When Sherman began his march to the sea, the regiment and corps went back with Gen. Thomas to attend to the rebel Hood in Tennessee. The subsequent movements of the regiment are told in the sketch relating to its companion regiment, the Fifteenth Ohio Infantry. It proceeded to Texas in June and landed at Victoria early in July, 1865. After remaining at San Antonio for some weeks, it returned to Victoria where it was mustered out of service on the 30th day of November, 1865.

The whole number of names borne upon the rolls of the regiment is fifteen hundred and fifty-two. Eight officers were killed in battle, and twenty wounded (six mortally). Of the enlisted men, one hundred and twenty-seven were killed in battle, seventy-one were mortally wounded, one hundred and sixty-five died from disease, seven others died in rebel prison pens, and six hundred and sixteen were discharged on account of wounds or disability.

Among the Wyandot County men who served in this regiment, were the following:

Company A—Capt. Daniel Hartsough.
First Lieut. John K. Gibson, died of wounds.
Sergts. John James, Cyrus DeWitt.
Corps. J. Bartison, D. H. Grindle, J. S. Grindle, Henry Stevens.
Privates, A. Willever, Allen Wilkins, C. K. Nye, Jerome Nye, James

---

*First Brigade, Second Division, Twentieth Army Corps.

Thompson, George W. Platt, L. Lambert, M. B. Hare, W. B. Leeper, William C. Gear, John Greek, Jacob Moyer, John I. Grindle, Dory Jackman, P. Grubb, S. T. Biles, Alfred De Witt, Salamas Bowlby, Solomon Bachar.
Company B—Second Lieut. Sheldon P. Hare.
Corp. James Burk.
Privates, Theodore Gibson, C. C. Conaghan, J. L. Bliss, H. H. Anderson, Job Baker, D. A. Bennett, A. F. Conaghan, A. P. Havens, Samuel Mays, David Mays, George Wagner, George Pancoast.
Company C—Capt. John Green.
Sergt. John Reiger.
Privates, John G. Markley, S. Bland, Sylvester Bowlby.
Company D—Capts. James Ewing, George W. Culver, George W. Pool.
First Lieut. M. Cowgill, J. Mosier.
Sergts. Samuel Bretz, Silas Barnhiser, W. R. Bliss, D. L. Kentfield, Charles Hoyt, Robert Gregg, James W. Ingle.
Corps. Joseph Battenfield, N. D. Bunn, S. S. Laird, Robert Cavit, Enos Goodman.
Drummers, W. H. Shuler, Jacob Funk.
Privates, William Updegraff, John Updegraff, Edward Marble, Martin Marble, Jesse Rifner, Henry Lowmaster, C. Morgan, B. Jewel, T. B. Hawkins, Kenry Kestner, Nathan Karr, David Hitchew, Fred W. Hine, George W. Greer, Otis S. Goodman, Anthony Kestner, J. B. Fox, Alfred Hitchew, David Cramer, John Bope, Jac Allion, Jr., Francis Beck, W. S. Karr, B. F. Bunn, Frank Babcock, James Barnhiser, S. W. Barnhiser, Samuel Burk, Fleming Ewing, Isaac Burk, Jacob Everhart, S. A. Durboraw, J. Enerson, Jesse De Long, W. W. Greer, H. L. Freet, William Hitchew, Lewis Corfman, William Rice, William Burk, P. Tracy, James Nye, Jesse Paulin, Levi Pennington, William Fruit, James Fruit, J. Young, Isaac Fruit, G. W. Mullholand, F. Roberson, Perry Rice, Sylvester Pontius, I. M. Winters, J. B. Weber, Charles Wigley, Jerome Williams, Benjamin Whetsel, Allen Smalley, John Rock, C. Shireman, E. S. Willson.
Company E—Private David Goodman.
Company G—Capt. Samuel M. Harper.
Sergts. J. S. Gibson, Walton Weber, F. J. Weber, Lewis Miller.
Corps. John Caldwell, P. C. Kitchen.
Wagoner, J. C. Kitchen.
Privates, John Solley, John Ingerson, F. M. Babcock, Seymour Culver, B. F. Culver, M. G. Clapsaddle, J. R. Ingerson, J. R. Lowry, Abner Willson, W. B. Kitchen, Ross Ingerson.
Company F—First Lieut. J. F. Harper.
Company H—First Lieut. James J. Zint.
Company I—Second Lieut. William F. Gibbs.
Corp. W. J. Loudermilch.
Privates, J. S. Thompson, E. C. Warner, John Stump, D. D. Armstrong, D. D. Cole, J. A. Bell, Joseph A. Liles, Thomas Petty, J. A. Petty.
Company K—Privates David Jacob, Rezin De Bolt, H. Bland, H. L. Eyestone, H. Badger, George De Bolt, Silas De Bolt, William Cummings, A. J. Miller, H. P. Jaqueth, D. R. Martin, Henry Jacoby, O. Lannon, G. P. Ogg, C. Whittem.
Attached to Companies not known—G. W. Sherwood, William Johnson, Ezra Phelps, Sergeant; Frank Johnson, James Stoner, W. M. Thomp-

son, Seth Kear, Willson Long, William Cowgill, Jackson Carter, Martin Heistand, Jackson Anderson, Conrad Bope, William Boyer, William Emerson, Bradford Dunn, George Inman, John Anderson, R. Baun, Joseph Barnhiser.

FIFTY-FIFTH OHIO INFANTRY.

This regiment was organized at Norwalk, Ohio, about the middle of October, 1861. On the 25th of January, 1862, it left Norwalk for Western Virginia, and soon after its arrival on the field of action was attached to Gen. Schenck's brigade. It participated in many minor movements against the redoubtable rebel leader—"Stonewall" Jackson—during the early part of that year, with varying success. When the "Army of Virginia" was organized in June, the Fifty-fifth was brigaded with the Twenty-fifth, Seventy-third and Seventy-fifth Ohio Regiments, and attached to Gen. Schenck's division.

On the 7th of July, the corps of which the regiment formed part, began a march to Sperryville, Va. After a few days' rest at that point, it again marched forward, and on the 1st of September, had passed through the various marches, skirmishes and battles, which marked Gen. Pope's brief but disastrous campaign. A re-organization of the army now took place, and in the many changes made, the Fifty-fifth was assigned to the Eleventh Army Corps. Subsequently, in the fall and winter of 1862, it engaged in the movement under Burnside, which was abruptly terminated by heavy rains and bad roads.

In the Chancellorsville campaign under Hooker, in May, 1863, the regiment lost heavily. It (with the entire Eleventh Corps), was driven in confusion from the field, and sustained a loss of 153 men killed, wounded and missing. About the middle of May, 1863, it was attached to the Second Brigade of the Second Division, and remained in the same brigade during the remainder of its term of service. At Gettysburg, the regiment lost in killed and wounded, about fifty men.

On the following 24th day of September, the Eleventh and Twelfth Army Corps took cars at Manassas Junction, Va., and moved over the Baltimore & Ohio Railroad, and through Columbus, Indianapolis, Louisville and Nashville to Bridgeport, Ala., arriving on the 30th. The Eleventh Corps moved to Chattanooga on the 22d of November. In the battle of Mission Ridge, the corps formed line to the left and front of Fort Hood, and moving forward rapidly, drove the rebel line beyond the East Tennessee Railroad. Immediately after the termination of the Union victories in the vicinity of Chattanooga, the regiment entered on the Knoxville campaign, and returned again to Lookout Valley on the 17th of December. This campaign was made over mountain ranges, amid the frosts and snows of winter, many men shoeless, and all without tents or blankets. On the 1st of January, 1864, 319 men of the Fifty-fifth re-enlisted. They started for Ohio on the 10th, and arrived at Norwalk on the 20th; on the 22d of February, the regiment re-assembled at Cleveland, and on the 4th of March it was again encamped in Lookout Valley, Ga. About this time the Eleventh and Twelfth Army Corps were consolidated, and denominated the Twentieth Corps (Gen. Hooker in command), and the regiment was attached to the Third Brigade of the Third Division.

During the Atlanta campaign, the regiment participated in all the movements, battles, etc., in which the Twentieth corps was engaged. At Resaca, on the 15th of May, it lost more than ninety men killed, wounded and missing. It was also engaged at Cassville, Dallas, New Hope Church, Kenesaw Mountain, and in the series of engagements around the city of Atlanta. It left Lookout Valley May 2, 1864, with about 400 men, and during the campaign of four months' duration had lost over 200.

On the 15th of November, the regiment and corps began the march, with Sherman's armies, from Atlanta to the sea. It entered Savannah on the 21st of December. On the 29th of January, 1865, the command got fairly started from Savannah on the march northward through the Carolinas. No incident worthy of particular notice occurred until the 16th of March, when at the battle of Averysboro, or Smith's Farm, N. C., the Fifty-fifth lost thirty-six men killed and wounded. The regiment was again engaged at Bentonville, N. C., on the 19th of March, and lost two killed, twenty-four wounded, and seven men missing. With Sherman's forces, it finally reached Washington, D. C., and paraded in the grand review May 24.

Upon the disbanding of the Twentieth Corps, the Ohio regiments belonging to it were organized into a Provisional Brigade, and assigned to the Fourteenth Corps. They proceeded to Louisville, Ky., starting on the 10th of June, where, on the 11th of July, the Fifty-fifth was mustered out of service. It was paid and discharged at Cleveland, Ohio, on the 19th of July.

Following are the names of officers and men from Wyandot County who served in this regiment:

Field and Staff--Maj. Rudolphus Robbins, killed at Resaca, Ga., May 15, 1864; commissioned Second Lieutenant January 20, 1862; Captain, December 20, 1862; Major, May 25, 1863.

Adjt. Frank W. Martin, commissioned June 22, 1862; promoted to Captain April 22, 1863; resigned June 6, 1863.

Company A—Capt. Robert W. Pool, resigned August 29, 1864.

Company B—Private, Joseph Earp.

Company C—Capt. Henry Miller, resigned September 28, 1864.

Privates, Philip Brewer, W. A. Gibson, George Hawk, William Thomas.

Company D—Private, W. H. Brewer.

Company F—This company, when first organized, was composed of the following members:

Captain, David S. Brown, resigned March 6, 1863.

First Lieutenant, Jacob Thomas, resigned July 17, 1862.

Second Lieutenant, Leander M. Craun.

Sergeants, Charles D. Robbins, promoted to Captain, resigned March 29, 1864; John S. Shaner, William H. Ashbrook, Butler Case (who subsequently became First Lieutenant, and resigned as such April 10, 1864), and J. Hallabaugh.

Corporals, J. R. Burkhart, J. Rumbaugh, William Rook, David Green, J. B. Gatchell, Martin Thomas, William J. Craun and Jacob Gatchell.

Drummer, Urias Swank.

Teamster, P. McLaughlin.

Privates, John H. Andrews, Samuel Adams, Anson Brewer, George W. Boyd, Amos Bowsher, John Byers, Moses Brown, J. W. Betz, John Burkhart, Samuel Cannon, Henry Casper, William B. Craven, R. W. Coots, E. P. Cole, William Clark, William Cupp, Henry Cowley, Noah Doll, Clark Edgington, William F. Edwards, Samson B. Flinchbaugh, Taylor Filson, Abraham Fulk, Abraham Freese, L. Fulmer, William Harley, J. Harley, Henry Hoppwood, John Henry, S. Hackenberger, George Hallabaugh, J. A. Kittle, James Kine, David Koble, John Lambright, C. Long, William C.

Law, Wesley Lane, Isaac Lambright, William Likins, William P. Mahon, George W. Michael, Benjamin Myers, John R. Myers, Levi Martin, J. McBee, J. McPherson, J. Malon, John O'Brien, Dorris Pike, Jeremiah Pisel, John Pierce, J. Robertson, Albert Roberts, Leander Riesenberger, Henry Ream, Andrew Robenalt, David Raymond, Israel Spoon, Adam J. Shaner, I. Smith, J. Saul, J. G. Sharp, J. Shuster, Michael Spout, Jacob Sprout, William Stoffulmyer, M. Tress, William C. Thomas, J. H. Vail, Hugh M. Van Wagoner, William H. Waters, S. Waggoner. Subsequently the folloging additional names appeared upon the rolls, Jacob Spoon, Thomas Corbin, Washington Michaels, A. J. Shannon, Fredrick Sipher, J. W. Sulliger and Anson Edgington.

Company K—First Lieut. J. F. Rieser; Sergts. Benjamin Welsh, H. W. Kramer; Corps. George Rice, Isaac Dippy, Christian Wise, W. H. Cole, Hugh Guthrie.

Privates, John Brand, M. C. Crass, —— Nuss, Fred Althauser, Joseph Hoover, H. J. Compton, W. H. Edgington, Hiram Gantz, Jacob Grunditsch, Levi Kotterman, Christian Gottier, Oscar Midlam, Curtis Hoff, George Harman, Jacob Yeager, William Winich, Edward McFarland, Henry Little, Aaron McCoy, George Lott, Peter Marquart, H. Huffman, Henry Carr, Jacob Shuler, Henry Vaughn, John Webb, George Wisenbarger, Henry Yeager, John Keller, Adam Wiswasser.

Company H—Sergt. W. B. Conger. Corp. G. W. Ragon. Privates, Adam Beer, James H. Cram, C. Linn, Samuel Stom, Z. W. Ahlefeld, J. G. Armstrong.

Company not reported—Capts. Augustus M. Wormley, Jesse Bowsher; First Lieut. Pliny E. Watson; Second Lieut. James K. Agnew; Privates, John Emerson, Patrick Laughrey, G. W. Price, R. Rolson, Isaac Price.

EIGHTY-FIRST OHIO INFANTRY.

The command first known as "Morton's Independent Rifle Regiment," but soon afterward designated the Eighty-first Ohio Volunteer Infantry, was recruited to the number of eight companies in the summer of 1861. The fourth Company (D), Capt. Peter A. Tyler in command, was composed almost entirely of Wyandot County men. Benton Barracks, near St. Louis, Mo., was the rendezvous in which the regiment entered upon its first military duties.

The regiment marched out of Benton Barracks September 24, 1861, and from that time until about March 1, 1862, was employed on the Northern Missouri Railroad, and its vicinity, in keeping the region free from bands of cowardly, yet murderous and destructive Missouri guerrillas. It was then ordered to report at St. Louis. It was armed with short Enfield rifles, was embarked on board the steamer Meteor, and about midnight of the 17th of March it disembarked at Pittsburg Landing. A few days later, the regiment was assigned to the Second Brigade (Col. McArthur in command) Second Division (Gen. C. F. Smith) of the Army of the Tennessee, then commanded by Gen. U. S. Grant.

During the battle of Pittsburg Landing, which was fought on Sunday the 6th and Monday the 7th days of April, 1862, the Eighty-first behaved most gallantly. Its members were ever ready to confront the enemy, many rebels fell lifeless before the furious and unceasing fire of their Enfields, and during the second day, in a wild and impetuous charge, the regiment captured many prisoners and a full battery of artillery. Until the early part of the following October, the regiment performed the various duties assigned it in West Tennessee and Northern Mississippi; but, after the evacuation of Corinth by the rebels, its actions were unimportant. However, in the battle of Corinth, fought October 3 and 4, the regiment, then part of the brigade commanded by Gen. Dick Oglesby, and the division commanded by Gen. Davies, was hotly engaged, losing eleven men killed, fourty-four wounded and three missing. This was one of the most fiercely contested fields of the war—one, where about eighteen or twenty thousand Union men, without reserves or intrenchments, defeated, pursued and scattered more than double their numbers.

As part of Gen. Dodge's command, the Eighty-first continued to campaign in the northern parts of Mississippi and Alabama, and the middle and western parts of Tennessee, until the latter part of April, 1864. It was then moved forward to Northern Georgia, and on the 5th of May was advanced to Lee & Gordon's mills, where, with the great army there assembled Gen. Sherman was just beginning the Atlanta campaign. Thereafter, until the final victory at Jonesboro and the occupation of Atlanta by the Union forces, the history of Gen. Dodge's command is the history of the regiment. "In the battle on the 22d of July (the day McPherson was killed), the Eighty-first, with three companies in reserve, was the second regiment from the right of Sweeney's division. The command stood like a rock, and never was there made a more daring or more effective resistance. At an opportune moment, the Eighty-first Ohio and Twelfth Illinois moved forward in a resistless charge, carrying everything before them. The Eighty-first captured a number of prisoners and three battle-flags. Later in the day, Gen. Logan called on Gen. Dodge for re-enforcements to assist the Fifteenth Corps in recovering its works. Mersey's brigade, which included the Eighty-fifth, was sent. It marched on the double-quick nearly two miles, and joined in a charge by which the lost lines were recovered. The Eighty-first furnished a detail to assist Capt. De Gress in serving his guns on the retreating rebels. Later, at night, Mersey's brigade was moved to Bald Hill, and there the Eighty-first Ohio and Twelfth Illinois built a perfect labyrinth of works."*

In September, 1864, the regiment was assigned to the Fourth Division of the Fifteenth Army Corps. With that command, it made a march to Savannah, and northward through the Carolinas and Virginia, to Washington, D. C. It participated in the review of Sherman's army at the National capital, May 24, 1865. Early in June, it proceeded to Louisville, Ky., via the Baltimore & Ohio Railroad to Parkersburg, W. Va., and thence by the Ohio River. The regiment remained at Louisville until July 13, when it was mustered out. It immediately started for Camp Dennison, where its members were paid in full and discharged July 21, 1865.

The Wyandot County men who served in this regiment were as follows:
Company D—Capts. Peter A. Tyler, Noah Stoker.
First Lieut. W. D. Tyler.
Second Lieut. J. W. Post; killed at Pittsburg Landing April 7, 1862.
Sergts. Noah M. Stoker, R. J. Earp.
Corps. Henry Hardly, David Agerter, David Hagerman, Benjamin Ellis, William D. Earp, Charles H. Willard.
Privates, Patrick Downey, James Anderson, Samuel Down, C. J. Fogle, Franklin Kating, J. P. Berry, Jacob Albert, J. R. Hagerman, H. H. Hawkins, William Helsel, Charles Caldwell, John Bushong, Henry Down, Anson Jones, Napoleon Crouse, David Dysinger, George Devine, William

---

*Whitelaw Reid.

Davis, J. A. Atkinson, W. R. Heffelfinger, M. W. Kimmell, Ephraim Hoy, T. M. Blake, H. T. Carlisle, Jacob Lime, C. S. Keys, J. K. Hagerman, Stephen Healy, Levi Keller, James Gillin, J. C. Groff, John Finan, J. W. Gillin, J. B. Graham, Patrick Kelly, Martin Lipp, Elijah Longabaugh, J. Mankin, Jared Mills, Henry Miller, Jacob Miller, J. M. Nelson, Jerome Kennedy, Patrick Mulhauser, William Stamford, W. A. Reed, R. M. Reed, William Mankin, J. L. Mills, J. H. Long, John Rose, O. H. P. Reed, J. P. Rose, J. F. Reidling, James Stol, Benjamin Stewart, W. Quaintance, M. Pendergast, Elias Stevens, James Surplus, Henry Stomb, J. F. Rose, Lawrence Smith, William Sanford, W. F. Savidge, J. E. Reed, Anderson Sullivan, A. H. Tyler, J. A. Vanorsdall, P. Whinery, Robert Whinnery, John Thompson, John Wilson.

Other companies.

B—John Albert.

C—William E. Reed, William Van Marter.

Company not reported—Fred Agerter, First Lieutenant; Henry Downing, W. C. Keller.

EIGHTY-SECOND OHIO INFANTRY.

This command was recruited during the months of November and December, 1861. It was mustered into service at Kenton, Ohio, its regimental rendezvous, December 31, and it proceeded toward Western Virginia on the 25th of January, 1862, where it was assigned to Gen. Schenck's brigade. Under Gens. Fremont and Sigel, the regiment performed arduous service and considerable fighting in the region mentioned. Subsequently it was attached to Gen. Milroy's Independent brigade (of Sigel's First Corps), and led by that officer, performed many gallant deeds. In September, 1862, Sigel's Corps was denominated the Eleventh, and was assigned to the Army of the Potomac. Thereafter, the Eighty-second engaged in all the movements of the Eleventh Corps in Virginia, Georgia and Tennessee. Finally, as already shown, the old Eleventh and Twelfth Corps were consolidated as the Twentieth Corps, and under Hooker and Slocum campaigned with Sherman through Georgia, the Carolinas and Virginia to the National capital. The regiment made a brilliant record throughout, and, mustered out of service at Louisville, Ky., July 25, 1865, was paid and discharged at Columbus, Ohio, on the 29th of the same month.

Among its members were the following Wyandot County men:

Company A—Sergt. Henry Robinson.

Privates, Joseph E. Johnston, J. Shever, Robert Couples, J. H. Robinson.

Company B—W. H. Hollinger, Isaac P. Adams, William Ginther, J. A. Hollinger.

Company C—Second Lieut. Morgan Simonson.

Sergt. A. D. Snyder.

Privates, C. P. Taylor, Francis Taylor. Thomas Ash, Sr., J. B. Dean, Samuel Garrett, Matthew Morrison, N. E. Sibert, J. E. Kirby, William Kirby, E. L. Ross, Ephraim Shever, Joseph C. Snyder, E. L. Ross.

Company G—Private, Philip Winslow.

Company I—Corps. J. C. Chadwick, John Holloway.

Privates, Charles Spencer, W. F. Williams.

Company K—Privates, Isaac H. Cole, Samuel Brown, W. H. Cole, Jonathan Harshbarger, George Eatherton, William Martin, Henry Martin.

Company not reported—Alfred Tracy, William Snyder, John Williams, F. J. Studebaker, Isaiah Williams, Caleb Dougherty, John Morrow.

HISTORY OF WYANDOT COUNTY. 457

ONE HUNDRED AND FIRST OHIO INFANTRY.

This organization was recruited in the counties of Erie, Huron, Seneca, Crawford and Wyandot, in the dark days of 1862. Its companies rendezvoused at Monroeville, Ohio, where the regiment was mustered into the United States service on the 30th day of August. Capt. Isaac M. Kirby's command in this regiment, afterward designated Company F, left Upper Sandusky for Monroeville, on Thursday morning, August 21, 1862. It was then stated that the company was composed of the flower of the young men of the county, with a commander who had withstood the fiery ordeal at Pittsburg Landing. The members of the company, as then published, were as follows:

Captain, Isaac M. Kirby; First Lieutenant, Franklin Pope; Second Lieutenant, Jacob Newhard; privates, Hubert Bixby, Theophilus D. Gould, John M. McLaughlin, C. J. Harris, Edwin Nye, David E. Carney, Aaron C. Shinely, A. H. Turner, Amos K. Slade, Frederick Ludwig, John H. Wells, W. J. Carney, William Shell, Edward W. Shaw, James M. Briggs, Alfred Dewitt, C. S. Vredenberg, Levi Shoemaker, Noah Sterm, Peter Sipes, George S. Myers, William H. Welter, Michael Stump, Amos Strycker, Levi Price, F. M. Sterling, S. H. Brown, James H. Herndon, W. H. Carothers, Cornelius J. Sibert, J. Loudermilch, William Stevens, F. G. Hill, James E. Barker, George Mann, John Liles, Joseph Harsh, William Swearingen, Elijah White, Thomas A. Clark, John Krider, William Carmichael, John Scott, Walter Foyer, John Shepard, Russel Shepard, S. F. Troup, Thomas Hollanshead, Josiah Shoafstel, C. Martin, Garret Taylor, George Gouldsby, Thomas Barry, Calvin J. Cutler, George Lawrence, J. W. Norton, J. W. Smith, William H. Kilmer, George W. Hale, David E. Hale, S. R. Myers, S. S. Waggoner, H. H. Lacy, Samuel Martin, John J. Gerstenstager, David Allison, James Stewart, John Hutter, A. A. Spafford, G. F. Spafford, J. D. Rex, W. J. Lawrence, William Good, James Reeves, Shepley H. Link, John A. Kerr, William Hallowell, R. Park, James H. Corning, H. H. Dixon, Christian H. Glazer, Andrew McElwain, H. D. Vroman, Franklin Culver, August Wise, August Sickfelt, Daniel Good, J. McAnderson, William Nichols, Oliver Bolander, David Good, Levi Scwartz, David Miller, John Grossell, Benjamin Ream, Jacob H. Flickinger, Jacob Good, Marcus L. Lowell, John H. Swinehart.

On the 4th of September, the regiment left Monroeville and was hurried by rail to Cincinnati, and thence to Covington, Ky., to assist in repelling a threatened attack by Kirby Smith. Remaining at Covington until September 24, it was sent by rail to Louisiville, Ky., and there attached to Gen. William P. Carlin's brigade of Gen. Robert B. Mitchell's division, Buell's army. When that army again moved southward, the battle of Perryville resulted, and in this, its first action, the regiment behaved handsomely. At Nashville, Gen. Jeff C. Davis took command of the division (vice Gen. Mitchell assigned to the command of the post of Nashville), and on the 26th it marched with the Army of the Cumberland, Gen. Rosecrans commanding, to battle with the rebel forces under Bragg in front of Murfreesboro.

The afternoon of the same day (December 26), the enemy was met and a line of battle formed. Gen. Jeff C. Davis' Second Brigade, consisting of the Twenty-first (Gen. Grant's original command in the rebellion) and Thirty-eighth Illinois, Fifteenth Wisconsin, and One Hundred and First Ohio Regiments of infantry and the Second Minnesota Battery, soon engaged the enemy with spirit, sustaining a sharp fire until he was dislodged.

Although the day was fast drawing to a close, and little was known of the precise nature of the ground over which the armies were moving, Gen. Davis resolved to follow up his advantage. The enemy retreated about two miles to a rugged hill, the road passing through a defile known as Knob Gap. Deploying on either side of the road, with one section of their artillery in the defile and other pieces on the crest of the hill, they waited another encounter. In the short, sharp action which ensued, Carlin's brigade performed its work most gallantly. The enemy was driven from his position and two bronze field pieces were captured from him on that part of the line covered by the One Hundred and First.

Four days later (December 30), Carlin's brigade was the first of the Union army to arrive on the battle-field of Stone River (a small, limpid stream named after a Pennsylvanian named Stone, who, with a party of three or four others, first discovered it about the year 1760). It at once engaged the enemy's outposts, and drove them back on his main line, and just at night became briskly engaged. The regiment lay on its arms through the night, and was fully prepared to receive the shock of battle that came with daylight on the following morning. The brigade stood firm, repulsing every attempt to break it, until Johnson's division and Post's brigade of the First Division on the right being driven from their positions, the enemy appeared on the right flank and rear of the brigade, when, in obedience to orders, it fell back and took up a new position, holding the enemy in check until he again threw a force on the flank and rear. The regiment continued in the hottest of the fight, taking up six different positions, and stubbornly maintaining them during the day. Col. Leander Stem was killed, and Lieut. Col. Wooster was mortally wounded while respectively leading the One Hundred and First on to victory. The regiment was held on the front line on the right of the army until the afternoon of January 2, 1863. When disaster was threatening the left of the Union forces, it was one of many regiments transferred to that part of the field, and with the bayonet helped to turn the tide of battle. During the series of actions termed the battle of Stone River, the regiment lost seven commissioned officers, and 212 men killed, wounded and missing.

During the remainder of the winter, the regiment was constantly engaged on expeditions through the regions surrounding Murfreesboro, suffering very much from fatigue and exposure. "It was no uncommon thing," says a writer, "to see as many as fifty men of the regiment marching without shoes on their feet,* and so ragged as to excite both the sympathies and risibilities of their companions. This marching up and down the country, the purposes or utility of which were oftentimes wholly unknown, lasted until April, when the regiment was allowed to go into camp at Murfreesboro for rest."

When the Tullahoma campaign was inaugurated during the last days of June, 1863, the One Hundred and First moved with that portion of the army that demonstrated in the direction of Liberty Gap, and was engaged with Cleburne's rebel division for two days at that place. It followed the fortunes of the army up to Chattanooga, and at the close of that campaign was with Davis' division at Winchester, Tenn. On the 17th of August, the

---

*We deem the imagination of Reid's informant too vivid in this statement. We were there, and we never saw fifty, nor even one man marching without shoes at or in the vicinity of Murfreesboro during the winter of 1862-63. True, some ragged men might occasionally be seen, or rather men who had stood or slept too near their camp fires and thus scorched and burned their garments, but there was no need at that time for men to march without shoes, for the army was near its base of supplies, and supplies of all kinds were issued in abundance. Besides, it is a well-known fact no general officer in the Union army was more thoughtful and zealous in seeing to it that his men were well supplied with food, clothing and equipments than Gen. Rosecrans.

regiment marched on the Chattanooga campaign, crossing the Tennessee River at Caperton's Ferry. From thence it marched over Sand and Lookout Mountains to near Alpine, Ga. It then countermarched over Lookout Mountain, up Will's Valley, and re-crossed Lookout Mountain to the field of Chickamauga, where it participated in that battle on the 19th and 20th of September, displaying great coolness and gallantry. During the second day, the 19th, the regiment re-took a Union battery from the enemy, fighting over the guns with clubbed muskets.

After retiring to Chattanooga, the army was re-organized, and the One Hundred and First Ohio became a part of the First Brigade, First Division, Fourth Army Corps. On the 28th of October, this brigade was ordered to Bridgeport, Ala., and thus missed taking part in the fighting at Mission Ridge and Lookout Mountain.

On the 3d of May, 1864, it marched with Gen. Sherman's armies on the Atlanta campaign, and from that time until the first days of September following was almost constantly engaged in marching and fighting. After the federal occupation of Atlanta, and in the sudden change of tactics adopted by the rebel Gen. Hood, it was actively employed with other Union forces in pursuing, fighting, and heading off the enemy in his designs on the railroad communications of the Union troops. It marched with the Fourth Corps from Atlanta to Pulaski, Tenn., and from there on to Nashville. At the battle of Franklin, which took place during the execution of the last-mentioned movement, just at nightfall, the One Hundred and First was ordered to retake a position held by the enemy, which it did at the point of the bayonet, and held the position until 10 o'clock P. M., notwithstanding the fact that the rebels were almost within bayonets reach during all that time.

The regiment was engaged in the battle of Nashville December 15 and 16, and participated in the assault on the enemy's center on the 15th. After the battle and rout, it followed in pursuit of Hood to Lexington, Ala., and marched thence *via* Athens to Huntsville, where it went into camp. It remained at that place until June 12, 1865, when it was mustered out of service. It was sent home by rail to Camp Taylor, near Cleveland, Ohio, where its members received final pay and discharge papers.

Among the officers and men mentioned at the close of the war as having served in this regiment from Wyandot County, were the following :

Field and Staff—Colonel and Brevet Brig. Gen. Isaac M. Kirby, who was mustered out with the regiment.

Company F—Capts. Franklin Pope, resigned January 28, 1863; William H. Kilmer, killed at battle of Chickamauga; George W. Hale, mustered out with regiment.

Second Lieut., Jacob Newhard, resigned December 23, 1862.

Sergts. F. G. Hill, J. W. Herndon, G. S. Myers, John Kerr, William Stevens, Harmon Lacy, C. N. Martin, David E. Hale, George F. Mann.

Corps. Joseph Lowdermilch, Andrew McElwain, Willam Hallowell, R. H. Parks, John Scott, Levi Price, Elijah White, John Shepherd, Alfred De Witt.

Privates, W. I. Lawrence, David Allison, Oliver Bolander, James N. Briggs, James M. Anderson, S. H. Brown, H. H. Dixon, C. P. Cutler, William Carothers, J. H. Corning, T. A. Clark, Walter Foyer, William Good, Herbert Bixby, August Lickfelt, Samuel Martin, David Good, John Liles, George Lawrence, William Carmichael, John McLaughlin, John Hutter, John Krider, C. J. Harris, Theopholis Gould, Joseph Harsh, P.

Heller, Thomas Hollanshead, S. H. Link, Benjamin Ream, Fred Ludwig, Claudius Martin, J. P. Gastenslager, John W. Norton, William Nichols, S. R. Myers, C. H. Glasser, Daniel Good, Russell Shepherd, George Quaintance, Amos K. Slade, S. S. Waggoner, Levi Shoemaker, Levi Swartz, F. Culver, William Shell, A. H. Turner, A. Stricker, A. A. Stafford, F. M. Sterling, C. J. Sibert, David Miller, August Wise, W. H. Welter, J. D. Rex, J. H. Flickenger, H. G. Vroman, John A. Wells, C. S. Vredenberg, Ellis Quaintance, Samuel F. Troup, Peter Sipes, J. A. Stewart, Noah Stinn, William Swearingen, Josiah Shaffstall, Edward Shaw, —— Spafford.

 Company A—Privates, Abel Thompson, Thomas Thompson.
 Company D—George Miller.
 Company E—Sergt. Enos B. Lewis.
 Privates, J. Y. Good, Michael Stump.
 Company H—Private, H. C. Cross.
 Company I—Corp. John Salyers.
 Privates, D. Funk, Joseph Funk, Valentine Wisebaker, P. Heckman, Christain Funk, S. P. Renisderfer.
 Company K—Private, M. W. Shumaker.
 Company not reported—Samuel Snyder, J. L. Miller.

 Brev. Brig. Gen. Isaac M. Kirby, whose name has already been mentioned in the foregoing sketch of the One Hundred and First Ohio Infantry, is a son of Moses H. Kirby, Esq., of Upper Sandusky, and was born at Cobumbus in 1834. In April, 1861, he was elected Captain of a company of Wyandot County volunteers, and with that command (afterward known as Company I, of the Fifteenth Regiment Ohio Volunteer Infantry) served during its term of three months. When the Fifteenth Ohio Infantry was re-organized for a three years' term, Capt. Kirby again took the field in command of Company D. He served with that regiment in Western Virginia and then in Buell's Army of the Ohio. He marched with it to Pittsburg Landing and participated in the second days' battle there, assisting Maj. Wallace in commanding the regiment. He resigned his position in the Fifteenth Regiment May 4, 1862. In July, of the same year, he recruited another company of volunteers for the One Hundred and First Ohio Infantry, of which he was (for the third time) commissioned Captain. The regiment soon after joined Buell's army in Kentucky, and in October, 1862, Capt. Kirby was promoted Major of that organization.

 Early in the morning of the first day's fight at Stone River, Col. Stem, commanding the One Hundred and First, was killed, and Lieut. Col. Wooster, of the same regiment, was mortally wounded. Maj. Kirby thus succeeded to the command of the regiment during the remainder of the battle. On the 27th of January, 1863, he was commissioned Colonel, to take rank from the date of Col. Stem's death—December 26, 1862. He continued in command of the regiment until the early part of the movement against Atlanta, when he was designated as the commander of the First Brigade, First Division, Fourth Army Corps, which he led throughout the campaign. Col. Kirby was now recommended by superiors in official reports for promotion. He commanded the brigade during the movement of Gen. Thomas' army from Northern Georgia to Nashville, and through the battles of Franklin and Nashville. In the latter, he led the first assault on the enemy's main line of works. He was now again recommended for promotion, and he finally received a commission as Brevet Brigadier General.

 Gen. Kirby continued in command of the First Brigade, First Division,

HISTORY OF WYANDOT COUNTY. 463

Fourth Army Corps, until the close of hostilities. He was mustered out of service with his regiment in June, 1865. At the present time, he is engaged in the sale of hardware, etc., etc., in Upper Sandusky, Ohio, a town which has been his place of residence during the past forty years.

ONE HUNDRED AND TWENTY-THIRD OHIO INFANTRY.

The military organization thus designated was recruited during the summer and early autumn of 1862. Its place of rendezvous was Monroeville, Ohio. On the 16th of October, it moved to Zanesville, whence it was taken down the Muskingum River to Marietta, thence by rail to Belpre, and across the Ohio River to Parkersburg, Va., thence by rail to Clarksburg, reaching that place October 20. From that time until early in January following, the command was constantly engaged in marching, and skirmishing with small parties of the enemy in Western Virginia.

On the 10th of January, 1863, the regiment left Moorefield for Romney. It arrived on the 12th, and remained about six weeks, engaged almost continually in scouting duty in that vicinity, protecting the line of the Baltimore & Ohio Railroad. While at this place, one whole company of the One Hundred and Sixteenth Ohio, of the brigade, and a small detail from the One Hundred and Twenty-third Ohio, were captured by McNiel's rebel cavalry, and the train in their charge burned. The men were at once paroled and sent back into the Union lines. On the 1st of March, the regiment was ordered to Winchester, Va., arriving at that place on the 4th. From that point it made several raids up the Shenandoah Valley, going as far as New Market.

Nothing further of interest occurred until the 13th of June, at which time Lee's entire rebel army, then on its march to Pennsylvania, surrounded Winchester. On the afternoon of that day, the One Hundred and Twenty-Third, with its brigade, under Brig. Gen. Elliott, had an engagement with Early's corps, in which it lost in killed, wounded and missing 105 men. On the 14th the Union forces were driven into their fortifications and hardly pressed by the overwhelming numbers of the rebel army. That afternoon they were under a severe artillery fire for two hours, during which time Gen. Milroy, the division commander, directed operations from the Crow's nest of the flag staff as coolly as if on parade. The outworks being carried by the enemy, it was then determined to evacuate the place. The troops marched out of the works in silence at 2 o'clock in the morning, leaving the heavy artillery in position, but spiked. At a point about four miles out on the Martinsburg road, at 4 o'clock in the morning, the rebels were found in position, and further retreat was cut off. In attempting to cut their way through, the regiment lost in killed and wounded about 50 men. In this affair, the regiment made three distinct charges, but to little purpose. While it was forming for a fourth charge, Col. Ely, of the Eighteenth Connecticut, then in command of the brigade, surrendered to the enemy, and the whole brigade, except Company D, of the One Hundred and Twenty-third, were made prisoners and marched away to Richmond, where the major portion of the officers of the One Hundred and Twenty-third, remained in Libby Prison about eleven months. Lieut. W. A. Williams and Capt. D. S. Caldwell made their escape. Col. William T. Wilson and Lieut. Beverton were exchanged and sent home. The remainder of the officers, after eleven months' confinement in Libby Prison, were sent to Macon, Ga., thence to Charleston, S. C., and placed under fire—by their inhuman captors—of the Union siege guns. Subsequently they were taken to Columbia, S. C. From that point several officers made their escape, among whom were Capts. J. F. Randolph, Alonzo Robbins and Oswell H. Rosenbaum; Lieuts. B. T. Blair, Frank B. Colver, Thomas W. Boyce, George D. Acker, J. B. Pumphrey and V. R. Davis. Capt. Randolph made his escape, with a number of the officers belonging to other States, in a wood-scow, down the Congaree and Santee Rivers, where they boarded the Union gunboat Neipsic. The remaining officers of the One Hundred and Twenty-third made their way successfully to the Union lines in Tennessee. Col. Wilson, Lieut. Col. Hunter, Capt. Chamberlain, Lieuts. Schuyler, M. H. Smith, Frank A. Breckenridge and Charles H. Sowers were exchanged. Capt. Charles H. Riggs died in Charleston, S. C., on the 15th of September, 1864, of disease contracted in prison. Capt. William H. Bender also died at Columbia, S. C., of yellow fever. The privates of the regiment were exchanged within a few months, and sent to the parole camps at Annapolis, Md., and Camp Chase, Ohio.

Maj. Kellogg, who was wounded and made his escape from the enemy at Winchester, collected the stragglers of the regiment at Martinsburg, Va., where the paroled men of the regiment, after exchange, joined him, about the 1st of September, 1863. At this place the regiment was newly armed and equipped; but being deficient in officers, it was engaged mainly in provost and picket duty until March 1, 1864, when it was distributed as guards along the line of the Baltimore & Ohio Railroad between Harper's Ferry and Monocacy Junction.

About the 1st of March, however, the regiment was collected together at Martinsburg, and, with the Army of West Virginia, began one of the most remarkable campaigns, without adequate results, performed during the war of the rebellion. First under Gen. Sigel, and subsequently under Gen. Hunter, this army was marched up and down the valleys, and from mountain range to mountain range throughout the northwest quarter of old Virginia. As pursuers or pursued, they visited, *en route*, Winchester, New Market (on the 15th of May, where, in a fight with Breckinridge, the regiment lost eighty men in killed and wounded), Woodstock, Port Republic, Staunton, Lexington, Buckhannon, Liberty, Lynchburg, Salem, Gauley Bridge, Camp Piatt, Charleston, Parkersburg, Cherry Run, Martinsburg, Harper's Ferry, and many other points. The regiment started on the Lynchburg raid with Hunter, with seven hundred men, and at the expiration of two months and a half it returned with two hundred and fifty present for duty.

However, a new era now dawned upon the Shenandoah Valley. Gen. Sheridan was placed in command of the Union troops assembled on the Upper Potomac, and with them he pressed forward to a round of victories. At Berryville, Winchester, Strasburg, Fisher's Hill and Cedar Creek, the enemy were signally defeated, and ere the close of October, 1864, the Shenandoah Valley was cleared almost entirely of rebels in arms. This had not been accomplished without great loss of life, and in the One Hundred and Twenty-third alone about one hundred and fifty brave spirits had either been killed or severely wounded.

In December, the regiment, with other troops, was ordered to report to Gen. Butler, commanding on the north side of the James River near Bermuda Hundred, and attached to the Twenty-fourth Army Corps, Gen. Ord commanding. It arrived at Deep Bottom on the 27th of December, 1864, where it remained until the 25th of March, 1865, at which time it broke camp and moved to the Chickahominy to aid Sheridan across that stream.

The Twenty-fourth Corps was then sent to the south side of the James, to the extreme left of the Union lines, on Hatcher's Run. On the 30th of March, an advance was made on the rebel works, and skirmishing continued until the morning of the 2d of April, when a general charge was made, and the rebel works were carried. The regiment during this time was for three days and nights on the skirmish line, without relief, and their rations had to be carried to them by Regimental Quartermaster, Lieut. Brown—a most dangerous duty. The loss of the regiment was quite severe while engaged in this long skirmish. It captured two battle-flags and a number of prisoners. The rebels were followed toward Petersburg, their forts on the way being captured, excepting at one or two points, where a sturdy resistance was made. On the 3d of April, the whole Union army marched in pursuit of Lee's rebel army toward Danville, the regiment reaching Burke's Junction in the night of the 5th, at 12 o'clock. At this point, the One Hundred and Twenty-third was included in a force sent on an expedition to burn High Bridge, fifteen miles in the advance, on the South Side Railroad. Within half a mile of the bridge, just as the regiment was opening a fight with a brigade of rebel home guards, the rebel cavalry, in advance of Lee's army, came on in their rear, and, after a fight of three or four hours, duration, with heavy loss on both sides, the Union command, including the One Hundred and Twenty-third, *was captured*. Capt. Randolph, of the regiment, was shot through the right lung in this fight, and Gen. Reed, the commander of the expedition, was killed. The One Hundred and Twenty-third, being a second time prisoners of war, was marched along with Lee's army to Appomattox C. H. At that point, the rebel army surrendered to the Union forces under Gen. Grant, and the prisoners were thus rescued.

Immediately after the surrender, the regiment proceeded to City Point; thence it embarked on transport for Annapolis, Md., and finally was sent to Camp Chase, Ohio, where its members remained until June 12, 1865, when they were mustered out of service.

Following is an almost complete list of the Wyandot County men who served in this regiment:

Field and Staff.—Col. and Brevet Brig. Gen. William T. Wilson, mustered out with regiment.

Maj. John W. Chamberlain, mustered out with regiment as Captain.
Surgeon Orrin Ferris, resigned November 10, 1864.
Assistant Surgeon J. H. Williams, resigned January 25, 1864.
Chaplain, Charles G. Ferris, resigned June 9, 1864.
Company A—Capt. J. W. Chamberlain.
First Lieut. J. B. Pumphrey.
Second Lieut. A. P. Ingerson.
Sergts. F. M. Anderson, J. H. Boroff, William F. Basom, J. P. Bear, Jac Clinger, D. D. Terry, Joseph Roll, H. S. Kaley, John Wentz.
Corps. D. L. Baker, W. S. Rifenberry, B. R. Reynolds, D. W. Nichols, S. A. McKenzie, W. H. Egeston, L. M. Zeigler, J. H. Ellis, D. P. Demarest, F. Egeston, T. C. Thompson.
Musicians, John Emerson, R. W. Lundy; A. S. Thompson, teamster.
Privates, Jacob Switzer, David Thompson, O. R. Torrey, E. H. Van Buren, John Thompson, Byal Tracy, W. Walters, Silas Wood, A. Davis, L. L. Wilcox, George B. Smith, George W. Smith, J. Suber, H. Stansberry, McKendree Smith, J. R. Cross, L. L. Wilson, Jacob Teal, John Davis, G. W. Davis, R. J. Craglow, E. P. Cozier, W. H. Crites, John Ellis, William Ellis, W. M. Ellis, R. J. Ewart, Elijah Emptage, George W. Finnell, R.

L. Ewart, A. Corwin, C. B. Drum, D. E. Gibson, Eli Frost, A. Debaugh, Albert Frost, D. Gipson, David Gibson, F. M. Harris, James Haner, W. J. Hildreth, H. Hunter, Edgar Haner, G. P. Hoysington, James Gregg, E. G. Emptage, D. H. Inman, A. Ingerson, Welcome Inman, J. W. Kemp, I. B. Kemp, W. K. Humbert, H. W. Karr, J. O. Heckathorne, W. Inman, A. Kennedy, C. M. King, H. P. King, Frank Leeper, S. C. Heckathorne, Hiram Long, J. W. Bower, Coonrod Hufford, David Mincer, H. M. McMillan, Isaac Michaels, H. Perrin, S. M. Parsons, J. H. Niebel, B. O. Neal, T. A. Miller, I. Price, Henry Palmer, John Parlet, L. Rickenbach, N. L. Robinson, E. S. Rummell, R. V. Rummell Jedediah Sears, J. Shannon, F. Robinson, R. W. Smith, J. C. Bear, Alexander Carothers, S. C. Cole, J. S. Anderson, John S. Anderson.

Company F—Capts. Curtis Berry, Sr., resigned January 31, 1863; Alonzo Robbins, mustered out with regiment.

First Lieuts. M. W. Willoughby, mustered out with regiment; James H. Gilliam, died in service.

Sergts. A. N. Sawyer, Eli Maskey, M. F, Allison, W. G. White, B. F. Willoughby, Jamuel Dunn, S. K. Cook.

Corps. F. Blond, Thomas Clark, W. R. Willoughby, William K. Fry, John Keys, G. G. White, N. McFarland, A. L. McBride.

J. B. Willoughby, John Swinehart, Eli Smith, musicians; J. P. Dry, color bearer; J. Gephart, teamster; N. B. Brisbine, hospital steward.

Privates, Isaac Van Doran, J. A. Smith, A. B. Smith, N. D. Young, Ezra Snyder, C. Washburn, Joseph Williams, L. P. Willoughby, J. Whinnery Levi Woodling, John Snyder, N. Cowgill, C. Cooper, R. B. Craig, J. Cook, E. L. Dunn, D. W. Dougherty, M. M. Gipson, David Galbreath, W. H. Fisher, David Hall. W. A. Gipson, Joel W. Gibson, Samuel Henley, W. H. Hefflebower, S. Hoffman, A. D. Hesser, Jacob Hayman, E. B. Holly, H. Hough, G. W. Hufford, Simon Huffman, Robert Irvin, C. H. Kiehl, J. A. Hefflebower, LaFayette Lee, Benjamin Kriechbaum, Peter J. Lott, John Mackey, W. L. Maurice, Lewis Corfman, George Mackey, E. W. McJenkins, R. N. McConnell, M. O. McClain, A. H. McClain, David McClain, S. R. Cook, John H. Miller, J. L. Milum, William Mitchell, D. McClain, J. G. Norton, Levi Noll, A. P. Reardon, H. B. Ragon, C. E. M. Oliver, J. B. Oliver, M. P. H. Oberlin, B. C. Rummell, I. H. Cathright, George Seager, O. J. Scott, J. S. Barclay, H. L. Simmons, Nelson F. Bowsher, R. Bulun, David Bowsher, N. Chambers, R. Cathright, A. Caylor, Peter Altvater, David Stalter, Charles Bolyard, Lewis Blond, Reuben Berleen.

Company D—Sergt. Thomas Parkin.

Corp. H. H. Pennington; Elias Osborn, musician.

Privates, C. C. Roberts, James Kenan, Isaac C. Stalter, Pitt Stevens, Peter Swartz, George Hatfield, B. Delapline, J. A, Heckman, B. L. Hoover, B. Kinney, W. A. Mitten, G. W. Naugle, D. C. Moron, Henry Reynolds, J. G. Reynolds, Gilbert Richmond, B, W. Moore, A. Folkner.

Company E—Privates, LaFayette Dunn, John Halsey, Calvin Dunn, Isaac Holden; John Loder, Corporal.

Company H—Capt. V. R. Davis, mustered out with regiment.

Privates, James Culver, Conrad Haas, G. W. Eyestone, W. L. Foy, J. C. Andrews, Charles Hotelling, Lewis Foy, Lewis Rank.

Company K—Privates, P. Hennessy, A. L. Ragon, William Montee, Isaac Nutter, G. R. Marvin, Thomas Irvin, Benjamin Spittle, W. Costoloe, W. Straub, Leonard Zent, Jacob Switzer, C. Simmon.

Other Companies:

First Lieut. R. D. Ferris, resigned March 12, 1863; T. C. Burnet, Samuel Hayman, William Hoover, J. H. Dunlap.

Brevet Brig. Gen. William T. Wilson, who served throughout its term of service as Colonel of the One Hundred and Twenty-third Ohio Infantry, was one of the most prominent residents of Upper Sandusky during what has been mildly termed "the late unpleasantness." He was also known both before and subsequent to that period as the publisher and editor of the Wyandot *Pioneer*, a Republican newspaper.

In April, 1861, he was commissioned Captain, and led into the field one of the three Wyandot County companies, which served in the Fifteenth Ohio Infantry during its first term of three months. Soon after its muster out, the same regiment was re-organized to serve for a period of three years. Many of the original members of the old organization returned to the front with the new, and among them was the Upper Sandusky editor, now the second officer in rank in the regiment. He was commissioned Lieutenant Colonel August 7, 1861, and served with credit until August 11, 1862, when he resigned and returned home. Like his townsman, Gen. Kirby, however, he could not remain in the rear while his country needed his services, and on the 26th day of September, 1862, he was appointed Colonel of the One Hundred and Twenty-third Ohio Infantry, with which regiment he served until it was mustered out June 12, 1865. Toward the close of his term he was commissioned Brevet Brigadier General, to take rank from March 13, 1865. He now resides in the city of Columbus, Ohio.

ONE HUNDRED AND FORTY-FOURTH OHIO NATIONAL GUARDS.

This regiment was formed by the consolidation of the Nineteenth Battalion Ohio National Guard, of Wyandot County, and the Sixty-fourth Battalion Ohio National Guard, of Wood County, at Camp Chase, on the 11th of May, 1864. The regiment was ordered to report without delay to General Wallace, at Baltimore, Md.

Upon its arrival in that city, Companies G and K were detached for duty in the fortifications, and the remainder of the regiment reported to Gen. Morris at Fort McHenry. From there, Company E was ordered to Wilmington, Del.; Company B, to Camp Parole, near Annapolis, Md., and Company I to Fort Dix, at the Relay House. On the 18th of May, the regiment was relieved from duty at Fort McHenry, and was ordered to the Relay House, where it enjoyed comparative quiet until the 1st of July, when the rebel Gen. Early came down the Shenandoah, threatening Baltimore and Washington. Companies B, G and I were in the engagement at Monocacy Junction, and suffered severely, losing in killed, wounded and prisoners about fifty men. On the 13th of July, the regiment was ordered to Washington, D. C., and from there moved toward Winchester, Va., passing through Leesburg. It was halted at Snicker's Gap, and after a day's delay was moved back toward Washington; but it was again faced toward the Shenandoah Valley, moving via Harper's Ferry, under the command of Maj. Gen. Wright.

At daylight on the 13th of August, a portion of the regiment, while guarding a train near Berryville, Va., was attacked by Moseby's command, with two pieces of artillery. Some confusion was caused by the first fire, but the men soon rallied, drove back the enemy and saved the train. The detachment lost five killed, six wounded and sixty captured. The men of the One Hundred and Forty-fourth were much fatigued and worn by the arduous service performed, but they never complained.

On the 31st of August, 1864, the regiment was mustered out of service, having lost during its term of a little more than one hundred days, about one hundred and twenty-five men killed, wounded and captured. Many of those taken prisoners were intentionally starved to death at Andersonville and other rebel prison pens.

The Wyandot County men who served in the regiment were as follows:
Field and Staff—Col. Samuel H. Hunt.
Adjt. Jonathan Ayers.
Chaplain, J. G. Baughman.
Company A—Capt. Henry H. Ragon.
First Lieuts. William McFee, James S. Leith.
Second Lieut. E. B. Ragon.
Sergts. Levi Shults, J. S. Bowers, H. J. Pool.
Corps. E. Pool, Benjamin Morris.
Privates, Fred Kinley, William Kurtz, Isaac Blackburn, John Blackburn, Hugh Mason, Isaac Ayres, John Gatchell, Jesse Smalley, H. J. Hunt, Leonard Cole, Charles Copler, A. R. Hunt, D. J. Hale, J. M. Pool, Henry Brown, H. C. Bowen, V. L. Obenchain, George Hayman, William Parker, E. Stansbery, John Walton.
Company C—First Sergt. H. M. Cunningham.
Company D—Capt. Asa Brayton.
First Lieut. F. R. Baumgardner.
Second Lieut. Amos Stetler.
Sergts. D. S. Nye, A. E. Gibbs, Byron Kear, W. H. Grindle, John W. Lime.
Corps. Oliver Brayton, Amos Bixby, Amos Nye, David Lindsay.
Privates, W. Plott, William Berry, John Battenfield, J. Barnhiser, J. S. Foster, J. J. Brunning, E. Goodman, W. Lowery, James McGarvey, Henry Kimmerly, Harrison Kimball, James Clark, M. A. Clark, A. A. Carothers, A. Carothers, A. S. Gear, S. J. Keeler, Lewis Bacher, J. A. J. Lang, W. Hurd, W. B. Hurd, J. W. Conn, Thomas Bliss, Gibson Busch, W. H. Davis, J. Duddleson, John Deardoff, Alonzo Ellison, James Myers, C. Humphrey, H. H. Hoysington, A. H. Hoysington, M. D. Grossell, W. H. Karr, L. D. Karr, J. H. Karr, J. C. Ish, J. E. Jones, C. L. Parker, J. W. Crum, C. R. McKenzie, E. H. Sage, James, Ritchie, O. P. Robinson, D. Sipes, Landline Smith, W. K. Nye, L. E. Nye, George A. Nye, A. Harshberger, J. D. Shireman, Elkanah Sherman, E. Sherman, E. H. Shellhouse, D. Shell, Joseph Shane, Wellington Nesbaum, S. C. Williams, S. Y. Williams, H. Straham, Luther Stone, S. Harpster, O. Whipple, J. W. Harpster, B. F. Swartz, W. C. Straw, W. H. H. Williams, G. F. Wonder, D. Wonder, A. J. Wonder, S. R. Wohlgamuth, S. Wohlgamuth, S. A. Wisner, Asa Wisner.
Company E—Private, E. Young.
Company F—Privates, Jacob Baldwin, Robert Lindsay, Miles Bowsher, William Bowsher, Andrew Baldwin.
Company G—Capt. William Frank.
First Lieut. Howard Kennedy.
Second Lieut. S. H. White.
Corps. G. W. Clark, John Shrank, Allen Parker, R. L. Willard, —— bugler.
Privates, Thomas Emptage, James Emptage, S. B. Cook, Irvine Straw, J. W. Atkinson, J. W. Bowers, Theodore Kellogg, —— McGha, Jerry O'Neal, John J. Inglehart, Orrin Long, John Runels, T. B. Mount, Marshall Cozier, S. D. Holland, R. Parks, E. L. Parker, Joseph Worthington,

Jacob Williams, Theodore Uncapher, D. H. Walker, W. A. Butler, John Campbell, D. D. Hildreth, William Hildreth, Robert Mitchell.
Company H—Capt. James A. Gibson.
Sergts. Samuel Phillips, T. B. Armstrong.
Privates, Clay Miller, John Milligan, J. W. Little, A. C. Hunt, J. W. Stinchcomb, W. H. Case, Alfred McCauley, Noble Emerson, G. W. Horrick, George H. Heistand, J. W. Shaffer, James Hibbins, Alva Bunn, T. A. VanGundy, G. W. Baldwin, Lewis Lupton, George Wilson, Benjamin Pontius, W. L. Clingman, J. O. Welty, H. C. Welty, T. C. Wood, C. C. Pancoast.
Company K—Corp. W. D. Cook, private Joseph Seager.
Company not reported—Jeremiah Kitchen, Captain; Aaron Kennedy, Sergeant; John Woessner, P. B. Oliver, Henry Karr, J. F. Myers, Ashford Nail, N. K. Eyestone, Vincent J. Flack, Warner Osborne, W. O. Phillips, W. J. Wilcox, P. P. Wilcox, C. Henry, William Hoffman, T. J. Frazer, L. Bloom, Aaron Price, J. R. Willson, Levi Willson, D. Shafer, John Midlam, J. Puffenberger.

ELEVENTH OHIO INDEPENDENT BATTERY.

The men who composed this battery were enlisted at Cincinnati, and from Athens, Butler, Hamilton, Vinton and Wyandot Counties, in August and September, 1861, and rendezvoused at St. Louis Arsenal, Mo., where they were mustered into service on the 27th day of October, 1861, with one hundred and fifty-one men, rank and file.

The battery consisted of two six-pounder rifled guns; two six-pounder smooth-bore guns, and two twelve-pounder field-howitzers, with gun carriages and caissons complete, and battery-wagon and blacksmith shop. The uniforms for the men were made to order, from actual measurement, of the best material, and each man was furnished with a pair of superior buck gauntlets in addition to the regular uniform. The non-commissioned officers, in addition to their regulation saber, were armed with Beal's patent revolvers, and the privates with saber-bayonets.

On the 26th of October, the battery marched to department headquarters, and was reviewed by Maj. Gen. Fremont, then commanding the Western Department, and was there presented by Mrs. Fremont with an elegant silk guidon. A few days later, the battery proceeded to Tipton, Mo. Subsequently it marched to Otterville, where a few weeks were passed; thence to Boonville and St. Charles. From there it was taken on transports to Commerce, Mo., where it joined a portion of Gen. Pope's Army of the Mississippi, then organizing for operations against New Madrid and Island No. 10. It participated in the Union victories at those points, and then moved with Gen. Pope's command to the re-enforcement of Grant's and Halleck's forces in front of Corinth, Miss. During the siege, and in the battles and skirmishes resulting in the occupation of Corinth the battery bore its full share.

With other troops, it remained in the vicinity of Corinth throughout the spring and summer of 1862, participating in the Ripley expedition under Gen. Rosecrans meanwhile. It was during this summer that the following incident occurred as narrated in a letter written by Lieut. Cyrus Sears at "Camp three miles beyond Corinth, Miss., July 2, 1862," to his brother, John D. Sears, Esq., of Upper Sandusky. "* * * Early Saturday morning last, Charles Rhodes and Robert Swegle, privates of our battery, were walking through the abandoned rebel camp, when having strayed incautiously too far, they suddenly came upon a couple of 'Secesh' sentinels armed with loaded double-barreled shot guns. Our men being unarmed were very unceremoniously taken prisoners and marched off toward the enemy's camp. Their captors proving very incautious, or mistaking the character of their prisoners, soon allowed them to get close along side. No sooner did they do this, than little Charley called out to Swegle to 'go in,' and suiting his actions to the words he grappled the gun of his man with one hand and, giving him a right-hander with the other, floored him. Meanwhile, Swegle, who is a big fellow, served his man in the same style, and disarmed him in short meter, and came to the rescue of Charley, who was having it rough and tumble, with his customer, among the bushes. The tables were now turned, and the 'Butturnuts' were marched into camp and turned over to Gens. Buford and Hamilton, who declared that it was the best and bravest incident that had come under their notice, and that it should be properly mentioned. * * *"

About the 1st of August, the battery with Gen. Hamilton's division moved to Jacinto, Miss., where it remained until 3 o'clock A. M., of the 16th of September, when it moved forward with the forces of Gen. Rosecrans, for the purpose of co-operating with Gen. Grant against the rebel Gen. Price at Iuka. Gen. Grant, with Ord's division, did not arrive in time. As a result, Gen. Rosecrans' command of about eight thousand men, after a march of nineteen miles, met Price, who had 12,000 men posted on a densely-wooded hill just southwest of the town of Iuka, at 4 o'clock P. M., of the 19th of September, and fought him single-handed. This battle, for the numbers engaged, was one of the most hotly contested and sanguinary fought during the war. The steady blaze and roar of musketry, as the opposing forces struggled to obtain and hold the crest of the hill, continued unceasingly until 9 o'clock P. M. During the remainder of the night, Rosecrans was engaged making his dispositions to seize some adjacent heights at daybreak for his artillery, and replenishing his ammunition. He had the men called to arms at 3 o'clock, and at daylight was moving. But meantime, Price had learned of the proximity of Ord's column of 6,000 men, and had hastily retreated, leaving his dead unburied, and his wounded either on the field or in hotel buildings, churches and dwellings in the town. The enemy's loss in this engagement was 1,078 prisoners, dead and wounded, left on the field, with 350 more wounded estimated to have been carried away. The Union loss was 782 killed, wounded and missing.

The Eleventh Ohio Battery went into this action 102 strong (three commissioned officers and ninety-nine enlisted men), under the command of First Lieut. Cyrus Sears. During the engagement, it was charged on three different times, suffering a loss of two officers and fifty-five men killed or wounded, eighteen being killed on the field and others dying afterward. Not a man flinched, and numbers were killed or wounded after the rebels, in their advance, had passed the muzzles of the guns, some of them nobly dying in the attempt to spike their pieces. More than sixty of the horses belonging to the battery were killed or disabled during the action, with the entire loss of harness and equipments. The assaulting rebel column suffered terribly, having received over a hundred rounds of canister and other shot, while moving forward less than a hundred yards. They (the rebels) made several attempts to drag off the guns by hand, but were thwarted each time by the hot fire of musketry poured in upon them by the Union regiments.

Although the battery suffered severely in the battle at Iuka, in the loss of men and equipments, it was, in a very short time again ready for the field, and took a prominent part in the battle of Corinth on the third and fourth days of October following (a battle in which eighteen thousand Union troops, under Rosecrans, signally defeated more than twice their number of rebels) nobly maintaining its reputation for efficiency and gallanty. On the 4th, after the first line in the center had given way, and when the rebels flushed with temporary success were pressing the second line with exultant shouts, the battery poured a destructive and continuous fire upon the advancing rebels, who, although coming within fifty yards, could no longer withstand the murderous discharge of canister from scores of Union guns, but broke and fled.

Subsequently the battery participated in various movements in Northern Mississippi and West Tennessee. In January, 1863, it was moved to Memphis, where its corps—the Seventeenth, under Maj. Gen. James B. McPherson—was preparing for the Vicksburg campaign. After a futile effort to reach the immediate vicinity of Vicksburg *via* the Yazoo Pass, the command to which the battery was attached steamed down the Mississippi to Milliken's Bend, Louisiana, where it remained a short time, and then started with the army, under Gen. Grant for the rear of Vicksburg. In the battles of Raymond, Clinton, Jackson, and Champion Hills, the battery bore a prominent part. Also throughout the siege of Vicksburg.

In the many changes consequent upon the re-organization of the army after the capture of Vicksburg, the battery was transferred from its old command—Seventh Division, Seventeenth Army Corps—to a provisional division, and soon after moved with its new command to Helena, Ark. Marching with Maj. Gen. Steele's command—the Army of Arkansas—from Helena, about the middle of August, for Little Rock, the battery passed through all the vicissitudes of a long and tedious campaign. In a short but decisive engagement fought near the capital of Arkansas on the 9th of September, 1863, the battery expended about one hundred rounds of ammunition, and both officers and men received the commendations of the General commanding for the ability with which the guns were handled, and for accurate firing at both long and short range. With this battle the active campaigning of the battery may be said to have ceased. It remained at Little Rock until the spring of 1864. About the 1st of April, with other troops, it proceeded to Pine Bluff, Ark., intending to co-operate with Banks in the Red River expedition, but Banks was defeated, and a portion of Steele's forces were halted at Pine Bluff, where the battery remained until its departure for Ohio, to be mustered out. It arrived at Columbus about the 1st of November, 1864, and on the 5th of that month its members were mustered out of service.

Lieut. Sears, already mentioned in the foregoing sketch, was, several months before the battery's term expired, appointed Colonel of a colored regiment. The men whom he enlisted at Upper Sandusky, and with whom he proceeded to St. Louis in September, 1861, joining "Constable's," soon afterward known as the Eleventh Ohio Independent Battery, were named as follows :

M. D. Butler, H. C. Worley, J. W. Bibby, C. Miller, Ira C. Swazze, M. N. Worly, John Crocheron, James Dewine, James B. Mitchell, M. V. B. Hall, Milo Allen, J. S. Barger, John Ettle, Jerome Woolsey, Lewis Ridling, Henry McLaughlin, Oscar Carpenter, Sherlock Stofer, John F. Hefflebower, John Holland, F. Welch, J. F. Hoover, J. B. Brooks, James W. Towers, J. B. Mowry, S. D. Welch, H. M. Welch, John R. Jury, J. W. Brewer, Stephen Trimble, W. H. Woodcock, W. H. Swazze, Louis B.

Henry, Elias Bringman, John Bringman, Amos B. Alger, D. Baughman, Theodore Allen, Matthew Free, Jacob Everhart, Zachariah Welch.

MISCELLANEOUS.

Besides the companies and regiments of which mention has already been made, there were many others containing Wyandot County men whose record is equally as brilliant. But from the fact that these men served in organizations in each of which the county had but very few representatives, it is an impracticable task to do otherwise than to arrange their names in classified lists as follows :

OHIO VOLUNTEER INFANTRY REGIMENTS.

Second—Company F, John Pausch.
Third—Company I, J. K. Waltermire ; Company —, E. Cowgill
Fourth—Company D, N. G. Case, Charles Case, Philip Wickiser; Company H, Joel Straub, Charles Warner, William Burns ; Company G, John F. Myers, A. W. Napers.
Sixth—Company I, John C. Lynch.
Eighth—Company A, Sergt. L. Snover, D. G. Watson, John Beatty, J. H. Nichols, Hiram B. Brown.
Ninth—Company A, Jonas Wohlgamuth ; Company F, Buell D. Chapman, Corporal ; Charles Moessner, private Company H, J. H. Warner.
Eleventh—Company A, William Reiber.
Fourteenth—Company —, Joseph Snider.
Sixteenth—Company G, Thomas Hanna.
Eighteenth—Company H, J. M. Huff, Fifer.
Twentieth—Company K, D. B. Rinehart, First Lieutenant ; Company A, R. B. Conant, Sergeant ; Company B, C. O. Oldfield ; Company —, Henry Inman.
Twenty-first—Company C, O. L. Cleveland ; Company H, J. W. Daish, Corporal.
Twenty-third—Company G, J. A. Brown ; Company F, Robert Ewart.
Twenty-fourth—Company K, Joseph Lehman.
Twenty-fifth—Company D, Sergt. T. A. Van Gundy ; Privates, Jonas Kamble, G. W. Long, W. H. Mann, Joel Milum, George W. Bogart ; Company G, Sergt. G. W. Kriling, Private J. K. Hawk.
Twenty-sixth—Company B, Francis Dawson, Barton Dawson.
Twenty-seventh—Company A, R. I. Murphy.
Thirty-second—Company I, Daniel Stam; Company H, J. S. Van Marter, Second Lieut.
Thirty-third—Company A, Jacob Reuter ; Company C, Jacob Stam ; Company D, Milton Tong ; Company K, D. W. McConnell.
Thirty-fourth—Company E, Edward Quaintance, Corporal; George W. Rex, G. W. Eckert, John Lumberson.
Thirty-sixth—Company D, J. E. Goodrich, Sergeant; A. G. Barger.
Thirty-seventh—Asst. Surg. A. Billhardt.
Company F—Eirst Lieut. M. W. Blucher.
Sergt. Jacob Schneider.
Privates, Henry Wuscher, Sebastian Glamser, Fred Fahrni, Peter Fahrni, John Michelfetter, J. Altenberger, Jacob Bastel, William Buehrle, Fredrick Waechter.
Other companies:
A—E. G. Bates.

K—Henry Gerster, John Keller, Oswald Voegel, Nicholas Volker.
Thirty-eighth—Company C, C. Stury.
Thirty-ninth—Company K, Joel Cole.
Forty fifth—Company B, W. R. Ramsdell; Company I, William Earp, George Morrison, George H. Morrison, J. W. Wickiser, William Wickiser; Company K, Adam Lambert, Jesse Lambert, Isaac N. Lane, A. G. Straw.
Company D—Nathan Rovert, Oliver Robinson.
Fifty-first—Company A, John Bart.
Fifty-third—Company H, H. W. Gillingham.
Fifty-fourth—Company G, Privates David Dysinger, David Kauble, Samuel Stalter, Oregon Kerr.
Company K—Capt. William H. Hunt; Private William Brown.
Fifty-seventh—Company F, Privates, Lewis Morehart, Leander Tong, Isaac Wohlgamuth, Lewis Switzer, Jerome Propes, James Switzer, Isaac Switzer, Joseph Glick, Joseph Newel, Andrew Amrine, Marion Esterly.
Other Companies in Fifty-seventh:
B—Sergt. J. F. Kemmel; Private Jacob Rumple.
C—Private George A. Gibbs.
D—Capt. David Ayres, Jr.
G—Capt. E. A. Gordon.
I—Private Samuel Gordon.
Fifty-eight—Company D, Christ. Woessner.
Sixty-first—Company K, Sergts. A. Bope, J. W. Brewer; Corp. Matthew Walton; Privates J. C. Spencer, Isaac Lott, H. Keller, Samuel Longabaugh, Jacob Greek, Nicholas Mott, P. H. Brewer.
Company G—Sergt. Israel Walterhouse.
Jac. Ludwig, Jacob Eckleberry.
Sixty-second—Company K, John Kriechbaum; Company A, Jacob Kennedy; Company D, Emmanuel Bowlby.
Sixty-fourth—Company A, Joseph Haupt; Company B, Joseph Richmond, E. B. Messenger; Company —, O. E. Fox.
Sixty-fifth—Company D, Privates, George W. Finnell, S. Perry, Theodore Stubbs, F. F. DeTray; Company C, Privates, J. C. Miller, George Zabriska.
Sixty-sixth—Company B, M. A. Parlet; Company E, Isaac Wood; Company H, S. H. Stricker; Company K, John Burk.
Sixty-seventh—Company C, J. C. Duffield.
Sixty-eighth—Company K, H. C. Kime.
Seventy-first—Company C, Jacob McPike; Company not known, John DeBolt, S. Barnhiser.
Seventy-second—Company C, A. P. Kelley; Company D, Orsin Bower, Corporal.
Seventy-third—Company A, Thomas Dawson.
Seventh-sixth—Company K, John McMullen.
Seventh-eighth—Company C, Rush Holloway; Company G, I. Hart, N. Willoughby, L. W. Scott.
Eightieth—Company A, Peter D. Newell.
Eighty-seventh—Company G, Theodore Dame.
Ninety-sixth—Company C, C. O. Oldfield, First Lieutenant; Company E, Thomas H. Carter; Company F, J. E. Breese.
One Hundredth—Company G, Patrick Farley.
One Hundred and Second—Company C, Samuel Miller; Company G, Chester Bowsell; Company D, Samuel Lutz.

One Hundred and Sixth—Company I, F. Shrank.

One Hundred and Seventh—Company D, John Russell; Company F, Frederick Bush.

One Hundred and Ninth—Company G; William Van Marter.

One Hundred and Thirteenth—George W. Kemp, Assistant Surgeon.

One Hundred and Twentieth—Company B, W. W. Chew.

One Hundred and Twenty-first—Company E, E. G. Bartram; Company G, Job Hoffmire.

One Hundred and Twenty-second—Company F, McDonald Savage.

One Hundred and Twenty-sixth—Company A, Titus Lowmiller, John Whittaker.

One Hundred and Twenty-eighth—Company C, M. M. Starr, Sergeant; George W. Starr; Company D, F. M. Brown.

One Hundred and Thirty-second—Company A, William Plott.

One Hundred and Seventy-fourth—Company H, W. E. Webber, First Lieutenant.

One Hundred and Seventy-fifth—Company I, Sergt. J. H. Plott; Corp. William Baker; Privates, Elias Wentling, J. D. Wickiser, David Spoon, Daniel Spoon, G. H. Carey, A. J. Shellhouse, W. H. Kimmell, Jesse Edgington, Henry Cram, L. A. Cole.

One Hundred and Seventy-sixth—Company B, G. Spitzer.

One Hundred and Seventy-seventh—Company B, S. B. Bechtel.

One Hundred and Seventy-eighth—Company G, W. Lundy; Company F, James Williams.

One Hundred and Seventy-ninth—Peter Grubb, Lieutenant Colonel; Company B, Privates, B. F. Smith, T. C. De Jean, John Keller, G. W. Gregg, G. S. Barber, Joseph Ralston, William Washburn, William Limberson, L. Wilson; Company G, Corp. E. Mutchelknaus; Company H, Jacob Hawdenshield; Company I, Privates, Uriah Bechtel, F. Caldwell, F. H. Chatlain.

One Hundred and Eightieth—Company C, Privates, E. Reynolds, Reuben Inman, J. E. Healey, Martin Inman; Company E, Private Samuel Bare; Company G, Corp. Frederick Scheufler; Company K, Privates, Jacob Opp, drummer, S. D. Blue, Simon Kachly, P. J. Liles, W. H. Moore, William Robey, Thomas M. White.

One Hundred and Eighty-second—Company K, E. R. Earp; Company I, S. G. Liles, Second Lieutenant; Company —, A. P. Inman.

One Hundred and Eighty-seventh—Company G, C. Wilt.

One Hundred and Eighty-eighth—Company G, Alfred Epley.

One Hundred and Ninety-second—Privates, Company E, John J. Mayer, John Tirey, J. L. Barick, John Weaver; Company H, Private G. W. Halsay; Company I, Privates, Isaiah McCleary, John Loubert, Theodore Henry, J. P. Berleen.

One Hundred and Ninety-fifth—Company B, Park Ludwig, John Wise, A. Hemrick; Company —, C. S. Sherwood.

One Hundred and Ninety-seventh—Company B, W. H. Spore; Company E, Hosea Tong.

One Hundred and Ninty-eighth—Company A, Robert Gerster, J. J. Gerster.

OHIO NATIONAL GUARDS, ONE HUNDRED DAYS' SERVICE.

One Hundred and Thirty-fifth—Company —, Charles Wooley; Company I, L. E. Landon.

One Hundred and Thirty-sixth—Company C, Wilbur Brown; Company E, Robert Seaton.
One Hundred and Fifty-fifth—Company F, Henry W. Peters.
One Hundred and Sixtieth—Company G, L. Chilcote.
One Hundred and Sixty third—Company C, Wesley Cashel, First Lieutenant.
One Hundred and Sixty-fourth—Company C, C. W. Longwell, Corporal; Company G, H. Dwire.
Regiment not known—Company E, John Freet.

OHIO VOLUNTEER CAVALRY REGIMENTS.

Second—Napoleon B. Brisbine, Surgeon; Company D, F. A. Singer.
Third—Company E, T. P. Miller; Company G, A. J. Caldwell, J. F. Gregg; Company L, Perry Roswell, Sergeant; G. M. Wisner, Corporal; Ashley Bixby, William Hewing, E. A. Nye, John L. Martin, Andrew Nye, S. A. Shepherd; Company M, J. S Chapin, First Sergeant; L. C. Chapin, John Lindsey, Sergeants; Daniel Clinger, C. H. Bradley, John Warner, Reese Hunter, Jacob Payne, W. H. Smith, Sergeant; William Young, Sims Irwin, G. B. Harness, William Hollanshead.
Company not known—Nelson Wilkins, Albert Harvey, Henry Lear.
Fourth—Company A, Henry Dodge.
Fifth—R. J. Brennen.
Eighth—Company L, J. M. Henry, First Lieutenant.
A. Fitzgerald, James Fitzgerald, J. Fitzgerald.
Ninth—Company F, L. C. Moody, Sergeant; H. W. Karr, John Karr, H. K. Inman, J. W. Holloway, J. C. Graham, Enos Gatchell, Jacob Gatchell, William J. Gatchell, William H. Branyen; Company —, Joseph McCutchen, Captain; George Sherman.
Tenth—Company B, John Venter; Company H, Daniel Dubbs, Sergeant; Company L, S. T. Jaqueth, Corporal.
Eleventh—Company H, Henry A. Hoffman.
Twelfth—Company A, Abraham Conger, F. M. Wert.
Thirteenth—Company —, S. A. Worley.
Thirtieth—Company L, Frank Kurtz.
————,—Company A, J. W. Lilley.

OHIO ARTILLERY COMMANDS, VOLUNTEERS.

First Ohio Heavy Artillery—David Gatchell, William Moore.
Second Ohio Heavy Artillery—Henry Larick.
Sixth Battery, Light Artillery—Second Lieutenant, Lemuel Krisher.

OTHER STATES.

INDIANA.

Fifth Infantry———Battery, John Kennedy, H. C. Worley.
Eighth Infantry—Company H, John Reiger.

ILLINOIS.

Seventy-seventh Infantry—Company B, J. A. Poyers.
One Hundred and Seventh Infantry—Company C, E. B. Norris.
One Hundred and Twenty-fifth Infantry—Company H, Joseph Coon, Daniel Williams.
Ninth Cavalry—William Walters.

PENNSYLVANIA.

Eleventh Cavalry—Company M, Irvin Bacon, Captain.
Seventeenth Cavalry—Company A, J. M. Walterhouse.
Fifth Artillery—Company B, John Andrews.

NEW YORK.

First Infantry—Company G, W. M. C. Durbarow.
Fifth Infantry—Company C, W. H. Spore.
Ninth Infantry—Company I, A. J. Shuler.
Thirty-second Infantry—Company H, George W. Cypher.
Thirty-fifth Infantry—Thomas Shuler.
Forty-second Infantry—Company H, J. M. Crawford, Sergeant.
Fifty-eighth Infantry—Company E, G. W. Nibloe, First Lieutenant.
One Hundred and Thirty-seventh Infantry—Company I, P. J. Van Marter.
Third Artillery—Company H, George W. Cypher.
Thirteenth Artillery—Company E, Christian Birk, Sergeant.
First Light Artillery—Company C, Edgar Ingerson.
Twenty-fourth Cavalry—Company A, James Morrison.

IOWA.

Fourth Infantry—Company D, John Swinehart.
Thirty-fourth Infantry—Company H, David Sheldon.
Thirty-first Infantry—Company D, Edward Brown.

MASSACHUSETTS.

Twenty-first Infantry—Company H, W. T. Durlow.
Fifty-fifth Infantry—Company E, I. W. Brickney, Color Sergeant.

MICHIGAN.

First Infantry—William High.
Third Infantry—Rolando Freet.
Eighth Infantry—Company D, Theodore Freet.
Second Cavalry—Company A, Alfred Foy.
Eleventh Cavalry—Company B, Willis Baker, First Sergeant.

MISSOURI.

Twelfth Infantry—Company E, Christian Birk.
Second Cavalry—Company C, J. B. Pool, Second Lieutenant.

KANSAS.

First Infantry—Company H, T. B. Armstrong.
Seventh Cavalry—Company A, George W. Kenan.

CALIFORNIA.

First Infantry—Company A, A. F. Smith, Captain.
Third Infantry—Company I, C. S. Swank, Sergeant.

NEW JERSEY.

Second Cavalry—Company M, George W. Karr.

MARYLAND.

Second Infantry—Company F, E. Thomas.

VIRGINIA.
Infantry—Samuel Hart.

LOUISIANA.
Second Infantry—Company A, Christian Birk, Corporal.

COLORADO.
First Infantry—John E. Shepherd.

UNITED STATES.
Eighteenth Infantry—Company F, John Leslie.
Forty-ninth Colored Infantry—Cyrus Sears, Colonel.
Seventh Cavalry—Edward Emptage.
United States Signal Corps—E. P. Shepherd, W. Strahan, M. B. Smith, Allen Smalley, J. W. McKenzie, Thomas C. McKenzie, A. McLeod, George Litle, J. L. Kaley, Nathan Jackson, C. B. Hare, D. D. Hare, Elijah Brayton, Ira J. Baker, John Carothers, Fred Harpster.
United States Engineer Corps—C. V. D. Worley.
Hospital Surgeon—John A. Royer.
James W. White, Surgeon of the United States.
Navy—Robert Bovard, John Reilly, W. H. Morris, R. S Mullholland.

The following soldiers whose regiments and companies were not reported were also accredited to Wyandot County:

G. B. Kelley, D. H. Walton, James F. Rich, I. B. Cross, P. Brashares, Page Blackburn, Peter Parsell, S. C. Anderson, W. S. Bowers, Martin Snyder, J. A. Dumm, William Sweet, Frank Switzer, Murray Switzer, J. A. Ankrum, J. O. Studebaker, J. G. Haner, John Kerr, Nathan Kimball, A. M. Johns, D. H. Young, E. W. Ekleberry, George Bowers, James M. Beam, James Miller.

We conclude this article by adding that Messrs. J. G. Roberts, Samuel H. Hunt, John D. Sears, S. H. White and T. E. Grisell, composed the county military committee during the last years of the war. That from 1861 to 1865 inclusive, the county received credit for one thousand five hundred and forty-five men, of whom only nineteen were drafted. That the total of all quotas called for amounted to one thousand five hundred and fifty; thus a deficit of five men was marked against the county at the close. However, thirty-five of the sixteen thousand non-enlisted "Squirrel Hunters" who hastened toward Cincinnati in August and September, 1862, at the time that city was threatened by the rebel forces under Kirby Smith— were Wyandot County men.

INDEX.

----, Old Hickory 331
ABBOTT, 303
ACKER, 464
ACKERMANN, 13
ADAMS, 375 453 456
AGERTER, 341-345 347 349 446 455 456
AGNEW, 341 343 454
AHLEFELD, 446 454
ALBERT, 447 455 456
ALDEN, 321 322
ALGER, 325 472
ALLEN, 290 321 343 344 471 472
ALLION, 451
ALLISON, 446 457 461 466
ALTENBERGER, 472
ALTHAUSER, 454
ALTVATER, 466
AMES, 431
AMRINE, 473
ANDERSON, 221 321 327 332 364 367 436 440 448 451 452 455 461 465 466 479
ANDREWS, 344 432 453 466 476
ANESHENSLEY, 445
ANKRUM, 479
ANNO, 446
APPLETON, 384 385
ARMSTRONG, 230 266 267 278 288 289 295 343 354 451 454 469 476
ARNOLD, 313

ASH, 448 456
ASHBROOK, 446 453
ASHLEY, 249 250
ASKEW, 444
ATHERTON, 446
ATKINSON, 456 468
AULTMAN, 397
AURAND, 432
AVERY, 359
AXT, 322
AYERS, 320-322 349 468
AYRES, 326 339 344 345 381 425 437 468 473
B, 380 411
BABBITT, 446
BABCOCK, 433 451
BACHAR, 451
BACHER, 468
BACHTELL, 446 447
BACKENSTOSE, 323
BACKUS, 337
BACON, 347 354 476
BADGER, 296 451
BAIRD, 326 332 335 337 350 436
BAKER, 339 340 348 407 408 451 465 474 476 479
BALDWIN, 346 349 447 468 469
BALLIET, 326 342 343
BALSLEY, 399
BANNING, 278
BARBER, 474
BARCLAY, 466
BARE, 372 474

BARGER, 445 471 472
BARGLEY, 304
BARICK, 474
BARKER, 457
BARLOW, 339
BARNES, 344 345 376
BARNET, 295
BARNHART, 321
BARNHISER, 451 452 468 473
BARRERE, 337
BARRY, 457
BART, 473
BARTISON, 450
BARTLEY, 337 339 359
BARTON, 354
BARTRAM, 474
BASELY, 446
BASHFORD, 293
BASOM, 446 465
BASTEL, 472
BATES, 304 323 337 338 345 349 472
BATTENFIELD, 451 468
BAUGHMAN, 304 468 472
BAUM, 304
BAUMGARDNER, 468
BAUN, 452
BAXTER, 431
BEAL, 469
BEAM, 342-344 349 479
BEAN, 242 245 248
BEAR, 322 325 465 466
BEARD, 439
BEATTY, 472
BEAUREGARD, 440
BEAVER, 303
BEBB, 332
BECHTEL, 474
BECK, 451
BECKLEY, 292
BEEBE, 339
BEER, 331 344 346 360 361 364 454
BEERY, 335 337 367 401 437
BEESON, 242
BEIDLER, 319 327 332 335 336 339-342 349 371 389 436 437
BELL, 325 344 451
BENDER, 464
BENJAMIN, 304
BENNETT, 344 451
BENTON, 345
BERLEEN, 445 466 474
BERRY, 303 323 328 331 335-341 348-350 368 372 429 430 437 455 466 468
BETZ, 453
BETZER, 304 400
BEVERTON, 463
BEVINGTON, 332
BIBBY, 446 471
BIGGS, 242 249 250 432
BILES, 344 349 451
BILLHARDT, 472
BINGHAM, 346 376
BIRCHARD, 327 328 359
BIRK, 476 479
BISHOP, 319 320 322 336 345 348
BIXBY, 314 317 327 332 335 350 457 461 468 475
BLACKBURN, 446 468 479
BLAIR, 464
BLAKE, 456
BLAND, 332 337 451
BLASER, 445
BLISS, 451 468
BLOND, 466
BLOOM, 446 469
BLOW, 446
BLUCHER, 472
BLUE, 474
BOGARD, 432
BOGART, 304 472
BOLANDER, 457 461
BOLYARD, 466

BOOKWALTER, 346
BOPE, 346 431 435 446 448 451 452 473
BOQUET, 230 237
BOROFF, 446 465
BOVARD, 479
BOWEN, 327 338 361-363 468
BOWENS, 360
BOWER, 337 466 473
BOWERS, 446 468 479
BOWLBY, 451 473
BOWMAN, 239 371 372 376
BOWSELL, 473
BOWSHER, 291 304 321 322 328 332 378 398 453 454 466 468
BOYCE, 464
BOYD, 453
BOYER, 446 452
BOYLE, 445
BOYNTON, 344
BRACKLEY, 335 336 342 348 432
BRADDOCK, 236 255
BRADLEY, 437 475
BRADSHAW, 339 340
BRADSTREET, 237
BRAGG, 457
BRAND, 454
BRANDENBURG, 445
BRANYEN, 475
BRASHARES, 479
BRAYTON, 313 468 479
BRECKENRIDGE, 464
BRECKINRIDGE, 464
BREESE, 446 473
BRENNEN, 475
BRETZ, 343 346 451
BREWER, 222 304 445 447 453 471 473
BRICKNEY, 476
BRIECHBAUM, 473
BRIGGS, 457 461
BRINGMAN, 472
BRINKERHOFF, 338 340 359 360 432
BRINTON, 242 245 248
BRISBINE, 466 475
BRISTOLL, 433
BROBST, 446
BRODHEAD, 239
BROOKE, 283
BROOKS, 372 471
BROUGH, 340
BROWN, 288 289 302 326 327 342 344 364 433 445 447 453 456 457 461 465 468 472-476
BRUCKEMILLER, 398
BRUNDIGE, 303
BRUNNER, 343 344 346-348 385 386 394-396 398 399 410 431 437
BRUNNING, 468
BRUSH, 338
BRYANT, 337 446
BUCHANAN, 440
BUCKINGHAM, 321
BUCKNER, 448
BUEHRLE, 472
BUELL, 444 449 457 462
BUFORD, 470
BUGH, 422
BULUN, 466
BUNN, 304 451 469
BURGOYNE, 238
BURK, 451 473
BURKE, 447
BURKHART, 453
BURN, 446
BURNET, 355 356 467
BURNS, 302 472
BURNSIDE, 444 450 452
BURSON, 332 335
BUSCH, 468
BUSH, 474
BUSHONG, 455
BUTLER, 260 464 469 471

BUTTERFIELD, 245
BYERS, 433 446 453
BYRON, 376
CADILLAC, 234
CALDWELL, 336 337 359 439
    446 447 451 455 463 474 475
CALHOUN, 287
CAMPBELL, 446 447 469
CANNON, 453
CAREY, 220 303 332 336 337
    339 340 346 348 372 408 429
    431 437 474
CARLIN, 348 457 458
CARLISLE, 456
CARMICHAEL, 457 461
CARNEY, 457
CAROTHERS, 457 461 466 468
    479
CARPENTER, 471
CARR, 432 445 447 454
CARTER, 371 433 447 452 473
CARTIER, 231
CARY, 219
CASE, 453 469 472
CASHEL, 475
CASPER, 453
CASS, 265 268 269 428
CASTLEMAN, 292
CATHRIGHT, 466
CATRELL, 292
CAVINS, 447
CAVIT, 451
CAWTHORN, 329 330
CAYLOR, 466
CHADWICK, 456
CHAFFEE, 320 322 332 364 390
CHAMBERLAIN, 464 465
CHAMBERLIN, 432
CHAMBERS, 322 466
CHAMPLAIN, 231-233
CHAPIN, 445 475
CHAPMAN, 472
CHASE, 338 362
CHATLAIN, 474

CHEMBERLIN, 335
CHESNEY, 432
CHEW, 474
CHILCOTE, 475
CHISNEY, 375
CHRISTEN, 343 350
CHRISTIAN, 321 344
CLAPSADDLE, 451
CLARK, 239 303 342 376 401
    445 447 453 457 461 466 468
CLAY, 331
CLAYTON, 347 349 372 408
CLEBURNE, 458
CLEMENS, 339
CLEVELAND, 472
CLINGER, 445 465 475
CLINGMAN, 435 469
CLOSE, 373
CLUGGAGE, 255
CLUGSTON, 327
COATS, 433
COFFAILD, 447
COFFINBERRY, 410
COLE, 304 410 451 453 454 456
    466 468 473 474
COLEMAN, 439
COLLINS, 365
COLVER, 322 464
COMBS, 304
COMPTON, 454
CONAGHAN, 451
CONANT, 472
CONE, 446
CONGER, 446 447 454 475
CONKLIN, 360 361
CONKLING, 398
CONN, 468
CONROY, 447
CONSTABLE?, 471
COOK, 341 342 344 466 468 469
COOKE, 340
COON, 303 475
COOPER, 446 466
COOTS, 453

COPE, 375
COPELAND, 429
COPLER, 446 468
CORBIN, 321 454
CORDRAY, 397
CORFMAN, 400 401 451 466
CORNING, 446 457 461
CORWIN, 331 359 466
CORWINE, 447
COSS, 294
COSTOLOE, 466
COTTER, 295
COUPLES, 456
COVER, 303 436 445
COVILL, 446
COWAN, 343
COWGILL, 446 451 452 466 472
COWLEY, 453
COX, 322
COZIER, 465 468
CRAGLOW, 465
CRAIG, 242 466
CRAM, 454 474
CRAMER, 342 451
CRANE, 377
CRASS, 454
CRAUN, 453
CRAVEN, 453
CRAWFORD, 224 239 241 242 245-252 254-258 275 290 294 339 340 349 368 410 413 438 445 476
CRITES, 465
CROCHERON, 471
CROCKER, 313
CROGHAN, 237 256
CROMWELL, 396
CRONISE, 335 348
CROOKS, 438
CROSS, 462 465 479
CROUSE, 447 455
CRUM, 468
CULBERTSON, 340 350 431 446 447
CULVER, 322 408 431 432 446 451 457 462 466
CUMMINGS, 444 448 451
CUMMINS, 444
CUNEO, 385 386 396-398 433
CUNNINGHAM, 468
CUPP, 453
CUPPALS, 321
CURLIS, 339 437
CURTIS, 366 431
CUTLER, 457 461
CYPHER, 476
D'AUBRY, 237
DABLON, 233
DAISH, 472
DALLAS, 331
DALZELL, 237
DAME, 399 473
DAVENPORT, 303 338
DAVID, 446 465
DAVIES, 455
DAVIS, 343 376 432 447 456-458 464-466 468
DAWSON, 444 472 473
DEAL, 346
DEAN, 456
DEARDOFF, 468
DEBAUGH, 466
DEBOLT, 409 431 451 473
DEBROUGH, 433
DEGRESS, 455
DEJEAN, 343 346 432 446 474
DELANGDALE, 237
DELANO, 362
DELAPLINE, 466
DELONG, 445 451
DEMAREST, 465
DEMMING, 446
DENNISON, 337-339 349 368 385 394
DEPLER, 343 344
DERMIGER, 303
DESHLER, 430
DETRAY, 321 473

DEVINE, 455
DEWINE, 471
DEWITT, 327 450 451 457 461
DICKENS, 303
DICKERSON, 372
DICKEY, 444 449
DICKINSON, 335
DIEGLE, 292
DIPPREY, 446
DIPPY, 454
DITTY, 446
DIXON, 432 457 461
DODGE, 345 360 455 475
DOHERTY, 257
DOLL, 453
DOLMETSK, 410
DONENWIRTH, 335
DONNELL, 325
DONNENWORTH, 348
DORMAN, 400
DOUGHERTY, 255 456 466
DOUGHTY, 259 446
DOUGLAS, 340
DOWN, 455
DOWNEY, 455
DOWNING, 456
DOYLE, 347
DRAKE, 294
DRESBACH, 335
DRISCOL, 447
DRUCKEMILLER, 448
DRUCKMILLER, 446
DRUM, 320-322 376 466
DRUMM, 479
DRY, 466
DUBBS, 475
DUBRE, 431
DUBUISSON, 234
DUDDLESON, 468
DUDLEY, 379
DUFFIELD, 473
DULY, 380 447
DUMM, 320 344 345 349 385 386 394-396 416 446

DUNLAP, 293 467
DUNN, 376 445 452 466
DURBAROW, 476
DURBIN, 446
DURBORAW, 451
DURLO, 476
DWIRE, 475
DYSINGER, 455 473
EARLY, 463 467
EARP, 446 453 455 473 474
EATHERTON, 456
EBERSOLE, 445
EBERSOLL, 325
EBY, 326
ECKERT, 472
ECKLEBERRY, 431 473
EDGERTON, 428
EDGINGTON, 340 341 453 454 474
EDWARDS, 453
EGESTON, 465
EGGLESTON, 446
EKLEBERRY, 446 479
ELKINS, 321
ELLIOTT, 246 283 432 463
ELLIS, 332 347 447 455 465
ELLISON, 468
ELY, 463
EMERSON, 446 448 452 454 465 469
EMPTAGE, 447 448 465 466 468 479
ENDERS, 433
ENERSON, 451
ENNINGER, 433
ENOS, 295
ENSMINGER, 400
EPLER, 321 322
EPLEY, 474
ERVIN, 322
ESTERLY, 473
ESTLE, 446
ETTLE, 471
EVANS, 409

EVERHART, 451 472
EWART, 465 466 472
EWING, 336 345 446 447 451
EYCK, 435 436
EYESTONE, 304 446 451 466 469
F, 413
FAHRNI, 472
FAILOR, 435 437
FAIRFAX, Lord 254
FARLEY, 473
FARRAGUT, 371
FEHL, 435
FERGUSON, 321
FERNWALT, 445
FERRIS, 327 375 376 435-437 445 447 465 467
FILLMORE, 383
FILSON, 453
FINAN, 456
FINCK, 344
FINK, 346
FINLEY, 271-274 276-278 282-284 286-290 295 344 345 410
FINNELL, 448 465 473
FIREING, 389
FISHEL, 341 342
FISHER, 466
FITCH, 303
FITZGERALD, 475
FLACK, 322 337-339 349 433 469
FLENNER, 320
FLETCHER, 376
FLICKENGER, 462
FLICKINGER, 457
FLINCHBAUGH, 453
FLOCK, 433
FLOWER, 303
FLOYD, 440
FOGLE, 455
FOLKNER, 466
FOLLETT, 346 347 426
FORAKER, 347

FORBES, 237 255
FORD, 335
FORNEY, 446
FOSTER, 345 346 376 432 468
FOUCHT, 344
FOUKE, 322 327 332 335 336 380 383 431
FOWLER, 314 317-319 322 324 331 332 337 338 340 348 376 380 435-437 447
FOX, 451 473
FOY, 446 466 476
FOYER, 457 461
FRANCIS THE FIRST, King of? 231
FRANK, 446 468
FRANKLIN, 381
FRASER, 255 321
FRAZER, 469
FRAZIER, 304
FRAZOR, 257
FREDERICK, 221
FREE, 376 446 472
FREES, 435 436
FREESE, 453
FREET, 339 346 347 349 432 433 451 475 476
FREMONT, 456 469
FROST, 273 466
FRUIT, 451
FRY, 466
FULK, 453
FULMER, 453
FUNK, 432 451 462
GADDIS, 242
GALBRAITH, 446 447
GALBREATH, 466
GALE, 303
GAMMELL, 328
GANTER, 432
GANTZ, 454
GARFIELD, 346
GARRETT, 456
GASTENSLAGER, 462

GATCHELL, 337 453 468 475
GATES, 238 432
GAULT, 432
GAY, 447
GEAR, 347 349 408 451 468
GEDDES, 346
GEE, 393
GEIGER, 396 446
GEORGE, King of ? 281
GEPHART, 466
GERSTENSTAGER, 457
GERSTER, 473 474
GETCHEL, 446
GHOLSON, 339
GIBBS, 341 347 432 433 451 468 473
GIBSON, 238 248 252 341 343 344 346 349 372 437 448-451 453 466 469
GIEGG, 432
GILES, 367 381-386 389-394 433
GILL, 430
GILLAN, 400
GILLETT, 437
GILLIAM, 466
GILLILAND, 444 446 448
GILLIN, 456
GILLINGHAM, 399 473
GILMAN, 355
GILMORE, 345
GILRUTH, 283 290
GINTHER, 456
GIPSON, 341 350 466
GIRTY, 246 250-252
GIST, 255
GLADWYN, 237
GLAMSER, 472
GLASSER, 462
GLAZER, 457
GLENN, 337
GLICK, 473
GLOVER, 444
GODFROY, 269
GOOD, 457 461 462
GOODBREAD, 341 349
GOODIN, 446
GOODMAN, 445 451 468
GOODRICH, 344 345 401 472
GOODSPEED, 449 450
GORDON, 313 344 437 455 473
GORMAM, 446
GORMAN, 447
GORMLEY, 327 435
GOTTFRIED, 223
GOTTIER, 454
GOULD, 384 457 461
GOULDSBY, 457
GRAHAM, 446 456 475
GRANGER, 450
GRANT, 237 398 449 454 457 465 469-471
GRAVELL, 447
GREEK, 344-346 349 451 473
GREEN, 335-337 451 453
GREENE, 430
GREER, 342 346 451
GREGG, 386 431 451 466 474 475
GRIFFITH, 304 314 317-319 322 324 327 331 335 347 348 380
GRINDLE, 304 450 451 468
GRISELL, 338 339 341 342 349 371 437 479
GRISWOLD, 320
GROFF, 456
GROSSCUP, 344
GROSSELL, 457 468
GRUBB, 451 474
GRUNDITSCH, 446 448 454
GUNDER, 446
GUTHERY, 446
GUTHRIE, 454
GWIN, 446
H, 219 414
HAAS, 466
HACKENBERGER, 453
HAFER, 347
HAGERMAN, 446 455 456

HAHN, 447
HALE, 446 457 461 468
HALL, 336 338 339 359 361 364
  365 375 446 466 471
HALLABAUGH, 453
HALLECK, 469
HALLOWELL, 457 461
HALSAY, 474
HALSEY, 466
HALSTEAD, 303 337 445
HAMILL, 397
HAMILTON, 470
HAMTRANCK, 259
HANCOCK, 346
HANER, 466 479
HANNA, 255 472
HARDER, 447
HARDIN, 259 445 448
HARDING, 256
HARDLY, 455
HARDY, 376
HARE, 337 342 347 349 371 372
  431 436 437 451 479
HARKEM, 447
HARKUM, 447
HARLEY, 453
HARMAN, 454
HARMER, 259
HARNESS, 475
HARPER, 304 326 332 335 336
  342 346 347 349 389 432 446
  451
HARPSTER, 343 344 468 479
HARRIS, 342 345-347 411 412
  437 457 461 466
HARRISON, 247 249 251 265
  272 340 342 368 411 422 438
  439 449
HARSH, 457 461
HARSHBARGER, 456
HARSHBERGER, 468
HART, 447 473 479
HARTER, 399 400
HARTLE, 219 446 447

HARTSOUGH, 343 446 450
HARVEY, 475
HARXTHOL, 435
HASTINGS, 410
HATFIELD, 466
HAUPT, 473
HAVENS, 451
HAWDENSHIELD, 474
HAWK, 446 453 472
HAWKINS, 451 455
HAYES, 341 342 344
HAYMAN, 321 466-468
HAYNES, 337
HAZEN, 446-448
HEALEY, 474
HEALY, 456
HECKATHORN, 219 303
HECKATHORNE, 466
HECKEWELDER, 228
HECKMAN, 462 466
HEDGES, 437
HEFFELFINGER, 456
HEFFLEBOWER, 446 466 471
HEFFLEFINGER, 446
HEISTAND, 452 469
HELLER, 462
HELSEL, 445 455
HEMRICK, 474
HENDERSON, 342 346 349 376
  395 448
HENKLE, 278 282 339
HENLEY, 466
HENNESSY, 466
HENRY, 446 453 469 472 474
  475
HENSEL, 447
HERNDON, 431 457 461
HERRING, 346 349
HESSER, 446 447 466
HETZELL, 386
HEWING, 475
HEYM, 350 376
HIBBINS, 469
HIGGINBOTHAM, 447

HIGH, 476
HILDRETH, 466 469
HILL, 321 457 461
HILLIARD, 431
HINCHMAN, 397
HINE, 451
HINKLE, 432
HITCHCOCK, 337-339 342 343 346 349 359 433 435
HITCHEW, 451
HITE, 328-331 437
HOADLEY, 347
HOAGLAND, 242
HOBBS, 408
HODGE, 422
HODGES, 303
HOFF, 454
HOFFMAN, 338 432 448 466 469 475
HOFFMIRE, 474
HOLDEN, 448 466
HOLDERMAN, 436
HOLDREDGE, 338
HOLDRIDGE, 329 339 348 436
HOLLAND, 468 471
HOLLANSHEAD, 408 457 462 475
HOLLENSHEAD, 341 342 348
HOLLINGER, 456
HOLLOWAY, 341 444 446 456 473 475
HOLLOWELL, 447
HOLLY, 466
HOLMAN, 396
HOLMES, 302 400 445
HONER, 435
HOOD, 242 450 461
HOOKER, 452 456
HOOPER, 283
HOOVER, 317 454 466 467 471
HOPPWOOD, 453
HORD, 432
HORICK, 446
HORRICK, 303 469

HOSFORD, 292
HOSTLER, 433
HOTELLING, 466
HOUCK, 327 433
HOUGH, 466
HOUK, 332
HOUPT, 320
HOUSTON, 345 346 350
HOWELL, 446
HOY, 456
HOYSINGTON, 466 468
HOYT, 337-339 341 349 368 437 451
HUBBARD, 433
HUBER, 302 320 321 439
HUDSON, 432
HUEY, 445
HUFF, 472
HUFFMAN, 218 447 454
HUFFNAGLE, 400
HUFFORD, 466
HUGHES, 321 431 435 446
HULBURD, 383 384
HULL, 264
HUMBERT, 466
HUME, 345
HUMPHREY, 468
HUNT, 330 431 432 468 469 473 479
HUNTER, 464 466 475
HUNTINGTON, 430
HURD, 468
HURXTHAL, 431
HUTTER, 345 457 461
INDIAN, Andauyouah 282
 Anthony Wayne 263 Ayenucere 291 Bearskin 299 Between-the-logs 264 265 269 277 278 282 283 288-290 Big River 283 299 Big Town 299 Big Tree 265 299 Big-tree 276 283 Billy Montour 291 Black Chief 295 Black Hoof 263 270 271 Black Racoon 291

HISTORY OF WYANDOT COUNTY. 491

INDIAN (Cont.)
Black Sheep 299 Bloody Eyes 277 Blue Jacket 263 299 Buckongehelas 263 Buckwheat 291 Bull Head 299 Capt Billy Doudee 292 Capt Billy Dowdee 292 Capt Dowdee 292 Capt Pipe 251 252 254 275 290 291 294 Capt Pipe Jr 290 294 Capt Wolf 291 Captain Pipe 268 Caryhoe 299 Cherokee Boy 267 268 Chop-the-logs 299 Comstock 377 Coon 377 Crane 263 Curly Head 299 De Un Quot 272 Deandoughso 282 Deunquot 282 284 288 296 Driver 283 George Punch 283 Grey Eyes 296 Grey-eyes 299 Grue 273 Half-John 377 Harrihoot 283 Hicks 377 Hoomaurou 291 Horonu 267 Isaac Hill 291 Jacques 299 James Armstrong 291 John Armstrong 291 John Hicks 278 282 283 299 John Hill 291 John Ming 291 Johnnycake 275 Johnnycake 291 Joseph Williams 283 Killbuck 275 Little Chief 283 Little Turtle 263 Lump-on-the-head 295 299 Lyons 275 291 Mahautoo 291 Mathew Peacock 283 Mononcue 277 278 282 283 285 288 289 295 377 Mudeater 299 Nickels 292-294 Old Tom Lyons 291 292 O-no-ran-do-roh 289 Peacock 278 299 377 Pipe 294 Pontiac 237 Porcupine 299 Prophet 264 265 Providence 299 Red Jacket 270 Robert Armstrong 283 Robinson 260

INDIAN (Cont.)
263 Rohyenness 283 Sanondoyourayquaw 267 Sanoudoyeasquaw 291 Sarrahos 377 Saw-yau-wa-hoy 295 Scuteash 278 283 Silas Armstrong 291 Solomon Johnycake 292 Soo-cuh-guess 295 Soo-de-nooks 295 Split-the-log 299 Squindatee 283 Squindecta 377 Squindighty 278 Squire Grayeyes 283 Squire Grey-eyes 299 Stand-in-thewater 299 Steele 377 Summundewat 265 283 288 296 377 Tahuwaughtarode 282 Tarhe 263 265 270-274 284 Tarhee 273 Tecumseh 264 265 272 281 The Crane 264 270 272 Thomas Lyons 291 Thunder 277 Tishatahooms 291 Tom 292 Tom Dowdee 292 293 Two Logs 283 Two-logs 277 Warpole 285 296 299 377 Washington 283 299 377 Whipping-stick 377 White Wing 299 Widow Armstrong 291 William Doudee 291 William Walker 299 Wingenin 251 Wingenund 254 Youdorast 291 Zeeshawan 267 Zeshauau 291
INGERSON, 341 446 451 465 466 476
INGLE, 451
INGLEHART, 447 468
INMAN, 304 341 344 345 347 349 452 466 472 474 475
IRVIN, 446 466
IRVINE, 240-242 248 336 340 348 433 446
IRWIN, 376 475
ISH, 468

JACKMAN, 451
JACKSON, 335 343 360 361 364
 452 479
JACOB, 451
JACOBY, 451
JAMES, 433 446 450
JAQUETH, 435 446 451 475
JAY, 431
JEFFERSON, 411
JENNER, 342 348
JEWEL, 451
JEWELL, 446
JEWETT, 340
JOHNS, 479
JOHNSON, 237 345 431 432 444
 449 451 458
JOHNSTON, 270 271 278 286
 295 336 456
JOHNYCAKE, 292
JONES, 327 385 391 392 437 447
 455 468
JUNKINS, 326 433
JUREY, 314 317 332 335 349
 380 446 448
JURY, 320 321 471
JUVINALL, 338 437
KACHLY, 474
KAIL, 342 344 371 372 437
KALEY, 465 479
KAMBLE, 472
KARR, 451 466 468 469 475 476
KATING, 455
KAUBLE, 473
KAYS, 322
KEAR, 303 331 332 336-338 347
 348 435 452 468
KECKLER, 220
KEELER, 468
KEEN, 384
KEIL, 398
KELLER, 219 331 445 447 454
 456 473 474
KELLEY, 473 479
KELLOGG, 464 468
KELLY, 456
KELSO, 410
KEMMEL, 473
KEMP, 436 466 474
KENAN, 327 338 345 433 437
 466 476
KENNEDY, 326 343 345 346 432
 447 456 466 468 469 473 475
KENNON, 338
KENTFIELD, 344 347 451
KERR, 325 337 445-447 457 461
 473 479
KESTNER, 451
KEYES, 447
KEYS, 445 447 456 466
KIBBLER, 218
KIBRY, 346
KIEHL, 466
KIGHTLINGER, 447
KILMER, 376 446 457 461
KIMBALL, 468 479
KIME, 473
KIMMELL, 456 474
KIMMERLY, 468
KINE, 453
KING, 328 429 433 446 466
KINKEAD, 321
KINLEY, 468
KINNEY, 336-349 466
KIRBY, 317 318 322 326 327 332
 335 337-345 348 349 360 361
 365 379 381 391 425 429 432
 433 436 439 443 444 446 447
 456 457 461 462 467
KIRK, 449
KIRTLAND, 399
KISER, 332
KISKADDEN, 332 376
KISOR, 303 304 340-343 348 435
 436
KISSEWITTER, 386
KITCHEN, 432 446 448 451 469
KITCHIN, 433
KITTLE, 453

HISTORY OF WYANDOT COUNTY. 493

KNAGGS, 269
KNAPP, 327
KNEAGEL, 327
KNIBLOE, 339
KNIGHT, 242 245-247 254
KNOX, 431
KOBLE, 453
KOTTERMAN, 454
KRAKAU, 335 337 338
KRAMER, 454
KRIDER, 457 461
KRIECHBAUM, 466
KRILING, 472
KRISHER, 475
KUNTZ, 446
KURTZ, 468 475
LACY, 457 461
LAIRD, 451
LAKE, 303
LAMBERT, 321 451 473
LAMBRIGHT, 447 453 454
LAMISON, 342
LANDON, 431 474
LANE, 454 473
LANG, 340 346 348 468
LANNON, 451
LARICK, 448 475
LATTA, 359 360
LAUGHREY, 454
LAURENS, 238
LAUTZENHEISER, 447
LAUTZENHISER, 447
LAUX, 446
LAW, 454
LAWRENCE, 359 361 363 379 457 461
LAWSON, 392
LAYTON, 446 447
LEAR, 475
LEE, 303 337 339 348 432 455 463 465 466
LEEPER, 304 313 451 466
LEET, 242
LEHMAN, 472
LEIB, 289
LEIGHTON, 336
LEITH, 303 326 327 337 341 361 364 437 447 468
LESLIE, 479
LETSON, 376
LEWIS, 282 332 336-338 346- 348 384 408 462
LICKFELT, 461
LIKINS, 454
LILES, 457 461 474
LILLEY, 475
LIMBERSON, 474
LIME, 344 456 468
LINCOLN, 340 367 439 440 443
LINDSAY, 345 446 468
LINDSEY, 345 475
LINK, 457 462
LINN, 454
LIPP, 456
LISH, 304 313
LITLE, 479
LITTLE, 320 454 469
LIVENSPIRE, 446 448
LOCHRY, 239 255
LODER, 448 466
LOGAN, 447 455
LONG, 303 431 433 452 453 456 466 468 472
LONGABAUGH, 446 456 473
LONGWELL, 475
LONGWORTH, 346
LOROMIE, 263 265
LOTT, 454 466 473
LOUBERT, 474
LOUDERMILCH, 451 457
LOVERICK, 293
LOVETT, 433
LOWDERMILCH, 461
LOWELL, 457
LOWERY, 468
LOWMASTER, 346 347 451
LOWMILLER, 474
LOWRY, 451

LUDLOW, 346
LUDWIG, 457 462 474
LUMBARD, 446 447
LUMBERSON, 472
LUNDY, 340 436 446 465 474
LUPFER, 323
LUPTON, 304 337 435 469
LUTE, 414
LUTZ, 343 346 473
LYLE, 335 349 367 391 392
LYNCH, 472
LYON, 365
MACKEY, 320 466
MADDOX, 432
MADDUX, 337 340 343 349 367 368 372
MAFFETT, 338-342 348 349 446
MAGEES, 288
MAHAN, 335
MAHON, 446 447 454
MALON, 454
MALONE, 431
MALOY, 446
MANKIN, 456
MANLEY, 323 408
MANN, 304 341 457 461 472
MANSFIELD, 295 354
MARBLE, 432 451
MARCH, 322
MARKLEY, 343 451
MARLOW, 340 341 350
MARQUART, 454
MARQUETTE, 233 236
MARSHALL, 241 248 343 354 433
MARTIN, 339 341 397 445 447 451 453 454 456 457 461 462 475
MARVIN, 466
MASKEY, 466
MASKY, 376
MASON, 304 322 327 375 376 468
MATTOCKS, 321

MAURICE, 466
MAVIS, 321
MAXWELL, 340 347 355 437
MAYER, 474
MAYS, 446 451
MCAFEE, 223
MCALMON, 338
MCANDERSON, 457
MCARTHUR, 265 268 269 454
MCBANE, 335 367
MCBEE, 454
MCBETH, 343-345
MCBRIDE, 466
MCCANDLISH, 433
MCCAULEY, 360 469
MCCLAIN, 342 343 349 446 447 466
MCCLARY, 446
MCCLEARY, 474
MCCLELLAND, 242 246
MCCLENAHAN, 444
MCCOLLOCK, 266
MCCONNELL, 255 320 321 376 377 425 436 466 472
MCCOOK, 342 444 449
MCCORKLE, 393
MCCORMICK, 446 447
MCCOY, 454
MCCRACKEN, 335
MCCULLOUGH, 288 432
MCCURDY, 325 426
MCCUTCHEN, 319-323 336-339 349 380 381 389 390 437 475
MCDONALD, 376
MCDOWELL, 322 345
MCELVAIN, 320-322 326 327 367 380 389-392 433 439
MCELVAINE, 290 342
MCELWAIN, 457 461
MCFARLAND, 447 454 466
MCFEE, 468
MCGARVEY, 468
MCGAVERN, 382 383
MCGEEHAN, 242

MCGHA, 468
MCGILL, 376 436
MCGLEN, 400
MCGOWAN, 440
MCILVAINE, 346
MCINTOSH, 238 257
MCJENKINS, 466
MCJUNKIN, 432
MCKEE, 255
MCKELLY, 328 336 337 339 343
  344 346 348 349 361 366 368
  372 380 381 389 425 426 428
  429 435 436
MCKENDREE, 285 286
MCKENZIE, 341 360 361 465
  468 479
MCKIBBIN, 432
MCKINLEY, 251
MCLANE, 337
MCLAUGHLIN, 446 453 457 461
  471
MCLEOD, 479
MCMILLAN, 356 466
MCMULLEN, 328 473
MCNIEL, 463
MCNULTY, 331
MCNURTY, 328
MCPHERSON, 454 455 471
MCPIKE, 473
MCRUFF, 323
MEARS, 338 339 350 431
MEDILL, 337 338
MEIGS, 283 355 439
MELLON, 446
MERRIMAN, 303 313 331 383
  432 435 436
MERSEY, 455
MESSENGER, 473
METCALF, 359
MICHAEL, 454
MICHAELS, 341 350 454 466
MICHELFETTER, 472
MIDLAM, 454 469

MILLER, 242 303 320 335 337
  340 341 343 344 348 349 366
  391 398 400 430 439 444 447
  451 453 456 457 462 466 469
  471 473 475 479
MILLIGAN, 409 469
MILLS, 429 456
MILROY, 456 463
MILUM, 466 472
MINCER, 466
MINER, 320 321 445
MITCHELL, 393 432 446 457
  466 469 471
MITTEN, 221 466
MOESSNER, 472
MONNETT, 344
MONROE, 287
MONTCALM, 237
MONTEE, 322 323 327 466
MONTGOMERY, 278
MOODY, 475
MOORE, 446 466 474 475
MOREHART, 473
MORGAN, 386 451
MORON, 466
MORRAL, 304 338 340 343 344
  348 349
MORRIS, 347 446 467 468 479
MORRISON, 314 317 326 332
  335 337 340 349 390 433 456
  473 476
MORROW, 456
MORTIMORE, 275
MORTON, 454
MOSIER, 451
MOTT, 314 317 320-323 327 328
  331 332 335 336 339 341 343
  348 349 360 361 363 365 366
  372 379 389 394 435 473
MOUNT, 468
MOWRY, 471
MOYER, 451
MUGG, 384 413

MULFORD, 446 447
MULHAUSER, 456
MULLHOLAND, 221 451
MULLHOLLAND, 479
MULLIGAN, 255
MUNGEN, 341 342
MUNGER, 446
MUNN, 242
MUNSON, 376 380 433
MURPHY, 446 448 472
MURRAY, 340-342 349
MUTCHELKNAUS, 474
MUTCHLER, 303
MYERS, 321 337 342 343 346 350 380 382 431 432 437 446 447 454 457 461 462 468 469 472
NAFZGAR, 447
NAGEL, 447
NAIL, 469
NAPERS, 472
NAUGLE, 466
NEAL, 466
NEISZ, 397
NELSON, 337 338 347 350 436 456
NESBAUM, 468
NEWEL, 473
NEWELL, 473
NEWHARD, 457 461
NEWMAN, 347
NIBLOE, 476
NICHOLS, 304 432 439 446 457 462 465 472
NIEBEL, 466
NIVER, 408
NOBLE, 338 340
NOEL, 422
NOLL, 466
NORRIS, 220 337 475
NORTH, 319
NORTON, 339 347 379 447 457 462 466
NOWELL, 432

NOYES, 342 343
NUGENT, 267
NUSS, 454
NUTTER, 466
NYE, 450 451 457 468 475
O'BRIEN, 221 446 447 454
O'DONNELL, 329 330
O'NEAL, 433 468
OBENCHAIN, 468
OBERLIN, 466
OFFICER, 439
OGG, 451
OGLE, 242 367
OGLESBY, 455
OKEY, 345 347
OLDFIELD, 472 473
OLIVER, 410 466 469
OPP, 474
ORD, 464 470
ORR, 339 348 389 390
ORTH, 321
OSBORN, 325 447 466
OSBORNE, 447 469
OWEN, 347 360
OWENS, 321
PAHL, 218
PAIGE, 345
PALMER, 359 435 436 447 466
PANCOAST, 451 469
PARK, 457
PARKER, 343 431 435 468
PARKIN, 466
PARKS, 461 468
PARLET, 466 473
PARSELL, 479
PARSONS, 340 354 355 466
PAULIN, 451
PAUSCH, 472
PAYNE, 338 431 475
PEASE, 314 317 320 327 332 338 350 432
PECK, 338 339
PEER, 313
PEN, 256

PENDERGAST, 456
PENDLETON, 342 360
PENN, 379
PENNINGTON, 361 451 466
PENTECOST, 255
PERDEW, 432
PERKINS, 408
PERRIN, 466
PERRY, 431 432 473
PETERS, 337 344 425 435-437 475
PETERSON, 435 446
PETTIT, 341 447
PHELPS, 361 451
PHILLIPS, 469
PICKET, 304 446
PIERCE, 454
PIKE, 454
PILLARS, 343 360 361
PISEL, 454
PITTSFORD, 408
PLANTS, 337 339 359 361 363
PLATT, 451
PLOTT, 468 474
PLUMMER, 401
POINTER, 272 276-278 285
POLK, 13 331 379
PONTIUS, 304 451 469
POOL, 323 327 342 345 346 372 446 451 453 468 476
POOLE, 335 336
POPE, 431 452 457 461 469
PORTER, 343 360
PORTERFIELD, 443
POST, 455 458
POTTER, 335 439
POWELL, 385
POYERS, 475
PRICE, 409 446 454 457 461 466 469 470
PROCTOR, 255
PROPES, 473
PUFFENBERGER, 469
PUMPHREY, 464 465
PUTNAM, 237 355
QUAINTANCE, 321 393 446 456 462 472
RAGON, 332 335 336 339 446 447 454 466 468
RALSTON, 474
RAMBO, 325
RAMSDELL, 473
RAMSEY, 376
RANDALL, 323
RANDOLPH, 464 465
RANGER, 376
RANK, 466
RANNEY, 338 339
RAPPE, 321 322 436 437
RASEY, 447
RATZ, 446
RAWSON, 336
RAYMOND, 454
REAM, 454 457 462
REAMY, 447
REARDON, 466
REBER, 436 437
REED, 320 336 337 350 359 446 456 465
REEVES, 457
REIBER, 472
REICHENEKER, 433
REICHMAN, 446
REID, 455
REIDLING, 446 456
REIGER, 451 475
REILLY, 479
REINHARD, 446
REISH, 447
REMINGTON, 321
RENICK, 326 327 335 336 361 364 435-437
RENISDERFER, 462
RENSHAW, 446 447
REUTER, 472
REX, 447 457 462 472
REYNOLDS, 338 340 341 347 349 432 446 465 466 474

RHODES, 469
RICE, 323 451 454
RICH, 479
RICHARDS, 313
RICHMOND, 466 473
RICKENBACH, 466
RICKER, 322
RIDDLE, 365
RIDLING, 446 471
RIESENBERGER, 454
RIESER, 342 343 433 454
RIFENBERRY, 465
RIFNER, 451
RIGGS, 464
RILEY, 283 343
RINEBARGER, 446
RINEHART, 448 472
RINGEISEN, 433
RIPLEY, 469
RISBY, 447
RISTERPHER, 446
RITCHIE, 242 303 468
ROBBINS, 320 436 453 464 466
ROBENALT, 454
ROBERSON, 451
ROBERTS, 394 433 436 437 446 454 466 479
ROBERTSON, 323 454
ROBEY, 474
ROBINSON, 321 456 466 468 473
ROCK, 451
ROCKWELL, 446 448
RODIG, 446 447
ROGERS, 237
ROLL, 465
ROLSON, 454
RONK, 320 322 325
ROOK, 453
ROOT, 314 317 318 327 332 335 349 371
ROSE, 249 360 446 456
ROSEBERRY, 303 304
ROSEBOROUGH, 347
ROSECRANS, 444 449 457 458 469-471
ROSENBAUM, 464
ROSENBERGER, 376
ROSS, 242 456
ROSWELL, 475
ROTH, 321
ROUSSEAU, 448
ROVERT, 473
ROWE, 380
ROWSE, 344
ROYER, 479
RUGGLES, 272
RUMBAUGH, 453
RUMMELL, 380 446 466
RUMPLE, 473
RUNELS, 468
RUSSEL, 389
RUSSELL, 327 474
RUST, 393
SAFFELT, 432
SAGE, 468
SAGER, 409
SAHN, 446
SAINTCLAIR, 255 257 259 263
SAINTJOHN, 390 433
SALTSMAN, 437
SALYARDS, 304
SALYERS, 462
SAMPSON, 327 337 339 376 377
SANDERS, 433
SANDERSON, 392
SANFORD, 456
SAUL, 454
SAVAGE, 327 474
SAVIDGE, 431 456
SAWYER, 446 466
SCHAEFER, 343 344 350
SCHANER, 409
SCHENCK, 452 456
SCHEUFLER, 474
SCHIDIGGER, 446
SCHNEIDER, 472
SCHNOOER, 447

SCHUG, 376
SCHULER, 346 347 350
SCHUMAKER, 347
SCHUYLER, 464
SCOTT, 338 340 344 359 360 365 366 379 389 432 457 461 466 473
SCROGGS, 389 393
SEAGER, 466 469
SEAMAN, 341 433
SEARLE, 338
SEARS, 313 321 327 332 339 361 366-368 378 379 389 414 429 432 435-437 466 469-471 479
SEATON, 475
SEITZ, 343 345 348
SELL, 320 329 330 382 446
SENEY, 339 347 359 361 431
SENSENEY, 337
SENSENY, 320
SEWARTZ, 457
SHAFER, 469
SHAFFER, 321 469
SHAFFSTALL, 462
SHALL, 394
SHANE, 468
SHANER, 446 453 454
SHANNON, 299 454 466
SHARP, 454
SHARROCK, 292 293
SHAW, 290 422 457 462
SHAY, 446
SHEEHY, 432 447
SHELDON, 476
SHELL, 457 462 468
SHELLHOUSE, 468 474
SHEPARD, 345 457
SHEPHERD, 217 304 461 462 475 479
SHERIDAN, 371 464
SHERMAN, 396 443 444 447-450 453 455 456 461 468 475
SHERWOOD, 320 321 451
SHEVER, 456
SHIELDS, 318
SHINELY, 457
SHIREMAN, 451 468
SHOAFSTEL, 457
SHOEMAKER, 340 457 462
SHORB, 317
SHOUP, 217
SHRANK, 468 474
SHRENK, 319 320 322 331 378 381
SHUE, 439
SHULER, 451 454 476
SHULTZ, 342 350 436
SHUMACHER, 347
SHUMAKER, 462
SHURR, 340
SHUSTER, 454
SIBERT, 456 457 462
SICKFELT, 457
SIGEL, 456 464
SIGLER, 376
SIMMON, 466
SIMMONS, 448 466
SIMONSON, 456
SIMPSON, 448
SINGER, 475
SIPES, 457 462 468
SIPHER, 454
SLADE, 457 462
SLOCUM, 456
SLOVER, 242 245-247
SMALLEY, 343 344 349 371 376 437 451 468 479
SMITH, 218 221 222 304 327 336 340 345 347 349 365 367 372 382 391 430 432 433 446 454 456 457 464-466 468 474-476 479
SMOOT, 373
SMUCKER, 258
SNERINGER, 446
SNIDER, 446 472
SNODGRASS, 336 348
SNOVER, 431 472

SNYDER, 303 304 436 456 462
  466 479
SOLLEY, 451
SOON, 448
SOWERS, 464
SPADE, 304
SPAFFORD, 457 462
SPALDING, 359 446
SPAYTH, 446 447
SPEELMAN, 325
SPELMAN, 338 348
SPENCER, 446 448 456 473
SPETLER, 433
SPICER, 267
SPINK, 336
SPITTLE, 466
SPITZER, 474
SPOON, 446 454 474
SPOONER, 446
SPORE, 474 476
SPOUT, 454
SPROAT, 447
SPROUT, 454
SPURGEON, 291
SPYBEY, 379
STAFFORD, 462
STALEY, 317
STALTER, 386 396 466 473
STAM, 472
STAMFORD, 456
STANLEY, 449
STANSBERRY, 303 433 465
STANSBERY, 468
STARN, 397
STARR, 304 345 437 474
START, 446
STATELER, 292 293
STAUM, 431
STEARNS, 439
STEELE, 471
STEM, 458 462
STERLING, 457 462
STERM, 457
STETLER, 468
STEVENS, 313 339 376 446 447
  450 456 457 461 466
STEVENSON, 398 431
STEWART, 265 274-278 281-283
  286 291 296 304 321 344 346
  446 456 457 462
STICKNEY, 344 348
STINCHCOMB, 469
STINN, 462
STOFER, 446 471
STOFFULMYER, 454
STOKELY, 321 331
STOKER, 446 455
STOKES, 327
STOL, 456
STOM, 454
STOMB, 456
STONE, 458 468
STONER, 446 451
STORM, 446
STORY, 354
STOUFFER, 439
STOVER, 431
STRAHAM, 468
STRAHAN, 479
STRASSER, 220
STRAUB, 466 472
STRAW, 303 327 433 446 447
  468 473
STREBY, 345 347
STRICKER, 462 473
STRYCKER, 457
STUBBS, 282 473
STUDEBAKER, 432 456 479
STUMP, 451 457 462
STURY, 473
STUTZ, 342 343 349
SUBER, 465
SULLIGER, 454
SULLIVAN, 456
SURPLUS, 446 456
SUTLIFF, 338 359
SWAN, 322
SWANK, 453 476

HISTORY OF WYANDOT COUNTY. 501

SWANN, 337 344
SWARTZ, 344 346 446 462 466 468
SWAZZE, 471
SWEARINGEN, 457 462
SWEENEY, 455
SWEET, 479
SWEGLE, 469 470
SWIGART, 338
SWINEHART, 446 457 466 476
SWITZER, 466 473 479
SYMMES, 354
TAGGART, 321 412 429
TAILOR, 436
TALLMAN, 399
TANNEHILL, 322
TANNER, 303
TAYLOR, 304 383 437 456 457
TEAL, 465
TERRY, 314 317-319 322 324 331 332 335 348 380 446 465
THAYER, 408 409
THEAKER, 379
THOMAS, 327 445 449 450 453 454 462 476
THOMPSON, 290 341 373 376 399 400 432 433 451 452 456 462 465
THURMAN, 336 341 359
TIDBALL, 364
TILGHAM, 256
TIREY, 474
TOD, 332 340
TONG, 472-474
TOWERS, 471
TOWNSEND, 346 347
TRACHT, 386 398
TRACY, 347 451 456 465
TRAGER, 393
TREES, 454
TREGO, 322
TRIBOLET, 345 350
TRIMBLE, 338 471
TRIPP, 321 398 399

TROUP, 446 457 462
TROWBRIDGE, 446
TUCKER, 447
TURK, 409
TURNER, 355 400 431 433 457 462
TURNEY, 433
TUTTLE, 321 326 327 335 346 347 365
TYLER, 13 337 345 348 366 372 380 443 444 446 454-456
ULRICH, 223
ULRICK, 432
UNCAPHER, 469
UNGER, 431
UPDEGRAFF, 451
UPSON, 347
VAIL, 454
VALENTINE, 380
VALLANDIGHAM, 340
VANCE, 336 337
VANCHOIK, 446
VANCLEVE, 449
VANDENBURG, 320 322
VANDORAN, 466
VANGUNDY, 304 322 437 446-448 469 472
VANHORN, 294
VANLUMP, 338
VANMARTER, 456 472 474 476
VANMETER, 267
VANORSALL, 303
VANORSDALL, 326 336 337 342 343 347 349 456
VANWAGONER, 454
VARNUM, 354
VAUGHAN, 396
VAUGHN, 454
VENTER, 475
VINTON, 336
VOEGEL, 473
VOIGHT, 410
VREDENBERG, 457 462
VROMAN, 446 447 457 462

WADSWORTH, 432
WAECHTER, 472
WAGGONER, 343 436 446 454
  457 462
WAGNER, 451
WALBORN, 432
WALKER, 267 272 275-277 282
  285 288 290 313 341 368 391
  447 469
WALLACE, 303 444 462 467
WALTER, 376 437
WALTERHOUSE, 473 476
WALTERMIRE, 472
WALTERS, 465 475
WALTON, 321 342 446 468 473
  479
WAMUS, 446
WARNER, 385 446 451 472 475
WARREN, 431
WASHBURN, 446 466 474
WASHINGTON, 236 238 254
  255 257 258 260 411
WATERS, 454
WATSON, 321 335-338 340-342
  361 375 376 380 454 472
WAYNE, 260 263 264 272 274
  289 291 300
WEAR, 367 379
WEAVER, 474
WEBB, 454
WEBBER, 474
WEBER, 451
WEBSTER, 331 386
WEDDLE, 323
WEEKS, 410
WEINANDY, 221
WEININGER, 327
WELCH, 317 327 335-338 348
  360 361 364 435-437 446 471
  472
WELK, 446
WELLER, 335 446 447
WELLS, 457 462

WELSH, 446 447 454
WELTER, 457 462
WELTY, 469
WENTLING, 474
WENTZ, 347 465
WERT, 475
WEST, 321 345 439
WESTENHOLM, 447
WHALEY, 328
WHARTON, 383
WHEATON, 385
WHEELER, 290
WHETSEL, 451
WHINERY, 335 456
WHINNERY, 447 466
WHIPPLE, 447 468
WHITAKER, 266 269
WHITE, 335 339 341 345 346
  348 349 360 368 376 437 446
  447 457 461 466 468 474 479
WHITEHEAD, 313
WHITELY, 335 338 348 359 361
WHITMAN, 338 339
WHITMORE, 446
WHITTAKER, 431 474
WHITTEM, 451
WICKISER, 472-474
WIDMAN, 323
WIGLEY, 451
WILCOX, 327 399 400 430 465
  469
WILKINS, 450 475
WILLARD, 455 468
WILLEVER, 450
WILLIAMS, 267 288 292 337-
  341 349 350 376 433 437 446
  447 451 456 463 465 466 468
  469 474 475
WILLIAMSON, 241 246-248 447
WILLICH, 449
WILLISTON, 347 348
WILLOUGHBY, 345 446 466 473
WILLSON, 451 469

WILMITH, 431
WILSON, 255-257 304 321 328
  329 331 335 336 338 348 375
  384 385 398 443-445 447 456
  463-465 467 469 474
WILT, 446 474
WINICH, 454
WINSLOW, 456
WINSTEAD, 303
WINTERS, 451
WISE, 454 457 462 474
WISEBAKER, 462
WISENBARGER, 454
WISNER, 468 475
WISWASSER, 454
WOESSNER, 469 473
WOHLGAMUTH, 304 335 348
  468 472 473
WOLF, 446
WOLFORD, 447
WOLKER, 473
WOLVERTON, 431
WONDER, 468
WOOD, 257 327 335 336 348 359
  446 447 465 469 473
WOODCOCK, 446 471
WOODLING, 466
WOODS, 255
WOOLEY, 474
WOOLSEY, 304 432 471
WOOSTER, 458 462
WORLEY, 340 447 471 475 479
WORLY, 471
WORMLEY, 447 454
WORRELLO, 218
WORTH, 314 317 320-322 327
  332 335 337-339 341 343 348
  349 380 389 425 426 431 435
WORTHINGTON, 302 468
WRIGHT, 432 467
WUSCHER, 446 472
YAGER, 446
YEAGER, 446 454
YENCER, 448
YENNER, 320
YENTZER, 344 345 349
YERK, 446
YORK, 303
YOUNG, 287 326 392 447 451
  466 468 475 479
ZABRISKA, 473
ZAHM, 394 398
ZANE, 242 245 278 288 289
ZEIGLER, 465
ZENT, 466
ZIMMERMAN, 386 394 447
ZINT, 451
ZOOK, 447

www.ingramcontent.com/pod-product-compliance
Lightning Source LLC
Chambersburg PA
CBHW071235230426
43668CB00011B/1454